A Fresh Assault
on the Synoptic Problem

REDATING MATTHEW, MARK & LUKE

John Wenham

INTERVARSITY PRESS
DOWNERS GROVE, ILLINOIS 60515

Published in the United States of America by InterVarsity Press, Downers Grove, Illinois, with permission from Hodder and Stoughton, 47 Bedford Square, London, WC1B 3DP, England.

InterVarsity Press is the book-publishing division of InterVarsity Christian Fellowship, a student movement active on campus at hundreds of universities, colleges and schools of nursing in the United States of America, and a member movement of the International Fellowship of Evangelical Students. For information about local and regional activities, write Public Relations Dept., InterVarsity Christian Fellowship, 6400 Schroeder Rd., P.O. Box 7895, Madison, WI 53707-7895.

ISBN 0-8308-1760-3

Printed in the United States of America

Library of Congress Cataloging-in-Publication Data

Wenham, John William.
    Redating Matthew, Mark, and Luke: a fresh assault on the synoptic
problem/[John Wenham].
        p.   cm.
    Includes bibliographical references and indexes.
        ISBN 0-8308-1760-3
        1. Synoptic problem.   2. Bible.   N.T.   Gospels—Chronology.
    I. Title.
    BS2555.2.R35   1991
226'.066—dc20   91-39328
                                                                          CIP

14	13	12	11	10	9	8	7	6	5	4	3	2	1
03	02	01	00	99	98	97	96	95	94	93	92		

To PETER

ACKNOWLEDGEMENTS

This book, which has had a long gestation, owes a great debt to a host of kind people who from time to time have read part or the whole of the manuscript and have made helpful suggestions. These include Christopher Band, Michael Goulder, Donald Guthrie, Peter Head, John Leach, Malcolm McDow, Howard Marshall, Tom Martin, Anthony Meredith, Bernard Orchard, Alan Padgett, Paul Rainbow, Andrew Saville, Alberic Stacpoole, Michael Thompson. It is somewhat invidious to make distinctions, but I feel I should give special thanks to five readers whose comments were particularly helpful: Fred Bruce, Martin Davie, Earle Ellis, Jim Scott, and my son David. I also owe a great debt to the two typists who faithfully typed and retyped for me: Elizabeth Carras in the early stages, and Lynne Knott who worked with marvellous selflessness in the later stages. I am also most grateful to my copy-editor David Mackinder, and to the staff of Hodder & Stoughton, who have been uniformly helpful throughout, and to Martin Davie, David Lambourn and Joe Martin for help in proof-reading. If this book proves to be of service to the church of God, a big share of the thanks will be due to all these folk.

John Wenham

ABBREVIATIONS

Adv. Haer.	*Adversus Haereses (Against Heresies)*
Aland	K. Aland, *Synopsis Quattuor Evangeliorum* (Stuttgart: Württembergische Bibelanstalt, 1964)
Alexander	L. C. A. Alexander, *Luke-Acts in Its Contemporary Setting*, Oxford D.Phil. dissertation, 1977
Alford	H. Alford, *The Greek Testament*, 4 vols (Cambridge: Deighton Bell, 7th ed., 1874)
Ant.	*Antiquities of the Jews*
Apol. 1	*First Apology*
BAG	W. Bauer, W. F. Arndt and F. W. Gingrich, *A Greek-English Lexicon of the New Testament*, rev. and augmented F. W. Gingrich and F. W. Danker (University of Chicago Press, 1979)
Balleine	G. R. Balleine, *Simon Whom He Surnamed Peter* (London: Skeffington, 1958)
Barnes	A. S. Barnes, *Christianity at Rome in the Apostolic Age* (London: Methuen, 1938)
Bellinzoni	A. J. Bellinzoni (ed.), *The Two-Source Hypothesis: A Critical Appraisal* (Macon: Mercer UP, 1985)
Bib	Biblica

Birks	T. R. Birks, *Horae Evangelicae*, ed. H. A. Birks (London: Bell, 1892)
BJRL	*Bulletin of the John Rylands Library*
BNTC	Black's New Testament Commentary
Bruce *Acts* Greek	F. F. Bruce, *The Acts of the Apostles*, Greek Text (London: Tyndale, 1951)
Bruce *Acts* NICNT	F. F. Bruce, *The Book of the Acts*, NICNT (Grand Rapids: Eerdmans, rev. ed., 1988)
Bruce *Chronology*	F. F. Bruce, 'Chronological Questions in the Acts of the Apostles' *BJRL* 68 (1968)
Bruce *Date*	F. F. Bruce, 'The Date and Character of Mark' in E. Bammel and C. F. D. Moule (edd.), *Jesus and the Politics of His Day* (Cambridge UP, 1984)
Bruggen	J. van Bruggen, *Die geschichtliche Einordnung der Pastoralbriefe* (Wuppertal: Brockhaus, 1981)
Butler	B. C. Butler, *The Originality of St Matthew* (Cambridge UP, 1951)
Buttrick	D. G. Buttrick (ed.), *Jesus and Man's Hope*, vol. 1 (Pittsburgh: Pittsburgh Theological Seminary, 1970)
c.	*circa*
Carmignac	J. Carmignac, *La naissance des Évangiles Synoptiques* (Paris: O.E.I.L., 1984) – also in *The Birth of the Synoptic Gospels*, ET (Chicago: Franciscan Herald Press, 1986)
CBQ	*Catholic Biblical Quarterly*
Chapman	J. Chapman, *Matthew, Mark and Luke* (London: Longmans, 1937)
Creed	J. M. Creed, *Gospel according to St Luke* (London: Macmillan, 1930)
Cullmann	O. Cullmann, *Peter: Disciple, Apostle,*

	Martyr, ET (London: SCM, 2nd ed., 1962)
De Vir. Ill.	*Concerning Illustrious Men*
Dodd	C. H. Dodd, *The Epistle of Paul to the Romans*, Moffatt New Testament Commentary (London: Hodder & Stoughton, 1932)
ed(d).	editor(s), edited by, edition
Edmundson	G. Edmundson, *The Church in Rome in the First Century* (London: Longmans, 1913)
Ellis *GC*	E. E. Ellis, 'Gospels Criticism' in P. Stuhlmacher (ed.), *Das Evangelium und die Evangelien* (Tübingen: Mohr, 1983)
Ellis *Luke*	E. E. Ellis, *The Gospel of Luke*, NCB (London: Nelson, 1966)
EQ	*Evangelical Quarterly*
ET	English Translation
ExpT	*Expository Times*
Farmer *NSS*	W. R. Farmer (ed.), *New Synoptic Studies* (Macon: Mercer UP, 1983)
Farmer *SP*	W. R. Farmer, *The Synoptic Problem* (London/New York: Macmillan, 1964)
Farmer *Synopticon*	W. R. Farmer, *Synopticon: The Verbal Agreement Between the Greek Texts of Matthew, Mark and Luke Contextually Exhibited* (Cambridge UP, 1969)
Fee	G. D. Fee, 'A Text-Critical Look at the Synoptic Problem' *NovT* 22 (1980) 12–28
Fitzmyer	J. A. Fitzmyer, *Gospel according to Luke*, Anchor Bible (New York: Doubleday, 1981)
France *Evangelist*	R. T. France, *Matthew: Evangelist and Teacher* (Exeter: Paternoster, 1989)
France *Gospel*	R. T. France, *The Gospel according to*

	Matthew, TNTC (Leicester: IVP, 1985)
Goulder	M. D. Goulder, *Luke: A New Paradigm* (Sheffield Academic Press, 1989)
GP	Gospel Perspectives
Gundry	R. H. Gundry, *Matthew: A Commentary on His Literary and Theological Art* (Grand Rapids: Eerdmans, 1982)
Harnack	A. von Harnack, *The Date of Acts and the Synoptic Gospels*, ET (London: Williams & Norgate; New York: Putnam, 1911)
Hawkins	J. C. Hawkins, *Horae Synopticae* (Oxford: Clarendon Press, 1899)
HDB	J. Hastings (ed.), *A Dictionary of the Bible*, 5 vols (Edinburgh: T. & T. Clark, 1898–)
HE	*Historia Ecclesiastica*
Hemer	C. J. Hemer, *The Book of Acts in the Setting of Hellenistic History* (Tübingen: Mohr, 1989)
Hengel *Johannine Q*	M. Hengel, *The Johannine Question* (London: SCM; Philadelphia: Trinity Press International, 1989)
Hengel *Mark*	M. Hengel, *Studies in the Gospel of Mark*, ET (London: SCM, 1985)
Hennecke	E. Hennecke, *New Testament Apocrypha*, ET (London: Lutterworth, 1965)
Hodges and Farstad	Z. C. Hodges and A. L. Farstad (edd.), *The Greek New Testament according to the Majority Text* (Nashville: Nelson, 1982)
HTR	*Harvard Theological Review*
Huck-Greeven	A. Huck, *Synopsis of the First Three Gospels*, rev. H. Greeven (Tübingen: J. C. B. Mohr, 1981)

Hughes	P. E. Hughes, *Paul's Second Epistle to the Corinthians*, NICNT (Grand Rapids: Eerdmans; London: Marshall, Morgan & Scott, 1962)
IBD	J. D. Douglas (ed.), *Illustrated Bible Dictionary*, 3 vols (Leicester: IVP, 1980)
ICC	International Critical Commentary
IDB	G. A. Buttrick (ed.), *The Interpreter's Dictionary of the Bible*, 5 vols (New York: Abingdon, 1962–)
Irenaeus	*Against all Heresies*
ISBE	G. W. Bromiley (ed.), *International Standard Bible Encyclopaedia*, vol. 2 (Grand Rapids: Eerdmans; Exeter: Paternoster, 1982)
IVP	Inter-Varsity Press
Jameson	H. G. Jameson, *The Origin of the Synoptic Gospels* (Oxford: Blackwell, 1922)
JBL	*Journal of Biblical Literature*
JSOT	JSOT Press, Sheffield
JTS	*Journal of Theological Studies*
Kittel-Friedrich	G. Kittel and G. Friedrich (edd.), *The Theological Dictionary of the New Testament*, ed. and trans. G. W. Bromiley, 10 vols (Grand Rapids: Eerdmans, 1964)
Kümmel	W. G. Kümmel, *Introduction to the New Testament*, ET (London: SCM, 1975)
Lindsey	R. L. Lindsey, *A Hebrew Translation of the Gospel of Mark* (Jerusalem: Dugith, *c*. 1971)
LSJ	H. G. Liddell and R. Scott, *A Greek-English Lexicon*, rev. and augmented H. S. Jones (Oxford, 1968)

Manson	T. W. Manson, *Studies in the Gospels and Epistles* (Manchester UP, 1962)
Marshall *Acts*	I. H. Marshall, *The Acts of the Apostles*, TNTC (Leicester: IVP; Grand Rapids: Eerdmans, 1980)
Marshall *Luke*	I. H. Marshall, *The Gospel of Luke*, NIGTC (Exeter: Paternoster, 1978)
Marucchi	O. Marucchi, *The Evidence of the Catacombs* (London: Sheed & Ward, 1929)
Massaux	E. Massaux, *Influence de l'Évangile de saint Matthieu sur la littérature chrétienne avant saint Irénée* (Leuven UP, 2nd ed., 1986)
Migne *PG*	Migne's *Patrologia Graece*
Morgan	R. Morgan and J. Barton, *Biblical Interpretation* (Oxford UP, 1988)
MS(S)	manuscript(s)
NCB	New Century Bible
NEB	New English Bible
Neirynck	F. Neirynck, *The Minor Agreements of Matthew and Luke Against Mark* (Leuven UP, 1974)
NICNT	New International Commentary on the New Testament
NIGTC	New International Greek Testament Commentary
NIV	New International Version of the Bible
NLC	New London Commentary
NovT	*Novum Testamentum*
NTS	*New Testament Studies*
O'Connor	D. W. O'Connor, *Peter in Rome: The Literary, Liturgical and Archeological Evidence* (New York/London: Columbia UP, 1969)
ODCC	F. L. Cross and E. A. Livingstone (edd.), *Oxford Dictionary of the*

	Christian Church (Oxford UP, 2nd ed., 1974)
Orchard *Synopsis*	J. B. Orchard (ed.), *A Synopsis of the Four Gospels in Greek* (Edinburgh: T. & T. Clark, 1983)
Orchard *Synoptics*	B. Orchard and H. Riley, *The Order of the Synoptics: Why Three Synoptic Gospels?* (Macon: Mercer UP, 1987)
passim	here and there throughout
Pickering	W. N. Pickering, *The Identity of the New Testament Text* (Nashville: Nelson, rev. ed., 1980)
RB	*Revue Biblique*
Reicke	B. Reicke, *The Roots of the Synoptic Gospels* (Philadelphia: Fortress, 1986)
Rist	J. M. Rist, *On the Independence of Matthew and Mark* (Cambridge UP, 1978)
Roberts	C. H. Roberts, *Manuscript, Society and Belief in Early Christian Egypt*, 1977 Schweich Lectures (Oxford UP, 1979)
Robinson	J. A. T. Robinson, *Redating the New Testament* (London: SCM, 1976)
RSV	Revised Standard Version
Sanders	E. P. Sanders, *The Tendencies of the Synoptic Tradition* (Cambridge UP, 1969)
Sanders and Davies	E. P. Sanders and M. Davies, *Studying the Synoptic Gospels* (London: SCM; Philadelphia: Trinity Press International, 1989)
SCM	Student Christian Movement
SNTS	Studiorum Novi Testamenti Societas
Stein	R. H. Stein, *The Synoptic Problem* (Grand Rapids: Baker; Leicester: IVP, 1987)
Stoldt	H.-H. Stoldt, *History and Criticism of the Marcan Hypothesis* (Macon: Mercer

	UP; Edinburgh: T. & T. Clark, 1980), ET of *Geschichte und Kritik der Markushypothese* (Göttingen, 1977)
Streeter	B. H. Streeter, *The Four Gospels* (London: Macmillan, 5th imp., 1936)
R. O. P. Taylor	R. O. P. Taylor, *The Groundwork of the Gospels* (Oxford: Blackwell, 1946)
Taylor *Mark*	V. Taylor, *The Gospel according to St Mark* (London: Macmillan, 1953)
Them.	*Themelios*
Thiede	C. P. Thiede, *Simon Peter* (Exeter: Paternoster, 1986)
Thompson	M. B. Thompson, *The Example and Teaching of Jesus in Romans 12:1–15:3*, Cambridge PhD thesis, 1988
TNTC	Tyndale New Testament Commentary
Torrey	C. C. Torrey, *Documents of the Primitive Church* (New York: Harper, 1941)
TU	Texte und Untersuchungen
Tuckett *SS*	C. M. Tuckett (ed.), *Synoptic Studies* (Sheffield: JSOT, 1984)
Tyn B	*Tyndale Bulletin*
Tyson and Longstaff	J. B. Tyson and T. R. W. Longstaff, *Synoptic Abstract*, The Computer Bible, vol. 15 (Wooster, Ohio: College of Wooster, 1978)
UP	University Press
v.l.	varia lectio (variant reading)
vol(s)	volume(s)
Walker	N. Walker, 'The Alleged Matthaean Errata' *NTS* 9 (1963) 391–94
War	*The Jewish War*
D. Wenham	D. Wenham, *The Rediscovery of Jesus' Eschatological Discourse*, GP 4 (Sheffield: JSOT, 1984)
Wenham *CB*	J. W. Wenham, *Christ and the Bible*

	(Leicester: IVP; Grand Rapids: Baker, 2nd ed., 1984)
Wenham *EE*	J. W. Wenham, *Easter Enigma* (Exeter: Paternoster; Grand Rapids: Zondervan, 1984)
Wenham *Luke*	J. W. Wenham, 'The Identity of Luke', *EQ*, forthcoming
Williams	C. S. C. Williams, *The Acts of the Apostles*, BNTC (London: Black, 1957)
Zahn	T. Zahn, *Introduction to the New Testament*, ET, 3 vols (Edinburgh: T. & T. Clark, 1909)
ZNW	*Zeitschrift für die neutestamentliche Wissenschaft*

INTRODUCTION: A RADICAL THESIS

A Radical Thesis

My active interest in the synoptic problem dates from 1937, when Dom John Chapman published his *Matthew, Mark and Luke*[1] in which he argued the 'Augustinian' view of the order of the gospels indicated in his title. My teachers, who held the priority of Mark and the two-document theory, virtually ignored Chapman and seemed to consider it unnecessary to take his arguments seriously. To me his arguments seemed at least as good as Streeter's, whose *The Four Gospels* had become (and was to remain for several decades) the standard work on the subject in English. I was not persuaded of all Chapman's positions, but I was sufficiently persuaded to become an undogmatic Augustinian. I have remained an undogmatic Augustinian ever since, though now I put very little weight on a literary dependence of one evangelist upon another. Rather, each evangelist writes in the way he habitually teaches, literary dependence being minimal in so far as his choice of words is concerned.

I continued to have an amateur interest in the subject over the years and noted with special attention such works as came my way which dissented from the standard view, including those of T. Zahn, H. G. Jameson, B. C. Butler, P. Parker, L. Vaganay, A. M. Farrer, N. Turner, A. W. Argyle, R. T. Simpson, W. R. Farmer, E. P. Sanders, R. L. Lindsey, M.-É. Boismard and J. M. Rist.[2] In 1979 I found myself in the Synoptic Problem Seminar of the Society for New Testament Studies, whose members were in disagreement over every aspect of the subject. When this international group disbanded in 1982 they had sadly to confess that after twelve years' work they had not reached a common mind on a single issue. My own views had been developing over the years on lines somewhat different from those of the other members, and I felt that in spite of the limitations of my reading I ought to try to commit my ideas to paper.

I have focused on the question of dating because of its intrinsic importance in the evaluation of the New Testament. But the book is in fact an investigation of the whole synoptic problem, considering both internal and external evidence, believing that there is an overall consistency between them.[3] Dating plays a significant part in the web of evidence.

The thesis of this book constitutes a radical departure from the commonly held view of the dates of the synoptic gospels. In spite of a few notable exceptions[4] there is wide agreement among New Testament scholars that no gospel should be put earlier than the late 60s. Usually Mark is placed first at ± 70 and Matthew and Luke somewhat later.[5] This book will argue that all three are probably to be dated before 55.

The title is of course a conscious echo of J. A. T. Robinson's *Redating the New Testament*, though in fact the two books are almost entirely independent in their treatment of the synoptic problem. On two major points, however, I greatly value his advocacy. In essence the argument of my book is quite simple. Its starting-point is the strange ending of the Acts of the Apostles, concerning which Robinson has revived the argument which so powerfully moved A. Harnack. For some nine chapters the book of Acts has been concerned, first with the story of Paul's fateful visit to Jerusalem which led to imprisonment and his appeal to Caesar, and then with the story of his journey to Rome. We are eager to know what happened at Paul's trial, but the author never tells us. He just says: 'he lived there two whole years at his own expense, and welcomed all who came to him, preaching the kingdom of God and teaching about the Lord Jesus Christ quite openly and unhindered'. The only satisfying explanation of the writer's silence concerning the trial, it will be argued, is that when Luke wrote these closing lines it had still not taken place. In other words the end of the story gives the date of the book: *c.* 62. But Acts was preceded[6] by an earlier treatise, the Gospel according to Luke, and this, it will be argued, can be dated with some assurance in the early 50s.

Further, there is wide (and, I am inclined to believe, justified) agreement that the author of Luke's gospel knew the gospel of Mark, which must therefore be dated earlier still. It will be shown that the usual reasons given for dating Mark around 70 have little weight and that it can be placed more satisfactorily in the mid-40s. Here again Robinson has done good service in resurrecting the long-forgotten Bampton lectures of G. Edmundson on *The Church in Rome in the First Century* which showed how strong was the case for the presence of Peter and Mark there in 42–44.

The question of Matthew is more complicated. The universal tradition of the early church is that Matthew 'in the Hebrew dialect' was the first gospel. It will be argued with some reserve that Matthew was indeed the first gospel, and that it may possibly have been written in Hebrew or Aramaic, and that it was known to Mark. I leave it an open question whether Mark knew Matthew in a Semitic or a Greek form.

A new approach to the synoptic problem is attempted which denies literary dependence as the primary explanation of the likenesses of the gospels and which also questions complete literary independence. The later evangelists are seen as probably writing with knowledge of the earlier gospels – adopting the newly invented genre and in the main following the same order. But they are not seen as systematically altering their predecessors' work. (The difficulty of following and adapting scrolls which did not even have word separation is stressed.) What they write is fundamentally what they themselves are accustomed to teach. So it is a case of some degree of structural dependence and a high degree of verbal independence.

As this book is an argument in favour of the high value of Christian tradition with regard to three major books of the New Testament, I am naturally predisposed towards the traditional authorship of its other books. They have all had able defenders and I shall provisionally assume that their conclusions are satisfactory and then try to see how the case looks when this assumption is made. Though the critical questions are important in themselves they are peripheral to our central argument and I shall not load the book with their detailed discussion.

xxiii

Similarly with Acts, I shall provisionally assume that the conclusions of Bernhard Weiss, E. Lekebusch, A. Wikenhauser,
Eduard Meyer, Harnack, W. M. Ramsay, W. W. Gasque,
Bruce, Marshall, Robinson, Hemer and others are broadly
satisfactory, and treat the book as a sound historical source.[7]

Setting a high value on the traditional attributions of authorship of the New Testament books leads naturally to setting a
fairly high value on other early Christian traditions. These
Christians were fallible and prejudiced like the rest of us, but by
and large they were, I believe, honest people trying to tell the
truth. It is best, therefore, to treat them as such and to beware of
the danger either of lightly rejecting their testimony or of
subjecting them to unreasonable hypercriticism.

The text of the gospels to be used is that of Aland's *Synopsis
Quattuor Evangeliorum* (13th ed.) and of the rest of the New
Testament that of the 26th edition of the Nestle-Aland *Novum
Testamentum Graece*, unless otherwise stated. The use of these
two great and readily accessible works of scholarship is for the
convenience of both writer and reader, though I feel bound to
say that I am far from convinced that we should give the
Nestle-Aland text the status of a new Textus Receptus.[8] The
choice of variant readings, however, is not often important to
the argument and the convenience of these editions can safely
be made the deciding consideration in the adoption of text.

With regard to the question of chronological framework, I
have not attempted any fresh investigation of the problems
involved, since absolute dating is not of importance to this
thesis, and I shall normally quote dates without calling attention to their approximate character. The chronological scheme
on the next page is based on a pre-publication version of the
1991 edition of F. F. Bruce's *Acts of the Apostles* (Greek Text),[9]
though I take leave to differ from him with regard to the date of
Peter's escape from prison, which I put in 42 rather than 43.[10] I
have also added dates for the Pastoral Epistles, following the
conclusions of J. van Bruggen's interesting study.[11] Bruce's
dating, in so far as it concerns Paul from his conversion to his
Roman imprisonment, is entirely corroborated by Hemer's
recent study.[12]

Chronological Table

Crucifixion, resurrection, ascension, Pentecost   30

Conversion of Saul of Tarsus (Acts 9:1–22; Gal. 1:15–17)   *c.* 33

Paul's first post-conversion visit to Jerusalem (Acts 9:26–30; Gal. 1:18–20)   *c.* 35

GOSPEL OF MATTHEW   *c.* 40

Accession of Herod Agrippa I; death of James son of Zebedee; Peter's imprisonment and escape to Rome (Acts 12:1–17)   42

Death of Herod Agrippa I (Acts 12:20–23)   March 44

Peter goes to Antioch   44

GOSPEL OF MARK   *c.* 45

Famine in Judea (Acts 11:28)   45–48

Barnabas and Paul visit Jerusalem (Acts 11:30; Gal. 2:1)   *c.* 46

Barnabas and Paul evangelise Cyprus and South Galatia (Acts 13:4–14:26)   *c.* 47–48

Letter to the Galatians   *c.* 48

Apostolic Council at Jerusalem (Acts 15:6–29)   *c.* 49

Paul, Silas and Timothy take the gospel to Macedonia (Acts 16:9–17:14; 1 Thess. 1:5–2:2)   *c.* 49–50

Paul in Corinth (Acts 18:1–18; 1 Cor. 2:1–5)   50–52

Letters to the Thessalonians   50

Gallio becomes proconsul of Achaia (Acts 18:12)   51

Paul's hasty visit to Judea and Syria (Acts 18:22)   52

Paul in Ephesus (Acts 19:1–20:1)   52–55

GOSPEL OF LUKE   *c.* 54

First Letter to the Corinthians   55

Paul in Macedonia and Illyricum (Acts 20:1f; Rom. 15:19)   55–56

Second Letter to the Corinthians   56

Paul in Achaia (Corinth) (Acts 20:2f)   56–57

Letter to the Romans   57

Paul's arrival and arrest in Jerusalem (Acts 21:17–33)   57

Paul detained at Caesarea (Acts 23:23–26:32); *1 Timothy, Titus*   57–59

Paul sets sail for Italy (Acts 27:1f)   59

Paul arrives in Rome (Acts 28:14–16)   60

Philippians, 2 Timothy (cf. 1:17)   *c.* 60–61

Theories about synoptic relationships

It may be helpful to give in somewhat simplified diagrammatic form some of the theories which will be discussed:

1. Oral Theory

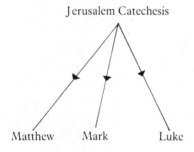

Jerusalem Catechesis

Matthew   Mark   Luke

2. Two-document Theory

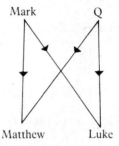

Mark   Q

Matthew   Luke

3. Four-document Theory
(Streeter)

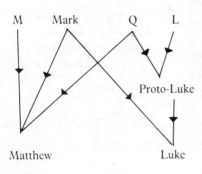

M   Mark   Q   L

Proto-Luke

Matthew   Luke

4. Markan priority, no Q
(Goulder)

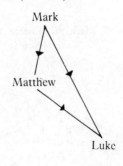

Mark

Matthew

Luke

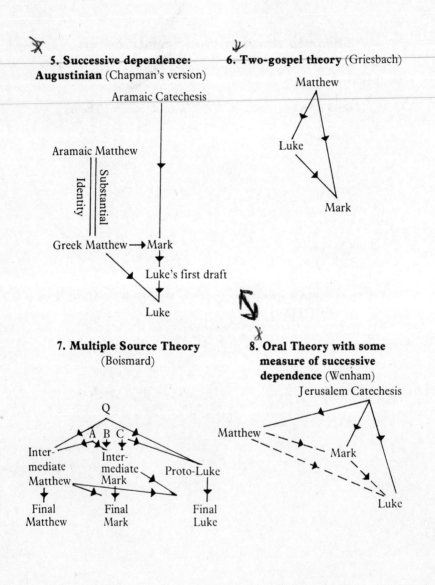

5. Successive dependence: Augustinian (Chapman's version)

Aramaic Catechesis

Aramaic Matthew

Identity | Substantial

Greek Matthew → Mark

Luke's first draft

Luke

6. Two-gospel theory (Griesbach)

Matthew

Luke

Mark

7. Multiple Source Theory (Boismard)

Q

A B C

Inter-mediate Matthew

Inter-mediate Mark

Proto-Luke

Final Matthew

Final Mark

Final Luke

8. Oral Theory with some measure of successive dependence (Wenham)

Jerusalem Catechesis

Matthew

Mark

Luke

1

THE INTRACTABLE PROBLEM

Chapter summary

The likenesses and differences between the three gospels present a problem of almost infinite complexity. The view that Matthew and Luke independently used Mark and a lost source Q is still held as a working hypothesis by most scholars, but with decreasing confidence. There is no new consensus among the dissentients. There can be no solution using faulty methods, but there is an answer, because the synoptic problem concerns something that actually happened.

For nearly a hundred years the search has been for literary solutions. Before that, belief in a common form of basic oral instruction was popular, Westcott being its most notable expositor. His views were eclipsed by the Oxford School: Sanday, Hawkins and Streeter. It is, however, perfectly possible for oral tradition to be accurately transmitted, and the oral theory has been revived by Rist, Reike, Scott and Chilton. But complete independence seems unlikely on three grounds: 1.) It means that a long list of pericopes was memorised, but was demonstrably not regarded as sacrosanct. 2.) It requires that the three gospels were published almost simultaneously. 3.) It seems to be contrary to church tradition.

There is a third way which stresses verbal independence with a measure of structural dependence.

Hans-Herbert Stoldt began his book *History and Criticism of the Marcan Hypothesis* with these words:

The critical analysis of the sources of the Gospels is justifiably regarded as one of the most difficult research problems in the history of ideas . . . one can truly say that no other enterprise in the

1

history of ideas has been subjected to anywhere near the same
degree of scholarly scrutiny.

When the three gospels are compared an almost infinitely
complex range of likenesses and unlikenesses is found, which
resolutely refuse to fit into any tidy scheme of relationships.
There is no need to spell them out; they are all too well known to
those who have looked seriously into the matter. The degree of
complexity can be seen in W. R. Farmer's *Synopticon*, which
takes the three gospels in turn and shows the points of agreement between them by means of a colour code, which is capable
of showing the relations in nine different ways.[1] These agreements show that there is *some* connection between them; the
question is, what?

It is true that throughout this century the great majority of
scholars have held to some form of the two-document
hypothesis,[2] believing that Mark came first and that Matthew
and Luke independently built their gospels out of Mark and
another source or sources known as Q. Probably, judging by the
attitude of the members of recent gospels conferences, most
scholars who have examined this theory critically have not been
particularly impressed with its logical weight,[3] yet they find no
other theory convincing, and, since life is short, they have been
content to go along with the majority and accept it as a working
hypothesis.

But throughout the century there has been a steady stream of
scholars who have been so dissatisfied with the theory on which
they have been brought up that they have felt bound to try to do
better, and a number have got to the point of publishing their
findings.[4] Yet, not only has no new consensus emerged, but the
debate has reached such an impasse that the problem begins to
look insoluble. In 1985 A. J. Bellinzoni assembled a collection
of the most significant articles in *The Two-Source Hypothesis: A
Critical Appraisal*. In its final essay J. B. Tyson concluded:
'After reading these essays it is difficult to avoid the conclusion
that nothing convincing has emerged from this long and
tortuous discussion.'[5]

The problem is insoluble if a solution is sought along the

2

wrong lines. As M. D. Goulder has said: 'Not tens but hundreds of thousands of pages have been wasted by authors on the Synoptic Problem not paying attention to errors of method.'[6] Much of the argumentation is worth very little, because so many of the arguments are reversible: they can be argued either way with approximately equal cogency.[7] This makes it essential to look for those arguments which have real weight. Another methodological snare is the temptation to fit the facts to a procrustean bed through looking for the wrong sort of solution.

Yet the problem is a real one to which there *is* an answer. It is not like a discussion of the contents or order of Q, where no one knows for certain whether a Q-document ever existed. The three gospels exist, there is *some* relation between them; if this relation could be correctly stated all the data would be satisfactorily explained without remainder. Has something gone wrong with our methodology?

It will be noticed that the research of the last hundred years has been dominated by a belief in direct literary connections, yet a century ago the then reigning view (at least in the English-speaking world) relied on common oral tradition to explain the likenesses between the gospels. H. Alford wrote: 'I do not see how any theory of mutual interdependence will leave to our three Evangelists their credit as able or trustworthy writers, or even as honest men: nor can I find any such theory borne out by the nature of the variations apparent in the respective texts.'[8] B. F. Westcott's *An Introduction to the Study of the Gospels* (1860), which had reached its seventh edition by 1887,[9] was the most influential advocate of the oral theory, and its influence continued strongly for most of the latter half of the century.

Westcott acknowledged that 'the explanation of the phenomena which [the Synoptic gospels] present is sought by universal consent in the presence of a common element' (177). He considered that this common element derived from the fact that the Twelve devoted themselves to the ministry of the word (Acts 6:4), remaining 'together at Jerusalem in close communion long enough to shape a common narrative, and to fix it with the requisite consistency' (157). This was a ministry to Judeans,

3

Galileans and Jews from the whole Diaspora. During this period, 'out of the countless multitude of Christ's acts, those were selected and arranged . . . which were seen to have the fullest representative significance' (157). In recounting the words spoken by Jesus and others a close unanimity was preserved, but in narrative each evangelist developed his individual style (183), making it 'a separate organic whole' (189).[10]

It was W. Sanday and his Oxford school who, towards the end of the nineteenth century, began to establish the two-document theory which became increasingly the received orthodoxy of the English-speaking world in the twentieth century, as it had already become in Germany.[11] It was felt that precise, detailed and objective work, as exemplified in J. C. Hawkins' *Horae Synopticae* (Oxford, 1899), gave hope of a 'scientific' solution to the problem, such as the oral theory could never provide. Precise, statistical studies to determine the redactional relationship between documents have formed a major part of the work on the problem throughout this century.[12]

That the relationship is primarily literary rather than oral has been the assumption underlying most of the work of the present century.[13] This is strikingly illustrated by Farmer in *The Synoptic Problem*, where Westcott is dismissed in a footnote.[14] It was illustrated even more strikingly by Sanders and Davies in 1989, who simply say that the synoptists 'often share the same Greek vocabulary, suggesting literary dependence' (vii) – they barely allude to the oral theory. After reviewing elaborated forms of the two-source hypothesis advocated by F. C. Grant and R. Funk and the multiple source hypothesis of M.-É. Boismard (with four sources and three intermediate 'gospels'), they too favour a complicated literary source theory – which, however, decisively rejects Q.[15]

The difficulty of distinguishing oral and literary relationships

The great question is: Have we been justified in placing so much emphasis on documentary relationships? Lying behind this is the even more basic question: Can one distinguish documentary dependence from indebtedness to a common oral tradition? A frequently used method of approach is simply to look at the parallel narratives and ask oneself about the closeness of parallelism. If the wording is largely different, one rejects a literary connection; if the wording has a good deal in common yet is not very close, one keeps an open mind; but as soon as there is identity of expression for more than about a dozen words in succession, one leaps to the conclusion that the connection must be literary. But this is not a safe conclusion. Even in our print-ridden era many Christians know a large number of ringing passages from the gospels and can quote them in their favourite version verbatim: 'Foxes have holes . . .', 'The harvest truly is great . . .', 'Ask and it shall be given you . . .', 'O Jerusalem, Jerusalem . . .' Much more would Greek-speaking Christians in the first century have memorised many of the sayings of Jesus in whatever form they were commonly taught.

There is no reason therefore why sayings of dozens of words in length should not occasionally be found in identical or nearly identical form and yet have no literary connection. As far as the wording of the individual pericopes is concerned, nearly all (if not all) could be explained by oral tradition. There are a few passages where the wording is so close for so long that it is difficult not to suspect literary dependence. The most noteworthy example is the γεννήματα ἐχιδνῶν sermon, which in Matthew (3:7–10) has sixty-three words and in Luke (3:7–9) sixty-four, with only three small differences between them. This is not a verbatim sermon of the Baptist, but a highly condensed summary which both authors must have got ultimately from a common source. Such a passage, given as part of the oral instruction, was easily memorised and could have been preserved intact in two retentive memories over a period of years. The passage concerning the faithful and wise steward in Luke 12:42–46 remains very close to Matthew 24:45–51 for more than a hundred words, but the two versions cannot be described as nearly identical, since some 15% of the words show differences. Such a concise and memorable parable could well have been preserved with that degree of similarity along two lines of

5

oral transmission from a single telling or from two slightly different tellings.[16]

In recent years there have been at least four brave souls (J. M. Rist, B. Reicke, J. W. Scott and B. Chilton) who have defied the modern consensus with regard to literary dependence and have declared their belief in the complete independence of two or more of the gospels. In 1978 Rist's SNTS monograph appeared under the title *On the Independence of Matthew and Mark*,[17] in which the author denied all literary dependence in the case of these two gospels. Rist was severely criticised by some reviewers, as for example by M. D. Goulder who said:

> The widely held belief that Matthew and Mark are related literarily rests on the following facts. (1) There are 661 verses in Mark, 606 of which, on a conservative count, have parallels in Matthew. (2) There are 11,078 words in Mark, the material parallel to which is given in 8,555 words in Matthew; of which 4,230 words are identical both in form and in sequence . . .
>
> . . . what is even more disturbing is his failure to use the argumentation which is common to the books he does refer to: all modern discussion includes the mention of word-counts, parallel usage elsewhere in the Gospel, etc.[18]

Others, equally wedded to the notion of literary dependence, were respectful. J. B. Orchard spoke of 'powerful advocacy' in a 'learned study'; T. R. W. Longstaff of the book's 'great strengths'; W. R. Farmer said that the 'book is full of vigorous and original argumentation'.[19] But (as we shall see) the author's reversion to total independence faces difficulties.

We shall look into the question of the order of the pericopes on pp. 44–7 (showing the closeness of Mark and Luke) and on pp. 89, 101–8 (showing the closeness of Mark and Matthew, in spite of three 'dislocations'). The closeness of order constitutes an objection to the notion of complete independence. Rist is inclined to allow 'that there are no particularly compelling reasons for denying that the author of Luke knew Mark' (4), but in the case of Matthew he considers that the sequence of pericopes in some parts of the preliterary tradition must have been firmly secured (13) and held in the memory (16). This means in Matthew 14–28 and Mark 6:14–16:8 seventy items all in order[20] (except for a minor difference in the way the cleansing of the temple and the cursing of the fig-tree are related), and this in spite of various omissions or additions by one or other evangelist. Unless there is strong evidence to the contrary, it seems more likely that one evangelist followed the other or that both followed a common written source, than that a standard order for reciting the oral tradition had been memorised, *but not consistently adhered to.*

In 1986 B. Reicke published his *The Roots of the Synoptic Gospels*, in which he argued the literary independence of all three gospels and dated them about 60 (180). He holds that Luke's prologue refers *exclusively* (45) to oral traditions 'delivered to us'; these traditions he considers were moulded over a long preliterary period (x) and were then collected at about the same time by Matthew, Mark and Luke. Luke and Mark were together in Caesarea (165, 170) and Luke indicates in his prologue that he knew that Mark and others were collecting material at the same time as he (166), yet Reicke insists that none of the three evangelists made use of the work of either of the others. He speaks of 'artificial source theories' (169); literary dependence is 'unnatural' (85), has 'bizarre consequences' (184), and there is a 'labyrinthian distribution of similarities and discrepancies . . . so that an irrational zigzag pattern emerges' (109). When, however, he comes to the question of the order of the pericopes, he can only say that 'some fundamental recollections . . . were apt to be kept in a certain order' (49).

J. W. Scott was made a PhD of St Andrew's University in 1986 for a dissertation arguing Luke's independence of Mark and Matthew. His unpublished thesis *Luke's Preface and the Synoptic Problem* is noteworthy for its learning, clarity and independence of thought.[21] The first nine chapters are devoted to exegesis of the preface, which, he maintains, makes no reference to Mark or Q, since, according to literary custom, Luke would have referred to them had he used them. He claims rather, in accordance with an interpretation widely favoured by the fathers, to have been a follower of all the apostles, probably having lived in Jerusalem for a considerable time in the 40s. He

7

became an expert in the oral traditions which they formulated and authorised, and it is these that he has written up accurately for his patron Theophilus. It is in his exegesis of the preface that Scott's most important single claim is made. He considers it to be almost certain that Luke is saying that his work is based virtually (if not completely) on oral traditions alone.

Chapters 10–12 of Scott's thesis present a two-tradition theory of the synoptic gospels, in which is argued, firstly, a basic narrative tradition, covering roughly the Markan material and half the Q-material. This had a generally recognised order and form of words, which were carefully taught, but which were not regarded as sacrosanct. In addition, there was a body of independent traditions of apostolic origin which were also regarded as authoritative. There were more of these independent traditions than traditions in the central cycle of stories. It was upon these two sources that Luke and the other evangelists drew. Scott supports his criticism of the two-document theory and his own analysis with a wealth of statistics.

Though impressive, the exegesis is inconclusive on many points, including the interpretation of παρέδοσαν. παραδίδωμι, though used predominantly of oral transmitting, can, as BAG says (and as Scott admits, 68), be used 'of oral *or written* tradition' to mean 'hand down, pass on, transmit, relate, teach', (see Acts 6:14; cf. 2 Thess. 2:15), and it may perfectly well include written tradition here. The exegete, however thorough he may be, is dealing all the time with probabilities rather than certainties. It is like examining a photograph under intense magnification. The exegete puts the text under a magnifying glass, but is defeated in his study of the detail by the limitations of his lens and the coarseness of the grain of his printing paper. Alexander, H. J. Cadbury, Fitzmyer, Marshall, J. W. Scott, W. C. van Unnik and the rest have brought great learning to Luke's famous sentence, but none can know all that was in the evangelist's mind and none can afford to lay great weight on his own tentative conclusions. Luke's words are in fact compatible with his knowing only oral traditions, or knowing Mark and Q, or knowing Matthew and Mark.[22] Scott's theory, though stated with great care (to which this summary does not do justice), to

8

me at least is not convincing. It posits an officially authorised oral ur-gospel, which had a well-established order which, however, was not immune from change. This seems to be too much like trying to have one's cake and eat it.[23]

There are three reasons for questioning independence:

1.) It is doubtful whether the order of the pericopes in the three gospels can be satisfactorily explained without recognition of literary connections. There would of course be no difficulty about putting the outstanding events in their natural order: the birth and baptism at the beginning and the death and resurrection at the end; and there would be no difficulty about retaining a standard sequence of events which followed one another in quick succession, as in Holy Week. But in the Galilean ministry, with its great number of events and its wealth of teaching (often with no obvious logical or chronological sequence), it is difficult to think that the correspondence of order would have arisen without a literary connection in a highly literate society as was first-century Judaism.

In the Huck-Greeven *Synopsis* the thirty-five parallel pericopes of the Galilean ministry in Mark and Luke follow in exactly the same order. In Huck's earlier editions there was one displacement, Luke 6:17–19 being put before 6:12–16. This was done to bring it alongside Mark 3:7–12, which also mentions a great crowd which came from Jerusalem, Judea, Tyre and Sidon to hear, to touch and to be healed. The parallel, however, is not at all close and Greeven seems fully justified in reverting to Luke's original order. The remaining thirty-seven parallel pericopes continue in the Markan order. It seems unlikely that this identity of order of seventy-two pericopes derives solely from an order preserved with the help of some mnemonic device in oral tradition. When it is remembered that in the sections covering the Galilean ministry and the Judean period Mark fitted in thirty-two other pericopes which are not found in Luke, and Luke twenty-eight which are not found in Mark, it is a little difficult to believe that the non-sacrosanct sequence would have survived all the subsequent additions and subtractions. Mark and Matthew also have long parallel sequences, though these are broken up by three major dislocations,

9

which makes the idea of an underlying memorised sequence look even less probable in their case.

2.) There was great mobility in both secular society and among the churches, as is witnessed not only by Acts, but in the constant comings and goings to which the epistles bear witness. Paul, having never set foot in Rome, knew at least twenty-nine members of that church when he wrote to them in 58.[24] The canonical gospels, especially Matthew and Luke, were major works, written by leaders of great competence, and it is unlikely that knowledge of their projected books was kept secret. Rather, we would expect one evangelist to be glad of another's help while preparing his own work.[25] Therefore complete independence suggests a sudden almost simultaneous inspiration of three men and a speedy execution of the task by all of them.[26] And they must all have found in their common oral tradition something sufficiently like the gospel genre to enable them thus independently to write in that genre. It seems a little improbable.

3.) There are (as we shall see, pp. 187–95) distinct (though occasionally mutually contradictory) traditions of gospel order in the early church, which most naturally presupposes that they were not all published at the same time. Rather, one evangelist invented the gospel genre and others copied him. This notion that the later evangelists knew the work of the earlier ones was held by Augustine, and may have been general.[27] (In due course we shall try to demonstrate life-settings for the gospels which are separate both in space and time.)

It seems, then, that solely literary theories reach an impasse[28] and that a simple oral theory is not adequate. But there is a third possibility: *There may be a large measure of independence as well as an important measure of interdependence.* It is along these lines that a new attempt may be made to solve the synoptic problem.

2

BUILDING A SYNOPTIC THEORY: (1) THE RELATION OF LUKE TO MARK

Chapter summary

This chapter considers the first three of five steps in building a synoptic theory.

Step 1: Luke knew Mark's gospel. We have already seen the wide scholarly consensus that Luke and Mark are not entirely independent. The Griesbach school argues that Mark followed Luke, being a composite narrative produced by the weaving together of Matthew and Luke, paragraph by paragraph, sentence by sentence, word by word. Such a procedure is improbable. There is very little of Luke's wording in Mark. The ready-made Q parallels are not used by Mark. The argument from order is invalid. Therefore Luke probably came after Mark.

Step 2: Fifty-two pericopes of Luke and Mark have a common origin (Category 1 passages), *fourteen others cover the same ground, but show no signs of common origin* (Category 2).

Step 3: Luke keeps to the sense of Mark in the truly parallel passages. In Category 1 passages the two gospels differ in wording five thousand times, but not in sense. Differences are complementary rather than contradictory, as in Jesus' eschatological discourse. The apparent contradiction about whether to carry a staff or not does not look like Luke's adaptation of Mark. The fourteen Category 2 passages, eleven in the passion/resurrection accounts and three earlier, are shown not to have a common origin by their vast differences of wording and by the differences of order within pericopes. To claim that Luke keeps

11

to the sense of Mark in Category 1 passages and not in Category 2 is not arguing in a circle since the two categories of material are self-evidently distinct.

In Chapters 2 and 3 an attempt will be made to establish the following steps in the argument:

Step 1: Luke knew Mark's gospel.

Step 2: There are fifty-two pericopes where Luke and Mark almost certainly have either a common oral origin or some measure of direct literary dependence. There are fourteen other pericopes covering much the same ground in the two gospels for which there is no *prima facie* evidence of this.

Step 3: In the former case Luke keeps to the sense of Mark.

Step 4: Luke may be presumed to keep to the sense of his other sources. This makes the existence of Q or large-scale borrowing from Matthew improbable, since the Lukan and Matthean forms of the Q-material often differ widely in sense.

Step 5: Matthew's relation to Mark can be satisfactorily explained on the lines of patristic tradition.

Step 1: Luke knew Mark's gospel. We have sufficiently shown that Mark and Luke are probably not entirely independent. The next question is: In which direction does the dependence lie? The great majority of scholars are agreed that Luke used Mark, but the Griesbach school holds that Luke is prior to Mark.[1]

Mark is noteworthy for its freshness and vigour, and many have seen this as evidence for its originality and so of its priority.[2] But of course freshness and vigour alone do not prove originality. Freshness and vigour may be the end product of a highly sophisticated literary process – the use of art to conceal art. The view that Mark's narrative is based on the reminiscences of Peter may seem a very natural inference, but it is certainly not the only conceivable one. That it might be the result of the interweaving of Matthew and Luke merits serious and imaginative consideration.

Perhaps the best way is to examine Mark with the aid of Farmer's *Synopticon*. Here by his use of different colours and different underlinings it is possible to see at a glance a) where

The author's movements in Mark 1 according to the Griesbach theory (showing sequences of 3 or more words)

Verse of Mark 1	Mark and partial agreements	Matthew	Matthew and Luke	Luke

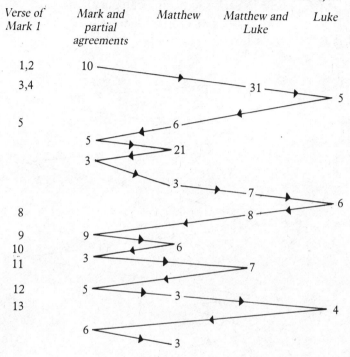

Verse of Mark 1:
1,2
3,4
5
8
9
10
11
12
13

10 — 31 — 5
6
5 — 21
3
3 — 7 — 6
8
9
6
3
7
5 — 3 — 4
6 — 3

The author's movements in Mark 1 according to the Griesbach theory (showing the number of words as they appear in each succeeding category)

Verse of Mark 1	Mark and partial agreements	Matthew	Matthew and Luke	Luke

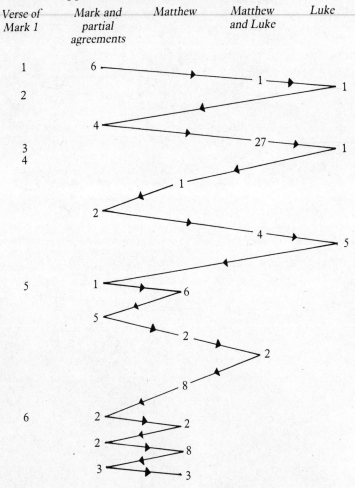

there is verbatim agreement between Matthew and Mark or between Luke and Mark or between all three; b) where there is material peculiar to Mark; and c) where there is partial agreement between Mark and one or both of the others. We can then set out in a chart (p. 13) the movements of the author in composing a typical passage (Mark 1:1–13) as supposed by the Griesbach theory. We can see the physical movements as he goes from one scroll to another, and the mental movements as he changes what he finds in his sources. There are four columns showing the number of successive words which came 1.) out of his own head (this comprises b) and c) above; since in both cases Mark is not just copying, all is in a sense Markan matter); 2.) from Matthew, 3.) from Matthew or Luke, 4.) from Luke.

It might be maintained with some reason that the verbatim agreement of a word or two is not likely in many cases to be evidence of the use of a particular source. So a fairer impression might be given if we concern ourselves only with sequences of more than two words, as shown in the chart on p. 14, in which single words or two-word sequences are left out of account.

This complex interweaving will be found to continue until we reach Mark 6:44. At that point Luke's 'Great Omission' begins and we simply have Matthean material, greatly modified by Mark. If we again discount single words or two-word sequences we get words taken from Matthew alternating with Mark's own words in this fashion:

Matthew

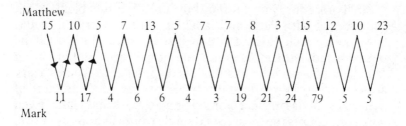

Mark

and so on to 8:10. In 8:11–21 there are small amounts of Luke in addition to the Markan and Matthean material; 8:22–26 is special Mark; then at 8:27 the two-source weaving is resumed, and for the rest of the book there continue different variations of the same highly complex processes.

That a process like this is envisaged by careful exponents of this view is shown by D. L. Dungan, who has made what is perhaps the most persuasive attempt at finding a *Sitz im Leben* for the Griesbach Mark. He takes seriously its association with Peter's ministry in Rome. Peter had found himself caught in crossfire between the hardline Torah party and the supporters of Paul, and the tension had been aggravated by the publication first of Matthew's gospel and then of Luke-Acts. When he came to Rome in the mid-60s, he took no sides, commending both gospels as being representative of apostolic teaching. After the death of Peter and Paul the Romans turned to Mark, who had worked with both apostles, and asked for a record of Peter's teaching. Being a practical people, they wanted the bedrock message. Taking Peter's public speeches as his guide and model, and making no attempt to be innovative, he got to work on the two gospels. He wove their accounts into a composite narrative, 'paragraph by paragraph, sentence by sentence and even word by word'.[3]

On somewhat similar lines Orchard maintained that Mark represents lectures delivered by Peter in Rome for the express purpose of giving apostolic approval to the new gospel of Luke. Knowing Matthew almost by heart Peter wove into it Lukan material and added his own recollections, Mark ensuring that a shorthand record was kept.[4]

Such procedures are *possible*, but surely improbable. If Mark had worked with Peter and taught Peter's converts, it would have been much easier for him just to write down what he remembered, either inventing the gospel genre or imitating Matthew's gospel if he had it at his disposal. The whole theory also seems to be made improbable by the small amount of material which is in fact common only to Mark and Luke. Even when one counts the most trivial single words like καί, there are (on my counting of the green words in Farmer's *Synopticon*) only some 1,070 words common to Luke and Mark which are not also in Matthew. As Mark's total word-count is, according to Morgenthaler, 11,229,[5] the distinctive Lukan vocabulary is

16

about 9.5%. There are no lengthy passages that are distinctively Lukan, in the way that 6:45–8:21 is distinctively Matthean. When one thinks of the huge quantity of special Lukan material, which by definition is not found in Mark, the small amount of distinctively Lukan material which is actually to be found there makes the theory implausible.

Again, if Mark is conceived as a book bridging the other two gospels, the material common to Matthew and Luke which Mark omits amounts to a surprisingly large total: the whole of Q. He is supposed to be conflating Matthew and Luke, yet he omits all those ready-to-use parallels.

The argument by which the Griesbach advocates set the greatest store seems to be (in Farmer's words):

> The rediscovery of its [the Griesbach hypothesis'] central and essential strength – viz. that it offers a credible explanation for the order of the episodes in the synoptic gospels . . . lacking in the alternative accounts . . . Mark on this view can *only* be third and *must* have known Matthew and Luke. There seems to be no other satisfactory solution.[6] (Italics mine)

Dungan puts the 'credible explanation' this way:

> Just when Luke goes off into a special passage, there appears at Mark's side faithful Matthew, as if by magic, and just when Matthew suddenly departs on an errand of his own, in the nick of time back comes Luke, as if in response to a providential *bath qol*. How is it possible?[7]

This sounds impressive, but on examination it amounts to very little. The argument is this: According to the two-document hypothesis, Matthew and Luke sometimes depart from the order of Mark. One would expect, if they were acting independently of one another, that they would sometimes depart at the same place. But they never do – is this not most improbable? C. M. Tuckett, writing from the standpoint of Markan priority, points out that the number of changes of order supposedly made by Matthew and Luke is relatively small; and, in spite of allowing (what seem to me) far too many changes of order, he shows that statistically the case goes the other way. He considers that there is in fact one point at which Matthew's and

Luke's changes of order may be held to coincide, so he works out two statistics:

> Luke changes the order of 4 Markan pericopes, Matthew changes the order of 6. These changes perhaps coincide once (Mark 3:13 –19). If one takes the range of the compass of Mark prior to the passion, this covers 80 Markan pericopes (using Huck's divisions). The probability of two authors independently choosing 4 and 6 respectively out of 80, and coinciding once is 0.246. The probability of their never coinciding is 0.726. This is perfectly acceptable in statistical terms. (It is usually assumed that a probability has to be at least as small as 0.05% before being considered statistically significant). There is thus nothing surprising in these figures, and nothing to suggest that the initial assumption, viz. the independence of Matthew and Luke, should be questioned.[8]

In fact (as we shall argue on pp. 45–47) none of the four supposed Lukan transpositions looks like a genuine transposition and (as we shall argue on pp. 101–8) the six Matthew/Mark transpositions are more helpfully regarded as three in number and are capable of a satisfactory explanation on the Augustinian order of Matthew, Mark, Luke. Thus the dogmatic and exclusive claim for the Griesbach argument from order vanishes into thin air.[9]

In reality it is quite difficult (as we shall see in Chapter 10) to conceive of anyone taking the great scrolls[10] of Matthew and Luke and treating them in a manner that would have produced our Mark. So, if Griesbach is wrong and total independence is wrong, it seems a virtual certainty that Mark was prior to Luke and to some extent used by Luke.

We will take Steps 2 and 3 together:

Step 2: There are fifty-two pericopes where Luke and Mark almost certainly have a common origin, either from a common oral source or through some measure of direct literary dependence (Category 1). There are fourteen other pericopes in which the two gospels cover more or less the same ground for which there is no prima facie evidence of this (Category 2).

Step 3: Luke keeps to the sense of Mark in the truly parallel passages.

The principle upon which these two categories are to be

distinguished is simply the impression given by laying the parallel passages side by side and looking at the closeness of wording. If this suggests either some process of common learning or of copying (along with a modest amount of modification), the passage comes in Category 1. If, however, differences of order and wording predominate, the passage comes in Category 2. This is a quite unsophisticated layman's test. As we shall see in due course (pp. 51ff), redaction critics who have accepted the two-document hypothesis (which for us is still *sub judice*), and are anxious as far as possible to explain the synoptic phenomena in terms of just these two documents, are inclined to see Luke sometimes modifying his material almost beyond recognition. Whether this seems plausible will depend considerably on how we take Luke's preface. If Luke is seriously trying to write καθὼς παρέδοσαν ἡμῖν οἱ ἀπ' ἀρχῆς αὐτόπται he will be careful about the sources he chooses and he will keep to the sense of those he utilises. If, however, he feels free to compose new material he might introduce almost unlimited change. When we assume the former we find that the material divides into the two categories quite naturally. Nearly all the material from the triple tradition and from the Mark-Luke tradition between Luke 4:31 and 22:13 (fifty-two pericopes) belongs to Category 1. In Category 2 are three pericopes from the Luke 4:14–22:13 section and eleven from the later part of the book, all of which have some sort of parallelism with Mark. We will look at the categories in turn and see how the passages fit into the two groups.

Category 1: Passages of common origin

There are something like five thousand differences of wording between Mark and Luke in the passages which belong to Category 1.[11] If we think of Luke as working directly on the scroll of Mark, we find that he often omits from, adds to or gives a more polished version of Mark's story, but he almost always does so without changing the basic meaning. This is particularly true with regard to the words of Jesus.[12] In the vast majority of cases the words are either identical, nearly identical or give the same sense in similar words; in some cases they give the same sense in markedly different words; in a few cases there are minor differences of sense; and there is just one case in the teaching of Jesus where Luke's account appears to contradict that of Mark.[13]

I use the language of 'omission', 'addition', and 'polishing' for convenience, rather than as a description of Luke's editorial work. With increasing study I become less inclined to think that Luke is directly dependent on Mark at the points where the two gospels are parallel and that he is modifying the text before him. So many of the huge number of changes seem pointless. Of course not every one of the five thousand changes would have involved a separate editorial decision, as groups of words would be considered together. But even so Luke would have had to make decisions to alter his text many hundreds of times. How much easier it would have been for him to have copied his source word for word at all points where he was in agreement with it, as on occasion the Chronicler did;[14] or to have contented himself at most with just a few omissions and a little polishing.

It may be better to think of him as an experienced teacher who had for years taught Theophilus and his kind the sort of things that we find in his gospel, the likenesses between the synoptic gospels being accounted for mainly by their common origin in the apostolic preaching. Thus what Luke wrote is fundamentally what he was accustomed to teach. That Luke actually knew and used Mark seems, however, to be shown by the closeness of order between the two books. It is therefore likely (as we shall argue more fully in Chapter 10) that when he came to write his work he from time to time refreshed his memory of what Mark (and perhaps, as I am inclined to believe, of what Matthew) had written and that he allowed them occasionally to influence what he eventually wrote. But it cannot be too strongly stated that one evangelist's knowledge of the work of another does not necessarily mean that his work is a modification of the other.

For the time being we will leave it an open question how far the differences between Mark and Luke are due to redaction of one by the other, and how far they represent separate traditions, and will go on to identify the main types of difference. In comparing the words of Jesus as given by the two evangelists we see a range of differences between complete identity and the one case of apparent contradiction. Luke and Mark of course often have single identical words and there are more than a dozen instances of common sequences of words ranging from two in number[15] to twenty-nine.[16] There are cases where they are identical except for word order and/or the addition,[17] subtraction[18] or change of a single word.[19] Then comes a large class in which there is a greater number of small differences,[20] some of these showing the omission of more or less otiose words.[21]

Then come instances where there are marked differences in wording, but where the sense remains substantially the same throughout. It is of course difficult to define what is meant by 'substantially the same'. A pedant can argue some difference in sense for a large proportion of the differences in wording, but as a test of substantial identity it is better to ask the question: Would one evangelist (who is not professing to give the *ipsissima verba* of his characters) recognise the parallel story of the other evangelist as a fair account (as far as it goes) of the same event or discourse? A measure of concurrence that passes this test can be found, for example, in the parable of the sower. In the story there are dozens of small differences, and occasionally quite a large one, e.g.

Mark	*Luke*
4:8 ἀναβαίνοντα καὶ αὐξανόμενα καὶ ἔφερεν ἐν τριάκοντα καὶ ἐν ἑξήκοντα καὶ ἐν ἑκατόν.	8:8 ἑκατονταπλασίονα.

In the interpretation of the parable there are scores of further differences, e.g.

Mark	*Luke*
4:14 ὁ σπείρων τὸν λόγον σπείρει.	8:11 ὁ σπόρος ἐστὶν ὁ λόγος τοῦ θεοῦ.

21

Another example can be seen in the story of the rich young ruler:

Mark 10:21, 22

21 ὁ δὲ Ἰησοῦς ἐμβλέψας αὐτῷ ἠγάπησεν αὐτὸν καὶ εἶπεν αὐτῷ· ἕν σε ὑστερεῖ· ὕπαγε, ὅσα ἔχεις πώλησον καὶ δὸς τοῖς πτωχοῖς, καὶ ἕξεις θησαυρὸν ἐν οὐρανῷ, καὶ
22 δεῦρο ἀκολούθει μοι. ὁ δὲ στυγνάσας ἐπὶ τῷ λόγῳ ἀπῆλθεν λυπούμενος· ἦν γὰρ ἔχων κτήματα πολλά.

Luke 18:22, 23

22 ἀκούσας δὲ ὁ Ἰησοῦς εἶπεν αὐτῷ· ἔτι ἕν σοι λείπει· πάντα ὅσα ἔχεις πώλησον καὶ διάδος πτωχοῖς, καὶ ἕξεις θησαυρὸν ἐν τοῖς οὐρανοῖς, καὶ δεῦρο
23 ἀκολούθει μοι. ὁ δὲ ἀκούσας ταῦτα περίλυπος ἐγενήθη, ἦν γὰρ πλούσιος σφόδρα.

The meaning is very close, but there are more than a score of differences in two verses.

In the parable of the wicked husbandmen, Luke has strikingly different wording:

Mark 12:5, 6

5 καὶ ἄλλον ἀπέστειλεν· κἀκεῖνον ἀπέκτειναν, καὶ πολλοὺς ἄλλους, οὓς μὲν δέροντες, οὓς δὲ
6 ἀποκτέννοντες. ἔτι ἕνα εἶχεν, υἱὸν ἀγαπητόν· ἀπέστειλεν αὐτὸν ἔσχατον πρὸς αὐτοὺς λέγων ὅτι ἐντραπήσονται τὸν υἱόν μου.

Luke 20:12, 13

12 καὶ προσέθετο τρίτον πέμψαι· οἱ δὲ καὶ τοῦτον τραυματίσαντες ἐξέβαλον.
13 εἶπεν δὲ ὁ κύριος τοῦ ἀμπελῶνος· τί ποίησω; πέμψω τὸν υἱόν μου τὸν ἀγαπητόν· ἴσως τοῦτον ἐντραπήσονται.

Further examples can be seen:

Mark

6:11 ὃς ἂν τόπος μή δέξηται.
8:36 ζημιωθῆναι τὴν ψυχὴν αὐτοῦ.
12:15 φέρετέ μοι δηνάριον ἵνα ἴδω.
10:52 ὕπαγε, ἡ πίστις σου . . .
12:36 ἐν τῷ πνεύματι τῷ ἁγίῳ.

Luke

9:5 ὅσοι ἂν μὴ δέχωνται.
9:25 ἑαυτὸν δὲ ἀπολέσας ἢ ζημιωθείς.
20:24 δείξατέ μοι δηνάριον.
18:42 ἀνάβλεψον· ἡ πίστις σου . . .
20:42 ἐν βίβλῳ ψαλμῶν.

22

The last two examples are not cases of two expressions having the same meaning, but of being complementary in sense.

Many omissions and additions take away or add a distinct piece of information without materially altering the sense of the rest, e.g.

2:26	πῶς εἰσῆλθεν εἰς τὸν οἶκον τοῦ θεοῦ ἐπὶ Ἀβιαθὰρ ἀρχιερέως.	6:4	ὡς εἰσῆλθεν εἰς τὸν οἶκον τοῦ θεοῦ.
4:23	εἴ τις ἔχει ὦτα ἀκούειν ἀκουέτω.	8:17	—
6:9	ἀλλὰ ὑποδεδεμένους σανδάλια	9:3	—
8:34	—	9:23	καθ᾽ ἡμέραν
10:19	μὴ ἀποστερήσῃς	18:20	—

In such cases the accounts are complementary without being contradictory.

This sort of complementarity is characteristic of the synoptic apocalypse of Mark 13 and Luke 21. The two gospels have here as elsewhere a number of sentences closely similar in wording and a number the same in sense in spite of considerable differences in wording. Occasionally also there are passages which have the same basic sense although the forms of words are quite different, e.g.

13:11	ὃ ἐὰν δοθῇ ὑμῖν ἐν ἐκείνῃ τῇ ὥρᾳ, τοῦτο λαλεῖτε.	21:15	ἐγώ γὰρ δώσω ὑμῖν στόμα καὶ σοφίαν, ᾗ οὐ δυνήσονται ἀντιστῆναι ἢ ἀντειπεῖν ἅπαντες οἱ ἀντικείμενοι ὑμῖν.

But the great characteristic of the discourse is its number of notable Lukan omissions and additions. There are half a dozen of each, yet all the material fits naturally into the respective gospels, and the two gospels dovetail harmoniously into each other.[22]

The sayings in Mark 13 which are not in Luke 21 include: 'this is but the beginning of the birth-pangs' (v. 8); 'the gospel must first be preached to all nations' (v. 10); 'Pray that it may not happen in winter' (v. 18); 'if the Lord had not shortened the

23

days, no human being would be saved; but for the sake of the elect, whom he chose, he shortened the days. And then if any one says to you, "Look, here is the Christ!" or "Look, there he is!" do not believe it. False Christs and false prophets will arise and show signs and wonders, to lead astray, if possible, the elect. But take heed; I have told you all things beforehand' (vv. 20–23); 'then he will send out the angels, and gather his elect from the four winds, from the ends of the earth to the ends of heaven' (v. 27); 'But of that day or that hour no one knows, not even the angels in heaven, nor the Son, but only the Father' (v. 32).

The sayings in Luke 21 which are not in Mark include: '"The time is at hand!" Do not go after them' (v. 8); 'there will be terrors and great signs from heaven' (v. 11); 'not a hair of your head will perish' (v. 18); 'For these are days of vengeance, to fulfil all that is written' (v. 22); 'they will fall by the edge of the sword, and be led captive among all nations; and Jerusalem will be trodden down by the Gentiles, until the times of the Gentiles are fulfilled' (v. 24); 'Now when these things begin to take place, look up and raise your heads, because your redemption is drawing near' (v. 28). Then Luke concludes (vv. 34–36) with an exhortation to watchfulness. The two versions are a remarkable example of harmonious complementarity, apart, possibly, from Luke's treatment of Mark's 'abomination of desolation', to which we refer below (p. 26).

There are two other instances of Luke giving a fuller account of the words of Jesus:

1.) 2:21 οὐδεὶς ἐπίβλημα ῥάκους ἀγνάφου ἐπιράπτει.

5:36 οὐδεὶς ἐπίβλημα ἀπὸ ἱματίου καινοῦ σχίσας ἐπιβάλλει.

Luke's version is at first sight hardly an improvement in sense; but Luke is presumably representing Jesus as humorously suggesting the absurd – the destruction not merely of a new piece of cloth, but a new garment, in order unsuccessfully to patch an old one. In Mark's shorter version no mention is made of where the new cloth is to come from. Here is a fuller account, but no conflict in sense.

24

2.) 14:13 ὑπάγετε εἰς τὴν
πόλιν . . .

22:8–10 πορευθέντες
ἑτοιμάσατε ἡμῖν τὸ
πάσχα, ἵνα φάγωμεν.
οἱ δὲ εἶπαν αὐτῷ· ποῦ
θέλεις ἑτοιμάσωμεν; ὁ
δὲ εἶπεν αὐτοῖς· ἰδοὺ
εἰσελθόντων ὑμῶν εἰς
τὴν πόλιν . . .

Again a filling out, but no conflict in sense.

We have now covered the main types into which the five thousand differences between Luke and Mark may be divided, which show no sign of the one setting out to change the sense of the other. We are left with a handful of differences which look like minor differences of sense, which Luke has allowed to stand:

1.) 1:38 εἰς τοῦτο γὰρ ἐξῆλθον.   4:43 ὅτι ἐπὶ τοῦτο ἀπεστάλην.

In the short pericopes (four verses in Mark, two in Luke) which conclude with these clauses, there is little verbal similarity. It does not look as though Luke is working on the text of Mark. For instance, he does not pick up the reference to Jesus praying. The theological slant of the concluding phrase is indeed different (Mark implying that Jesus came out from God willingly, Luke stressing that Jesus was sent by the Father), but in no way contradictory.

2.) 2:5 τέκνον   5:20 ἄνθρωπε

This pericope on the healing of the paralysed man is typical of the triple tradition, with Mark and Luke having many verbal likenesses and many differences and Luke having echoes of Matthew, e.g. ἰδοὺ ἐπὶ κλίνης (v. 18), καὶ περιπάτει (v. 23). It seems unlikely that the differences, including a change to ἄνθρωπε, were deliberate alterations. Rather it is Luke's way of telling the story.

3.) 2:17 ἰσχύοντες.   5:31 ὑγιαίνοντες.

Much the same applies to this passage on the call of Levi. Luke the physician may well have preferred ὑγιαίνοντες, but this does not mean that it is a deliberate adaptation of Mark.

4.) 2:28 ὥστε κύριός ἐστιν ὁ   6:5 ἔλεγεν αὐτοῖς κύριός ἐστιν
       υἱὸς τοῦ ἀνθρώπου   τοῦ σαββάτου ὁ υἱὸς τοῦ
       καὶ τοῦ σαββάτου.   ἀνθρώπου.

In Mark's previous verse (27) Jesus refers to the sabbath having been made for man. Luke and Matthew agree against Mark in not having this saying. They also agree in explicitly attributing the above saying about the Son of Man being Lord of the sabbath to Jesus himself, whereas in Mark it could be a comment of the evangelist. Luke *might* be clarifying Mark, but it is more likely that both he and Matthew are giving the saying in their own accustomed way.

5.) 4:25 ὃ ἔχει.   8:18 ὃ δοκεῖ ἔχειν.

This pericope about hiding one's light, which in Luke (8:16–18) contains sixty-one words has, according to Farmer's *Synopticon*, only twelve words identical with Mark. Luke's addition of δοκεῖ merely makes explicit what was already implicit in Mark. This again looks like Luke's own version of the sayings rather than his alteration of Mark.

6.) 8:31 μετὰ τρεῖς ἡμέρας   9:22 τῇ τρίτῃ ἡμέρᾳ ἐγερθῆναι.
       ἀναστῆναι.

This is another of Luke's minor agreements with Matthew against Mark in the triple tradition. It could of course be Luke safeguarding himself from a literalistic misunderstanding of Mark, but this is in fact the normal usage of both Matthew and Luke, so it is unnecessary to suppose it to be an alteration of Mark.

The eschatological discourse provides an example of a much greater change of sense, if indeed Luke is intending his version to explain that of Mark:

13:14 ὅταν δὲ ἴδητε τὸ   21:20 ὅταν δὲ ἴδητε
       βδέλυγμα τῆς ἐρημώσεως   κυκλουμένην ὑπὸ
       ἑστηκότα ὅπου οὐ δεῖ, ὁ   στρατοπέδων Ἰερουσαλήμ,
       ἀναγινώσκων νοείτω.   τότε γνῶτε ὅτι ἤγγικεν ἡ
                                               ἐρήμωσις αὐτῆς.

26

Here Mark's version is obscure, and deliberately so (ὁ ἀναγινώσκων νοείτω). Luke's version is clear, and is commonly taken as proof that it must post-date the siege of Jerusalem. This is not necessarily so, since attempts to interpret the obscure warning of Jerusalem's desolation are likely to have been current long before that time.[23] This passage is carefully discussed by D. Wenham. He comes to the conclusion:

> To recognize that the three synoptic accounts are complementary is important, but it is not the same as saying that they are identical. It remains the case that Luke refers to one aspect of the coming event (the arrival of hostile armies) and that Matthew and Mark refer to a different aspect (the profanation of the temple). And this difference calls for explanation. It is possible that Luke, faced with the obscurity of the phrase in Matthew and Mark, has simply drawn on his knowledge of Daniel and/or his historical imagination for something more straightforward. But in the light of the previous discussion, it is also possible that the pre-synoptic tradition was like Dan 11:31 and contained both the Lukan and the Matthew/Mark phraseology, reading perhaps
>
> When you see Jerusalem surrounded by armies and the desolating sacrilege standing where it should not let the reader understand. Then let those in Judea . . . (187)

He regards this as a well-grounded possibility, which shows that we should be rash to jump to the conclusion that Luke is here redacting Mark.

Finally, we have the one apparently straightforward case in the teaching of Jesus of Luke seeming to contradict Mark:

Matthew	*Mark*	*Luke*
10:9f μὴ	6:8f μηδὲν	9:3 μηδὲν αἴρετε
κτήσησθε . . .	αἴρωσιν . . . εἰ	μήτε ῥάβδον
μηδὲ	μὴ ῥάβδον	
ὑποδήματα	μόνον . . . ἀλλὰ	
μηδὲ ῥάβδον.	ὑποδεδεμένους	
	σανδάλια.	

If it is true that Luke had before him Matthew as well as Mark, and that he was primarily dependent on them at this point, he had two traditions to choose from: Matthew, which said, 'Do not procure sandals or a staff,' and Mark, which said that they should not take anything except only a staff and that they were to wear sandals. Luke would then probably have interpreted Matthew, not as demanding an exercise in asceticism, but as bidding them not to procure anything new (spare clothing, shoes, staff)[24] as if making provision for a long journey: and Mark similarly as telling them to go just as they were, shod simply with sandals, looking for support from those who heard them as they went along. So he decides to adopt Matthew's imperatival form, to use Mark's verb αἴρω (which leaves open the question whether it means 'procure' or 'carry'),[25] and to let Matthew's prohibition of a staff stand; and he omits all reference to footwear. Alternatively and more likely, Luke may already have had the version which appears in his text and saw no need to change it, especially if he knew Matthew's form of words, and if he knew that the generally received understanding of Jesus' instruction was, 'Do not make provision as if for a long journey.'

The upshot of this is that, in spite of all the differences between the two gospels, Luke is demonstrably most reluctant to write anything which alters – less still, contradicts – the sense of Mark, especially in his reporting of the words of Jesus.

This is certainly true of the passages in Category 1, which are by definition closely parallel. But the question arises whether it applies to the fourteen passages in Category 2 which, though covering much the same ground, are markedly different in sense.[26]

Category 2: Passages showing no *prima facie* evidence of common origin

There are fourteen of these, eleven of which virtually constitute Luke's passion and resurrection narrative and three of which come earlier in the book.

Luke 4:14, 15 – Jesus' appearance in Galilee

Mark 1:14, 15	Luke 4:14, 15
Καὶ μετὰ τὸ παραδοθῆναι τὸν	Καὶ ὑπέστρεψεν ὁ Ἰησοῦς ἐν τῇ

'Ιωάννην ἦλθεν ὁ 'Ιησοῦς εἰς
τὴν Γαλιλαίαν, κηρύσσων τὸ
εὐαγγέλιον τοῦ θεοῦ καὶ λέγων
ὅτι πεπλήρωται ὁ καιρὸς καὶ
ἤγγικεν ἡ βασιλεία τοῦ θεοῦ·
μετανοεῖτε καὶ πιστεύετε ἐν τῷ
εὐαγγελίῳ.

δυνάμει τοῦ πνεύματος εἰς τὴν
Γαλιλαίαν. καὶ φήμη ἐξῆλθεν
καθ' ὅλης τῆς περιχώρου περὶ
αὐτοῦ. καὶ αὐτὸς ἐδίδασκεν ἐν
ταῖς συναγωγαῖς αὐτῶν,
δοξαζόμενος ὑπὸ πάντων.

These passages appear in the same context, immediately after the temptation, but the only words in common are ὁ 'Ιησοῦς and εἰς τὴν Γαλιλαίαν; otherwise the treatment is quite different. Luke's version is closely linked to the account of Jesus' preaching in Nazareth (vv. 16–30) which immediately follows and which has no parallel in the other gospels. The pericopes do not appear to come from a common source. This is in effect granted both by those (like H. Schürmann) who take the view that Luke is dependent on a non-Markan source at this point and by those (like J. Delobel) who regard it as Luke's own composition. To quote J. Fitzmyer 521f:

> This summary statement is most likely inspired by Mark 1:14–15. H. Schürmann ('Der "Bericht vom Anfang"') has tried to argue that Luke is here dependent on a variant non-Marcan source. Similarly, B. H. Streeter (*The Four Gospels*, 206–207): . . . 'from Q, not Mark'. But this is highly questionable and has been examined at length by J. Delobel ('La rédaction'), who rightly argues rather for Lucan redaction [i.e. composition]. These verses are to be regarded as an editorial statement, composed by Luke, who differs with his Marcan source, by which he is otherwise inspired.

Luke 5:1–11 – The call of the fishermen

In verses 1–3 we have Jesus standing by the Lake of Gennesaret, seeing two empty boats and fishermen nearby washing their nets. He gets into one of the boats and teaches the people from it. In verses 4–10 he tells Peter to put out into the deep; Peter, James and John are awed by the catch of fish; Peter acknowledges his sinfulness and is told that he will catch men.

In verse 11 they come to land, leave everything and follow Jesus. Mark has no parallel to the main story: Peter's call after the great catch of fish. He has, however, an account of the call of Peter, James and John, and also Andrew, which is remarkable for its completely different treatment. There are a few verbal coincidences: in verses 1–3 παρά, εἶδεν, ἁλεεῖς, τὰ δίκτνα; verses 4–9 are quite independent; in verses 10, 11 the coincidences (underlined) and differences can be clearly seen:

Mark 1:17–20

17 καὶ εἶπεν αὐτοῖς ὁ ᾽Ιησοῦς· δεῦτε ὀπίσω μου, καὶ ποιήσω ὑμᾶς γενέσθαι
18 ἁλεεῖς ἀνθρώπων. καὶ εὐθὺς ἀφέντες τὰ δίκτνα
19 ἠκολούθησαν αὐτῷ. καὶ προβὰς ὀλίγον εἶδεν ᾽Ιάκωβον τὸν τοῦ Ζεβεδαίου καὶ ᾽Ιωάννην τὸν ἀδελφὸν αὐτοῦ καὶ αὐτοὺς ἐν τῷ πλοίῳ καταρτίζοντας τά δίκτνα. καὶ εὐθὺς
20 ἐκάλεσεν αὐτούς· καὶ ἀφέντες τὸν πατέρα αὐτῶν Ζεβεδαῖον ἐν τῷ πλοίῳ μετὰ τῶν μισθωτῶν ἀπῆλθον ὀπίσω αὐτοῦ.

Luke 5:10, 11

10 ὁμοίως δὲ καὶ ᾽Ιάκωβον καὶ ᾽Ιωάννην υἱοὺς Ζεβεδαίου, οἳ ἦσαν κοινωνοὶ τῷ Σίμωνι. καὶ εἶπεν πρὸς τὸν Σίμωνα ὁ ᾽Ιησοῦς· μὴ φοβοῦ· ἀπὸ τοῦ νῦν ἀνθρώπους ἔσῃ ζωγρῶν.
11 καὶ καταγαγόντες τὰ πλοῖα ἐπὶ τὴν γῆν, ἀφέντες πάντα ἠκολούθησαν αὐτῷ.

There are also some slight parallels between Luke 5:1–3 and the later scene in Mark 4:1, 2 which introduces the parable of the sower: there was a crowd, which he taught, out of the boat. It is of course possible to suppose with Fitzmyer that the episode is 'composed by Luke from transposed and redacted Marcan material [from both chapters 1 and 4] and other material from Luke's private source ("L")' (560), but it is certainly not an edited version of what Mark wrote in 1:16–20, nor a recollection by Mark and Luke of the same carefully learnt oral tradition.

The end of the eschatological discourse

Mark 13:33–37

33 Βλέπετε, ἀγρυπνεῖτε· οὐκ οἴδατε γὰρ πότε ὁ καιρός
34 ἐστιν. ὡς ἄνθρωπος ἀπόδημος ἀφεὶς τὴν οἰκίαν αὐτοῦ καὶ δοὺς τοῖς δούλοις αὐτοῦ τὴν ἐξουσίαν, ἑκάστῳ τὸ ἔργον αὐτοῦ, καὶ τῷ θυρωρῷ ἐνετείλατο ἵνα
35 γρηγορῇ. γρηγορεῖτε οὖν· οὐκ οἴδατε γὰρ πότε ὁ κύριος τῆς οἰκίας ἔρχεται, ἢ ὀψὲ ἢ μεσονύκτιον ἢ
36 ἀλεκτοροφωνίας ἢ πρωΐ· μὴ ἐλθὼν ἐξαίφνης εὕρῃ ὑμᾶς
37 καθεύδοντας. ὃ δὲ ὑμῖν λέγω, πᾶσιν λέγω, γρηγορεῖτε.

Luke 21:34–36

34 Πποσέχετε δὲ ἑαυτοῖς μήποτε βαρηθῶσιν ὑμῶν αἱ καρδίαι ἐν κραιπάλῃ καὶ μέθῃ καὶ μερίμναις βιωτικαῖς, καὶ ἐπιστῇ ἐφ' ὑμᾶς αἰφνίδιος ἡ ἡμέρα
35 ἐκείνη ὡς παγίς· ἐπεισελεύσεται γὰρ ἐπὶ πάντας τοὺς καθημένους ἐπὶ πρόσωπον πάσης τῆς
36 γῆς. ἀγρυπνεῖτε δὲ ἐν παντὶ καιρῷ δεόμενοι ἵνα κατισχύσητε ἐκφυγεῖν ταῦτα πάντα τὰ μέλλοντα γίνεσθαι, καὶ σταθῆναι ἔμπροσθεν τοῦ υἱοῦ τοῦ ἀνθρώπου.

The discourse of Luke 21 has its own problems. There is much verbatim agreement in the triple tradition, and Luke has occasional coincidences with Matthew and Mark separately. There are also several sections where the contents of Mark and Luke are similar, but the wording different. Some common origin is evident in the main part of the discourse. When, however, we come to the respective conclusions, we find that they are too unlike (linked only by the word ἀγρυπνεῖτε) to make the idea of a common origin probable. Fitzmyer says categorically: 'This conclusion is peculiar to Luke; part of it may depend on material from his source "L", but Lucan composition cannot be wholly excluded' (1354).

Luke 4:31–22:13 follows the Markan outline consistently. He has made large additions (6:20–8:3; 9:51–18:14) and some subtractions (e.g. Mk. 6:17–29; 6:45–8:26), but he has kept steadily to Mark's order, recording his narratives with a closeness of wording which suggests either a literary relationship or derivation from an early common oral tradition or both. The three cases mentioned above are quite exceptional in this the major part of Luke's gospel, but from Luke 22:14 the situation changes. The three gospels continue to cover much the same ground and therefore continue to have verbal coincidences, but Luke has a great amount of material entirely his own, often his order of narration within a pericope is different, and in general the differences are more conspicuous than the coincidences.

Luke 22:14–23 – The institution of the Lord's Supper

In the columns below, the Markan account is given in the order of the text and the Lukan parallels are put alongside out of order. The order is strikingly different; the forecast of the betrayal is put by Mark near the beginning and by Luke at the end; Mark puts the taking of the bread before the taking of the cup, whereas Luke puts it after and then adds a second cup. Luke also has unique sayings at verses 15b and 16. Furthermore, where there are clear parallels the verbal forms are almost always different.

a) He sat at table with his disciples:

Mark 14	*Luke 22*
17 καὶ ὀψίας γενομένης ἔρχεται μετὰ τῶν δώδεκα.	14 καὶ ὅτε ἐγένετο ἡ ὥρα, ἀνέπεσεν, καὶ οἱ ἀπόστολοι σὺν αὐτῷ.
18 καὶ ἀνακειμένων αὐτῶν καὶ ἐσθιόντων ὁ Ἰησοῦς εἶπεν·	15 καὶ εἶπεν πρὸς αὐτούς· ἐπιθυμίᾳ ἐπεθύμησα τοῦτο τὸ πάσχα φαγεῖν μεθ' ὑμῶν πρὸ τοῦ με παθεῖν·
	16 λέγω γὰρ ὑμῖν ὅτι οὐκέτι οὐ μὴ φάγω αὐτὸ ἕως ὅτου πληρωθῇ ἐν τῇ βασιλείᾳ τοῦ θεοῦ.

b) The forecast of the betrayal, put by Mark near the beginning of the narrative and by Luke at the end:

18 ἀμὴν λέγω ὑμῖν ὅτι εἷς ἐξ ὑμῶν παραδώσει με, ὁ	21 πλὴν ἰδοὺ ἡ χεὶρ τοῦ παραδιδόντος με μετ' ἐμοῦ

19 ἐσθίων μετ' ἐμοῦ. ἤρξαντο
λυπεῖσθαι καὶ λέγειν αὐτῷ
εἷς κατὰ εἷς· μήτι ἐγώ;
20 ὁ δὲ εἶπεν αὐτοῖς· εἷς τῶν
δώδεκα, ὁ ἐμβαπτόμενος
μετ' ἐμοῦ
21 εἰς τὸ τρύβλιον. ὅτι ὁ μὲν
<u>υἱὸς τοῦ ἀνθρώπου</u> ὑπάγει
καθὼς γέγραπται περὶ
αὐτοῦ· οὐαὶ δὲ τῷ ἀνθρώπῳ
<u>ἐκείνῳ δι' οὗ ὁ υἱὸς τοῦ</u>
<u>ἀνθρώπου παραδίδοται·</u>
καλὸν αὐτῷ εἰ οὐκ ἐγεννήθη
ὁ ἄνθρωπος ἐκεῖνος.

22 ἐπὶ τῆς τραπέζης. ὅτι ὁ υἱὸς
μὲν τοῦ ἀνθρώπου κατὰ τὸ
ὡρισμένον πορεύεται, πλὴν
οὐαὶ τῷ ἀνθρώπῳ ἐκείνῳ δι'
23 οὗ παραδίδοται. καὶ αὐτοὶ
ἤρξαντο συζητεῖν πρὸς
ἑαυτοὺς τὸ τίς ἄρα εἴη ἐξ
αὐτῶν ὁ τοῦτο μέλλων
πράσσειν.

c) He took the bread, gave thanks, broke and distributed it:

22 καὶ ἐσθιόντων αὐτῶν <u>λαβὼν</u>
<u>ἄρτον</u> εὐλογήσας <u>ἔκλασεν</u>
<u>καὶ ἔδωκεν αὐτοῖς</u> καὶ
εἶπεν· λάβετε· <u>τοῦτό ἐστιν</u>
<u>τὸ σῶμα μου.</u>

19 <u>καὶ λαβὼν ἄρτον</u>
εὐχαριστήσας <u>ἔκλασεν καὶ</u>
<u>ἔδωκεν αὐτοῖς</u> λέγων· <u>τοῦτό</u>
<u>ἐστιν τὸ σῶμά μου</u> τὸ ὑπὲρ
ὑμῶν διδόμενον· τοῦτο
ποιεῖτε εἰς τὴν ἐμὴν
ἀνάμνησιν.

d) He took the cup and gave thanks:

23 <u>καὶ λαβὼν ποτήριον</u>
<u>εὐχαριστησας</u> ἔδωκεν
αὐτοῖς, καὶ ἔπιον ἐξ αὐτοῦ
24 πάντες. καὶ εἶπεν αὐτοῖς·

17a <u>καὶ δεξάμενος ποτήριον</u>
<u>εὐχαριστήσας εἶπεν·</u>

e) The words accompanying the cup(s) have striking differences of form and order:

17b λάβετε τοῦτο καὶ
διαμερίσατε εἰς ἑαυτούς·

24 <u>τοῦτο ἐστιν τὸ αἷμα μου</u> τῆς
<u>διαθήκης τὸ ἐκχυννόμενον</u>
25 <u>ὑπὲρ</u> πολλῶν. ἀμὴν λέγω
ὑμῖν ὅτι οὐκέτι οὐ μὴ πίω ἐκ
τοῦ γενήματος τῆς ἀμπέλου

18 λέγω γὰρ ὑμῖν, οὐ μὴ πίω
ἀπὸ τοῦ νῦν ἀπὸ τοῦ
γενήματος τῆς ἀμπέλου ἕως
οὗ ἡ βασιλεία τοῦ θεοῦ ἔλθῃ

ἕως τῆς ἡμέρας ἐκείνης ὅταν 20 καὶ τὸ ποτήριον
αὐτὸ πίνω καινὸν ἐν τῇ ὡσαύτως μετὰ τὸ
βασιλείᾳ τοῦ θεοῦ. δειπνῆσαι, λέγων· τοῦτο τὸ
ποτήριον ἡ καινὴ διαθήκη
ἐν τῷ αἵματί μου, τὸ ὑπὲρ
ὑμῶν ἐκχυννόμενον.

There are verbal coincidences – notably in the taking, breaking and giving of the bread, and τοῦτό ἐστιν τὸ σῶμά μου, and in the not drinking of the fruit of the vine until the kingdom of God – but there are many remarkable differences of order and content. On the face of it this does not look like a case of Luke adapting Mark, or even of variant versions of a carefully memorised oral tradition. Luke appears to be giving his own version of the story without any attempt to bring it into line with Mark. Luke's text, as Marshall says, is 'similar to Mk 14:22 and 1 Cor 11:23–25, but is sufficiently different from them to make it improbable that it is a literary derivation from them' (Marshall *Luke* 800).[27]

Luke 22:31–39 – Prediction of Peter's denial; the two swords

According to Farmer's *Synopticon*, only ten of the 142 words in Luke's pericope are found in Mark: λέγω σοι σήμερον τρίς με ἀπαρνήσῃ and the hardly significant ὁ δὲ, αὐτῷ, ὁ. The accounts appear to be quite independent. Luke places the incident before the departure to the Mount of Olives, while Mark places it after; and the common words are surrounded by entirely different matter in the two accounts, as is the case in John 13:38 where the same prediction is made. Fitzmyer's comment is:

> Luke seems to be following a tradition, known also from the Johannine Gospel, according to which the foretelling of Peter's denial takes place in the room where the Last Supper was eaten and not on the way to the Mount of Olives, as in the Marcan and Matthean tradition. (1421)

Luke 22:40–46 – Gethsemane

Fitzmyer here notes nine major differences:

1) In Luke Jesus proceeds to the Mount of Olives (generically

named) followed by unnamed disciples, whereas in Mark he goes to Gethsemane, on the Mount of Olives.

2) In Luke Jesus exhorts the disciples to pray, whereas in Mark he tells them to sit there, while he goes to pray; he further singles out Peter, James, and John and tells them of his distress and anxiety – none of which is noted in Luke.

3) In Luke Jesus withdraws from (all) the disciples 'about a stone's throw' (v. 41) and prays, whereas in Mark he withdraws 'a little further' from Peter, James, and John.

4) In Mark part of Jesus' prayer is recounted in indir. discourse, but in Luke the content of his prayer is given entirely in dir. discourse.

5) Though the substance of what he utters to the Father is the same in Mark and Luke, the latter eliminates the Aramaic address *àbbā'* and its Greek literal translation, *ho patēr*, using the more correct voc. *páter*.

6) In Mark Jesus prays three times and returns to Peter, James and John after each prayer, whereas in Luke he prays only once and then returns to (all) the disciples.

7) In Mark Jesus finds Peter, James and John asleep, whereas in Luke he finds all the disciples asleep – and because of grief.

8) Jesus' counsel to pray lest they enter into temptation is common to Mark and Luke, but in the latter it forms an *inclusio* which frames his own prayer.

9) If vv. 43–44 in the Lucan account are authentic, Jesus receives heavenly reassurance and strength in his traumatic experience, a detail that is wholly lacking in Mark. (1437)

There are only two sentences which even approximately coincide in the eleven verses of Mark and the seven verses of Luke. They have in common προσηύχετο, παρένεγκε, τοῦτο, τὸ ποτήριον, ἀπ' ἐμοῦ, ἀλλά and προσεύχεσθε ἵνα μή, εἰς πειρασμόν. This is insufficient ground for Fitzmyer's assertion: 'The Lucan account is clearly inspired by the Marcan.' Clearly? There is in fact no *prima facie* evidence that Luke is adapting the text of Mark or that both are using a standard oral tradition.

Luke 22:47–53 – The arrest

There are considerable coincidences with Mark's eight verses (ἔτι αὐτοῦ λαλοῦντος, ὄχλος, Ἰούδας εἷς τῶν δώδεκα, τοῦ ἀρχιερέως, τὸν δοῦλον, καὶ ἀφεῖλεν, ὡς ἐπὶ λῃστήν, μετὰ μαχαιρῶν καὶ ξύλων, καθ' ἡμέραν, ἐν τῷ ἱερῷ) in these seven verses (and also half a dozen minor coincidences with Matthew), which suggest the influence of a common oral source at some stage, but there are big additions and omissions and 'conspicuous' (Marshall *Luke*) differences of wording and word order.

Fitzmyer 1447 notes considerable changing of Mark (including omissions of 'details that one would consider necessary for comprehension') and a good deal of free composition. This does not suggest that Luke is based on the text of Mark.

Luke 22:54–23:1 – Jesus before the high priest; Peter's denials

Within this section of nineteen verses there are major differences of order. The passages which correspond approximately with Mark come in this verse order: 54, 55, 67–71, 63–65, 56–62, 66, 23:1. The accusers of Peter in Mark are a maid, the maid again and the men standing by; in Luke they are a maid, a man and another man. There are considerable additions and omissions and many verbal differences, which have led to great conflict of opinion among critics as to what may be derived from a highly redacted form of Mark and what may come from a non-Markan source. According to Farmer's *Synopticon*, 72% of the pericope does not reproduce the words of Mark and there are important parallels with Matthew, including ἐξελθὼν ἔξω ἔκλαυσεν πικρῶς and τίς ἐστιν ὁ παίσας σε; This does not look like either literary adaptation or the product of a common oral tradition.

Luke 23:2–16 – Jesus before Pilate and Herod

Here Pilate's five-word question and Jesus' two-word reply in verse 3 are identical in Mark and Luke, but the other fourteen verses are quite different. In Mark's account of Jesus before Pilate in 15:2–5 as printed in the Aland *Synopsis* only verse 2 is printed alongside a Lukan parallel (v. 3). Luke's verses 2, 4, 5 and the Herod account in verses 6–16 have no parallel.

Building a Synoptic Theory: (1)

Luke 23:18–25 – Barabbas and the condemnation

In spite of verbal coincidences with Mark 15:6–20a (τὸν Βαραββᾶν, φόνον, πάλιν δὲ ὁ Πιλᾶτος, τί γὰρ κακὸν, ἐποίησεν, ἀπέλυσεν, τὸν Ἰησοῦν, παρέδωκεν) and a substantial agreement in content, the story is treated quite differently. The order is different, the wording never coincides for long, and there are differences of detail in content: Mark includes the *privilegium paschale*, the stirring up of the crowd by the chief priests, the taunts about the king of the Jews and the mocking of the soldiers, which Luke does not mention; and Luke has Pilate's declaration of Jesus' innocence, which Mark does not mention. It is of course possible that Luke was working from the Mark scroll, abbreviating, adding, rearranging, rewording, but on the face of it it does not look like it.

Luke 23:26–32 – The way to the place of crucifixion

Nearly half the words of verse 26 are identical with those in Mark 15:21 (Σίμωνά τινα Κυρηναῖον ἐρχόμενον ἀπ' ἀγροῦ, τὸν σταυρόν), after which (vv. 27–32) follows the 'special-Luke' account of the daughters of Jerusalem. Since so much of the surrounding material is not derived from Mark, it is better to assume that these eight words were part of Luke's own material, rather than an extract from Mark.

Luke 23:33–49 – The crucifixion

Here there are massive differences in order. The passages in Luke which correspond approximately to those in Mark 15:22–26 are in this verse sequence: 33a, 34, 35a, 38, 33b, 37, 35b, 39, 36, 46, 45, 47, 49. Several Markan items are not included: Golgotha, wine mixed with myrrh, Jesus' refusal to drink, the third hour, wagging of heads, 'the destroyer of the temple', 'King of Israel'. Details peculiar to Luke include the term κακοῦργοι, the prayer for forgiveness (assuming this to be the correct text), the title 'the Chosen One' and the distinguishing of the scoffing rulers from the watching people. And

37

there are many verbal differences. This does not look like literary adaptation, but an independent version.

Luke 23:50–56 – The burial

Verses 50–53 have verbal correspondences with Mark 15:42, 43, 46 (Ἰωσήφ, βουλευτής, ἀπὸ Ἀριμαθαίας, τὴν βασιλείαν τοῦ θεοῦ, ᾐτήσατο τὸ σῶμα τοῦ Ἰησοῦ, καθελών, σινδόνι, ἐν μνήματι) and with Matthew 27:57–59 (οὗτος προσελθὼν τῷ Πιλάτῳ, ἐνετύλιξεν αὐτό, ἔθηκεν and the omission of Mark 15:44), yet there are so many verbal differences that there is no good reason to regard Luke as based on Mark. Verses 54–56 are 'special-Luke'.

Luke 24:1–11 – The empty tomb

There is a handful of coincidences between Mark 16:1–8 and Luke (μιᾷ τῶν σαββάτων, ἐπὶ τὸ μνῆμα, ἀρώματα, τοῦ μνημείου, εἰσελθοῦσαι, ζητεῖτε, οὐκ ἔστιν ὧδε, ἠγέρθη, ἀπὸ τοῦ μνημείου), but there are huge differences in every verse.

In the fourteen examples cited above there seems to be no *prima facie* evidence that Luke has been adapting the text of Mark. From Luke 22:14 right to the end of the gospel, the evangelist appears to have his own account of the passion and resurrection. It is possible that the wording of Mark may have influenced Luke's phraseology occasionally, but it seems to be a fundamental mistake to try to explain Luke as an adaptation of Mark in this section of the book and in the three earlier cases examined.

But is it not a case of arguing in a circle to include the passages which fit the argument and to exclude those which do not?[28] It is not a case of arguing in a circle, since the two categories are clearly distinguishable. It is a matter of observation: the passages in Category 1 are self-evidently closely parallel, whereas those in Category 2 are almost self-evidently not.[29] The first two passages in Category 2 are mainly about different things: in the case of Jesus' appearance in Galilee, Mark 1:14, 15 is concerned about the content of Jesus' teaching, while Luke 4:14, 15 is concerned about the power and fame of his teaching; in the case of the summoning of the fishermen, Mark 1:16–20 is concerned with their call and Luke 5:1–11 with an experience which preceded their call. In the third passage (the closing section of the apocalyptic discourse) the two gospel accounts simply have little in common. In the eleven examples in the passion and resurrection narratives, Mark and Luke are writing about the same things and therefore of necessity have a few words in common, but they are written in a way so different that it is difficult to think that Luke is adapting Mark. Not only is there the wholesale juggling with order when Jesus is before the high priest and in the account of the crucifixion and to some extent at the last supper, but in every case the supposed alterations are on a big scale.

The clarity of distinction between the two sets of passages is quite remarkable – there is no grey area where it is difficult to know in which class to put a passage; there is no gentle shading of one category into the other. Perhaps the nearest to a grey area is the institution of the Lord's Supper, where there is a good deal of common wording. Both accounts purport to describe the origin of certain words and actions which were regularly repeated in the early church, and in *that* sense of course they have a common source. But the wording, order and content are so different that Luke's redaction of Mark would perforce have been a tortuous process to have achieved this result, and, in view of its likenesses to the account in 1 Corinthians 11:23–26, it is better to regard it as a separate line of tradition followed perhaps in the Pauline churches.

So we conclude: in the truly parallel passages Luke keeps to the sense of Mark.

3

BUILDING A SYNOPTIC THEORY: (2) THE RELATION OF LUKE TO MATTHEW

Chapter summary

The case to be argued is *Step 4: Luke may be presumed to keep to the sense of his other sources. The differences of sense between the Q-material of Matthew and of Luke make dependence on Q or large-scale borrowing from Matthew improbable.*

Luke's preface makes the strongest claims to trustworthiness, which means that he would only have used sources which he trusted and the sense of which he would have adhered to.

The Q-material is first examined on the supposition that a Q-source existed substantially in the Matthean form, and that Luke was responsible for the changes. *In Luke's Central Section* the Q-material has no common order. (Before discussing wording it is necessary to look at the origin of redaction criticism and understand how Goulder and others have come to see literary relationships even where verbal likenesses are few. The plain man's test which requires strong verbal likenesses to make literary relationship probable is sounder.) Likenesses in wording may sometimes be due to the repetitions of an itinerant preacher, sometimes to independent recollection or transmission of the same discourse; it hardly ever looks like the adaptation of someone who is copying. There are nine examples of difference in sense of a kind that Luke could not have made if his aim was the faithful following of reliable sources. Luke's central section may have come from one of the seventy. *In the Great Sermon* there is common order, but many verbal differences, suggesting independent condensed reports of one discourse. *In the rest of Luke* there are two passages concerning the Baptist so close to Matthew as to suggest that Luke is actually copying Matthew.

If we suppose that Matthew is the innovator, we find that in spite of eight thousand verbal changes, he too keeps close to the sense of Mark, and can be presumed therefore not to have been likely to have created the great differences to be found in the Q-material. The supposition that both Matthew and Luke substantially changed Q is equally improbable.

The differences in the Q-material also rule out large-scale use of Matthew by Luke, though small-scale borrowing seems likely.

Luke's fidelity to the sense of Mark leads at once to *Step 4: Luke may be presumed to keep to the sense of his other sources. The differences of sense between the Q-material of Matthew and of Luke make dependence on Q or large-scale borrowing from Matthew improbable.*

Luke's preface makes strong claims.[1] It assumes that all worthwhile accounts of Jesus' life and teaching must be in accord with what the apostles and their assistants have handed on to the church: καθὼς παρέδοσαν ἡμῖν οἱ ἀπ' ἀρχῆς αὐτόπται καὶ ὑπηρέται γενόμενοι τοῦ λόγου. The writer then claims equal authority with them: 'It seemed good to me, having followed all things accurately from a long time back, to write to you in order, *so that you might know the certainty* of the things concerning which you have been instructed.' He could hardly have made a stronger claim to accuracy and veracity. When comparing Luke with Mark we have seen how consistently he keeps to Mark's sense. Since his aim was to confirm Theophilus in the truth, it follows that he would only have used sources which he believed to be trustworthy, and that he would have been as faithful to them as he was to Mark.

The problem of Q

To establish Step 4 it is necessary to examine the Q-material in Matthew and Luke and see whether their forms are compatible

41

with the hypothesis of a Q-document. When we try to put the Q-theory to the test the matter is of course complicated by the fact that we have no text of Q to work with. The text of Q cannot in fact be firmly delineated. S. Petrie in his *Novum Testamentum* 3 (1959) article ' "Q" is Only What You Make It' has shown this in a colourful way. He speaks of the 'exasperating contradictoriness' of scholarly views as to its nature:

'Q' is a single document; it is a composite document, incorporating earlier sources; it is used in different redactions; it is more than one document. The original language of 'Q' is Greek; the original language is Aramaic; it is used in different translations. 'Q' is the Matthean Logia; it is not the Matthean Logia. 'Q' has a definite shape; it is no more than an amorphous collection of fragments. 'Q' is a gospel; it is not a gospel. 'Q' includes the Crucifixion story; it does not include the Crucifixion story. 'Q' consists wholly of sayings and there is no narrative; it includes some narrative. All of 'Q' is preserved in Matt. and Luke; not all of it is preserved; it is better preserved in Luke. Matt.'s order is the correct order; Luke's is the correct order; neither order is correct. 'Q' is used by Mark; it is not used by Mark. (29f)[2]

We can, however, assume (for the sake of argument) the existence of a document Q and look at the possibilities, 1.) that the Q-text was like the Matthean form, 2.) that it was like the Lukan form, 3.) that both the Matthean and the Lukan form are the result of considerable redactional change. We can also look at 4.) the possibility that Luke extracted his material direct from Matthew.

Assuming that Luke is the innovator

If Matthew keeps to the sense of Q, it is easy to show that Luke frequently fails to do so. It will be found that in about half the material usually classified as Q Luke would appear *not* to keep to the sense of his source. It will be well to look at Luke's Q-material in three parts: 1.) the Central Section, which covers the bulk of the material; 2.) the Sermon on the Level Place; 3.) the rest of Luke.

42

The Central Section (9:51–18:14)

Luke's Central Section has no major parallels to Mark but consists of Q-material intermingled with much special-Lukan material. If Q is regarded as a single Greek document roughly coterminous with the material not found in Mark which is common to Matthew and Luke, the Q theory is sufficiently precise for thorough investigation. For example, it is possible to investigate whether there is evidence of common order in the Q-material, and whether there is evidence of a distinctive vocabulary, style or content which differentiates it from the other strata of the gospels. But when Q is broken up into a plurality of possible sources, or is conceived as a source known to the evangelists in different recensions, or the sources are considered to be heavily redacted in the only forms known to us, these tests become difficult if not impossible to apply, and the theory's scientific status becomes dubious. There is left to us a variety of theories which are possible, but which lack solid foundations because of an absence of testable evidence. It seems best, therefore, to look at the theory in its simplest form, that of a single Q-document, before exploring more elusive theories.

So let us consider whether a) the argument from order or b) the wording of parallel passages supports the use of such a Q-document.

THE ARGUMENT FROM ORDER

The order of the Q-material in Matthew and Luke contrasted
Where several pericopes, which have no apparent logical or chronological succession, are found in the same order, a natural possible inference is a literary connection. Similarly, if a sequence of material is broken by an omission or by the intrusion of new matter and is then resumed again, a literary connection is a natural explanation. Such sequences are found at a number of places in the synoptics, especially in the triple tradition. In Luke's Central Section, however, it is hard to demonstrate a common order for the Q-material. Just the opposite appears to be the case. For instance, if the passages in the Central Section

43

which have parallels in Matthew are taken in order, it will be found that their Matthean counterparts come in a totally different order. As given in the Aland *Synopsis*, these parallels come in turn from the following chapters of Matthew: 19, 8, 9, 10, 11, 10, 11, 13, 22, 6, 7, 12, 5, 6, 15, 16, 10, 12, 10, 6, 24, 10, 16, 5, 13, 7, 8, 23, 22, 10, 5, 18, 6, 11, 19, 18, 17, 24. Conversely, many of the sayings of Matthew's Sermon on the Mount are not found in Luke's Sermon on the Level Place, but in the Central Section, and in this order of chapters: 14, 16, 12, 16, 11, 12, 11, 16, 12, 11, 13. Vincent Taylor[3] laboured hard to support the Q-hypothesis by showing that there were sequences common to Luke and Matthew within particular sections of Matthew (this is obvious, for instance, in the case of the Sermon on the Mount). But apart from this one case the sequences are too short and too broken to have any statistical value.

Attempts to show a Matthean origin for Luke's Q-material were made by a series of writers who sought to show that Q in any form is an unnecessary hypothesis which needlessly multiplies entities, and that the Q-material in Luke can all be explained by direct derivation from Matthew. At least two of these writers tried to show that there was a significant relation of order in this material in the two gospels. This approach was pioneered by E. W. Lummis, *How Luke was Written* (Cambridge, 1915) and worked out more fully and with great skill by H. G. Jameson, *The Origin of the Synoptic Gospels* (Oxford: Blackwell, 1922). Jameson argued that Luke combed through Matthew a number of times, picking up on each new combing fresh items which appear in his gospel in the same order as he found them in Matthew. His scheme, however, seemed to me on careful scrutiny to prove too complex to be credible. More recently Farmer, with no greater plausibility, has espoused the same theory, arguing that Luke 'worked forward in Matthew not once, but repeatedly'.[4]

Luke's relation to Mark and to Matthew contrasted:
The order of Luke and Mark
The contrast between Luke's demonstrable following of Mark's order and Luke's putative following of Matthew's order can be

vividly pictured by plotting one gospel against another in a graph (p. 46). The graph representing Luke's use of Mark is extremely simple if one confines oneself to the order of peri-copes. (It is impracticable in such a graph to plot the small changes of order within pericopes.) The diagonal lines show the passages where Luke is following Mark. (The latter part of the final diagonal, representing Luke 22:14–24:11, is shown as a broken line, since it is all Category 2 material, covering much the same ground as Mark, though with many differences of wording and various small changes of order within pericopes.) The horizontal lines show the passages where Luke is using material not in Mark, and the vertical lines show where he is omitting from Mark. It will be observed that except for two small irregularities at Mark 3:7–12 and 3:31–35 the diagonal lines follow an uninterrupted course.

The first irregularity has been included because Mark 3:13–19 and Luke 6:12–16 (which record the calling and the names of the twelve) are customarily printed as parallel passages, but it is far from obvious that Luke is following Mark at this point. The calling is handled quite differently in the two cases – of the thirty-six words of Mark and the thirty-seven of Luke the only common ones are εἰς τὸ ὄρος, δώδεκα and καί (twice). Even in the names, in spite of a certain stereotyping (which is found in all four apostolic lists), there are two differences of order, one change of name and five major differences of description. The errant pericope could equally well be regarded as special-Lukan material and be represented by a horizontal line, leaving the upward movement of the diagonal entirely uninterrupted.

The dubiousness of this supposed parallelism is further illustrated by the fact that Tuckett[5] allows that Luke 6:12–16 could be paralleled either by Mark 3:13–19 or by 3:7–12 (Orchard adopts the latter in his *A Synopsis of the Four Gospels*). 3:7–12 (a pericope of 103 words) has a few identical words: καί, πλῆθος, πολύ, ἀπό, τῆς Ἰουδαίας, καί, ἦλθον, and a few others with the same root but different morphology. The fact is that Luke is so different from both pericopes that it is implausible to regard Mark as either an adaptation of Luke or as a conflation of Matthew and Luke. *Literary* dependence is just not suggested.

45

The relation of Luke to Mark

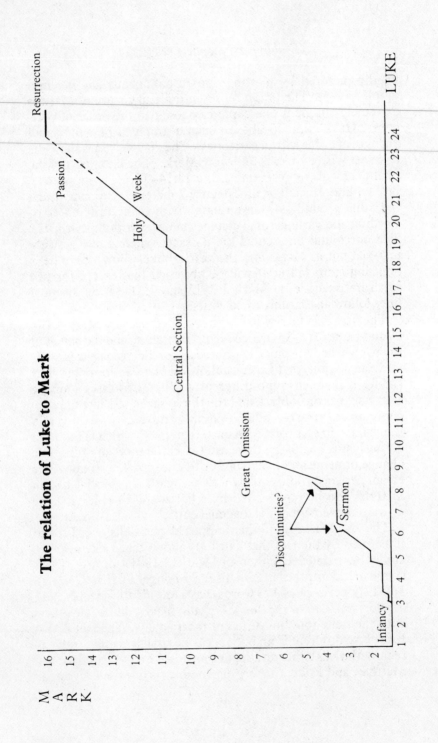

M
A
R
K

16
15
14
13
12
11
10
9
8
7
6
5
4
3
2

Resurrection
Passion
Holy Week
Central Section
Great Omission
Discontinuities?
Sermon
Infancy

1 2 3 4 5 6 7 8 9 10 11 12 13 14 15 16 17 18 19 20 21 22 23 24

LUKE

In the second irregularity Luke records how Jesus' mother and brothers tried unsuccessfully to reach him (8:19–21); this he places after his parable section (8:4–18), whereas Mark (3:31–35) puts it before his. In Mark the context is that of blasphemous denigration of Jesus: 'He is beside himself . . . He is possessed by Beelzebul . . . whoever blasphemes against the Holy Spirit never has forgiveness, but he is guilty of an eternal sin – for they had said, "He has an unclean spirit."' The coming of οἱ παρ' αὐτοῦ to seize him in Mark 3:21 is thus followed almost immediately by the shocking revelation that even his own mother and brothers apparently tried to dissuade him from his activities. Vincent Taylor and C. E. B. Cranfield[6] regarded οἱ παρ' αὐτοῦ as his family and saw the second story as the sequel to the first. Luke, however, only records the second incident, which he tells in a form which stresses the importance of hearing the word of God and doing it, which fits admirably after his parable section (note especially the interpretation of the parable of the sower) and before his account of the stilling of the storm (which obeys his word) in 8:22–25. The two accounts, in spite of the common use by both of lengthy expressions: 'his mother and his brothers', 'your mother and your brothers', 'my mother and my brothers', have less than half their words in common and have several major differences. In addition, neither writer professes to give the story a chronological setting. (The RSV is misleading in translating δέ at Luke 8:19 by 'then'.) It therefore seems likely enough that both writers are recording the story in the way and with the associated incidents with which they are accustomed to tell it and that Luke is neither redacting nor dislocating Mark. In any case Luke's departures from Mark's order are very small[7] – the upward movement of the graph is at least *almost* unbroken.

Luke's relation to Mark and to Matthew contrasted:
The order of Luke and Matthew
If on the other hand Luke's supposed use of Matthew is plotted, a very different graph results (p. 49). Luke's raids upon Matthew are so brief and so dispersed that it is almost impossible to draw them. The most that we can do is to take the longer

Q-passages and set them out on their own, ignoring the possibility of Luke using Matthew in the triple tradition.

The result is a quite impressive sequence at the beginning which covers the Baptist, the temptation, the Sermon on the Level Place, the centurion's boy, and the Baptist again (Luke 3:7–7:35), and a suspicion of a sequence towards the end where Luke 17:22–37 has parallels with the discourse on the day of the Son of Man in Matthew 24:26–41, and Luke's parable of the pounds in 19:11–27 has parallels with Matthew's parable of the talents in 25:14–30. But in between all is chaos, in spite of the fact that the material has been immensely simplified. In the Central Section six of the longer pericopes have been given their usual little sloping lines and ten medium length pericopes (too short for sloping lines) have been marked simply by crosses (and nine even shorter ones have been omitted altogether). In this section, an attempt has been made to show Luke's movement backwards and forwards in Matthew's scroll by drawing lines to connect up the items in order. The result looks like a seismographic record of a force 8 earthquake.

Goulder's view

The sequences at the beginning and end of the graph enabled R. Morgenthaler to make an impressive computation. He reckoned that the Q-material consists of 3,861 words in Matthew and 3,663 in Luke, and of these 1,851 are identical in form and sequence – that is, about half the material.[8] This impressed M. D. Goulder, who has been the great protagonist in recent years of the theory of the Matthean origin of the Q-material. But, being also impressed by the improbability of Luke working in the fashion suggested by the graph, he attempted another theory, which he set out in a paper read at Ampleforth, which was published in 1984 under the title 'The Order of a Crank'.[9] This title was a response to a remark of Streeter, who had declared that 'an author capable of such a proceeding' would be 'a crank'.[10] Goulder reckoned that Luke was a preacher who, as he worked through Matthew collecting material not to be found in Mark, recalled from memory many other appropriate Matthean sayings, which he inserted into his

Luke's supposed use of Matthew's Q-material

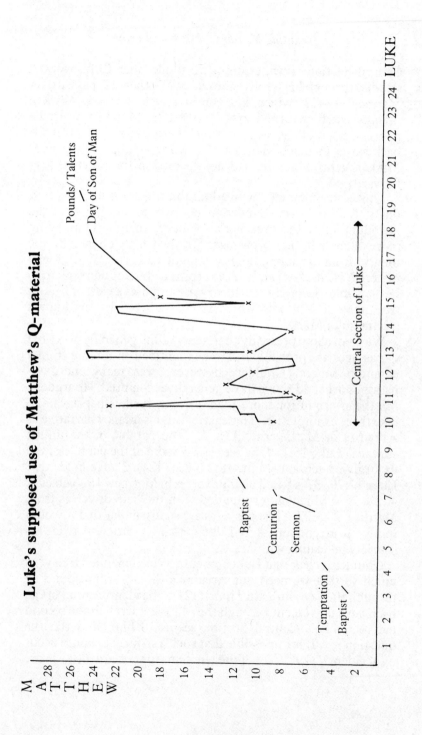

Central Section. Furthermore, he thinks that Luke worked steadily through his scroll to the end of Matthew 12, passed over Matthew 13–22 (which has comparatively few non-Markan sayings) and then turned on to Matthew 23, 24 and 25. When he had extracted all he wanted from these chapters he worked backwards through Matthew 23 to 16 picking up the non-Markan gems which he had not gleaned in the previous leap forward.

This is all expounded with admirable ingenuity and lucidity, but it fails to carry conviction on two counts. Firstly, the introduction of the preacher's memory, thereby eliminating more than half the Q-passages (those which do not fit the theory) from the supposedly systematic gathering of Matthean material, is a *deus ex machina* too arbitrary and too convenient to be plausible. Secondly, the theory presupposes a view of Luke's treatment of Matthew which is contradicted by his known treatment of Mark.

We shall show presently that many of the generally accepted Q-passages are probably not to be identified as coming from a common source. Goulder, however, sees many more Q-passages over and above those generally recognised. He argues a Matthean origin for more than a dozen further passages. To take three examples: 1.) He regards Luke's infancy narrative as a rewrite of Matthew's (113). 2.) The parable of the unjust steward (Luke 16:1–9) he sees as a rewrite of the parable of the unforgiving servant (Matt. 18:23–25) (124). 3.) He holds that Luke 17:20–37 is based on four verses in Matthew 16 – verses 1, 4, 21, 25 – which are expounded with the help of verses from Matthew 24 (127). The passages are so dissimilar that it would imply an inventiveness in Luke strikingly different from his sobriety in dealing with Mark.

Goulder is clear that Luke sometimes 'has emended freely, so much so that we need our Ariadne's thread to find our way through the labyrinth after him' (121). His identification of the backward movement through the Matthew scroll in the second half of Luke's Central Section seems to him 'to settle the question . . . It is impossible that such a sequence should occur by accident' (129f). Yet of the ten items in the sequence, six are

50

not recognised as parallels in the Aland *Synopsis* and two are out of order.[11] It is not likely that many will think that these supposed correspondences settle the question.[12] So the argument from order on the supposition that Luke followed either Q or Matthew must be deemed to have failed as far as Luke's Central Section is concerned.

THE ARGUMENT FROM WORDING

The methodology of redaction criticism

Before proceeding to the argument from wording a serious question of methodology must be faced, which necessitates a digression. Redaction critics tend to see the redactionary process as something quite complex, so it may seem naive to try to assess the probability of a literary connection by simply laying parallel passages side by side and asking ourselves whether they *look* as though one is adapting the text of the other. It has been believed for so long that the synoptic problem must be solved in terms of literary relationships, that likenesses between passages are explained almost exclusively in a literary way however great the differences may be. It must be remembered, however, that the gospels were produced in a society where much learning was acquired by rote, and they were produced for communities who were trying to propagate the common teaching of the apostolic church. In such circumstances verbal likenesses would survive in oral transmission, and there is no need to invoke literary sources unless there is consistent evidence of actual copying. Only if it is assumed that Luke had little knowledge not obtained from literary sources, will it appear probable that all resemblances to Mark came directly from Mark, or that all Matthew/Luke resemblances came from Q.

Redaction criticism as it has been practised in recent years is the end product of a long process. By the early nineteenth century, New Testament study had reached something of an impasse. It was a case of Christians versus unbelievers. You either adhered to a theory of inerrancy handed down in the church from first-century Judaism via such as Origen,

Augustine, Aquinas and the Reformers or you were classified as anti-Christian. It was the desire of Christians strongly influenced by the Enlightenment to escape from this straitjacket (as they felt it to be) which provoked the modern critical movement.[13] They dropped attempts at gospel harmonisation, and they laid emphasis on the purely human aspects of scripture. With this loosened framework the battle raged between those who believed in the soundness of the gospel tradition and those who did not. In the early part of the twentieth century broad agreement had been reached that Mark was the earliest gospel. One group (including such as A. C. Headlam[14] and B. H. Streeter[15]) made Mark the basis of their reconstruction of the historical Jesus, and they were inclined to see good historical material in all the four main strata of the synoptic gospels. They upheld the 'Markan hypothesis' which accepted the outline of Mark as basically good history. The other group was inclined to consider Mark theologically motivated and historically unreliable.

The influence of W. Wrede and J. Wellhausen had done much to create a climate of distrust of the 'Markan hypothesis'. W. Wrede in *Das Messiasgeheimnis den Evangelien* (1901)[16] had argued 1.) that Mark's tradition knew nothing of Jesus as Messiah; 2.) that belief in the Messiahship of Jesus only developed in the early church after the death of Jesus; 3.) that Mark wrote this belief back into his narrative of the ministry; 4.) that Mark disguised its absence in his tradition by inventing the idea of Jesus imposing secrecy on those who recognised him – this he made an important motif of his gospel. Thus Wrede makes Mark a redactor of considerable inventiveness.

Wellhausen towards the end of his life turned to New Testament study, and between 1903 and 1905 published commentaries on the three synoptic gospels as well as an *Introduction to the First Three Gospels*.[17] As N. Perrin says, 'In these works many of what came to be the characteristic emphases of twentieth century synoptic scholarship first found expression.'[18] Bultmann (who was to build on his conclusions and become a pioneer in New Testament form criticism) says that one of Wellhausen's most important conclusions was that the oldest tradition consisted almost entirely of small fragments (sayings or words of Jesus) and did not present a continuous story of the deeds of Jesus or any complete collection of sayings . . . He showed that the evangelist's narratives connecting the fragments were secondary, but also that oral tradition was already steadily producing more and more new sayings of Jesus . . . In the primitive community at Jerusalem the Spirit of Jesus continued to be active, and his ethical teaching was progressively elaborated and expressed in utterances which were then transmitted as the sayings of Jesus himself. Thus tradition shaped and handed down, in the form of words of Jesus, conceptions actually arising from the faith of the community.[19]

These ideas were developed by the form critics in the early part of the twentieth century and, although some used the methods while retaining a belief in the general soundness of the tradition, a profoundly sceptical view of the historical value of the gospels generally prevailed.

In the 1950s, when the era of form criticism was giving way before that of redaction criticism, some scholars felt free to impute a high degree of inventiveness to the evangelists, as they adapted their traditions to current needs and composed new material into which to incorporate them. (The alternative term 'composition criticism' seems aptly to describe this sort of activity.) Other scholars, like I. H. Marshall and E. E. Ellis, having accepted the two-document hypothesis, have felt free to follow the redaction-critical line while arguing still for the basic soundness of the tradition. Ellis further holds that the evangelists felt themselves consciously moved by the Holy Spirit as they wrote, giving them the mind of Christ, so that modifications and reapplications of Jesus' teaching in the later evangelists were as truly words of Jesus as those in Mark.[20] It is doubtful whether this claim, which makes the gospels to some extent like prophecies,[21] can really be sustained. Paul is clear as to the distinction between words handed down from Jesus and instructions of later origin,[22] and the gospels were accepted by the early church as giving us the former. Before accepting the validity of composition criticism, the prior question has to be faced, Is a *literary* relationship the key to an understanding of the likenesses and differences in parallel pericopes? We shall try to show that in most cases this seems improbable.

Ultimately the acceptability of redaction theories will turn on what we think of the evangelists and their aims. If we believe that they were well informed, anxious to pass on their story in accordance with the apostolic tradition, we shall be sceptical of theories which allow great scope to the evangelist to modify and transpose his source material and to create new material to serve his purposes. (Also it needs to be remembered that the more complex such redactionary work is held to be the less likely it is that we have identified it correctly.) The only safe criterion of literary dependence is the plain man's test: Is there consistent evidence of either copying of order or copying of the actual wording?

Examples of verbal likeness and agreement in sense

If the argument from order tells against the derivation of Luke's Central Section from Q or Matthew, this is reinforced by the argument from sense. In the case of Mark (as we have seen) Luke almost invariably keeps to his sense, but this (as we shall now show) is not so in the Q-material. Even in the ten fairly long passages (pp. 55–66 below) where there is general agreement in wording and sense the relation does not appear to be a literary one; in the nine examples (pp. 67–76) where the sense is markedly different a literary connection is improbable in the extreme.

If one disregards context and treats the sentences of Jesus as isolated units, there are indeed more than ninety verses or part verses[23] in Luke's Central Section in which the language is identical or very close, or where the sense is virtually the same, even though the wording is somewhat different. Sometimes these are embedded in similar material in the two gospels, sometimes in otherwise dissimilar material. Many of these are pithy sayings or short memorable passages which could well have been spoken on more than one occasion and might easily have survived in oral tradition without major alteration.

For example, several sayings of the Sermon on the Mount reappear in Luke's Central Section, e.g. 11:2–4 – the Lord's

Prayer; 11:9–11, 13 – 'ask . . . seek . . . knock'; 11:34, 35 –
'Your eye is the lamp of your body; when your eye is sound,
your whole body is full of light'; 12:34 – 'where your treasure is,
there will your heart be also'; 16:13 – 'No servant can serve two
masters; for either he will hate the one and love the other, or he
will be devoted to the one and despise the other. You cannot
serve God and mammon.' Words about the harvest being
plentiful, which are given by Matthew (9:37f) to introduce the
mission of the twelve, are found at Luke 10:2 introducing the
instructions to the seventy.

There are ten examples of longer passages: 1.) *The parable of
the leaven* of Matthew 13:33 reappears at Luke 13:20, 21 with
small differences (underlined):

Matthew 13:33

ὁμοία ἐστὶν ἡ βασιλεία τῶν
οὐρανῶν ζύμῃ, ἣν λαβοῦσα
γυνὴ ἐνέκρυψεν εἰς ἀλεύρου
σάτα τρία, ἕως οὗ ἐζυμώθη
ὅλον.

Luke 13:20, 21

τίνι ὁμοιώσω τὴν βασιλείαν
τοῦ θεοῦ; ὁμοία ἐστὶν ζύμῃ,
ἣν λαβοῦσα γυνὴ ἔκρυψεν
εἰς ἀλεύρου σάτα τρία, ἕως
οὗ ἐζυμώθη ὅλον.

2.) *The theme of bold confession* in the mission charge of
Matthew 10 reappears at Luke 12:2–9, but in a form sufficiently different to reinforce what the context implies, namely,
that similar things were said on two different occasions. The
differences are underlined:

Matthew 10:26–33

26 Μὴ οὖν φοβηθῆτε αὐτούς·
οὐδὲν γάρ ἐστιν
κεκαλυμμένον ὃ οὐκ
ἀποκαλυφθήσεται, καὶ
κρυπτὸν ὃ οὐ γνωσθήσεται.
27 ὃ λέγω ὑμῖν ἐν τῇ σκοτίᾳ,
εἴπατε ἐν τῷ φωτί· καὶ ὃ εἰς
τὸ οὖς ἀκούετε, κηρύξατε
ἐπὶ τῶν δωμάτων.
28 καὶ μὴ φοβεῖσθε ἀπὸ τῶν
ἀποκτεννόντων τὸ σῶμα,

Luke 12:2–9

2 Οὐδὲν δὲ συγκεκαλυμμένον
ἐστὶν ὃ οὐκ
ἀποκαλυφθήσεται, καὶ
κρυπτὸν ὃ οὐ γνωσθήσεται.
3 ἀνθ' ὧν ὅσα ἐν τῇ σκοτίᾳ
εἴπατε ἐν τῷ φωτὶ
ἀκουσθήσεται, καὶ ὃ πρὸς τὸ
οὖς ἐλαλήσατε ἐν τοῖς
ταμιείοις κηρυχθήσεται ἐπὶ
4 τῶν δωμάτων. Λέγω δὲ ὑμῖν
τοῖς φίλοις μου, μὴ φοβηθῆτε

τὴν δὲ ψυχὴν μὴ δυναμένων
ἀποκτεῖναι· φοβεῖσθε δὲ
μᾶλλον τὸν δυνάμενον καὶ
ψυχὴν καὶ σῶμα ἀπολέσαι
ἐν γεέννῃ.

29 οὐχὶ δύο στρουθία
ἀσσαρίου πωλεῖται; καὶ ἓν
ἐξ αὐτῶν οὐ πεσεῖται ἐπὶ
τὴν γῆν ἄνευ τοῦ πατρὸς
30 ὑμῶν. ὑμῶν δὲ καὶ αἱ τρίχες
τῆς κεφαλῆς πᾶσαι
31 ἠριθμημέναι εἰσίν. μὴ οὖν
φοβεῖσθε· πολλῶν
στρουθίων διαφέρετε ὑμεῖς.
32 Πᾶς οὖν ὅστις ὁμολογήσει
ἐν ἐμοὶ ἔμπροσθεν τῶν
ἀνθρώπων, ὁμολογήσω
κἀγὼ ἐν αὐτῷ ἔμπροσθεν
τοῦ πατρός μου τοῦ ἐν τοῖς
οὐρανοῖς·
33 ὅστις δ' ἂν ἀρνήσηταί με
ἔμπροσθεν τῶν ἀνθρώπων,
ἀρνήσομαι κἀγὼ αὐτὸν
ἔμπροσθεν τοῦ πατρός μου
τοῦ ἐν τοῖς οὐρανοῖς.

ἀπὸ τῶν ἀποκτεννόντων τὸ
σῶμα καὶ μετὰ ταῦτα μὴ
ἐχόντων περισσότερόν τι
5 ποιῆσαι. ὑποδείξω δὲ ὑμῖν
τίνα φοβηθῆτε· φοβήθητε
τὸν μετὰ τὸ ἀποκτεῖναι
ἔχοντα ἐξουσίαν ἐμβαλεῖν εἰς
τὴν γέενναν. ναὶ λέγω ὑμῖν,
6 τοῦτον φοβήθητε. οὐχὶ πέντε
στρουθία πωλοῦνται
ἀσσαρίων δύο; καὶ ἓν ἐξ
αὐτῶν οὐκ ἔστιν
ἐπιλελησμένον ἐνώπιον τοῦ
7 θεοῦ. ἀλλὰ καὶ αἱ τρίχες τῆς
κεφαλῆς ὑμῶν πᾶσαι
ἠρίθμηνται. μὴ φοβεῖσθε·
πολλῶν στρουθίων
8 διαφέρετε. λέγω δὲ ὑμῖν, πᾶς
ὃς ἂν ὁμολογήσῃ ἐν ἐμοὶ
ἔμπροσθεν τῶν ἀνθρώπων,
καὶ ὁ υἱὸς τοῦ ἀνθρώπου
ὁμολογήσει ἐν αὐτῷ
ἔμπροσθεν τῶν ἀγγέλων τοῦ
θεοῦ·
9 ὁ δὲ ἀρνησάμενός με
ἐνώπιον τῶν ἀνθρώπων
ἀπαρνηθήσεται ἐνώπιον τῶν
ἀγγέλων τοῦ θεοῦ.

Although there is parallelism throughout the passage, more than half Luke's words are different from Matthew's. Luke is considerably the fuller – note the additions ἐν τοῖς ταμιείοις, 'I say to you my friends', and note major differences: Luke has 'whatever you have said in the dark shall be heard' for 'what I say to you in the dark tell'; 'and after these things they have no more that they can do. But I will warn you whom to fear' for 'but cannot kill the soul'; 'five sparrows sold for two ossaria' for 'two sparrows sold for one ossarion'; 'angels of God' for 'my

Father in heaven'; 'he will be denied' for 'I will deny him'. Some of these differences (notably the five or two sparrows) seem greater than those which Luke allows himself when he is parallel to Mark, which confirms the view that he is neither copying Matthew nor copying the same document as Matthew. It is of course commonly held (e.g. by Fitzmyer and Marshall)[24] that Luke and Matthew are both here using Q. But it becomes necessary to postulate deliberate changes of sense which are difficult to explain and/or the use of different recensions of Q. Thus Marshall *Luke* says that Luke's

> v. 3 conveys a different sense from Mt. 10:27, and this affects the force of v. 2 . . . Some alterations of the wording to suit new contexts appear to have been made . . . the strange differences in v. 6 . . . are hard to explain redactionally . . . the wording of v. 12 . . . is a puzzle and lends support to the idea that two different recensions of the Q material are used. (510)

There are two other passages of some length where a strong case for a documentary connection could have been made had they been in similar contexts: 3.) *The lament for Jerusalem* of Luke 13:34, 35, given in the context of Jesus' 'journeying toward Jerusalem' and of his reply to 'this fox Herod' about the necessity for prophets to perish there, reappears in Matthew 23:37–39 just before the discourse concerning the destruction of the city. Though the wording is very close there are a dozen little differences between the two versions (underlined):

Matthew 23:37–39	Luke 13:34, 35
37 Ἰερουσαλὴμ Ἰερουσαλήμ, ἡ ἀποκτείνουσα τοὺς προφήτας καὶ λιθοβολοῦσα τοὺς ἀπεσταλμένους πρὸς αὐτήν, ποσάκις ἠθέλησα ἐπισυναγαγεῖν τὰ τέκνα σου, ὃν τρόπον ὄρνις ἐπισυνάγει τὰ νοσσία αὐτῆς ὑπὸ τὰς πτέρυγας, καὶ οὐκ 38 ἠθελήσατε. ἰδοὺ ἀφίεται 39 ὑμῖν ὁ οἶκος ὑμῶν. λέγω γὰρ	34 Ἰερουσαλὴμ Ἰερουσαλήμ, ἡ ἀποκτείνουσα τοὺς προφήτας καὶ λιθοβολοῦσα τοὺς ἀπεσταλμένους πρὸς αὐτήν, ποσάκις ἠθέλησα ἐπισυνάξαι τὰ τέκνα σου ὃν τρόπον ὄρνις τὴν ἑαυτῆς νοσσιὰν ὑπὸ τὰς πτέρυγας, 35 καὶ οὐκ ἠθελήσατε. ἰδοὺ ἀφίεται ὑμῖν ὁ οἶκος ὑμῶν. λέγω δὲ ὑμῖν, οὐ μὴ ἴδητέ με

ὑμῖν, οὐ μή με ἴδητε ἀπ᾽
ἄρτι ἕως ἂν εἴπητε·
εὐλογημένος ὁ ἐρχόμενος ἐν
ὀνόματι κυρίου.

ἕως ἥξει ὅτε εἴπητε·
εὐλογημένος ὁ ἐρχόμενος ἐν
ὀνόματι κυρίου.

4.) *The parable of the faithful and wise slave* of Matthew 24 has no parallel in Luke 21, but comes in Luke 12:39, 40, 42–46. In spite of many verbal identities there are some thirty-five[25] differences between these seven verses and Matthew 24:43 –51a; if the twenty-eight extra words of Luke 12:41 and Matthew 24:51b are included, the differences total sixty-three:

Matthew 24:43–51

43 Ἐκεῖνο δὲ γινώσκετε ὅτι εἰ ἤδει ὁ οἰκοδεσπότης ποίᾳ φυλακῇ ὁ κλέπτης ἔρχεται, ἐγρηγόρησεν ἂν καὶ οὐκ ἂν εἴασεν διορυχθῆναι τὴν

44 οἰκίαν αὐτοῦ. διὰ τοῦτο καὶ ὑμεῖς γίνεσθε ἕτοιμοι, ὅτι ᾗ οὐ δοκεῖτε ὥρᾳ ὁ υἱὸς τοῦ ἀνθρώπου ἔρχεται.

45 Τίς ἄρα ἐστὶν ὁ πιστὸς δοῦλος καὶ φρόνιμος ὃν κατέστησεν ὁ κύριος ἐπὶ τῆς οἰκετείας αὐτοῦ τοῦ δοῦναι αὐτοῖς τὴν τροφὴν ἐν

46 καιρῷ; μακάριος ὁ δοῦλος ἐκεῖνος ὃν ἐλθὼν ὁ κύριος αὐτοῦ εὑρήσει οὕτως

47 ποιοῦντα· ἀμὴν λέγω ὑμῖν ὅτι ἐπὶ πᾶσιν τοῖς ὑπάρχουσιν αὐτοῦ

48 καταστήσει αὐτόν. ἐὰν δὲ εἴπῃ ὁ κακὸς δοῦλος ἐκεῖνος ἐν τῇ καρδίᾳ αὐτοῦ·

49 χρονίζει μου ὁ κύριος, καὶ

Luke 12:39–46

39 Τοῦτο δὲ γινώσκετε, ὅτι εἰ ἤδει ὁ οἰκοδεσπότης ποίᾳ ὥρᾳ ὁ κλέπτης ἔρχεται, οὐκ ἂν ἀφῆκεν διορυχθῆναι τὸν οἶκον αὐτοῦ.

40 καὶ ὑμεῖς γίνεσθε ἕτοιμοι, ὅτι ᾗ ὥρᾳ οὐ δοκεῖτε ὁ υἱὸς τοῦ ἀνθρώπου ἔρχεται.

41 Εἶπεν δὲ ὁ Πέτρος· κύριε, πρὸς ἡμᾶς τὴν παραβολὴν ταύτην λέγεις ἢ καὶ πρὸς

42 πάντας; καὶ εἶπεν ὁ κύριος· τίς ἄρα ἐστὶν ὁ πιστὸς οἰκονόμος ὁ φρόνιμος, ὃν καταστήσει ὁ κύριος ἐπὶ τῆς θεραπείας αὐτοῦ τοῦ διδόναι ἐν καιρῷ

43 σιτομέτριον; μακάριος ὁ δοῦλος ἐκεῖνος, ὃν ἐλθὼν ὁ κύριος αὐτοῦ εὑρήσει

44 ποιοῦντα οὕτως. ἀληθῶς λέγω ὑμῖν ὅτι ἐπὶ πᾶσιν τοῖς ὑπάρχουσιν αὐτοῦ

45 καταστήσει αὐτόν. ἐὰν δὲ

ἄρξηται τύπτειν τοὺς
συνδούλους αὐτοῦ, ἐσθίῃ δὲ
καὶ πίνῃ μετὰ τῶν
50 μεθυόντων, ἥξει ὁ κύριος
τοῦ δούλου ἐκείνου ἐν
ἡμέρᾳ ᾗ οὐ προσδοκᾷ καὶ ἐν
51 ὥρᾳ ᾗ οὐ γινώσκει, καὶ
διχοτομήσει αὐτόν, καὶ τὸ
μέρος αὐτοῦ μετὰ τῶν
ὑποκριτῶν θήσει· ἐκεῖ ἔσται
ὁ κλαυθμὸς καὶ ὁ βρυγμὸς
τῶν ὀδόντων.

εἴπῃ ὁ δοῦλος ἐκεῖνος ἐν τῇ
καρδίᾳ αὐτοῦ· χρονίζει ὁ
κύριός μου ἔρχεσθαι, καὶ
ἄρξηται τύπτειν τοὺς
παῖδας καὶ τὰς παιδίσκας,
ἐσθίειν τε καὶ πίνειν καὶ
46 μεθύσκεσθαι, ἥξει ὁ κύριος
τοῦ δούλου ἐκείνου ἐν
ἡμέρᾳ ᾗ οὐ προσδοκᾷ καὶ ἐν
ὥρᾳ ᾗ οὐ γινώσκει, καὶ
διχοτομήσει αὐτόν, καὶ τὸ
μέρος αὐτοῦ μετὰ τῶν
ἀπίστων θήσει.

There is no reason in these two cases why they should not be taken, as Luke's setting suggests they should be, as records of similar but distinct utterances. If to some the wording seems too close for separate utterances retained in separate minds over several years, it needs to be remembered that in addition to a tendency towards divergence there could also have been a tendency towards assimilation when similar sayings were taught in the church.

5.) *Luke's mission charge to the seventy* (10:2–12) provides a further example of fairly (but not very) close wording when compared with the mission charge to the twelve in Matthew 10. Matthew's order is quite different: the corresponding verses have the sequence 16, 9, 10a, 11, 12, 13, 10b, 7, 8, 14, 15; and according to Farmer's *Synopticon* identical words are fewer (eighty-three) than differing words (one hundred and three). If the order and the context were the same, we should naturally think that we had two (considerably variant) accounts of the same discourse. Even then they would still be too different (with 55% of non-identical words) to suggest a common literary origin. But as it is, with the jumbled order and the clearly stated different contexts, it is far more plausible to take them as different missions containing (as might be expected) similar charges given on different occasions. On the face of it the comments of Fitzmyer and Marshall do not seem to be justified:

Since none of the other Gospels know of a separate sending-out of 'other' disciples than the Twelve and since what is addressed here to the 'others' is already found in part in the charge to the Twelve in Matthew, Luke has clearly created this literary 'doublet' from the 'Q' material that is parallel to Mark 6:6b–13. Information that was preserved in the 'Mk' and 'Q' sources about a sending-out of disciples by Jesus has been used by Luke to fashion two separate mission-charges, one to the Twelve and one to the 'seventy(-two) others'. (Fitzmyer 843)

Luke based his account of the mission of the Twelve on Mk. (with some influence from Q), but Matthew conflated material from Mk. with parallel material from Q; both the Marcan and Q material were probably based ultimately on the same tradition . . . The task of determining the precise extent, order and wording of Luke's source is far from easy. The beginning and ending (10:2, 13–16) appear in almost identical form in Mt. and must be from Q. The same is true of 10:3, although it appears in a different position in Mt. The wording in 10:4–12 differs considerably from that in Mt., but it is probably based on the same source; many of the differences are due to Matthew's conflation with Mk. and his own special source material, and the possibility that Matthew and Luke used different recensions of Q should also be borne in mind. (Marshall *Luke* 412f)

There are three examples of close wording (especially close in the words of Jesus) in which the contexts are not precisely defined, but in which the two gospels are probably referring to the same incident. (We revert to underlining the identical words.)

6.) *'I will follow you wherever you go.'*

Matthew 8:18–22	*Luke 9:57–62*
18 Ἰδὼν δὲ ὁ Ἰησοῦς ὄχλον περὶ αὐτὸν ἐκέλευσεν	57 Καὶ πορευομένων αὐτῶν ἐν τῇ ὁδῷ εἶπέν τις πρὸς αὐτόν· ἀκολουθήσω σοι
19 ἀπελθεῖν εἰς τὸ πέραν. Καὶ προσελθὼν εἷς γραμματεὺς εἶπεν αὐτῷ· διδάσκαλε, ἀκολουθήσω σοι ὅπου ἐὰν	58 ὅπου ἐὰν ἀπέρχῃ. καὶ εἶπεν αὐτῷ ὁ Ἰησοῦς· αἱ ἀλώπεκες φωλεοὺς ἔχουσιν
20 ἀπέρχῃ. καὶ λέγει αὐτῷ ὁ Ἰησοῦς· αἱ ἀλώπεκες	καὶ τὰ πετεινὰ τοῦ οὐρανοῦ κατασκηνώσεις, ὁ δὲ υἱὸς

φωλεοὺς ἔχουσιν καὶ τὰ
πετεινὰ τοῦ οὐρανοῦ
κατασκηνώσεις, ὁ δὲ υἱὸς
τοῦ ἀνθρώπου οὐκ ἔχει ποῦ
τὴν κεφαλὴν κλίνῃ.
21 ἕτερος δὲ τῶν μαθητῶν
εἶπεν αὐτῷ· κύριε,
ἐπίτρεψόν μοι πρῶτον
ἀπελθεῖν καὶ θάψαι τὸν
22 πατέρα μου. ὁ δὲ Ἰησοῦς
λέγει αὐτῷ· ἀκολούθει μοι,
καὶ ἄφες τοὺς νεκροὺς
θάψαι τοὺς ἑαυτῶν
νεκρούς.

τοῦ ἀνθρώπου οὐκ ἔχει ποῦ
59 τὴν κεφαλὴν κλίνῃ. Εἶπεν
δὲ πρὸς ἕτερον· ἀκολούθει
μοι. ὁ δὲ εἶπεν· ἐπίτρεψόν
μοι πρῶτον ἀπελθόντι
θάψαι τὸν πατέρα μου.
60 εἶπεν δὲ αὐτῷ· ἄφες τοὺς
νεκροὺς θάψαι τοὺς ἑαυτῶν
νεκρούς, σὺ δὲ ἀπελθὼν
διάγγελλε τὴν βασιλείαν τοῦ
61 θεοῦ. Εἶπεν δὲ καὶ ἕτερος·
ἀκολουθήσω σοι, κύριε·
πρῶτον δὲ ἐπίτρεψόν μοι
ἀποτάξασθαι τοῖς εἰς τὸν
62 οἶκόν μου. εἶπεν δὲ [πρὸς
αὐτὸν] ὁ Ἰησοῦς· οὐδεὶς
ἐπιβαλὼν τὴν χεῖρα ἐπ᾽
ἄροτρον καὶ βλέπων εἰς τὰ
ὀπίσω εὔθετός ἐστιν τῇ
βασιλείᾳ τοῦ θεοῦ.

This incident is not recorded by Mark, so Luke had no guidance from that quarter as to where it should be placed. In neither Matthew nor Luke is the context precisely defined. Matthew sandwiches the two offers of discipleship between a command to cross the sea and the storm. Luke puts his three offers at the beginning of the travel narrative between the rejection by a Samaritan city and the commissioning of the seventy. He just says that they were 'in the way'. It is conceivable that Luke got the story from Matthew, but it would be difficult to account for his addition of the third offer if that were so. It is better to suppose that Luke left it as he found it in his travel narrative material, and that we have independent accounts of the same event.

7.) *Woes on Chorazin and Bethsaida.* (Note the transference of Luke's verse 12 to the end to align it with Matthew.)

Matthew 11:20–24
20 Τότε ἤρξατο ὀνειδίζειν τὰς

Luke 10:12–15
13 Οὐαί σοι, Χοραζίν, οὐαί

61

πόλεις ἐν αἷς ἐγένοντο αἱ
πλεῖσται δυνάμεις αὐτοῦ,
21 ὅτι οὐ μετενόησαν· οὐαί
σοι, Χοραζίν· οὐαί σοι,
Βηθσαϊδά· ὅτι εἰ ἐν Τύρῳ
καὶ Σιδῶνι ἐγένοντο αἱ
δυνάμεις αἱ γενόμεναι ἐν
ὑμῖν, πάλαι ἂν ἐν σάκκῳ
καὶ σποδῷ μετενόησαν.
22 πλὴν λέγω ὑμῖν, Τύρῳ καὶ
Σιδῶνι ἀνεκτότερον ἔσται
ἐν ἡμέρᾳ κρίσεως ἢ ὑμῖν.
καὶ σύ, Καφαρναούμ, μὴ
ἕως οὐρανοῦ ὑψωθήσῃ; ἕως
ᾅδου καταβήσῃ· ὅτι εἰ ἐν
Σοδόμοις ἐγενήθησαν αἱ
δυνάμεις αἱ γενόμεναι ἐν
σοί, ἔμεινεν ἂν μέχρι τῆς
σήμερον. πλὴν λέγω ὑμῖν ὅτι
γῇ Σοδόμων ἀνεκτότερον
ἔσται ἐν ἡμέρᾳ κρίσεως ἢ
σοί.

σοι, Βηθσαϊδά· ὅτι εἰ ἐν
Τύρῳ καὶ Σιδῶνι
ἐγενήθησαν αἱ δυνάμεις αἱ
γενόμεναι ἐν ὑμῖν, πάλαι ἂν
ἐν σάκκῳ καὶ σποδῷ
καθήμενοι μετενόησαν.
14 πλὴν Τύρῳ καὶ Σιδῶνι
ἀνεκτότερον ἔσται ἐν τῇ
κρίσει ἢ ὑμῖν.
15 καὶ σύ, Καφαρναούμ, μὴ
ἕως οὐρανοῦ ὑψωθήσῃ; ἕως
τοῦ ᾅδου καταβήσῃ.

12 Λέγω ὑμῖν ὅτι Σοδόμοις ἐν
τῇ ἡμέρᾳ ἐκείνῃ
ἀνεκτότερον ἔσται ἢ τῇ
πόλει ἐκείνῃ.

This passage comes in both gospels in the chapter following the mission of the twelve and is therefore roughly in the same context, suggesting two versions of the same utterance.

8.) *Thanksgiving to the Father.*

Matthew 11:25–27

25 Ἐν ἐκείνῳ τῷ καιρῷ
ἀποκριθεὶς ὁ Ἰησοῦς εἶπεν·
ἐξομολογοῦμαί σοι, πάτερ,
κύριε τοῦ οὐρανοῦ καὶ τῆς
γῆς, ὅτι ἔκρυψας ταῦτα ἀπὸ
σοφῶν καὶ συνετῶν, καὶ
ἀπεκάλυψας αὐτὰ νηπίοις·
26 ναί, ὁ πατήρ, ὅτι οὕτως
εὐδοκία ἐγένετο ἔμπροσθέν
27 σου. Πάντα μοι παρεδόθη

Luke 10:21, 22

21 Ἐν αὐτῇ τῇ ὥρᾳ
ἠγαλλιάσατο τῷ πνεύματι
τῷ ἁγίῳ καὶ εἶπεν·
ἐξομολογοῦμαί σοι,
πάτερ, κύριε τοῦ οὐρανοῦ
καὶ τῆς γῆς, ὅτι ἀπέκρυψας
ταῦτα ἀπὸ σοφῶν καὶ
συνετῶν, καὶ ἀπεκάλυψας
αὐτὰ νηπίοις· ναί, ὁ πατήρ,
ὅτι οὕτως εὐδοκία ἐγένετο

ὑπὸ τοῦ πατρός μου, καὶ
οὐδεὶς ἐπιγινώσκει τὸν υἱὸν
εἰ μὴ ὁ πατήρ, οὐδὲ τὸν
πατέρα τις ἐπιγινώσκει εἰ
μὴ ὁ υἱὸς καὶ ᾧ ἐὰν
βούληται ὁ υἱὸς
ἀποκαλύψαι.

22 ἔμπροσθέν σου. πάντα μοι
παρεδόθη ὑπὸ τοῦ πατρός
μου, καὶ οὐδεὶς γινώσκει τίς
ἐστιν ὁ υἱὸς εἰ μὴ ὁ πατήρ,
καὶ τίς ἐστιν ὁ πατὴρ εἰ μὴ ὁ
υἱὸς καὶ ᾧ ἐὰν βούληται ὁ
υἱὸς ἀποκαλύψαι.

This thanksgiving follows the pericope of the woes on the unrepentant cities in both gospels, in Matthew immediately and in Luke almost immediately. Closeness of wording and similarity of context suggest a common incident.

9.) *The Beelzebul controversy* (11:14–32) has perhaps the most plausible claim to a literary connection. It has nineteen verses which run parallel to the twenty-four verses of Matthew 12:22–45. Not only are several of the sayings of Jesus found in identical or nearly identical form, but there is a sustained similarity of order throughout much of the passage. In addition the setting, including the reactions of Jesus and of the crowds, is similar. If on other grounds there were reasons for believing in literary dependence for the Q-material, this would undoubtedly provide plausible confirmation of it. If, however, literary dependence is regarded as something still to be established, this passage cannot be said to prove it. The relation here between Luke 11 and Matthew 12 is in fact highly complex (see p. 64).

It will be observed that in both gospels the teaching of Jesus is broken up into two sections – in Matthew by an intervention of Pharisees (v. 38) and in Luke by the cry of the woman (v. 27). In the first section the same logical sequence is followed as far as 'He who is not with me is against me; and he who does not gather with me scatters.' The wording in this concluding saying is identical. It is also very close in the preceding Matthew 12:26–28 and Luke 11:18–20, 'If I cast out demons by Beelzebul . . . then the kingdom of God has come upon you', though in this case there is the striking difference between Matthew's 'Spirit of God' and Luke's 'finger of God'. In the rest of the passage, however, the differences are many and varied. Matthew 12:22 recounts the healing of a man who is blind and

The contents may be set out as follows:

	Kingdom, city, house divided		Kingdom divided, house falls
26	Satan divided	18	Satan divided
27	sons your judges	19	sons your judges
28	If I by the Spirit of God	20	If I by the finger of God
29	need to bind strong man	21	strong man armed at peace
		22	a stronger takes his armour
30	He not with me	23	He not with me
		24-26	unclean spirit in waterless places
31,32	blasphemy against Spirit		
33-37	man judged by his words		
		27, 28	A woman said: Blessed the womb
38	Pharisees seek sign	29a	Jesus said, This generation seeks a sign
39,40	no sign but Jonah	29b	no sign but Jonah
41	Ninevites rise in judgement	30	Jonah a sign to Ninevites
42	queen of south	31	queen of south
		32	Ninevites rise in judgement
43-45	unclean spirit in waterless places		
46-50	mother and brothers seek Jesus		
		33-36	sayings on light

dumb, whereas Luke mentions only the dumbness (and he does so in remarkably different wording, which has closer affinities with the Matthean doublet in 9:32–34 than with Matthew 12:22). Luke makes no mention of 'Can this be the Son of David?' nor of the part played by the Pharisees. The accusation about Beelzebul is differently phrased and Luke inserts an extra sentence about others seeking a sign (vv. 15, 16). Verses 17–20, though close in sense, have numerous differences. In verses 21 and 22 Luke's treatment of the strong man has virtually nothing in common with Matthew's (which is very close to Mark's treatment at 3:27). Luke ends his first section with the saying (which ends Matthew's *second* section) concerning the unclean spirit which seeks seven spirits more evil than himself, whereas Matthew ends his first section with sayings concerning blasphemy against the Spirit and man's judgement according to his words.

It is by no means obvious that a common document lies behind the two passages in this first section. They could be independent accounts of a single occasion considerably modified in transmission; or they could be accounts of different occasions when the same slander was similarly dealt with by Jesus. It is likely enough that this line of attack was deliberately thought out and then pressed home against Jesus during the latter part of his ministry.

In the second briefer section there are two verses which are nearly identical, but in the reverse order – the easily remembered sayings about the queen of the south and the men of Nineveh. The setting, however, is different – Matthew introduces Pharisees and they ask for a sign, whereas Luke speaks simply of increasing crowds. In verses 39 and 40 Matthew's phraseology differs at a number of points from Luke's and he tends to write more fully (e.g. 'and adulterous', 'the prophet', 'three days and three nights in the belly of the whale'), though Luke too has his own expressions (e.g. 'a sign to the men of Nineveh', 'this generation'). Matthew concludes with the saying about the unclean spirit, while Luke concludes with sayings about light. Again, it is by no means obvious that there is a literary connection between the two passages. It is possible that a demand for a sign, like the charge of demonic inspiration, was a favourite way of attempting to discredit Jesus and that more than one audience heard his rebuttal, but on the whole the passage suggests some common (but not quite direct) origin of the two accounts.

10.) *Earthly possessions and heavenly treasure* (12:22–31) has similar characteristics. There are ten consecutive verses which run very close to two passages in the Sermon on the Mount. These two Matthean passages of nine and three verses respectively (6:25–33; 6:19–21) come in the reverse order in Matthew and are there separated by sayings paralleled elsewhere in Luke. Compared with most Q-passages, these are very close to one another, yet there are over sixty differences between them, some of them striking, like Luke's ταμεῖον, μετεωρίζεσθε. Marshall writes: 'there are marked differences . . . Some of these go well beyond what can be explained by editorial activity on the part of the two Evangelists, and suggest that we have two variant forms . . . the theory that the Q material existed in more than one form receives further support' (*Luke* 525). Though these two passages provide the most plausible evidence for literary dependence, neither considered singly nor taken together do they demand it.

Looking at the Q-material studied thus far, it does not look as though the Luke who followed Mark so closely would have constructed passages out of Matthew in this way. Nor does it look as though the two evangelists followed a single common Q-source, since it would have entailed (particularly as we shall see, in the nine most divergent passages) one or other or both of them treating its different parts in too inconsistent a way. Of course, if the supposed common source is broken up into sufficiently small units of mixed written and oral tradition, which at a number of points had already diverged considerably from one another, a theory might result which does not run contrary to the facts. But if the Q-hypothesis has to be so diluted it undermines the cogency of the original postulation of the two-source hypothesis.

Examples of differences of sense

There are nine passages (some of them fairly long) in which the differences between Luke and Matthew are far greater than the differences between parallel passages of Luke and Mark.

1.) In Luke 11:39–52 Jesus delivers a severe *rebuke to the Pharisees* when he goes to dine with one of them. This occupies fourteen verses which have parallels occurring in Matthew 23 in this order: verses 26f, 23, 6f, 27, 4, 29–31, 34–36, 13. The passages are too long to set out in full, but the contents may be seen in the following table:

Matthew 23: 4-39		Luke 11:39-52	
		*39,40	Cleanliness (no Woe)
4	*Burdens (no Woe)		
5	Phylacteries		
6,7a	*Love of honour (no Woe)		
7b-10	Titles		
11,12	Humility		
13	*Shutting men out		
15	Proselytes		
16-22	Oaths		
23,24	Tithes	42	Tithes
		*43	Love of honour (Woe)
25,26	*Cleanliness (Woe)		
27,28	Tombs	44	Tombs
		45	Lawyer's interjection
		*46	Burdens (Woe)
29-36	Prophets	47-51	Prophets
(33	Vipers)		
37-39	O Jerusalem		
		*52	Shutting men out

Fitzmyer remarks: 'one senses a great similarity between these two passages in content and generic topics and wording, but specific phrasing and the order of the topics vary considerably' (942). The beginning of the two discourses illustrates the degree of variation:

Matthew 23:25, 26, 23   *Luke 11:39–42*

(Identical words are underlined. Matthew's verse 23 has been transferred to align it with Luke.)

25 Οὐαὶ ὑμῖν, γραμματεῖς καὶ
   Φαρισαῖοι ὑποκριταί, ὅτι
   καθαρίζετε τὸ ἐξωθεν τοῦ
   ποτηρίου καὶ τῆς
   παροψίδος, ἔσωθεν δὲ
   γέμουσιν ἐξ ἁρπαγῆς καὶ
26 ἀκρασίας. Φαρισαῖε τυφλέ,
   καθάρισον πρῶτον τὸ ἐντὸς
   τοῦ ποτηρίου ἵνα γένηται
   καὶ τὸ ἐκτὸς αὐτοῦ
   καθαρόν.
23 Οὐαὶ ὑμῖν, γραμματεῖς καὶ
   Φαρισαῖοι ὑποκριταί, ὅτι
   ἀποδεκατοῦτε τὸ ἡδύοσμον
   καὶ τὸ ἄνηθον καὶ τὸ
   κύμινον, καὶ ἀφήκατε τὰ
   βαρύτερα τοῦ νόμου, τὴν
   κρίσιν καὶ τὸ ἔλεος καὶ τὴν
   πίστιν· ταῦτα δὲ ἔδει
   ποιῆσαι κἀκεῖνα μὴ
   ἀφεῖναι.

νῦν ὑμεῖς οἱ Φαρισαῖοι τὸ
ἔξωθεν τοῦ ποτηρίου καὶ
τοῦ πίνακος καθαρίζετε,
τὸ δὲ
40 ἔσωθεν ὑμῶν γέμει ἁρπαγῆς
καὶ πονηρίας. ἄφρονες, οὐχ
ὁ ποιήσας τὸ ἔξωθεν καὶ τὸ
41 ἔσωθεν ἐποίησεν; πλὴν τὰ
ἐνόντα δότε ἐλεημοσύνην,
καὶ ἰδοὺ πάντα καθαρὰ
ὑμῖν ἐστιν.
42 ἀλλὰ οὐαὶ ὑμῖν τοῖς
Φαρισαίοις, ὅτι
ἀποδεκατοῦτε τὸ ἡδύοσμον
καὶ τὸ πήγανον καὶ πᾶν
λάχανον, καὶ παρέρχεσθε
τὴν κρίσιν καὶ τὴν ἀγάπην
τοῦ θεοῦ ταῦτα δὲ ἔδει
ποιῆσαι κἀκεῖνα μὴ
παρεῖναι.

Matthew's address, set in the temple, makes a coherent whole. Luke's account, though shorter and interrupted in the middle by a lawyer's question, also hangs well together. Matthew has seven woes, Luke has two series of three woes. The commentators are agreed that 'the source of this material . . . is not easily determined' (Fitzmyer 942), 'far from clear' (Marshall *Luke* 491). The latter thinks the differences 'sufficiently great to suggest that different recensions' of Q were made (493). This of course is a way of saying that the two accounts do not have an immediate common literary source. Judging by Luke's use of Mark in parallel passages, Luke would not have altered this passage from Matthew 23 into his version in Luke 11.

Building a Synoptic Theory: (2)

2.) In Luke 12:49–59 on the *Coming crisis* we have three pericopes with clear parallels, yet manifesting a host of differences – additions, subtractions and differences of wording.
a) Division in households.

Matthew 10:34–36

34 Μὴ νομίσητε ὅτι ἦλθον
βαλεῖν εἰρήνην ἐπὶ τὴν γῆν·
οὐκ ἦλθον βαλεῖν εἰρήνην
35 ἀλλὰ μάχαιραν. ἦλθον γὰρ
διχάσαι ἄνθρωπον κατὰ
τοῦ πατρὸς αὐτοῦ καὶ
θυγατέρα κατὰ τῆς μητρὸς
αὐτῆς καὶ νύμφην κατὰ τῆς
36 πενθερᾶς αὐτῆς, καὶ ἐχθροὶ
τοῦ ἀνθρώπου οἱ οἰκιακοὶ
αὐτοῦ.

Luke 12:49–53

49 Πῦρ ἦλθον βαλεῖν ἐπὶ τὴν
γῆν, καὶ τί θέλω εἰ ἤδη
50 ἀνήφθη. βάπτισμα δὲ ἔχω
βαπτισθῆναι, καὶ πῶς
συνέχομαι ἕως ὅτου
51 τελεσθῇ. δοκεῖτε ὅτι
εἰρήνην παρεγενόμην
δοῦναι ἐν τῇ γῇ; οὐχί, λέγω
ὑμῖν, ἀλλ᾿ ἢ διαμερισμόν.
52 ἔσονται γὰρ ἀπὸ τοῦ νῦν
πέντε ἐν ἑνὶ οἴκῳ
διαμεμερισμένοι, τρεῖς ἐπὶ
δυσὶν καὶ δύο ἐπὶ τρισίν·
53 διαμερισθήσονται, πατὴρ
ἐπὶ υἱῷ καὶ υἱὸς ἐπὶ πατρί,
μήτηρ ἐπὶ θυγατέρα καὶ
θυγάτηρ ἐπὶ τὴν μητέρα,
πενθερὰ ἐπὶ τὴν νύμφην
αὐτῆς καὶ νύμφη ἐπὶ τὴν
πενθεράν.

This passage which Matthew puts in the mission charge is not put in either of Luke's mission charges, but in a discussion with his disciples in the presence of a great multitude.
b) Interpreting the times.

Matthew 16:2, 3

2 ὁ δὲ ἀποκριθεὶς εἶπεν
αὐτοῖς· [ὀψίας γενομένης
λέγετε· εὐδία, πυρράζει γὰρ
3 ὁ οὐρανός· καὶ πρωΐ·
σήμερον χειμών, πυρράζει
γὰρ στυγνάζων ὁ οὐρανός.

Luke 12:54–56

54 Ἔλεγεν δὲ καὶ τοῖς ὄχλοις·
ὅταν ἴδητε νεφέλην
ἀνατέλλουσαν ἐπὶ δυσμῶν,
εὐθέως λέγετε ὅτι ὄμβρος
ἔρχεται, καὶ γίνεται οὕτως·
55 καὶ ὅταν νότον πνέοντα,

τὸ μὲν πρόσωπον τοῦ
οὐρανοῦ γινώσκετε
διακρίνειν, τὰ δὲ σημεῖα τῶν
καιρῶν οὐ δύνασθε;]

λέγετε ὅτι καύσων ἔσται,
56 καὶ γίνεται. ὑποκριταί, τὸ
πρόσωπον τῆς γῆς καὶ τοῦ
οὐρανοῦ οἴδατε δοκιμάζειν,
τὸν καιρὸν δὲ τοῦτον πῶς
οὐ δοκιμάζετε;

Luke either has no parallel here (if the ℵ B reading in Matthew is adopted) or (if the longer reading is followed) a form of words almost wholly different till the last sentence, which still has twelve differences in the course of seventeen words. Matthew sets the saying in a Galilean context.

c) Agreement with one's accuser.

Matthew 5:25, 26

25 Ἴσθι εὐνοῶν τῷ ἀντιδίκῳ
σου ταχὺ ἕως ὅτου εἶ μετ'
αὐτοῦ ἐν τῇ ὁδῷ·
μήποτέ σε παραδῷ ὁ
ἀντίδικος τῷ κριτῇ καὶ ὁ
κριτὴς τῷ ὑπηρέτῃ, καὶ εἰς
26 φυλακὴν βληθήσῃ· ἀμὴν
λέγω σοι, οὐ μὴ ἐξέλθῃς
ἐκεῖθεν, ἕως ἂν ἀποδῷς τὸν
ἔσχατον κοδράντην.

Luke 12:57–59

57 Τί δὲ καὶ ἀφ' ἑαυτῶν οὐ
58 κρίνετε τὸ δίκαιον; ὡς γὰρ
ὑπάγεις μετὰ τοῦ ἀντιδίκου
σου ἐπ' ἄρχοντα, ἐν τῇ ὁδῷ
δὸς ἐργασίαν ἀπηλλάχθαι
ἀπ' αὐτοῦ, μήποτε
κατασύρῃ σε πρὸς τὸν
κριτήν, καὶ ὁ κριτής σε
παραδώσει τῷ πράκτορι,
καὶ ὁ πράκτωρ σε βαλεῖ εἰς
59 φυλακήν. λέγω σοι, οὐ μὴ
ἐξέλθῃς ἐκεῖθεν, ἕως καὶ τὸ
ἔσχατον λεπτὸν ἀποδῷς.

The saying in the Sermon on the Mount expresses the same idea as Luke but in markedly different words, until the last short memorable sentence which still has five differences in its twelve words.

Marshall says at this point that 'Luke's use of sources here is . . . a puzzle' (*Luke* 545). Fitzmyer 994 gives verse 49 to L; verse 50 'has been so heavily modified by Luke that it borders on Lucan composition'; verse 51 is Q; verse 52 is Luke's redaction; verse 53 is Q. In verses 54–56, where 'only six Greek words out of forty-seven . . . in the Lucan text of this passage agree with the Matthean vocabulary', verse 54a 'is of Lucan composition, the rest . . . should be regarded as "L"' (999). Verse 57 is 'composed by Luke'; verses 58 and 59 are Q (1001). Such inventiveness, however, and such jumping from source to source, is not reminiscent of Luke when he is following Mark.

3.) *Exclusion from the kingdom* (13:24–29) has parallels of a sort in the following chapters of Matthew: 7, 25, 7 and 8. The narrow entrance is treated quite differently in the two gospels:

Matthew 7:13, 14	*Luke 13:24*
13 Εἰσέλθατε διὰ τῆς στενῆς πύλης· ὅτι πλατεῖα ἡ πύλη καὶ εὐρύχωρος ἡ ὁδὸς ἡ ἀπάγουσα εἰς τὴν ἀπώλειαν, καὶ πολλοί εἰσιν	24 ἀγωνίζεσθε εἰσελθεῖν διὰ τῆς στενῆς θύρας, ὅτι πολλοί, λέγω ὑμῖν, ζητήσουσιν εἰσελθεῖν καὶ οὐκ ἰσχύσουσιν.
14 οἱ εἰσερχόμενοι δι' αὐτῆς· ὅτί στενὴ ἡ πύλη καὶ τεθλιμμένη ἡ ὁδὸς ἡ ἀπάγουσα εἰς τὴν ζωὴν, καὶ ὀλίγοι εἰσὶν οἱ εὑρίσκοντες αὐτήν.	

In 13:25 it is not virgins who are shut out, but 'you':

Matthew 25:10–12	*Luke 13:25*
10 ἀπερχομένων δὲ αὐτῶν ἀγοράσαι ἦλθεν ὁ νυμφίος, καὶ αἱ ἕτοιμοι εἰσῆλθον μετ' αὐτοῦ εἰς τοὺς γάμους καὶ	25 ἀφ' οὗ ἂν ἐγερθῇ ὁ οἰκοδεσπότης καὶ ἀποκλείσῃ τὴν θύραν καὶ ἄρξησθε ἔξω ἑστάναι καὶ
11 ἐκλείσθη ἡ θύρα. ὕστερον δὲ ἔρχονται καὶ αἱ λοιπαὶ παρθένοι λέγουσαι· κύριε	κρούειν τὴν θύραν λέγοντες· κύριε, ἄνοιξον ἡμῖν, καὶ ἀποκριθεὶς ἐρεῖ
12 κύριε, ἄνοιξον ἡμῖν. ὁ δὲ ἀποκριθεὶς εἶπεν· ἀμὴν λέγω ὑμῖν, οὐκ οἶδα ὑμᾶς.	ὑμῖν· οὐκ οἶδα ὑμᾶς πόθεν ἐστέ.

Verse 26 has virtually nothing in common with Matthew 7:22, but verse 27 is close in sense, though very different in wording:

71

Matthew 7:22, 23

22 Πολλοὶ ἐροῦσίν μοι ἐν
ἐκείνῃ τῇ ἡμέρᾳ· κύριε
κύριε, οὐ τῷ σῷ ὀνόματι
ἐπροφητεύσαμεν, καὶ τῷ σῷ
ὀνόματι δαιμόνια
ἐξεβάλομεν, καὶ τῷ σῷ
ὀνόματι δυνάμεις πολλὰς
23 ἐποιήσαμεν; καὶ τότε
ὁμολογήσω αὐτοῖς ὅτι
οὐδέποτε ἔγνων ὑμᾶς
ἀποχωρεῖτε ἀπ' ἐμοῦ οἱ
ἐργαζόμενοι τὴν ἀνομίαν.

Luke 13:26, 27

26 τότε ἄρξεσθε λέγειν·
ἐφάγομεν ἐνώπιόν σου καὶ
ἐπίομεν, καὶ ἐν ταῖς
πλατείαις ἡμῶν ἐδίδαξας·
27 καὶ ἐρεῖ λέγων ὑμῖν· οὐκ
οἶδα πόθεν ἐστέ· ἀπόστητε
ἀπ' ἐμοῦ πάντες ἐργάται
ἀδικίας.

Verse 28a has a short and memorable sentence identical with its parallel, though in the one case it comes at the beginning and in the other at the end of the section. The rest of verses 28 and 29 differ much in wording:

Matthew 8:11, 12

11 λέγω δὲ ὑμῖν ὅτι πολλοὶ ἀπὸ
ἀνατολῶν καὶ δυσμῶν
ἥξουσιν καὶ
ἀνακλιθήσονται μετὰ
'Αβραὰμ καὶ 'Ισαὰκ καὶ
'Ιακὼβ ἐν τῇ βασιλείᾳ τῶν
12 οὐρανῶν· οἱ δὲ υἱοὶ τῆς
βασιλείας ἐκβληθήσονται
εἰς τὸ σκότος τὸ ἐξώτερον·
ἐκεῖ ἔσται ὁ κλαυθμὸς καὶ ὁ
βρυγμὸς τῶν ὀδόντων.

Luke 13:28, 29

28 'Εκεῖ ἔσται ὁ κλαυθμὸς καὶ
ὁ βρυγμὸς τῶν ὀδόντων,
ὅταν ὄψησθε 'Αβραὰμ καὶ
'Ισαὰκ καὶ 'Ιακὼβ καὶ
πάντας τοὺς προφήτας ἐν τῇ
βασιλείᾳ τοῦ θεοῦ, ὑμᾶς δὲ
29 ἐκβαλλομένους ἔξω. καὶ
ἥξουσιν ἀπὸ ἀνατολῶν καὶ
δυσμῶν καὶ ἀπὸ βορρᾶ καὶ
νότου, καὶ ἀνακλιθήσονται
ἐν τῇ βασιλείᾳ τοῦ θεοῦ.

Marshall says, 'The origins of this section are particularly obscure' (*Luke* 563). Luke has 'probably taken over a set of sayings from Q which were available to Matthew in a variant form' (564). Fitzmyer says:

the episode has been fashioned by Luke . . . Though I ascribe vv. 24–29 to 'Q' . . . I have to admit that the parallel Matthean material is at times quite diverse. How much of the difference is to

72

be ascribed to Matthean redaction, or to Lucan redaction – or, in the extreme, to the use rather of 'L' – who can say? (1021f)

4.) Both Luke 14:15–24 and Matthew 22:1–14 give an extended story concerning a *great banquet*, to which there is a gracious invitation, which is greeted with ungrateful excuse-making, which in turn is received with anger and is followed by a call to outcasts. This is customarily held to be Q-material, but according to Farmer's *Synopticon* the 180 words of Luke and the 223 words of Matthew have only eleven identical: εἶπεν, καὶ ἀπέστειλεν, αὐτοῦ, ἕτοιμα, ἀγρόν, τότε, αὐτοῦ, εἰς τὰς ὁδούς. (A further seventeen have significant, but incomplete, agreement.) This is no basis for a theory of a common literary source.

5.) *Forsaking family, taking up the cross*: in Luke 14:26, 27 are two sayings conveying the same ideas as two consecutive sayings in Matthew's mission charge, yet the differences could scarcely be greater:

Matthew 10:37, 38

37 Ὁ φιλῶν πατέρα ἢ μητέρα ὑπὲρ ἐμὲ οὐκ ἔστιν μου ἄξιος·καὶ ὁ φιλῶν υἱὸν ἢ θυγατέρα ὑπὲρ ἐμὲ οὐκ

38 ἔστιν μου ἄξιος· καὶ ὃς οὐ λαμβάνει τὸν σταυρὸν αὐτοῦ καὶ ἀκολουθεῖ ὀπίσω μου, οὐκ ἔσττν μου ἄξιος.

Luke 14:26, 27

26 εἴ τις ἔρχεται πρός με καὶ οὐ μισεῖ τὸν πατέρα αὐτοῦ καὶ τὴν μητέρα καὶ τὴν γυναῖκα καὶ τὰ τέκνα καὶ τοὺς ἀδελφοὺς καὶ τὰς ἀδελφὰς, ἔτι τε καὶ τὴν ψυχὴν ἑαυτοῦ, οὐ δύναται

27 εἶναί μου μαθητής. ὅστις οὐ βαστάζει τὸν σταυρὸν ἑαυτοῦ καὶ ἔρχεται ὀπίσω μου, οὐ δύναται εἶναί μου μαθητής.

6.) *Parable of the lost sheep*

Matthew 18:12–14

12 Τί ὑμῖν δοκεῖ; ἐὰν γένηταί τινι ἀνθρώπῳ ἑκατὸν πρόβατα καὶ πλανηθῇ ἓν ἐξ αὐτῶν, οὐχὶ ἀφήσει τὰ ἐνενήκοντα ἐννέα ἐπὶ τὰ

Luke 15:4–6

4 τίς ἄνθρωπος ἐξ ὑμῶν ἔχων ἑκατὸν πρόβατα καὶ ἀπολέσας ἐξ αὐτῶν ἓν οὐ καταλείπει τὰ ἐνενήκοντα ἐννέα ἐν τῇ ἐρήμῳ καὶ

73

ὄρη καὶ πορευθεὶς ζητεῖ τὸ
13 πλανώμενον; καὶ ἐὰν
    γένηται εὑρεῖν αὐτό, ἀμὴν
    λέγω ὑμῖν ὅτι χαίρει ἐπ'
    αὐτῷ μᾶλλον ἢ ἐπὶ τοῖς
    ἐνενήκοντα ἐννέα τοῖς μὴ
14 πεπλανημένοις. οὕτως οὐκ
    ἔστιν θέλημα ἔμπροσθεν
    τοῦ πατρὸς ὑμῶν τοῦ ἐν
    οὐρανοῖς ἵνα ἀπόληται ἓν
    τῶν μικρῶν τούτων.

πορεύεται ἐπὶ τὸ ἀπολωλὸς
5 ἕως εὕρῃ αὐτό; καὶ εὑρὼν
    ἐπιτίθησιν ἐπὶ τοὺς ὤμους
6 αὐτοῦ χαίρων, καὶ ἐλθὼν εἰς
    τὸν οἶκον συγκαλεῖ τοὺς
    φίλους καὶ τοὺς γείτονας,
    λέγων αὐτοῖς· συγχάρητέ
    μοι, ὅτι εὗρον τὸ πρόβατόν
    μου τὸ ἀπολωλός.

The basic story is the same, but the context is different, the details are different (Matthew: strays, on the hills, rejoices; Luke: is lost, in the desert, they rejoice together) and the application is different. Marshall comments 'The differences between the Lucan and Matthaean forms are sufficiently great to make it unlikely that both Evangelists are directly dependent upon the same source. Even when allowance is made for their editorial work, we are still left with two independent versions of the parable' (*Luke* 600).

7.) *Law and violence in the kingdom of God*: these two adjacent Lukan sayings do not look as though they have a literary connection with their widely separated Matthean parallels:

Matthew 11:12, 13; 5:18
12 Ἀπὸ δὲ τῶν ἡμερῶν
    Ἰωάννου τοῦ βαπτιστοῦ
    ἕως ἄρτι ἡ βασιλεία τῶν
    οὐρανῶν βιάζεται, καὶ
    βιασταὶ ἁρπάζουσιν αὐτήν.
13 πάντες γὰρ οἱ προφῆται καὶ
    ὁ νόμος ἕως Ἰωάννου
    ἐπροφήτευσαν.
18 Ἀμὴν γὰρ λέγω ὑμῖν, ἕως
    ἂν παρέλθῃ ὁ οὐρανὸς καὶ ἡ
    γῆ, ἰῶτα ἓν ἢ μία κεραία οὐ
    μὴ παρέλθῃ ἀπὸ τοῦ νόμου,
    ἕως ἂν πάντα γένηται.

Luke 16:16–17
16 Ὁ νόμος καὶ οἱ προφῆται
    μέχρι Ἰωάννου· ἀπὸ τότε
    ἡ βασιλεία τοῦ θεοῦ
    εὐαγγελίζεται καὶ πᾶς εἰς
    αὐτὴν βιάζεται.
17 εὐκοπώτερον δέ ἐστιν τὸν
    οὐρανὸν καὶ τὴν γῆν
    παρελθεῖν ἢ τοῦ νόμου μίαν
    κεραίαν πεσεῖν.

8.) *Offences, forgiveness and faith*: a series of sayings with Matthean parallels which do not suggest a literary connection:
a) Warning against offences.

Matthew 18:7
7 Οὐαὶ τῷ κόσμῳ ἀπὸ τῶν σκανδάλων· ἀνάγκη γὰρ ἐλθεῖν τὰ σκάνδαλα, πλὴν οὐαὶ τῷ ἀνθρώπῳ δι' οὗ τὸ σκάνδαλον ἔρχεται.

Luke 17:1
1 Εἶπεν δὲ πρὸς τοὺς μαθητὰς αὐτοῦ· ἀνένδεκτόν ἐστιν τοῦ τὰ σκάνδαλα μὴ ἐλθεῖν, οὐαὶ δὲ δι' οὗ ἔρχεται·

Matthew 18:6
6 Ὃς δ' ἂν σκανδαλίσῃ ἕνα τῶν μικρῶν τούτων τῶν πιστευόντων εἰς ἐμέ, συμφέρει αὐτῷ ἵνα κρεμασθῇ μύλος ὀνικὸς περὶ τὸν τράχηλον αὐτοῦ καὶ καταποντισθῇ ἐν τῷ πελάγει τῆς θαλάσσης.

Luke 17:2, 3a
2 λυσιτελεῖ αὐτῷ εἰ λίθος μυλικὸς περίκειται περὶ τὸν τράχηλον αὐτοῦ καὶ ἔρριπται εἰς τὴν θάλασσαν, ἢ ἵνα σκανδαλίσῃ τῶν μικρῶν τούτων ἕνα.
3 προσέχετε ἑαυτοῖς.

Note the reversal of order in Matthew and the verbal differences. Luke here has echoes of the Markan parallel.
b) Forgiveness.

Matthew 18:15
15 Ἐὰν δὲ ἁμαρτήσῃ ὁ ἀδελφός σου, ὕπαγε ἔλεγξον αὐτὸν μεταξὺ σοῦ καὶ αὐτοῦ μόνου. ἐάν σου ἀκούσῃ, ἐκέρδησας τὸν ἀδελφόν σου·

Luke 17:3b, 4
3b Ἐὰν ἁμάρτῃ ὁ ἀδελφός σου, ἐπιτίμησον αὐτῷ, καὶ ἐὰν μετανοήσῃ, ἄφες αὐτῷ.
4 καὶ ἐὰν ἑπτάκις τῆς ἡμέρας ἁμαρτήσῃ εἰς σὲ καὶ ἑπτάκις ἐπιστρέψῃ πρὸς σὲ λέγων· μετανοῶ, ἀφήσεις αὐτῷ.

A quite different reference to forgiving seventy times seven comes in Matthew 18:22.
c) Faith.

Matthew 17:19, 20
19 Τότε προσελθόντες οἱ μαθηταὶ τῷ Ἰησοῦ κατ' ἰδίαν

Luke 17:5, 6
5 Καὶ εἶπαν οἱ ἀπόστολοι τῷ κυρίῳ· πρόσθες ἡμῖν πίστιν.

εἶπον· διὰ τί ἡμεῖς οὐκ
ἠδυνήθημεν ἐκβαλεῖν αὐτό;
20 ὁ δὲ λέγει αὐτοῖς· διὰ τὴν
ὀλιγοπιστίαν ὑμῶν· ἀμὴν
γὰρ λέγω ὑμῖν, ἐὰν ἔχητε
πίστιν ὡς κόκκον σινάπεως,
ἐρεῖτε τῷ ὄρει τούτῳ·
μετάβα ἔνθεν ἐκεῖ, καὶ
μεταβήσεται καὶ οὐδὲν
ἀδυνατήσει ὑμῖν.

6 εἶπεν δὲ ὁ κύριος· εἰ ἔχετε
πίστιν ὡς κόκκον σινάπεως,
ἐλέγετε ἂν τῇ συκαμίνῳ
ταύτῃ· ἐκριζώθητι καὶ
φυτεύθητι ἐν τῇ θαλάσσῃ·
καὶ ὑπήκουσεν ἂν ὑμῖν.

The power of faith like a grain of mustard seed is expounded in different contexts, different words and with different applications. In verses 5–6 there is no *prima facie* case for literary dependence.

9.) *Day of the Son of Man* (17:22–37): a long passage with parallels in the Mount of Olives discourse of Matthew 24. The Matthean sayings come in this order in Luke: verses 23, 27, 37, 38b, 39, 17, 18, 40, 41, 28. (None of these is paralleled in Luke's Mount of Olives discourse.) The context of Matthew is Jerusalem in Holy Week; the context of Luke is well prior to the final journey up from Jericho. In Luke's sixteen verses only verses 27 and 37b approximate to Matthew in wording. Though the sense of verses 23, 24, 26, 34, 35 is close to Matthew, the language is very different. Luke also has additional matter in verses 25, 28–32, 37a; 33 is parallel to a different Matthean passage (10:39). Fitzmyer sees the passage as a complex of composition, redaction and weaving together of putative sources (1164f): verse 23a is Lukan composition; verse 22b redaction; verses 23, 24 Q; verse 25 redaction; verses 26, 27 Q; verses 28–32 L; verses 33–35 Q; verse 37a, and 37b redaction; verse 37c Q. But with order, context and wording so different a literary connection seems on the face of it improbable.

THE ORIGIN OF LUKE'S CENTRAL SECTION

If the Q-material of the Central Section does not come from the one or more Qs or from Matthew, what is the alternative? The simplest answer is the most revolutionary. The answer could be that these Q-passages have no common literary, or even oral, origin, but derive from different sayings of Jesus. Their similarities derive from a common source in the mind of Jesus, rather than from a single utterance of his lips. It is inevitable that an itinerant preacher must repeat himself again and again, sometimes in identical words, sometimes with slight variations, sometimes with new applications; sometimes an old idea will appear in an entirely new dress. All Q-passages set in different contexts in the two gospels (from cases of complete identity to cases of similar imagery) could quite well have come from a preacher who on one occasion had used the Matthean form and on another the Lukan. It could be that we are distorting the material when we insist upon asking which of the two is the more original.

I have further suggested[26] that the whole section may have come from one of the seventy. There are five arguments which might be thought to support this hypothesis.

1.) *It fits the claims of the narrative.* Luke's gospel has a broad chronological outline which includes an extensive Galilean ministry and a detailed account of the final happenings in Jerusalem. The Central Section is placed between them and is ostensibly a record of what happened in the interval. Luke writes at length about the Great Sermon in chapter 6 and about the destruction of Jerusalem in chapter 21, yet he puts much important material paralleled at those points in Matthew in his Central Section. He would appear *prima facie* to be indicating that his material does not belong either in Galilee or in Jerusalem.

2.) *It fits Luke's claims for his sources.* Luke expresses the utmost confidence in his sources, which he considers to be as reliable as the apostolic tradition handed on by the-from-the-beginning-eyewitnesses and ministers of the word. They are (he affirms) calculated to give Theophilus an orderly and trustworthy account of what happened. This accords better with records of someone present in the later stages of the ministry than with free manipulations of words of Jesus found in other contexts.

3.) *It would explain the extraordinary interest in the mission of the*

77

seventy. The twelve played an important part not only in the leadership of the early church but also in its constitution and thought. The seventy, on the other hand, seem to have had no permanent importance in the structure of the church. Yet Luke deals with the mission of the twelve in six verses (9:1–6), and then proceeds to devote twenty-four verses (10:1–24) to tell of the appointment, instruction, despatch and return of the seventy and of the subsequent disclosures to them. He enters into considerable and intimate detail: he 'sent them on ahead of him, two by two, into every town and place where he himself was about to come'; and when they returned 'with joy', Jesus told them of his own experience of seeing Satan fall from heaven. He then 'exulted in the Holy Spirit' and turned to the disciples and spoke to them 'privately'. It is true that the instructions to the seventy have much in common with those to the twelve, but this need not mean borrowing, since not only is it intrinsically probable that the instructions would be similar, but there are also many differences between them to be accounted for. This otherwise strange phenomenon would be explained if the narrative concerning the seventy stood almost at the beginning of the records of one who took part in that mission and stayed with Jesus until the end. It would supply a gap in the church's knowledge of Jesus' ministry and it would reinforce and add to its knowledge of this teaching.

4.) *It would explain the order of the material.* It is no longer necessary to suppose that Luke darted hither and thither in search of material, which he put together sometimes without revealing his connections of thought. It is only necessary to suppose that Luke trusted his source, and that he copied faithfully even when the notes were too concise to make clear the relations between the sayings.[27]

5.) *It would account for the verbal likenesses and unlikenesses.* It is quite improbable that the great sayings which find a place in both Matthew and Luke, many of which are hauntingly memorable, were uttered only once by Jesus. He would have enjoyed them and would have wished them remembered far and wide. He would have repeated them again and again. These sayings would have become known in a common Greek form, through the instructions given by the Jerusalem church to the diaspora Jews who came to the festivals from all over the world. The identical or almost identical sayings in Luke's Central Section, which at first suggest literary dependence, could in fact easily have come from a saying uttered on two different occasions. It is exceedingly unlikely that Jesus taught about prayer only once; it is natural that he should have given the Lord's Prayer and his 'ask . . . seek . . . knock' sayings more than once, and not always in identical words.[28] As for the passages where common ideas are presented in quite different dresses, this is all so natural. Indeed if we release the Central Section from the procrustean bed of literary dependence and accept it for what it purports to be, the strains and distortions of the other theories vanish.

Furthermore, if Luke had such an informant, he would have been well informed about earlier stages of the ministry, since any man chosen for this mission work must have been around long enough to show his mettle; and it is likely that he would also have been with Jesus in the final stages of the ministry after the journeyings which brought them eventually to Jerusalem. So it is possible that eyewitness information from this man may explain small special-Lukan elements in other parts of his narrative. It may also explain the appearance of Q-sayings in new contexts. Knowing his material intimately and suffering limitations of space, Luke may have omitted Matthean sayings which he found in earlier contexts, aware that the same or similar sayings would be recorded later in his Central Section.[29]

The Great Sermon

The Sermon on a Level Place in Luke 6:20–49 is remarkable in that all but five of its thirty verses have parallels in the Sermon on the Mount, *mostly in the same order*. Its five main sections: the beatitudes, loving one's enemies, judging, 'by their fruits', the house built on the rock, come in the same order, and in three of those sections the sayings within the sections also come in the same order. But the completeness of the parallelism is broken in the loving one's enemies pericope of 6:27–36, where the parallel verses of Matthew 5 come in the order: 43, 44, 39, 40, 42, 12, 46, 44, 45, 48. In the short 'by their fruits' pericope the parallel verses of Matthew 7 come in the order 18, 16, to be followed by a parallel from 12:35. Further, there are no parallels to the five verses peculiar to Luke (the woes of 6:24–26 and the sayings of 6:34 and 6:38a) and there are very many verbal differences, such as 6:44b: οὐ γὰρ ἐξ ἀκανθῶν συλλέγουσιν σῦκα, οὐδὲ ἐκβάτου σταφυλὴν τρυγῶσιν, which parallels Matthew's μήτι συλλέγουσιν ἀπὸ ἀκανθῶν σταφυλὰς ἢ ἀπὸ τριβόλων σῦκα;

This sermon does not show such great differences from its Matthean counterpart that a common origin is ruled out, but the differences are too great to suggest a common *literary* source. If there was such a source either Matthew or Luke or both of them must have introduced many seemingly gratuitous changes of order or wording. A case can be made out for both accounts being highly condensed reports of the same discourse,[30] one designed to meet the needs of a Jewish environment and the other of a Gentile situation. The idea that they are extracts from the same discourse is somewhat confirmed by the context, which is roughly the same in the two gospels – in both it follows the call of the fishermen and a highly successful preaching tour, and in both it is followed by a return to Capernaum and the healing of the centurion's boy there. But they could have been separate discourses.[31]

The rest of Luke

There are five major Q-passages in the rest of Luke: 1.) the preaching of the Baptist, 3:7–9, 16, 17; 2.) the temptation, 4:1–13; 3.) the centurion's boy, 7:1–10; 4.) Jesus and the Baptist, 7:18, 19, 22–28, 31–35; 5.) the parable of the pounds, 19:11–27.

1.) The 'brood of vipers' denunciation (3:7–9), consisting of sixty-three or sixty-four words, is the longest Q-passage in which almost complete verbal identity is to be found. (Luke has καρποὺς ἀξίους for Matthew's καρπὸν ἄξιον and ἄρξησθε for his δόξητε, and he has an extra καί not found in many Matthean texts.) This provides a strong case for a common literary origin, even for direct copying of Matthew by Luke at this point. The same applies (though slightly less strongly) to verse 17. Verse 16 has affinities with both Matthew and Mark.

2.) The temptation narratives have many verbal identities (notably in Luke's third temptation), yet the order of the temptations is different and verbal differences in the first two temptations are considerable. There are traces of Markan phraseology in 4:1 – ἐν τῇ ἐρήμῳ (if this is the correct reading) and in 4:2 – πειραζόμενος. This looks more like two versions of carefully memorised teaching than literary dependence. If (as seems likely) Luke's account is basically the way he was accustomed to tell this story, there is of course no reason, if he had access to Matthew and Mark why they may not have influenced the final form of his wording.[32]

3.) In Matthew 8:5–13 and Luke 7:1–10 the story of the centurion's boy (Matt. παῖς; Luke δοῦλος) seems to be in the same context in the two gospels: the soldier approaches Jesus following his entrance into Capernaum after the great discourse. Matthew's account of the direct approach by the man himself in 8:5 and Luke's account of the mediation of the elders in 7:3–6a have scarcely a word in common, but when it comes to the dialogue in 6b–9 the language becomes very close, including a sequence of twenty-five identical words. It is difficult to think that these two accounts come from a common literary source, for, if Matthew approximates to the original source, Luke must have totally recast it, and, if Luke approximates to the original source, Matthew represents a daring simplification. Marshall here inclines somewhat towards the likelihood of two different versions of Q (*Luke* 278). It is better to regard the accounts as independent with Matthew perhaps suggesting the content to Luke and possibly influencing Luke's wording at some stage.

4.) Luke 7:18–35 is a long passage about Jesus and the Baptist which parallels Matthew 11:2–19. Luke has four verses with no Matthean equivalent and Matthew has four with no Lukan equivalent, but the fourteen common verses are all in the same order and with very close wording. According to Farmer's *Synopticon* there are 163 verbal identities, averaging, that is, about twelve per verse.[33] We appear to have here more clearly than in any other Q-passage a documentary relationship. If we suppose that Luke was using Matthew, he was faithful to his order, sense and wording. His additional verses (vv. 20f and 29f) look very much like interpolations into Matthew's text. Matthew's additional verses (about the kingdom of heaven suffering violence, 11:12–15) could have been omitted by Luke in view of his intention to include a similar saying at 16:16.

5.) The identifying of Luke's parable of the pounds (19:11–27) with Matthew's parable of the talents (25:14–30) is one of the least plausible of the Q identifications. There is of course in each case an ἄνθρωπος who has δούλους to whom he gives money to trade with; the faithful are commended: ἀγαθὲ δοῦλε, and the lazy one is rebuked: πονηρὲ δοῦλε, and there is a common conclusion saying that to everyone who has shall be given and from him who has not shall be taken away what he has. But the context is different and four-fifths of the content is different. In Matthew the context is teaching given to disciples on the Mount of Olives to encourage watchfulness; in Luke it appears to be directed to the people in general on Jesus' way from Jericho to Jerusalem, in order to discourage the idea that his arrival in the holy city would mean the immediate coming of the kingdom.

As to content, in Matthew the man goes abroad for a long time on unspecified business; in Luke it is a nobleman who goes to receive a kingdom, and while he is away his citizens send an embassy (to the emperor?) saying that they do not want him to reign over them. In Matthew he gives large sums of money; in Luke he gives small sums. In the one case three slaves receive respectively five, two and one talents; in the other ten slaves receive one pound each. In Matthew's account two of them double what they receive; in Luke one of them adds ten more pounds to his one pound and another adds five. In Matthew the lazy one digs a hole in the ground and hides his money; in Luke he wraps it in a cloth. In Matthew the judgement is: 'cast the worthless slave into the outer darkness; there men will weep and gnash their teeth'; in Luke it is: 'as for these enemies of mine, who did not want me to reign over them, bring them here and slay them before me'.

Prima facie the two parables do not at all look as if they come from a common written source. It is far more plausible to suppose that Jesus used the same idea on more than one occasion and developed it in two different ways. It is commonly argued that there was one original parable and that this was modified in transmission and so came to have two different forms; and then at a later stage the nobleman motif was added to Luke's recension. Marshall, for instance, says (*Luke* 701):

[Matthew] lacks the element of the rejection of the king . . . which in any case fits rather awkwardly into Luke's parable. It is, therefore, almost universally agreed that this theme is a secondary addition to the parable (19:12, 14, 15a, 27; *contra* Lagrange, 497) . . . Once this addition has been removed, there are still considerable differences between the two parables.

Probably 'we have further evidence for the two recensions of the Q material' (702).

This brings us back to the question of method in redaction criticism. Thus far we have simply laid the Q-passages side by side and asked the question: Does the similarity necessitate a belief that there is a direct literary connection between them? And the answer (except in rare cases) seems plainly to be, No. But of course modern writers do not conceive the relationship in this simplistic fashion. We have quoted from Fitzmyer, who presents his theory of Luke's composition with elegant sophistication. We saw in his treatment of the Coming Crisis in Luke 12:49–59 on p. 69 a case in point. He found there in succession: L, L heavily modified, Q, redaction, Q, a passage where six words out of forty-seven agree with Matthew – partly Lukan composition partly L, Lukan composition, Q. This is all right, if one is assured a) that the relationship is primarily literary, b) that Luke was in the habit of altering the substance of his sources, c) that Q actually existed, d) that L source(s) actually existed, e) that Luke (whether by inspiration or not) created a good deal of his material *de novo*. But all these propositions are debatable and they beg the very question that we are investigating.

This postulation of sources, followed by a juggling of the data to find the best way of fitting them into the sources so postu-lated, is a fascinating intellectual exercise, but whether it bears any relation to what the author actually did as he wrote his book is more than doubtful. An alternative to heavy redaction and large-scale invention is the possibility that the author's know-ledge of the facts extended beyond the narrative of Mark. This knowledge could have come third-hand from well-trained ὑπηρέται τοῦ λόγου, or second-hand from apostles and other eyewitnesses, or even first-hand if Luke had literally 'followed everything from a long time back'.[34]

The difficulty of reconstructing sources

This matter is so important that it merits a further digression. The difficulty of reconstructing supposed sources can be vividly illustrated by considering one hypothetical case. Let us suppose that the authors of Matthew and Luke had met in AD 90 and had discovered that they had independently used Mark as their main source; and that they had signed a joint affidavit, which had been preserved till today, asserting this to be so; and that Mark's gospel had disappeared, leaving no trace in Christian history. Who would dare to claim that from Matthew and Luke alone he would have reconstructed anything like our Mark in style, content or order? (No one could have guessed his style; content would have been problematical – there would be no means of knowing what part of the common material came from Mark and what from Q, or even whether parts of M or L might not have come from Mark. The order might have been partially recovered, but with much uncertainty.) *A fortiori* any recon-struction of a possible Q-document is exceedingly unlikely to be anywhere near the real thing. Even more, a reconstruction of different recensions of Q or of a collection of supposed oral and literary sources is almost certain to be wrong, as the number of possible permutations and combinations is enormous. In a case like the parables of the talents and the pounds there are no solid grounds for refusing to take them at their face value as different utterances.

To sum up our conclusions concerning Luke's Q-material. It

is broadly of four types. 1.) There are nine major passages in the Central Section, totalling sixty verses, where the differences between Luke and Matthew are considerably greater than the differences between the parallel passages of Luke and Mark. The same applies to the seventeen verses of the parable of the pounds – giving seventy-seven in all. 2.) There are short sayings where the degree of similarity is akin to that in the passages where Luke is parallel to Mark.[35] 3.) In the Baptist passages there are nineteen verses which suggest direct literary dependence. 4.) In the Beelzebul/sign-seeking passage there are nineteen, in the heavenly treasure passage ten, in the Great Sermon thirty, in the temptation thirteen and in the narrative of the centurion's boy ten verses (in total eighty-two) suggesting not direct literary dependence, but some remoter common origin. This eliminates the idea that Luke's Q-material is largely derived from Matthew or from a Q of the Matthean form – the order does not correspond, and much of the wording would show departure from Matthew's sense.

Assuming that Matthew is the innovator

But might it not be that Luke has kept to the sense of Q and that Matthew has done nearly all the changing? We will leave open for the present the question whether Matthew or Mark came first. In due course we shall be arguing the priority of Matthew, but for the moment let us suppose, as virtually all supporters of Q do, that much of Matthew is an adaptation of Mark. It can be shown that Matthew, like Luke, keeps to the sense of Mark and therefore can be presumed to do the same with his other sources. In spite of the perplexing changes of order in the first half of Matthew and the large amount of extra material (Q and special-Matthew) incorporated in it, the parallels between Matthew and Mark are more clear-cut than between Mark and Luke – all of it comes in what we have described as Category 1, there is nothing corresponding to Category 2. It has been estimated that about eleven-twelfths of Mark's subject-matter appears in Matthew. But, as Rist has shown, there is a large measure of independence between the two gospels, and there is a vast number of verbal differences between them. The number of additions, subtractions, alterations and changes of order in the parallel passages amounts to well over eight thousand.[36] (This calculation leaves out of account the special-Markan passages which form separate entities not embedded in material which parallels Matthew, i.e. 3:20, 21 – 'he is out of his mind'; 4:26–29 – the seed growing secretly; 7:31–37 – the deaf-mute; 8:22–26 – the blind man of Bethsaida; 9:49, 50 – salt; 14:51, 52 – the naked young man.) Yet in spite of this, differences in sense are strikingly few.

There are about ten small additions, subtractions or alterations in the current critical texts which might perhaps be said to show some change of sense.[37] At the baptism, οὗτός ἐστιν for σὺ εἶ; at the mission charge, the question of footwear and staff; at Nazareth, carpenter or carpenter's son? Magadan or Dalmanoutha? Gadarenes or Gerasenes? Matthew 19:9 adds μὴ ἐπὶ πορνείᾳ; at 19:17 τί με ἐρωτᾷς περὶ τοῦ ἀγαθοῦ; for τί με λέγεις ἀγαθόν; (a better text would seemingly eliminate this discrepancy);[38] at 21:19 the withering is said to be immediate; at 26:34 he omits the δίς preferred by most editors;[39] before the high priest (26:64) we have σὺ εἶπας for ἐγώ εἰμι. This is about all that we can muster from the sixteen parallel chapters. For all their thousands of differences and their considerable degree of apparent independence, Matthew (if he is redacting Mark) demonstrably keeps close to Mark's sense; he makes a handful of tiny changes or allows a handful of tiny differences to stand.

Did both Matthew and Luke innovate?

It is thus clear that, just as Luke would not have altered a Q of the Matthean type in the way supposed, neither would Matthew have done so to one of the Lukan type. That both Matthew and Luke would have made major changes sufficient to account for the divergences between the two known versions of the Q-material is of precisely equal improbability – for, if Luke made x changes and Matthew made y, the result would be the same as if all the x + y changes had been made by one of them. In other words, Luke's known use of Mark and Matthew's supposed use of it render the Q-hypothesis (whether regarded as a single or multiple source) improbable.

Did Luke use Matthew?

Finally, we must consider the possibility that Luke got his Q-material direct from Matthew. In this case the Q-hypothesis is ruled out since the Matthean Q-material is simply Matthean material. We have already seen (pp. 47f above) that attempts to find a common order of Q-material in Luke and Matthew have failed to convince. Equally, no argument can be based on the wording. Luke cannot have got his main Q-material from Matthew, since this would have entailed changing the sense of his source in a manner belied by his known fidelity to Mark. However (as we saw in our discussion of the two Baptist passages in Luke 3:7–17 and 7:18–35), a modest use of Matthew by Luke would seem likely on this supposition; and where Luke seems to be following Matthew, he is found to follow him closely. Thus Step 4 in the argument is established.

The picture which is emerging would suggest that Luke had two documents which are known to us which he used quite differently but equally scrupulously. He took Mark as his guide to the basic framework of the gospel, following the order and main substance of Mark's pericopes in the first third and final third of his book, though seldom following his actual wording. Matthew he seems to have used in a minor way to provide some supplementary information in the early part of the book. (That he used so little of Matthew would not be surprising a) if Luke intended his gospel to supplement rather than to replace the earlier work, and b) if he was hard pressed for space.) In addition he had a great quantity of new material, not only the commonly recognised L-material, but a different account of the Great Sermon and of the healing of the centurion's boy, the whole Central Section and the parable of the pounds; and he probably had his own version of the eschatological discourse and the passion narrative prior to his final composition of the gospel. This is tantamount to a great enlargement of the category special-Luke.[40]

4

BUILDING A SYNOPTIC THEORY: (3) THE RELATION OF MATTHEW TO MARK

Chapter summary

Step 5: Matthew's relation to Mark can be satisfactorily explained on the lines of patristic tradition. The argument from order renders the entire independence of Matthew and Mark unlikely. Recognition of the miscalled Lachmann fallacy means that four of Streeter's five heads of evidence only show Mark as the middle term between Matthew and Luke, not necessarily as first. Styler's defence of Markan priority is very thin. The arguments for Matthean priority, though not overwhelming, are substantial. Matthew looks original. His eight thousand supposed departures from Mark's text are cleverly disguised. It looks early and Palestinian, reflecting a terrible clash between Jesus and the religious authorities, rather than a post-70 clash between church and synagogue. Mark looks like Peter's version of the same Palestinian tradition composed for Jewish and Gentile readers outside Palestine. Mark shows signs of consciously making omissions, e.g. parables. The three differences of order can be explained as Peter's recollection of the original order of events. The cure of two demoniacs and two blind beggars and the mention of two donkeys for Mark's one are better explained on Matthean priority. The tradition of Matthew being originally in Hebrew should not be summarily dismissed. Goodspeed shows the tax-collector to be suited for authorship and he affirms the likelihood that notes were made of Jesus' teaching during his lifetime.

88

Having shown the probable relation of Luke to Mark and Matthew, it now remains to show the probable relation of Matthew to Mark. This brings us to Step 5: *Matthew's relation to Mark can be satisfactorily explained on the lines of patristic tradition.* (The patristic tradition, as we shall see in the next chapter, may be summarised in two propositions: a) The apostle Matthew was the first to write a gospel, which he wrote for Hebrews in the Hebrew tongue; b) The second gospel, by Mark, was a record of the teaching of the apostle Peter as given in Rome.)

There are three main possibilities as to the relation of the first two gospels: 1.) They are independent; 2.) Matthew used Mark; 3.) Mark used Matthew. The first (as we saw on p. 6) is argued by Rist. He examines many of the parallel passages in detail and concludes that it is difficult to find rational grounds for the supposed redaction either of Mark by Matthew or of Matthew by Mark. He summarises one part of his argument thus: 'Sometimes the theory that Matthew depends on Mark entails extraordinary carelessness on the part of Matthew. Sometimes the theory that Mark depends on Matthew entails an extraordinarily unlikely genesis for the brilliant and graphic Markan narrative' (62). Rist certainly makes a strong case for a large measure of independence in the case of the two gospels,[1] based on the evidence of the huge number of differences between them in parallel passages; but when he goes on to argue total literary independence he is unconvincing.

Great sections of the two gospels have the pericopes in the same order. The identity of order is almost complete in the last half of Matthew (from 14:1 onwards) and the last two-thirds of Mark (from 6:14), and this provides evidence of some literary connection between them.

The relationship which is still usually favoured makes Matthew the redactor of Mark. One achievement of the modern reopening of the synoptic debate by Butler, Farmer and the rest has been the recognition of the worthlessness of so many of the arguments which have been deployed. Most of the arguments are reversible and can be used with comparable effectiveness either way. So often reasons purporting to support a given redactional view are simply *possible* reasons which *might* have influenced a redactor *if* there was a redactor – which has yet to be proved.

The so-called Lachmann fallacy[2] has also been generally recognised. Though he was not the first to spot it, Butler succeeded in bringing this home to many. He showed[3] that four out of the five supposedly converging heads of evidence adduced by Streeter to 'establish beyond reasonable doubt' that both Matthew and Luke used Mark in fact did nothing of the sort. They showed merely that Mark was the middle term between the other two and they favoured an Augustinian view as much as the two-document view.

That Victorian headmaster and polymath E. A. Abbott had not only perpetrated this fallacy in his massive *Diatessarica*, but had illustrated it in an amusing, yet horrifying, way. He says:

> Matthew and Luke are in the position of two schoolboys, Primus and Tertius, seated on the same form, between whom sits another, Secundus (Mark). All three are writing (we will suppose) a narrative of the same event . . . Primus and Tertius copy largely from Secundus. Occasionally the two copy the same words; then we have . . . agreement of three writers. At other times Primus (Matthew) copies what Tertius (Luke) does not . . . At others, Tertius (Luke) copies what Primus (Matthew) does not . . .[4]

He goes on to show that, since Primus and Tertius cannot see each other's work, agreement of any importance against Secundus will be non-existent. But, *as the same results would follow if Secundus copied from Primus and was himself copied by Tertius,* one can imagine the indignation of an innocent Primus if he was summoned to the headmaster's study and falsely accused. The Lachmann fallacy might be called the Abbott howler!

When this fallacy has been recognised, all that is left of Streeter's evidence is his head number 4 (162ff), which argues the primitive nature of Mark from its use of phrases likely to cause offence and from its roughness of style and its use of Aramaic words. He says, 'Mark reads like a shorthand account of a story by an impromptu speaker', while 'Matthew and Luke use the more succinct and carefully chosen language of one who writes and then revises for publication' (163). It is immediately clear that this conclusion in no way conflicts with the patristic tradition, which regards Matthew as a carefully prepared written work and Mark as an account, based upon the discourses of Peter, which deliberately retains the characteristics of the spoken word.

This seemingly devastating undercutting of the two-document hypothesis has not brought the great edifice tumbling down, even if it has revealed the insecurity of its foundations. One of the best-known defences of the old position is that of G. M. Styler in his excursus in C. F. D. Moule's *The Birth of the New Testament*.[5] Styler's essay in the third edition was written in the light of Butler's and Rist's work. He makes four main points.

1.) *It is difficult to believe that Mark would have omitted so much important Matthean material had he known of its existence* (290). This objection is widely felt and often repeated. But is it not based on a groundless supposition? If it is supposed that Mark was intended as a replacement of Matthew, it has great weight – we should indeed be much the poorer without the great discourses and all Matthew's unique contributions. But whoever suggested that this was the intention? All modern Augustinians regard Mark as an additional apostolic witness which confirms, illumines and supplements Matthew, and which would have been particularly appreciated by Peter's hearers, as indeed it is by most of us. The supplement is hardly at all that of new incidents and new teaching, it is that of Petrine vividness and Markan emphases, with restriction probably to the most standard elements of the apostle's evangelistic teaching. It is a new portrait.

2.) *Mark's wealth of detail is a* prima facie *indication of priority* (291). But is it? Wealth of detail would make it an acceptable supplement, but in itself it has nothing to do with order of production. This is one of the points brought out in E. P. Sanders' book *The Tendencies of the Synoptic Tradition*. He says in fact that 'on the whole, there was a tendency to make the material more detailed'[6] as the tradition developed. Wealth of detail can be the product of an inventive imagination or it can be the product of a vivid recollection. If as we shall argue (pp.

91

179–82) Mark is faithfully recording the eyewitness touches of Peter's spoken word, this could have been put on paper just as well after the writing of Matthew as before.

Styler then cites six key passages which he thinks put Markan priority beyond doubt, two of which he singles out as decisive: the death of the Baptist and Pilate's offer to release a prisoner. So his next main point is: 3.) *Matthew's account of the death of the Baptist requires a knowledge of Mark's account* (293). Mark 6:17–29 (248 words) is a much fuller narrative than Matthew 14:3–12 (136 words). Matthew says that Herod wished to kill John, but he feared the populace, because they held John to be a prophet. He then goes on to tell how Herod was trapped by his oath into giving the Baptist's head to Herodias' daughter, and that he was *grieved* about it – 'a plain contradiction' to his earlier words, about wishing his death. Matthew does not attempt to explain Herod's ambivalence, but Mark does: he shows that Herod feared and respected John at the same time as wishing to be rid of him. So we can see, according to Styler, that 'Matthew has over-simplified his introduction, and now betrays knowledge of the more complicated account' in Mark. But this statement of Styler is unsatisfactory on two counts. a) 'Plain contradiction' is an overstatement. It is perfectly possible that Herod was torn between great annoyance that John had repeatedly (ἔλεγεν) denounced his sexual sin in public, and respect for one he knew to be a good man. b) There is no need for Matthew to have known Mark's gospel, it is sufficient that he should have known the fuller story, which may well have been current in the early church.

4.) *Matthew 27:15–18 has destroyed the logic of Mark 15:6–10.* This is how Styler states this 'decisive' argument:

Mark's sequence is comparatively clear and intelligible: he mentions (a) the custom of releasing a prisoner on the people's request; (b) the existence of Barabbas and the circumstances of his arrest; (c) Pilate's offer to release 'the King of the Jews', meaning Jesus; and (d) his awareness that Jesus had been handed over to him out of envy on the part of the Jewish leaders. The logic seems to be that Pilate expected the release of Jesus to please the people, because he took it that Jesus was popular with them, and, perhaps for that very reason, was the object of their leaders' envy and hatred. Mark goes on to relate that the chief priests urged the 'crowd' to ask for the release of Barabbas instead.

But Matthew blurs the picture badly. At point (c) in the sequence he makes Pilate offer a choice between Jesus and Barabbas; nevertheless he continues with (d), 'he knew that it was out of envy that they had delivered him up'. It is very hard to find any clear logic in Matthew's sequence. Once again, the inference is that Matthew has retained, without quite assimilating, some words that had a good logic in Mark. (296)

The claim is that Mark's 'comparatively clear' sequence 'seems' to have a logic which has been blurred by Matthew, whose account lacks 'clear logic'. This appears to be hypercriticism with no real basis. The point of the statement 'For he knew that it was out of envy that they had delivered him up' may not be immediately obvious – but this applies equally to both gospels. They are both making the point that Pilate knew Jesus to be innocent, and he hoped that the demand of the people would get him out of his predicament.

My own view is that in any case the whole discussion of this pericope is beside the point, as there is no firm evidence for a literary connection between the two stories. Styler's four other passages, which he does not regard as decisive, carry even less weight. In general I am bound to say that the revised arguments for the priority of Mark seem to give every encouragement to those who incline towards the priority of Matthew.

The third main possibility is that Mark was written with a knowledge of Matthew. Although this is the position which I hold, I do not claim that there are knock-down arguments which prove it beyond reasonable doubt. For one thing, my belief in a large measure of independence between the two gospels (which I share with Westcott, Rist, Chilton, Reicke and Scott) means that in many cases there is no evidence either way, and Augustinian writers have been as prone to overstatement as anyone else in instances where the enquiry about priority is probably a non-question. There are, I think, some good arguments not only from tradition, but also of a literary kind. But it needs to be remembered that the source critic studying an ancient text can usually say no more than 'It looks as though . . .' The impressions that follow make no pretence of being proofs, they merely present ways of looking at things which to some of us seem more plausible than their opposites.

To many holders of Matthean priority:

Matthew looks original

As the title of his book suggests, the originality of Matthew particularly struck Butler – as it had done Jameson[7] and Chapman before him. They were struck by the quality of its composition, which did not look to them like a patchwork from various sources. As Jameson put it:

> The elaborate and well-considered arrangement of the book . . . [would] be more naturally found in an original composition than in an adaptation from other documents, while the masterly presentation of its subject, implying even in an original work an author of unusual skill, is very difficult to account for in a mere compiler, who is supposed . . . to have conflated and interwoven these sources in a complicated patchwork of paragraphs and sentences which (like Aaron's calf) have somehow emerged from the process in the shape of a complete and wonderful whole. (91f)

From the earliest patristic times Matthew's gospel was held in the very highest esteem; indeed it seems to have been regarded as the premier document of the Christian church, quoted far more than any other gospel, and it is not exaggerating when Butler calls elements of the book 'this magnificent composition', 'his own freely soaring and monumental structure', 'a stroke of genius'.[8] If Matthew is indeed following Mark, his many departures from his text are cleverly disguised, and it is surprising that he has obliterated so much of Mark's vivid narrative. Whether he assembled recollections and testimonies of his own or whether his work was based on Mark and other sources, all must admit that it was a careful and brilliantly successful operation. It is difficult to see it as the result of making eight thousand alterations to someone else's work. But of course it is not impossible.

Matthew looks early and Palestinian

In its beginnings Christianity was a wholly Jewish movement and it seems natural that the gospel most evidently designed for Jewish readers should be early. Matthew is an apologetic showing that Jesus was the Messiah (1:1, 17; 2:4; 16:16; 26:68; 27:22), hence its constant appeal to the fulfilment of the scriptures. It is insistent on the sharpness of Jesus' conflict with the Pharisees, a topic which would have been far more relevant to the churches in Palestine, which had to live cheek by jowl with so many of them, than for the churches in the Gentile world.

It is sometimes held by those who date Matthew late that the book does not really reflect the conflict of Jesus with the Pharisees so much as the conflict of the post-70 church with the now sharply separated world of Judaism.[9] It is even held by some that the outlooks of Jesus and of contemporary Pharisees were in fact very close and that there would have been no reason for them to quarrel and therefore that Matthew's 'anti-semitic' picture is exaggerated and unhistorical. But it is evident that Jesus succeeded in uniting almost the whole Sanhedrin against himself, which must have meant that many leading Pharisees deeply resented what he had said. Doubtless the official ideals were irreproachable, but their practice did not match their ideals, and their teaching made a life of legal rectitude almost impossible to the common man. Jesus' sweeping denunciations were of course generalisations, which allowed of exceptions – Nicodemus may not have been the only Pharisee who was to some extent well disposed towards him[10] – but as generalisations we have no reason to think them unfair. Matthew's account looks like a vivid record of a terrible clash between Jesus and the religious leaders, rather than a veiled polemic of church against synagogue. Some of the apologetic (e.g. the account of the suicide of Judas and the account of the guard at the tomb) seems of no great theological significance, yet of particular interest to those who frequented Jerusalem.

Mark looks like Peter's version of the same Palestinian tradition composed for Jewish and Gentile readers outside Palestine

We have already noted Streeter's judgement that 'Mark reads like a shorthand account of a story by an impromptu speaker'. This is certainly the impression gained by many readers. Although Mark is not bad Greek, it is a very informal, unliterary sort of Greek, such as one might expect from an oral discourse. He eschews almost entirely the periods beloved of the great prose writers, preferring parataxis and the frequent use of καί. His addiction to εὐθύς and the historic present, the number of anacolutha and parentheses, his fondness for vivid detail, his tautological expressions, all comport well with the picture of a dynamic speaker. It is of course possible that all these characteristics are the product of lively traditional material worked up by the author's literary skill. But the patristic tradition of its Petrine origin is a simpler hypothesis, and it gives greater credit to Mark as one anxious to hand on the apostolic teaching faithfully.

It is sometimes objected that Peter is not more prominent in Mark than in the other gospels. As Stoldt puts it:

> one would have every right to expect that the figure of Peter would not only take a central position in the Gospel of Mark, but also, beyond that, would stand out considerably more than in the other Gospels. *This, however, is not the case – on the contrary.* The following important passages which refer to Peter in the two parallel texts have no equivalent in Mark:

Mt 14:28–31   Simon walks on the water, sinks and is rescued by Jesus: 'O man of little faith, why do you doubt?'

16:17–20   Simon's beatitude: the bestowal of the name Peter; the granting of the keys.

17:14–27   The questioning of Simon by the tax collectors as to whether Jesus paid the half-shekel tax; Jesus' charge to Peter; the shekel in the fish's mouth.

18:21, 22   Peter's question about how often one should grant forgiveness.

Lk 5:3–10   Peter's miraculous catch of fish. 'Depart from

me, for I am a sinful man.' – 'Henceforth you
will be catching men.'

22:31–32   'Simon, Simon, behold, Satan demanded to have
you, that he might sift you like wheat, but I have
prayed for you that your faith shall not fail; and
when you have turned again, strengthen your
brethren.'

22:8   In order to prepare the Passover feast, Jesus
sends out Peter and John (Mark: 'two of his
disciples').[11]

But others would contend that this expectation that Peter
would have frequently called attention to his own doings is
quite unjustified. Mark in fact faithfully records incidents
which are to Peter's discredit. As Butler puts it:

> [Mark contains] all that the Gospels tell us in disparagement of him;
> that he rebuked our Lord at Caesarea Philippi and was rebuked by
> Him; that he presumed to promise loyalty, though all others should
> fail, and yet alone in set terms denied Him . . . in telling the
> Caesarea Philippi incident he has, in that case, torn out of the story
> the high praise of himself and the promise of his peculiar status
> *vis-à-vis* the Church, while leaving the stinging rebuke. And again,
> he has omitted the incident of the Temple-tribute, which seems to
> put him into a peculiarly close relation with his Master, and that of
> his walking on the waters . . . Ought we to wonder that the Prince
> of the Apostles had learnt the lesson of Christian humility well
> enough to lay bare not only his strength but his weakness? (167f)

It looks as though Mark is omitting Matthean material at certain points

It was this observation which precipitated Chapman into his
repudiation of the two-document theory. In his *Matthew, Mark
and Luke* he told of his rather dogmatic and vocal commitment
to the standard theory and of his disappointment when the
Pontifical Biblical Commission in 1911 and 1912 ruled against it
and in favour of the Augustinian order. He set about trying to
disprove the Commission's case. He recognised the Lachmann
fallacy at once and saw that 'the ordinary bases of the two-
document theory are just as consistent with the view that

Matthew was first and Mark second, provided Luke is third'
(3). They merely showed that Mark was the mean between the
other two. But he reckoned (5–7) that there was a test which
should be capable of disproving Matthean priority:

> If Mk. abbreviated Mt., omitting much, adding next to nothing,
> since Mk. is carelessly written with less literary ability than the
> other Gospels, wherever it makes long omissions we shall find some
> sign of the gap, – perhaps merely want of sequence, for Mt. is very
> systematic, or even illogical sequence. If there are no such signs –
> *and there cannot well be, since nobody has noticed them* – I shall
> conclude quite securely that Mk. is indeed prior to Mt.

Here was a practical test, and I applied it at once. The omission of
the first two chapters of Mt. by Mk. was hardly a case in point; the
omissions of the Sermon on the Mount (three chapters) is accompanied by a considerable dislocation of order; so is that of the next
great Matthean discourse, the charge to the twelve in ch. 10. So I
started with Mk. 4:1 which is parallel to Mt. 13:1, where our Lord
teaches from a boat.

St. Matthew gives a series of parables and the explanations, given
in private to the disciples, of two of them: (1) the Sower; (2) the
disciples ask for explanation; (3) a prophecy of Isaiah, and blessings
on those who see and hear; (4) Explanation of the Sower; (5) the
Wheat and the Tares; (6) the Mustard Seed; (7) the Leaven; (8) 'All
this was said in parables'; (9) to fulfil a prophecy of Psalm 78:2; (10)
then, indoors, in the house, the explanation of 'Wheat and Tares';
(11) the Hidden Treasure; (12) the Merchant and the Pearl; (13) the
Drag-net of Fishes; (14) the final verse, 'things new and old'.

Of all this Mk. gives (1), (2), (4), (6), (8) and he interpolates four
quasi-proverbial verses (which are found elsewhere in Mt.) and a
short parable peculiar to himself. Therefore Mk. has three parables
and one explanation, against the seven parables and two explanations of Mt. Does Mk. show any sign of having omitted anything? He does. Twice.

A. Mt. 13:3
καὶ ἐλάλησεν αὐτοῖς πολλὰ
ἐν παραβολαῖς λέγων.

Mk. 4:2
καὶ ἐδίδασκεν αὐτοὺς ἐν
καραβολαῖς πολλὰ, καὶ ἔλεγεν
αὐτοῖς ἐν τῇ διδαχῇ αὐτοῦ.

Here Mt. has πολλά, and proceeds to give actually many parables.
Mk. retains πολλά, and intends to give only three parables, so he

adds: 'And in the course of His instruction He said'. Mk. has before him a series of many, πολλά, and he has not given the whole, – or so it seems. Other explanations might be invented, no doubt.

B. Mt. 13:34

Mk. 4:33–4

34. <u>ταῦτα πάντα</u> ἐλάλησεν ὁ Ἰησοῦς ἐν παραβολαῖς τοῖς ὄχλοις,

33. καὶ <u>τοιαύταις παραβολαῖς πολλαῖς</u> ἐλάλει αὐτοῖς τὸν λόγον, καθὼς ἠδύναντο ἀκούειν.

καὶ χωρὶς παραβολῆς οὐδὲν ἐλάλει αὐτοῖς,

34. χωρὶς δὲ παραβολῆς οὐκ ἐλάλει αὐτοῖς, κατ' ἰδίαν δὲ τοῖς ἰδίοις μαθηταῖς ἐπέλυεν πάντα.

Here St. Matthew sums up ταῦτα πάντα, but Mk. of necessity changes this into τοιαῦτα πολλά: and because Mt. is about to add the explanation (10) of a parable (5) which Mk. had omitted, the latter supplies its place by the general statement that 'in private' (Mt. 13:36, 'in the house') Christ explained all the parables to his disciples.

I wonder whether the reader can imagine my surprise on lighting upon A and B, perfectly familiar passages. *I had proposed a test, and I was already answered.* I had imagined, I suppose, some illogical sequence at most, and I expected to find nothing at all; and I found (apparently) two definite statements by Mk. that he had omitted some outdoor parables and indoor explanations. This was astounding. I did not wait. I went on in haste to another passage.

Mt. 23:1–39 contains a long discourse of Christ against the Pharisees and the scribes, ending with an appeal to Jerusalem, which had slain the prophets. Of these 38 verses (2–39) Mk. has *two and a half* only, very freely and pointedly given. The chapter was of great importance in Palestine; but at Rome it was valueless, except as a moral lesson against vanity and ambition. Now let us see how it is introduced:

C. Mt. 23:1

Mk. 12:38

τότε ὁ Ἰησοῦς ἐλάλησεν τοῖς ὄχλοις καὶ τοῖς μαθηταῖς αὐτοῦ λέγων.

καὶ <u>ἐν τῇ διδαχῇ αὐτοῦ ἔλεγεν</u>.

This, coming immediately after A and B, completely bowled me over. No reply is possible. Mk. tells us once more, 'In the course of His teaching, He was saying'. What teaching? Look at Mt.; there it is, shoals of it.

All this does seem to suggest that Mark is conscious of omitting material at these points. This does not necessarily mean that he was working on the Matthew scroll and editing it. It would be sufficient that he was well acquainted with its contents.

Chapman argues that the didrachma incident also looks more like an omission by Mark than an addition by Matthew:

> After Mt. 17:22–3 = Mk. 9:30–2 = Lk. 9:43–5, where Mt. and Mk. march together in the usual manner, Mt. interpolates the story of the Didrachma and the Stater in the fish's mouth, after which again the three Gospels agree, Mt. 18:1 = Mk. 9:34 = Lk. 9:46. But we notice that in Mk. there is a half verse 33a which refers to Mt. and has been omitted as unnecessary by Lk.

Mt. 17:24–7	Mk. 9:33
24. Ἐλθόντων δὲ αὐτῶν εἰς Κ. προσῆλθον οἱ τὰ δίδραχμα λαμβάνοντες τῷ Πέτρῳ καὶ εἶπαν· ὁ διδάσκαλος ὑμων οὐ τελεῖ δίδραχμα; λέγει· ναί. καὶ ἐλθόντα εἰς τὴν οἰκίαν προέφθασεν αὐτὸν ὁ Ἰησοῦς λέγων· τί σοι δοκεῖ, Σίμων; . . .	Καὶ ἦλθον εἰς Κ.,
	Καὶ ἐν τῇ οἰκίᾳ γενόμενος

> It is natural to suppose that St. Peter, wishing (as usual) to omit a story about himself, but remembering it perfectly and also the incident which immediately followed (the question who should be greatest), retains from Mt. the local detail, Capharnaum and the house there, which was the scene of the discourse.
>
> One alternative explanation is possible, that Mt., using Mk., noticed the mention of Capharnaum and of the house, and inserted his story about Peter before and after the mention of the house. I commend this explanation to the consideration of those who still hold the view I formerly clung to; but I certainly do not recommend them to defend it.[12]

It may in general be said that, although Mark looks like Peter's version of it, Mark and Matthew are basically the same tradition – something which cannot be said if either are compared with Luke or John.

If Acts is to be believed, Peter was the leading figure in the early Jerusalem church and doubtless played a large part in moulding the form of the teaching given to those who flocked to the city from all over the world. Presumably there was a core of instruction which had been carefully rehearsed by the twelve and the seventy before they went out telling the words and deeds of Jesus. To this would have been added later incidents, particularly emphasising the passion and resurrection. If Matthew was the first approved record of this teaching it is natural that it should be strong in its Jewish and Palestinian matter, with stress on Messiahship, the fulfilment of prophecy and Jesus' conflict with the Pharisees. When this tradition was taken to a Gentile environment one would expect to see a great reduction in the Jewish emphasis and one would expect something very like Mark to be the staple content of Peter's instruction. One would expect to see Mark true to the sense of Matthew, with here and there additional details and clarifications. And this is very much what we appear to have. Mark gives, for instance, a fuller and clearer account of the death of the Baptist (Matt. 14:3–12; Mark 6:17–29) and he provides explanations of things Jewish which Matthew's original hearers would not have needed: e.g. οἱ Ἰουδαῖοι ἐὰν μὴ πυγμῇ νίψωνται τὰς χεῖρας οὐκ ἐσθίουσιν (7:3); the Mount of Olives is κατέναντι τοῦ ἱεροῦ (13:3); the passover was killed τῇ πρωτῇ ἡμέρᾳ τῶν ἀζύμων &14:12?; παρασκευή ὅ ἐστιν προσάββατον (15:42).

Matthean priority provides the better rationale for the differences in order between the two gospels

Supporters of Markan priority have found it difficult to account satisfactorily for Matthew's changing of the order of Mark. There are three major dislocations in the Matthew/Mark order, two comparatively short and one quite long. It will be convenient to deal with the short ones (the first and the third) first and leave the long one (the second) till last.

First dislocation

Matthew 3:1–4:22 and Mark 1:1–20 follow the same general outline:

John the Baptist
Baptism of Jesus
The temptation
Beginning of Galilean ministry
Call of four fishermen

(The verbal likenesses are not on the whole very close until the last pericope, when they become much closer.) At this point the sequence diverges (p. 103).

Matthew's arrangement is quite coherent. The first four items are all concerned with teaching, of which the centrepiece is the Sermon on the Mount, which is given a suitable introduction and conclusion. The last four items are all concerned with healing. If, however, Matthew is based on Mark, the author indulged in a complex process to achieve his result. Having reached Mark 1:20 he passed over verses 21–38 to secure the one verse 39, which he rewrites and adds to. He then adds a section on the gathering of crowds which Jesus addressed on the hillside. (This has some resemblances to the gathering of the crowds at the lakeside in Mark 3:7–12, which he addressed from the boat. The many striking differences, however, make literary dependence unlikely.) He then inserts his great sermon, which he rounds off by going back to Mark 1:22. So he completes his teaching section. For his section on healings he passes over verses 23–39: the vivid story of the cure of the demoniac in the Capernaum synagogue, the healing of Peter's mother-in-law, the sabbath-evening healings, the night prayer and the preaching tour, and then at verse 40 he takes up the leper story to start his series. He adds his new story of the centurion's boy, then goes back again to Mark's earlier healings. He decides to omit altogether the demoniac's cure, and rounds off his series with Peter's mother-in-law and the evening healings in verses 29–34. Thus in the Mark scroll he goes from verse 19 to 39 to 22 to 40 to 29. In doing this he omits a notable healing and he breaks up Mark's clearly indicated chronological sequence.

If, however, Mark is changing Matthew's order a simple hypothesis will explain it. The whole sequence of events (if they actually happened) would have formed a memorable period in

102

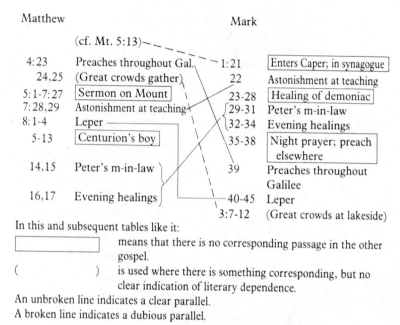

In this and subsequent tables like it:

<table>
<tr><td>⬚</td><td>means that there is no corresponding passage in the other gospel.</td></tr>
<tr><td>( )</td><td>is used where there is something corresponding, but no clear indication of literary dependence.</td></tr>
</table>

An unbroken line indicates a clear parallel.

A broken line indicates a dubious parallel.

Peter's life – the call of the four fishermen, the healing in his synagogue at Capernaum, the cure of his wife's mother after service, the great crowds arriving after sunset when the sabbath was over, Peter's following Jesus after his early rising for prayer, and his recollection of Jesus' new resolve to take his disciples on a preaching tour throughout Galilee. It is only necessary to suppose that Mark is relating this section in chronological order to explain the rearrangement.

Third dislocation

Matthew and Mark have kept fairly closely in step from the time of the

third passion prediction, which is followed by
the request of the sons of Zebedee,
the healing of the blind at Jericho,
the entry into Jerusalem.

Then come divergences:

Matthew		Mark	
		11:11b	Retirement to Bethany
		12-14	Next day: fig-tree cursed
21:12,13	Temple cleansing	15-17	Temple cleansing
14-16	Healings, controversy	18	Plot of chief priests
17	Retirement to Bethany	19	Leave city in evening
18,19	Fig-tree cursed, withers	20	Morning: fig-tree withered
20-22	Prayer and faith	21-25	Prayer, faith, forgiveness

In this passage there are short sections of close verbal similarity, but there are also very great differences, suggesting a common oral tradition rather than literary adaptation by either evangelist. One feature that distinguishes Mark from Matthew here is Mark's greater chronological precision. In verse 11 it is ὀψέ, in verse 12 it is ἐπαύριον, in verse 19 it is ὀψέ again, in verse 20 it is πρωΐ. If we suppose that Matthew is an adaptation of Mark, it means that the evangelist again performed a complex operation on his source, destroying its coherence and being positively misleading in his use of the twofold παραχρῆμα (21:19, 20). It is simpler to assume that Mark's material is arranged as it is in the interest of chronological accuracy. Walker points out that historically 'certainly an interval is suggested, for how could Jesus, surrounded by cheering children in the Temple (Matt. 21:15), have overturned tables and seats, and driven out cattle and traders? The following day provided a better opportunity.'[13]

Will the same principle work for the much larger second dislocation?

Second dislocation

The table on p. 106, when the boxed and bracketed items are omitted, shows two common sequences, in Mark covering 2:1–4:34 (indicated by horizontal lines) and 4:35–6:11 (indicated by sloping lines), with only one anomaly – the Nazareth visit being inserted into the second sequence. If Matthew is based on Mark, the process of compilation is obviously highly complicated,[14] and the reasons for making the changes are notoriously obscure. If Mark is based on Matthew, however, the same number of changes has to be made, but conceptually the process is simple. We shall consider the mechanics of Mark's operations in more detail in Chapter 10, but broadly his plan may be described thus. There were evidently some passages that Mark wished to omit and some that he wished to defer. It seems likely that he would first have gone through Matthew's text, listing the contents and marking on this list what he wished to omit (the boxed passages) and what he wished to defer (those with an asterisk). To compile his own order of contents he would simply have noted down in order first the unmarked material from 8:23 to 13:52 and then (again strictly in order) the six deferred items. He would then have inserted a short section of his own (3:13–21) into the first sequence and the Nazareth visit into the second.

There is no doubt that this account of the complicated dislocation (which I owe largely to Jameson) has the merit of simplicity; but will the chronological explanation fit here too? The answer is that it can be verified at one crucial point and be shown to be plausible at two others, but there is no point-by-point verification. So let us take these three cases in turn.

1.) Note that the link which joins the two Markan sequences (the first ending with the parables section and the second beginning with the storm) says specifically (4:35): 'He says to them *on that day when evening had come*, "Let us go across to the other side."' So the scene in which Jesus had been teaching in the boat (4:1) passes easily into the evening scene where 'they took him, just as he was, in the boat' (4:36). If the account is indeed history, it would have been another memorable day for

105

Second Dislocation

Matthew		Mark	

8: 18-22 Following Jesus

23-27 *Storm

28-34 Gadarene demoniacs

9: 1-8 Paralytic ⎫   2: 1-12 Paralytic ⎫

  9-13 Call of Matthew ⎬   13-17 Call of Levi ⎬

 14-17 Fasting ⎭   18-22 Fasting ⎭

18-26 *Jairus & haemorrhaged woman

27-31 Two blind

32-34 Dumb

35 *Summary of Jesus' activity

36-38 Sheep without shepherd

10: 1 *Commission of twelve

  2-4 (Names of twelve)

 5-42 *Missionary discourse

11: 1-19 Witness to Baptist

20-24 Woe to cities

25-27 Jesus thanks Father

28-30 'Come'

12: 1-8 Plucking grain ⎫   2: 23-28 Plucking grain ⎫

 9-14 Withered hand ⎬   3: 1-6 Withered hand ⎬

15-21 Crowds ⎭   7-12 Crowds ⎭

                        13-15 (Choice of twelve)

                        16-19 (Names of twelve)

22,23 Blind-dumb   20,21 Supporters' anxiety

24-32 Beelzebul, blasphemy — 22-30 Beelzebul, blasphemy

33-37 Tree and fruits

38-42 No sign but Jonah's

43-45 Return of unclean spirit

46-50 Mother and brothers — 31-35 Mothers and brothers

13: 1-52 Parables — 4: 1-34 Parables

- -

                       *⎧ 35-41 Storm

                        ⎩5: 1-20 Gerasene demoniac

                        *21-43 Jairus & haemorrhaged w.

53-58 Nazareth — 6: 1-6a Nazareth

                        *6b Summary of J's activity

                        *7 Commission of twelve

                        *8-11 Missionary discourse

Controversy Section

Peter, and Mark may well have heard his mentor recall the connection between the two events on more than one occasion. The next occurrence, the demoniac healing on the other side of the lake, follows naturally in both gospels.

Beyond this point there is no direct confirmation of the chronological suggestion. The incidents related after the return to the Capernaum shore are not given any note of time by Mark, they are introduced simply by a series of καίς (5:21; 6:1, 6b, 7, 8). So it is impossible to say whether Mark thought that the incidents followed the recrossing of the lake in that order.

2.) However, in the case of the Jairus story, the fact that Mark has deliberately detached the narrative from the fasting discussion, to which it is rather firmly attached in Matthew 9:18 (ταῦτα αὐτοῦ λαλοῦντος) might lend some weight to the hypothesis. The Nazareth incident he leaves roughly in the same position as it is in Matthew.

3.) In the case of the mission of the twelve it is not unreasonable to think that the calling of twelve 'to be with' Jesus (Mark 3:14) was in fact separated (as Mark suggests) by a considerable time from his despatch of them two by two on mission. It would seem that, although Matthew is concerned with the broad outline of the history, he is also concerned to put as early as possible the great statement of the church's standards in the Sermon on the Mount and the charter of her ministry in chapter 10. For his purposes this is more important than strict chronology.

The chronological explanation of Mark's alterations is a simple and possible one in all three dislocations. Perhaps Luke's καθεξῆς (1:3) may suggest that he too was aware of Mark's interest in chronological order. If Luke knew Matthew (as I am inclined to believe), it is nonetheless Mark's order that he follows with great fidelity.

Some further points might be made in favour of Matthean priority. For instance, Walker says boldly:

The 'two' Gadarene demoniacs (8:28), the 'two' blind beggars at Jericho (20:30) and the 'two' donkeys of Palm Sunday (21:1–6) recorded by Matthew, as against one in each case by Mark, point also to the improbability that Matthew was copying Mark. The Matthean text with 'two' is more likely to have been original rather than the Marcan without 'two'.[15]

There could well be something in this assertion, for in all three instances Matthew gives the shorter and more restrained account, altogether belying the customary notion that Matthew is heightening the miraculous. (One extra individual in the content of Jesus' myriad cures only heightens the miraculous in a most trivial sense.) Those of us who have had the experience of trying to get the same Christian message over to successive groups of listeners, notice how the forms of the stories and anecdotes gradually change. We tend to drop out details which are true in themselves, but which do not contribute to the point we are trying to make, and we add other details. If there are two individuals in an anecdote, one more prominent than the other, the impact is more direct if the story confines itself to one and does not risk creating a side-track by calling attention to the other. Walker may well be right about Mark dropping a demoniac and a beggar.

The two donkeys present a somewhat different case. Here it is a question whether Matthew's mention of the presence of the mother alongside the unbroken foal is a bit of history, which called attention to the curious verbal form of Zechariah's prophecy (Zech. 9:9); or whether Matthew just invented the extra beast, thinking that it would fulfil the prophecy better. Such invention would lack integrity and it would have been poor apologetics if there were people alive who had witnessed what actually happened. Matthew's wording, which leaves it ambiguous as to whether Jesus sat on the clothing or upon two donkeys simultaneously, has certainly provided a first-class side-track for commentators! Mark would have been wise to leave out the mother donkey.

Again, Matthew's account of the man-handling of Jesus at 26:67f records 'Prophesy to us, you Christ, Who is it who struck you?' but says nothing about his face being covered, which piece of information is necessary to the intelligibility of the story. It is easy to imagine Mark supplying it, difficult to

108

imagine Matthew leaving it out if it was in the document before him.

Chapman and Butler are both impressed by the convenient way in which Matthew seems to have just the right material to insert into the Markan text. For example, after discussing the parable of the labourers in the vineyard (Matt. 20:1–15) Chapman says: 'This instance adds one more improbability to the theory that Mt., in using Mk., had ready to hand an indefinite number of incidents, parables, discourses, which he could fit so neatly into Mk. that the suture is unseen, unfelt, indiscoverable' (17).

If we look over the ground covered, we seem to be justified in claiming that the case for Matthean priority is not negligible. We have seen signs of Markan omissions and a number of other indications suggesting that Matthew looks original, early and Palestinian, while Mark looks like a later version of the tradition as told by Peter. We have seen how well the differences in order can be explained as Mark's rearrangements. We have seen the deliberate falsification involved in Matthew's supposed twofold addition of παραχρῆμα to the fig-tree narrative. We have seen that there is a case for Matthean priority in the didrachma incident, in the stories where Matthew has 'two' and Mark has 'one', in the 'Prophesy to us' incident and in the convenient way in which Matthew seems to have just the right material. Further points will emerge as we consider one more item in the Matthean tradition.

Matthew looks as though it may have been originally in a Semitic language

An objective consideration of the question of Matthew's original language is made difficult by the entrenched status of the hypothesis of Markan priority. If Matthew is based upon the Greek Mark (as most scholars believe), that is the end of the matter. However, I venture to think that if there was no pressure from this angle, it would be generally recognised that the case for a Semitic original is considerable. Of course Semitic idioms will often appear in the writings of those whose first language is Aramaic, but with Matthew it seems to be more than Semitic idioms.

The sentence 'You shall call his name Jesus, for he will save his people from their sins' (1:21) makes good sense in Hebrew, but it makes no more sense in Greek than it does in English without further explanation. It looks as though a translator did not think to explain the meaning of the well-known name Jesus, although two sentences later he gave the translation of the more unusual Emmanuel.

Matthew's use of οὐρανοί for 'God' makes strange Greek: it is 'never used in plural by classical writers'[16] and the use of the plural in any sense is rare in the pre-Christian Greek-speaking world. Biblical Hebrew on the other hand uses the plural term *shamayim* with great frequency. In consequence the plural οὐρανοί obtained a grudging foothold in Greek through the Septuagint, where it is used (almost exclusively in poetry) fifty-one times as against 616 cases of the singular. As Traub says, 'This use is almost completely alien to profane Greek.'[17] On top of this, by metonymy and for reasons of reverence, it became customary among Jews to substitute 'heavens' for 'God', thus introducing a usage which was doubly unGreek. There are traces of this sort of figurative use of 'heaven' elsewhere in the gospels (though in the singular, not the plural, e.g. Luke 15:18; 20:4), but Matthew uses it habitually in the key expression ἡ βασιλεία τῶν οὐρανῶν, which appears thirty-four times. It is conceivable that an author capable of writing good Greek might have continued so to think in Aramaic that he came to use this unGreek expression habitually. But Matthew by no means avoids θεός, employing it fifty-one times (three times in the expression 'kingdom of God'), so it may be that a translator is simply rendering literally the text that lay before him. Be that as it may, it is easier to imagine Mark dropping this strange expression than to think that Matthew wrote it into Mark's text thirty-four times.

Chapman remarks on the difficulty of supposing that a Greek or Hellenist interpolated τότε into Mark and Q 'by the bushel' (185). τότε appears ninety times in Matthew as compared with six times in Mark and fourteen times in Luke. Fifty-one of these are in passages paralleled in Mark; that is to say, he introduced forty-five new τότε's into the Markan material in addition to the six already there. Often they appear to have very little force and represent a light 'after this' rather than the classical 'at that time'. This reflects a common Aramaic usage: *'edayin* or *bĕ'dayin,* and the τότε's would be neatly accounted for if Matthew was a translation. It is easier to understand Mark dropping forty-five of these, than Matthew adding them.

Similarly ἰδού, which occurs sixty-two times, is also Semitic. Thirty-four of these are in passages parallel to Mark, but Mark retains only six of them. Butler says:

> It is hardly conceivable that St Matthew added ἰδού on all these occasions when engaged in improving Mark's Greek style; but it is entirely natural that St Mark should dislike and eschew the word whenever he meets it in Matthean narrative, and in all except six occurrences in Matthean discourse.[18]

Of the thirty-one instances of Ἀμὴν λέγω ὑμῖν Chapman says: 'The explanation . . . might be that the Greek compiler of Mt. added ἀμήν though it was not Greek, twice to Mk.'s and six times to Q's simple λέγω ὑμῖν, and even changed ναί and ἀληθώς to ἀμήν and then added twenty more examples of the formula. I do not commend this hypothesis.'[19] In both these cases a Semitic original would explain the usage.

It is of course impossible for a non-specialist to hope to prove this case. Carmignac, an expert in this field, believed that Matthew, Mark and the sources of Luke were originally in Hebrew and at the time of his death he was endeavouring to prove it in a scientific manner.[20] Zahn sets out his reasons for believing our Matthew to be an accurate translation of an Aramaic original (2.573–601). He favours the view that 'Mark could have used the Aramaic Matthew, and the person who translated Matthew into Greek could have used Mark' (602). Many others, equally learned, however, are perfectly content with their belief that all three, though containing many Semitisms, were Greek compositions. Since the evangelists are competent in the Greek language, it is difficult to find clear cases of mistaken renderings and it is impossible to find criteria that will sharply distinguish between Semitic influences and Semitic originals. All that the non-expert can say is that there seem to be considerable empirical data supporting the patristic tradition, and that these are likely to be felt with increasing force once the two-document hypothesis loses its hold over our minds.

There is one further consideration which should be taken into account at this point: that is the unique fittedness of Matthew to be the author of the first gospel. This matter has been examined with great thoroughness in an undeservedly neglected book by E. J. Goodspeed, *Matthew, Apostle and Evangelist*.[21]

Goodspeed has no doubts about the priority of Mark, but at the same time he believes in the traditional authorship of Matthew, arguing that it was normal practice to use sources without acknowledgement. But he considers it improbable that in the Greek world of books the author should have been forgotten. He stresses the sheer greatness of this gospel, which throughout the whole history of the Christian church has usually been regarded as the greatest of the four. Its very quality presupposes a writer who knew his subject at first-hand. How could his name have been forgotten, and why was Matthew's name adopted if he was not in fact the author? Goodspeed suggests that Jesus found himself in a similar position to Isaiah, when it became clear that his message was going to be rejected by the people as a whole. He deliberately took steps for the preservation of his teaching among his disciples. He observed the faith and commitment of Levi the tax-collector and recognised him as one who was capable of making a record of his teaching. The other leading disciples could doubtless read and write, but from what we know of them they all seem to have been essentially practical men. The only one who was a professional pen-pusher was Matthew.

Goodspeed shows how sophisticated the tax system was. It is known that in Egypt at this date there were 111 kinds of tax, and many of the tax-collectors knew shorthand. Matthew's livelihood was earned by interviewing tax-payers and discussing their affairs (usually in Aramaic) and then writing up his reports in Greek. He had a lifelong habit of noting things down and of preserving what he had written. It cannot be too strongly stressed that the world of Jesus' day was highly literate and that (whether or not Goodspeed's notion that Jesus made Matthew his recorder is true) it is altogether likely that there were people who made notes of what Jesus said. He made a tremendous impact on a wide variety of listeners, and it seems unlikely that no one attempted to make a record of what he taught.

This point was commonly made in an earlier generation, for example, by such scholars as W. M. Ramsay and G. Salmon.[22] But, as it is now unfashionable, it may be well to quote some modern writers on the subject. R. H. Gundry says:

> The only hypothesis with enough flexibility to meet the require-
> ments is that a body of loose notes stands behind the bulk of the
> synoptic tradition. The wide use of shorthand and the carrying of
> notebooks in the Graeco-Roman world, the school practice of
> circulating lecture notes and utilizing them in published works,
> and the later transmission of rabbinic tradition through shorthand
> notes support this hypothesis. As a former publican, the Apostle
> Matthew would have been admirably fitted to fill a position as
> note-taker in the band of uneducated apostles.[23]

M. Lowe and D. Flusser write: 'It was common practice for the disciples of rabbis to make notes of their sayings. It is also notable that Justin Martyr repeatedly refers to the gospels as ἀπομνημονεύματα . . . a technical term for memoirs.'[24] (It is particularly important to observe this note-taking in rabbinical circles since learning by rote was the method of education favoured by the rabbis. Goodspeed 48 summarises the Jewish rule as 'Commit to memory', and the Greek rule as 'If you have no paper, write it on your garments!') L. C. A. Alexander observes in connection with the training of professional men in the Greek-speaking world that note-taking was 'necessary in academic life'.[25]

D. A. Carson says: 'Recent research has argued for *written* records that go back to Jesus' ministry,' and he gives further references from the works of H. Schürmann (1961), and R. Riesner (1981).[26] E. E. Ellis (1987) says: 'Traditions of Jesus were carefully cultivated, transmitted by an authorised leadership and fixed in writing much earlier than was formerly supposed.' And in 1988 he wrote: 'There are good grounds, then, for supposing not only that the traditioning of Jesus' acts and teachings began already during his earthly ministry, as H. Schürmann has argued, but also that some of them were given written formulation at that time.'[27] P. H. Davids writes:

There is no reason to assume that the early transmission was *exclusively* oral. The apostles may not have been studied in the Jewish law (so Acts 4:13), but due to the prevalence of education in Jewish communities many, if not most, of them must have been literate. We should not therefore be surprised if at least a minimal amount of the *testimonia*, narratives, and teaching which found their way into the gospels was recorded in writing before or soon after Easter . . . The pre-Easter *Sitz-im-Leben* of such material was the mission of the twelve and the need to leave teaching behind as the itinerant band travelled. The post-Easter setting was the teaching needs of the growing church and especially the mission outside Jerusalem. The Hellenists of the Stephen group had reduced much of the Gospel to writing in Greek.[28]

Another element in the gospel fits into place if Matthew is the author: the story of his call in 9:9. Matthew was doubtless of interest as a living illustration of Jesus' care for tax-collectors and sinners, as the ensuing narrative relates. But if it was universally known from the beginning that he was the author of the gospel, the wider significance of his call would have been apparent. The fame of the four fishermen, whose call is narrated collectively, who were senior leaders of the Christian community, was self-evident. Of the remaining eight, Matthew's call alone is singled out for mention by the three evangelists. In the case of his own gospel, it could be the author modestly stating his credentials. Similarly Mark and Luke were recalling the credentials of the man who had no distinction in the church except for one thing: he had given the world his magnificent book – and that would have made him of interest to all Christian readers.

To sum up our investigation of the internal evidence of the synoptic problem thus far: There seems to be a good case for believing that Matthew, possibly in a Semitic language, was the first gospel; that Mark is substantially the teaching of Peter, who knew Matthew's gospel; and that Luke knew and used both Matthew and Mark. However, Mark shows a large measure of independence of Matthew, and Luke shows a large measure of independence of both. These conclusions (which have already to some extent anticipated it) will be seen to fit the external evidence remarkably well.

5

ANCIENT TESTIMONY TO
MATTHEW'S GOSPEL

Chapter summary

The fathers are almost unanimous in asserting that Matthew the
tax-collector was the author, writing first, for Hebrews in the
Hebrew language: Papias (*c*. 60–130), Irenaeus (*c*. 130–200),
Pantaenus (died *c*. 190), Origen (*c*. 185–254), Eusebius (*c*.
260–340), Epiphanius (*c*. 315–403), Cyril of Jerusalem (*c*.
315–86) and others write in this vein. The medieval Hebrew
gospel of Matthew in *Even Bohan* could be a corrupted version
of the original. Though unrivalled, the tradition has been
discounted on various grounds, particularly on the supposed
unreliability of Papias, from whom some would derive the
whole tradition. But Papias is very early, having had direct
contact with two of Jesus' actual followers. It is quite unsafe to
assume that all the later writers got an incorrect tradition from
him and had never heard the correct story. Vincent Taylor
argues against Matthean authorship on the ground that an
apostle would not have used a work by Mark, but this would not
necessarily have been felt to be plagiarism. Acceptance of belief
in Matthew's dependence on Greek Mark tends irresistibly to
govern the argument. Eusebius was anxious to prove the existence of two Johns and so deny first-hand information to Papias
from the apostle John. One attempt to show how Papias might
have got his idea wrong was the proposal that the Matthean
λόγια referred to the lost document Q. The λόγια, however, are
scriptures. Eusebius had the same gospels as ourselves. Papias
was concerned with their proper *interpretation*, which he preferred to get from living individuals who were in touch with the

116

apostles. The attempt of Kürzinger to interpret Ἑβραΐδι διαλέκτῳ as 'in a Hebrew style' is strained. The uncontradicted tradition of the church is weightier than Papias alone. Hengel shows that our gospel titles are very early.

The common witness to authorship

In the case of the first gospel the external testimony, although it has been rejected in all its main particulars by most modern scholars, is almost unanimous.

The fathers regularly make the following points:

1.) Matthew the tax-collector, otherwise known as Levi, one of the twelve, was the author.
2.) His was the first gospel to be written.
3.) He wrote for Hebrews in the Hebrew language (and in the Hebrew script).

The most important testimonies are as follows:

Papias (*c.* 60–130): 'Matthew collected the oracles in the Hebrew language, and each interpreted them as best he could'[1] (Eusebius, *HE* 3.39.16 – first edition published before 303).

Irenaeus (*c.* 130–200): 'Matthew indeed among the Hebrews, in their own dialect put forth also a writing of the gospel while Peter and Paul were evangelizing in Rome and founding the church.[2] (*Adv. Haer.* 3.1.1).

Pantaenus (died *c.* 190): 'It is said that he [Pantaenus] went to the Indians, and the tradition is that he found there that among some of those there who had known Christ the Gospel according to Matthew had preceded his coming; for Bartholomew, one of the apostles, had preached to them and had left them the writing of Matthew in Hebrew letters' (*HE* 5.10.3). (Jerome (*c.* 342–420) says similarly: 'He [Pantaenus] found that [in India] Bartholomew, one of the twelve apostles, had preached the coming of the Lord Jesus according to the Gospel of Matthew, which, written in Hebrew letters, he brought with him when he returned to Alexandria' (*De Vir. Ill.* 36).)

Origen (*c.* 185–254): 'As having learnt by tradition concerning the four gospels, which alone are unquestionable in the Church of God under heaven, that first was written that

according to Matthew, who was once a tax-collector but afterwards an apostle of Jesus Christ, who published it for those
who from Judaism came to believe, composed as it was in
the Hebrew language' or 'composed in Hebrew letters'
(γράμμασιν ʽΕβραϊκοῖς συντεταγμένον) (*HE* 6.25.4).

Eusebius (*c.* 260–340): 'Matthew had first preached to
Hebrews, and when he was on the point of going to others he
transmitted in writing in his native tongue, the Gospel according to himself, and thus supplied by writing the lack of his own
presence to those from whom he was sent' (*HE* 3.24.6). In
another work, *On the Discrepancies of the Gospels*, Eusebius
comments on the phrase ὀψὲ τοῦ σαββάτου (cf. Matt. 28:1),
saying it 'has been written by him who translated the scripture,
for the evangelist delivered it in the Hebrew tongue' (*Ad
Marinum*, Question 2).

Epiphanius (*c.* 315–403) says of the Ebionites and the Nazoraeans: 'they have the Gospel according to Matthew complete
and in Hebrew. For this is evidently still preserved among
them, as it was originally written, in Hebrew script.' Also (of
the Ebionites) 'they too receive the Gospel according to Matthew. For this they too use . . . to the exclusion of all others. But
they call it [the Gospel] according to the Hebrews, for, to speak
truthfully, Matthew alone of New Testament writers presents
and proclaims the gospel in Hebrew and in the Hebrew script'
(*Adv. Haer.* 29.9.4; 30.3.7).

Cyril of Jerusalem (*c.* 315–86): 'Matthew who wrote the
gospel wrote it in the Hebrew tongue' (*Catecheses* 14.15).

Jerome has several references to the subject, notably: 'The
first evangelist is Matthew . . . he published a gospel in the
Hebrew tongue, especially for their sake who had believed in
Jesus among the Jews' (*Preface to Matthew*). Also:

> Matthew, who is also Levi, from a publican an apostle, was the
> first to compose a gospel of Christ in Judea for the sake of those who
> had believed from the circumcision, in Hebrew words and letters;
> who it was that afterwards translated it into Greek is not sufficiently
> certain. Further, the Hebrew itself is preserved up to the present
> day in the library at Caesarea which Pamphilus the martyr very
> diligently collected. I had leave also given me to copy it by the

118

Nazaraeans [evidently the equivalent of the Nazoraeans of Epiphanius] in Beroea a city of Syria who use this work. In which it is to be observed that wherever the evangelist, either in his own person or the person of the Lord the Saviour, uses testimonies of the Old Testament, he does not follow the authority of the Septuagint, but of the Hebrew. (*De Vir. Ill.* 3)

Similar testimonies are found in Gregory of Nazianzus (329–389), Chrysostom (*c.* 347–407), Augustine (354–430)[3], and in Syrian and Coptic authorities, and they continue in this vein in the later fathers.

Recent research has added another consideration of great interest. One argument long deployed against the patristic tradition was the total disappearance of the Hebrew original. G. Howard is now arguing that the medieval Hebrew Matthew found in the *Even Bohan* of *c.* 1380 was not (as was often supposed) a translation of its Jewish author Shem-Tob, but an original composition in use many centuries earlier 'in primitive times', though now in a somewhat debased form.[4] It is not impossible that a copy of the original Matthew may have survived in Jewish hands when the Christians had lost almost all knowledge of the Hebrew language.

The quotations given above come from the best authorities in the early church, including those best acquainted with Hebrew (i.e., Origen and Jerome), none of whom seem to find the tradition suspicious. The tradition, as R. H. Gundry says, is 'persistent and unrivalled'[5] and many of the older scholars thought it so strong as to be virtually unquestionable. Yet to those who on other grounds are convinced that the tradition is wrong, it has not been difficult to find arguments to discount it.

The tradition discounted

To begin with, the references to Jewish Christian gospels in the fathers and in later writers form a notoriously complex study concerning which no consensus has yet emerged.[6] There may well be three or more different works referred to. Jerome's statements are particularly perplexing. He frequently refers under different names to what he apparently believes to be one and the same book, which he usually calls 'The Gospel according to the Hebrews', which he regards as the original Matthew. For instance, he says in *De Viris Illustribus* (ch. 2):

> The Gospel called according to the Hebrews which was recently translated by me into Greek and Latin, which Origen frequently uses, records after the resurrection of the Saviour: And when the Lord had given the linen cloth to the servant of the priest, he went to James and appeared to him. For James had sworn that he would not eat bread from that hour in which he had drunk the cup of the Lord until he should see him risen from among them that sleep. And shortly thereafter the Lord said: Bring a table and bread! And immediately it is added: he took the bread, blessed it and brake it and gave it to James the Just and said to him: My brother, eat thy bread, for the Son of man is risen from among them that sleep.

Hennecke in his careful study considers that Jerome's statements merit 'a very small measure' of confidence. His statement that the gospel 'was recently translated by me' he rejects as untrue, and he considers that Jerome worked only with fragments, which probably came from two different gospels neither of which Jerome had actually seen. Certainly some of his quotations do not come from our Matthew, as the above quotation shows.[7]

Similarly, the copy of the Ebionite gospel that Epiphanius knew was in Greek, not Hebrew, and from his own account it clearly contained matter not found in Matthew, some of it heretical. There is no firm evidence that Jerome or Epiphanius or anyone else had actually seen a copy of Matthew in Hebrew, in spite of the common belief that such had existed. Again, the best that Eusebius can say about the story of Pantaenus in India is that 'it is said' to have been so. If, as may well be, the story has a basis in fact,[8] it could be that the gospel in Hebrew letters which Pantaenus was shown was similar to that known to Jerome. Further, the evidence of Irenaeus may carry little weight since he had read Papias and his wrong notions may have come from him (*Adv. Haer.* 5.33.4). In such ways it is possible to argue that some of the tradition is worthless and that all of it stems from Papias.

But, while it is possible to find arguments that whittle away the whole tradition, it needs to be remembered that these arguments only open up the possibility that all came from a single erroneous source, they constitute no proof. As we shall see, Papias claimed to have many informants, and it is unlikely that they passed on their information only to Papias. If Papias got his ideas about Matthew from them it would be almost inevitable that others would acquire the same beliefs. It is true that Irenaeus had read Papias, but it does not mean that he had no other sources of information. We know on his own testimony that as a boy he heard Polycarp (*c.* 69–155), who had (he says) 'intercourse with John and with the rest of those who had seen the Lord'.[9] Thus Irenaeus was separated from the apostles only by a single intermediary. The extra information which he and later writers supply may or may not have come out of their own heads. In the case of Irenaeus, as we shall see (pp. 239–42), it is probable that he is not trying to supply new information. But the testimony of Pantaenus hardly looks like an expansion of Papias, and the learned Origen (whose writings, according to Zahn 2.517, 'betray not the slightest trace of acquaintance' with Papias' work) specifically appeals, not to a single informant, but to tradition. And, as Lagrange pertinently asks, Was Eusebius with his mediocre view of Papias just accepting the latter's opinion with his eyes shut?[10] It is true that Jerome wrongly identified his gospel, but it does not alter the fact that he firmly believed in the existence of a Hebrew Matthew and expected to find his version to be such. As far as we know, there was only one tradition known to the scholars and historians of the early and medieval church which they considered worth recording, and we need not lightly assume that it all sprang from an erroneous statement of one denigrated Phrygian bishop which obliterated knowledge of the true facts.

Supposing, however, that Papias was the sole source of the tradition, what is his evidence worth?

The testimony of Papias

The evidence suggests that the date of Papias' writing was very early. To quote Gundry again:

Modern handbooks usually put the date of his writing at ca. AD 135. Early though it is, this date is not early enough. The only hard evidence in its favor comes in a statement of Philip of Side, who makes Papias refer to the reign of Hadrian (117–138; see the citation in Aland, *Synopsis Quattuor Evangeliorum*, 531). But we have good reasons to distrust Philip's statement. He is notoriously unreliable and wrote approximately a century later than Eusebius did (Philip – ca. 430; Eusebius – ca. 324). Hence, if Eusebius leads us to an earlier date for Papias's writing, we should probably prefer the earlier. In fact, Eusebius does lead us to an earlier date by saying that Papias became famous during the time of Polycarp and Ignatius, with whom he associates Clement of Rome (*HE* 3.36.1–2; 3.38. 1–5). Polycarp did not die till the middle of the second century; but Ignatius died ca. 107 and Clement ca. 100. Eusebius' discussion of Papias's writings comes right at this point, i.e. before Trajan's persecution, which started ca. 110 and which Eusebius does not describe till Book 4 of his *Ecclesiastical History*, whereas the fragments of Papias appear in Book 3.

Then Gundry shows how Philip appears to have garbled Eusebius, transferring what Eusebius says about Quadratus the apologist to Papias. He says in summary:

A number of considerations unite to disfavor a date ca. 135 in accordance with Philip of Side and to favor a date before Trajan's persecution (i.e. before ca. 110) for Papias's report concerning Mark and Matthew: (1) the late date of Philip of Side; (2) his generally acknowledged unreliability; (3) the ease with which he might have confused Papias's writing with the apology by Quadratus; (4) the earlier date and greater reliability of Eusebius, who had in his hands the writings of both Papias and Quadratus; (5) Eusebius's associating Papias with Ignatius and, through Ignatius, with Clement of Rome; and (6) Eusebius' discussing the fragments of Papias prior to his description of Trajan's persecution.[11]

So we have a bishop of Hierapolis in Asia Minor completing his work probably in the first decade of the second century, writing five books from which we have fragmentary quotations in Irenaeus, Eusebius and some other writers. The account which Eusebius gives of him merits quotation at length. In Book 3 of his *Ecclesiastical History* he tells of the last days of the apostolic age and of the opportunity that the passing of the apostles provided for the growth of heresy, and he tells of the faithful men of the next generation who preserved the true faith, mentioning in particular Polycarp, Ignatius (*c.* 35–107), Clement of Rome (flourished *c.* 96) and Papias. Of the last he says:

Of Papias five treatises are extant which have also the title of *Interpretation of the Oracles of the Lord* [Λογίων κυριακῶν ἐξηγήσεως]. These are also mentioned by Irenaeus as though his only writing, for he says in one place, 'To these things also Papias, the hearer of John, who was a companion of Polycarp and one of the ancients, bears witness in writing in the fourth of his books, for five books were composed by him.' So says Irenaeus. Yet Papias himself, according to the preface of his treatises, makes plain that he had in no way been a hearer and eyewitness of the sacred Apostles, but teaches that he had received the articles of the faith from those who had known them, for he speaks as follows: 'And I shall not hesitate to append to the interpretations all that I ever learnt well from the presbyters and remember well, for of their truth I am confident. For unlike most I did not rejoice in them who say much, but in them who teach the truth, nor in them who recount the commandments of others, but in them who repeated those given to the faith by the Lord and derived from truth itself; but if ever anyone came who had followed the presbyters, I inquired into the words of the presbyters, what Andrew or Peter or Philip or Thomas or James or John or Matthew, or any other of the Lord's disciples, had said, and what Aristion and the presbyter John, the Lord's disciples, were saying. For I did not suppose that information from books would help me so much as the word of a living and surviving voice.' (*HE* 3.39.1–4)

He then discusses the significance of the two mentions of a John:

It is here worth noting that he twice counts the name of John, and reckons the first John with Peter and James and Matthew and the other Apostles, clearly meaning the evangelist, but by changing his statement places the second with the others outside the number of the Apostles, putting Aristion before him and clearly calling him a presbyter. This confirms the truth of the story of those who have said that there were two of the same name in Asia, and that there are two tombs at Ephesus both still called John's. This calls for

123

attention: for it is probable that the second (unless anyone prefer
the former) saw the revelation which passes under the name of
John. The Papias whom we are now treating confesses that he had
received the words of the Apostles from their followers, but says
that he had actually heard Aristion and the presbyter John. He
often quotes them by name and gives their traditions in his
writings. (*HE* 3.39.7)

He then goes on to tell of two miracles related by Papias, before
continuing:

> The same writer adduces other accounts, as though they came to
> him from unwritten tradition, and some strange parables and
> teachings of the Saviour, and some other more mythical accounts.
> Among them he says that there will be a millenium after the
> resurrection of the dead, when the kingdom of Christ will be set up
> in material form on this earth. I suppose that he got these notions by
> a perverse reading of the apostolic accounts, not realizing that they
> had spoken mystically and symbolically. For he was a man of very
> little intelligence,[12] as is clear from his books. But he is responsible
> for the fact that so many Christian writers after him held the same
> opinion, relying on his antiquity, for instance Irenaeus and who-
> ever else appears to have held the same views. (*HE* 3.39.11–13)

After this he recounts the traditions of John the Presbyter
concerning Mark, and then concludes with this statement by
Papias concerning Matthew, also presumably (though not
explicitly) from the presbyter:

> About Matthew this was said, 'Matthew collected the oracles in the
> Hebrew language, and each interpreted them as best he could.'
> [Ματθαῖος μὲν οὖν Ἑβραΐδι διαλέκτῳ τὰ λόγια συνετάξατο,
> ἡρμήνευσεν δ' αὐτὰ ὡς ἦν δυνατὸς ἕκαστος.] (*HE* 3.39.16)

Papias emphasises that he got his information from those who
had known the apostles Andrew, Philip, Thomas, James, John,
Matthew and others, and he is able to say of his interpretations
'of their truth I am confident'. He is writing self-consciously as a
particularly well-informed person, who has multiple sources
and who is only removed from Matthew himself by a single link.
Papias implies indeed that during the time of his enquiries most
of 'the Lord's disciples' to whom he refers were dead, hence his

124

dependence on those 'who had followed the presbyters'. He shows, however, by his change of tense from 'had said' to 'are saying' that two of 'the Lord's disciples', Aristion and the presbyter John, were still alive at the time when he received information from them. Thus he had informants of great reliability whose reports his readers could safely trust.

Discounting the evidence of Papias

On the face of it, Papias has testimony of the highest quality, but he has had detractors both in the modern and in the ancient world. Four means have been used to discredit his testimony:
1.) insistence on Matthew's derivation from Mark;
2.) emphasis on the ambivalence of Eusebius;
3.) attempted explanations of how Papias got it wrong;
4.) attempted reinterpretations of Papias.

Matthew's use of Mark

Modern critical opinion has for a long time been almost unanimous that Papias was wrong – certainly about the first gospel being originally in Hebrew and probably about Matthew being the author. This derives principally from the vast measure of assent given to the theory that our Greek Matthew was based on the Greek Mark.[13] This makes it impossible to believe that Matthew is a translation from a Semitic original, and difficult to believe that it is the work of an eyewitness apostle.

As to the latter, Vincent Taylor called it 'improbable in the extreme that an Apostle would have used as a source the work of one who was not an eyewitness of the ministry of Jesus'.[14] But it is not perhaps quite so hard to believe as is usually thought, since attitudes towards literary borrowing were different in the ancient world from those of today. What to us would be disgraceful plagiarism might be to them an honourable and faithful preservation of tradition. So it is conceivable that Matthew the apostle could have taken Mark as his starting-point, adding fresh material and weaving into it his special emphases.

This is the more credible if Matthew had recognised that

Mark's gospel had the authority of Peter behind it. It is true that Matthew has not the vividness of narrative of Mark, which has been commonly attributed to the lively descriptiveness of Peter's spoken word. But the degree of vividness of narrative in an eyewitness account depends upon the temperament of the writer and upon his mood and aim at the time of writing. A literary record of a remembered event can be stated in a quite matter-of-fact way. So it is possible to believe that Matthew the apostle could have used Mark, even though it seems unlikely. In Chapters 1–4 we challenged the basic premise of Markan priority, but it is important to realise that, when a hypothesis has reached the stage that it is accepted virtually as fact, it exerts an almost irresistible pressure on the whole course of an argument. So the supposed dependence of the Greek Matthew upon the Greek Mark has been felt to be an unanswerable objection at least to that part of the tradition which says that Matthew was originally in the Hebrew language.

The ambivalence of Eusebius

On the one hand Eusebius commends Papias as the author of important works bearing witness to the apostolic understanding of the faith, on the other he denigrates him as an evil influence, teaching many Christian writers to believe that the kingdom of Christ was to be set up in material form on this earth. As to the latter, it is far from obvious that these ideas about the millenium were the invention of Papias, and furthermore it is demonstrable that Eusebius himself was by no means unbiased in his assessment of Papias. A. Meredith summarised a paper entitled 'The Evidence of Papias for the Priority of Matthew' which he read at the 1982 Gospels Conference at Ampleforth as follows:

> (He first gives the commonly accepted argument.)
> *Major premise*: All available external evidence pointing to the priority of Matthew is derived from Papias.
> *Minor premise*: Papias was a man of 'small intelligence' (Eusebius' term).
> *Conclusion*: All traditional evidence based on Papias is probably false.

126

(He then examines the evidence, showing that Eusebius is not impartial: he gives great play to Origen and Dionysius in their denigration of the Apocalypse of John.)

> Eusebius turns out to be a devout proConstantinian antichiliast, a caesaropapalist who would have abhorred the physical millenialism of earlier Fathers such as Papias and Irenaeus. Hence his slighting reference to the former as 'of small intelligence.'

(He then states his conclusion.)

> Ergo, the minor premise falls, and the major premise is left standing. [15]

It would be unwise therefore to take Eusebius' estimates of Papias' intelligence too seriously and lightly attribute to him a foolish mistake with regard to Matthew's gospel. Irenaeus certainly trusted him and on Eusebius' own reckoning 'so many Christian writers after him' did the same. Eusebius cannot really have it both ways. He must either indict the great body of early witnesses as ill-informed or of insufficient intelligence or he must take Papias as a representative witness to an apparently uncontradicted tradition.

Eusebius is generally recognised as an honest transcriber of valuable sources, but also as a person of unreliable critical judgement. [16] As we have seen in the passage quoted above, he argues that there were two Johns. Papias, he says, counts one of these with the apostles, 'clearly meaning the evangelist', and one as outside the number of apostles, 'clearly calling him a presbyter . . . [who] it is probable . . . saw the revelation'. Eusebius has a certain animus against the Apocalypse, [17] and this interpretation of Papias was doubtless convenient to him, but the fact is that Papias calls all the seven whom he names (including the first John) 'presbyters' and 'the Lord's disciples', just as he does the second John. It is more natural, especially in view of the great age attributed to the apostle, to interpret Papias as referring first to those (most of whom were then dead) who had instructed his informants in the past; and then (changing to the present tense) to two who were still alive, who had instructed them comparatively recently. But even if a second

John did exist, he would still be a direct link between Jesus and Papias – he and Aristion are called 'the Lord's disciples' by Papias in exactly the same way as the seven named apostles.[18]

It is difficult to exaggerate the importance of testimony of this quality. Papias claimed (and why should we doubt him?) that he made it his practice to get his information from those who had got it direct from the apostles, a good deal of it before the last of those who had accompanied Jesus were dead, and some of it may well have come from the apostle John himself. Thus a critical examination of the ambivalence of Eusebius actually enhances the witness of Papias. Furthermore, Papias makes it clear that he was not dependent on a single source of information. There were many people passing on what they had learnt from the apostles and doubtless they had many listeners. If Papias was garbling what he learnt one would have expected a more correct version to have reached the ears of some of the early writers. But the fact remains that there is no alternative tradition about the authorship of Matthew's gospel, as there is in the case of Hebrews, nor was there doubt of its apostolic authorship, as there was in the case, for instance, of 2 Peter.

Attempts to explain how Papias got his ideas wrong

Those who rule out Matthean authorship or a Semitic original realise that they must try to explain how Papias got it wrong. One initial difficulty is to explain how the name of such an undistinguished apostle became attached to this gospel. We are so used to thinking of Matthew as the traditional author of the premier document of Christianity that we tend to forget that, apart from his role as tax-collector, his call, the meal at his house and his membership of the twelve, the gospels tell us nothing about him as an individual. Why then choose Matthew as the supposed author, either originally if it was pseudonymous or later if it was anonymous?

One highly influential answer was that of F. D. E. Schleiermacher (*Theologische Studien*, 1832), who took Papias' λόγιον to be a diminutive of λόγος and interpreted it as a short saying. Stoldt quotes him thus: 'Matthew has written a collection of statements made by Christ which may have been only single proverbs or extended ones, or most probably both. *Papias' expression simply cannot mean anything else'* (365; Stoldt's italics). But Schleiermacher rejected just as firmly an identification of this logia compilation with our gospel of Matthew: 'Let us ask ourselves if it is really probable that this very same Matthew would still have written our Gospel after writing the collection of these speeches: my answer has to be entirely in the negative' (367). And also: 'Eusebius has not found a trace of two distinct works by Matthew in his Papias; thus it is probable that only the one existed, and it was not our Gospel' (368). However, Schleiermacher also expressed the opinion: *'The Gospel of Matthew embraces this collection.'* Further, he was of the view that 'the reason it bears the name is because it is based on this work by Matthew' (372; Stoldt's italics).[19] Lexicographically Schleiermacher was doubly wrong. In the first place λόγιον is almost certainly not a diminutive; secondly, the natural and obvious meaning of Papias' title λογίων κυριακῶν ἐξηγήσεως is *Exposition of the Gospels*. B. B. Warfield wrote a fifty-five page article 'The Oracles of God'[20] (which strangely has been overlooked by BAG and Kittel's *Wörterbuch* and which has not been superseded by any other treatment in English) in which he demonstrates both points. There is a solid body of evidence from classical Greek, the Septuagint, Philo and the fathers showing that λόγιον meant divine utterance, an oracle, which could be used for a short saying or for a whole body of inspired literature (though in the latter case the plural τὰ λόγια is the normal use). Warfield's conclusion is:

> it means, not 'words' barely, simple 'utterances', but distinctively 'oracular utterances', divinely authoritative communications, before which men stand in awe and to which they bow in humility: and this high meaning is not merely implicit, but is explicit in the term. It would seem clear again that there are no implications of brevity in the term: it means not short, pithy, pregnant sayings, but high, authoritative, sacred utterances; and it may be applied equally well to long as to short utterances. (387)

Warfield's conclusions have been underlined by an important study of R. Gryson,[21] which shows that the second-century fathers consistently use the term for the sacred scriptures.

Quite apart from lexicographical difficulties and the inherent difficulties of the Q-hypothesis (which we looked at in Chapter 3), Schleiermacher's identification of τὰ λόγια with Q has a further difficulty. Those who regard Q as a single document do not in fact think of it precisely as a collection of short sayings, since it includes lengthy parables and at least one narrative passage (the healing of the centurion's servant), so τὰ λόγια (even if taken as a diminutive) is not as apt as might first appear.

This means that Papias' work is an exposition of scriptures comprising the Lord's oracles, and Matthew's gospel is one of the books of divine oracles which he expounds. Eusebius complains that Papias has got false notions by 'a perverse reading of the apostolic accounts'. This is not a complaint that he has an incorrect version of the oracles (he had the same written apostolic records which Eusebius knew); his fault is that he misreads their meaning, 'not realising that they had spoken mystically and symbolically'. And when Papias says, 'I did not suppose that information from books would help me so much as the word of a living and surviving voice', *he is not contrasting the value of written scripture with that of oral tradition*, he is contrasting the value of unauthoritative books (possibly of gnosticising tendency) purporting to interpret the Lord's words, with the answers to his questions which he got from eye- and earwitnesses, that is, those who had had first-hand touch with the apostles.[22] What he was concerned about was not what the logia *said*, but what they *meant*. That was the whole theme of his *Interpretation*.

Others have thought that τὰ λόγια may have been a collection of Old Testament testimonia compiled by Matthew, which was later incorporated in the gospel. But in this case it is difficult to imagine how authorship of so small a proportion of the gospel could have been transferred to the whole. G. D. Kilpatrick[23] thought that the gospel may have been pseudonymous; but if so, neither Papias nor any other early writer seems to have suspected it. K. Stendahl's[24] idea that the gospel derived from a school for advanced study which owed its inspiration to Matthew has a very slender foundation and appears to have been quite unknown to early Christian writers.[25]

Another suggestion is that the mistaken notion of a Hebrew original arose simply from a conjecture of Papias. He knew from his distant Phrygia that Palestine was bilingual and he knew that the gospel was preached first to the Jew and then to the Greek. Seeing that Matthew's gospel had striking Jewish features which linked it closely to the Old Testament, it was natural to suppose[26] that it was written for the Hebrews in the Hebrew language and that it was only afterwards translated into the language of the other gospels. Papias was interested in the question of gospel harmony, and it is possible that he developed the idea of a Hebrew Matthew to resolve discrepancies between the gospels. The snag with this theory is that Papias gives no hint that he is guessing. He writes as if his report was fact, and those who come after do the same.

Attempts to reinterpret Papias' expression ῾Εβραΐδι διαλέκτῳ

Another way of discounting the evidence of Papias has been to reinterpret the expression ῾Εβραΐδι διαλέκτῳ. διάλεκτος in all its six New Testament uses means 'language'. J. Kürzinger,[27] however, has argued that the whole passage is concerned with the distinctive styles of Mark and Matthew. Papias lived in Hierapolis, which had a strong school of rhetoric. He is acknowledging Mark's deficiencies in style, while defending his accuracy and apostolic orthodoxy. Mark did not write 'in order', but he was the middle man faithfully rendering Peter's message. Matthew, on the other hand, put his material together in an orderly fashion (συνετάξατο) and according to a Jewish way of doing things. 'Each [Mark, Matthew and any others] interpreted and arranged the divine oracles as best he could.'

It is true that διαλέγω was used in the sense of 'to discourse or argue', especially in connection with the dialectic method of the Socratics, and διάλεκτος was used of 'a way of speaking' or 'style'. To interpret it this way is particularly attractive to those like Gundry, who see Matthew as a writer of midrash. He says:

131

'a Hebrew dialect' means a Hebrew way of presenting Jesus' messiahship. Immediately we think of all those Jewish features of Matthew – the stress on Jesus as the Son of David and Messiah, the tracing of his genealogy back to Abraham, the frequent and unique citations of OT passages as fulfilled by Jesus, and so on – that capture a large amount of attention in modern introductions to this gospel. To these traditionally recognized features must now be added Matthew's midrashic style.[28]

But if one reads the whole context in Eusebius it does not seem to be about style. Chapter 37 is about the generation that followed the apostolic age, the writers who took the first rank in the apostolic succession, who were zealous to preach and to hand on the divine gospels. Eusebius' method is to mention a miscellany of facts which he thinks will be of interest to his readers and at the same time to get over to them his own understanding of the history. He is particularly interested in canonicity and in Chapter 38 discusses the Epistle to the Hebrews and the Clementine writings. The long Chapter 39 is devoted to Papias' *Exposition*. In this treatise he gives us miscellaneous interesting facts: he tells us the story about the raising of a corpse and another concerning Justus Barsabbas, who drank poison unharmed (presumably in illustration of Mark 16:18). He tells us of Papias' quotations from 1 John and 1 Peter and of his use of the story about the woman who was accused before the Lord of many sins. But his deeper concerns are 1.) to use Papias in defence of the apostolicity of Mark; 2.) to use him to further his case against the Apocalypse; 3.) to berate Chiliasm. As far as Eusebius is concerned it is not a rhetorician's discussion of style; he is giving interesting information about Papias' book, including what he says about the origin, apostolicity and mode of composition of two gospels.

But, it is argued, Eusebius has misunderstood Papias; he did not recognise the remarks of Papias as being a rhetorician's discussion of style. This, however, seems improbable, since Eusebius, unlike ourselves, had the whole work in front of him. Furthermore, Papias is not giving his own views as a rhetorician, he is quoting the Presbyter. Are we to believe that this Palestinian follower of Jesus was using the language of the rhetorical schools? The comment of R. T. France (in a review of Gundry) on Kürzinger's suggestion will be widely echoed: 'that Papias' Ἐβραΐδι διαλέκτῳ must be translated "in a Jewish *style*" . . . seems to me to stretch the elastic of Papias' reported words to the limit'.[29] It is unlikely that this interpretation, which never occurred to the fathers, would have occurred to modern writers had they not been under great pressure to dispose of the natural meaning of his words. If however in the end we do feel compelled to dispose of the natural meaning, this seems to offer the best hope of a reasonable explanation.

There is also the less important question: Does Ἐβραΐδι mean 'in Aramaic' (Aramaic being the main Semitic language used in common speech in first-century Palestine) or should it be understood as literally 'in Hebrew'? Until recently Hebrew was thought to be a dead language in the first century, although the Hebrew scriptures were read regularly in the synagogue lections and were taught to the children in school. But the discovery of the Bar-Kokhba letters showed that Hebrew was still in use for literary purposes well after the time of Matthew. It was indeed the language of most of the Qumran writings. So it is an open question which language Papias meant.

We are led to the conclusion that the testimony of Papias to the authorship of the first gospel is weighty and that attempts to discredit it have not succeeded. We cannot disprove the theory that he is the sole source of patristic tradition, but far less can we prove that he is. We must recognise that the uncontradicted tradition of the church as a whole is weightier than that of Papias alone. It provides a datum which must not be too readily surrendered.

The significance of the titles

Further light on the date and authorship of the gospels is provided by the study of their titles. Martin Hengel has investigated this subject at some depth in his *Studies in the Gospel of Mark*.[30] He calls attention to the unusual form of the gospel titles as found in the superscriptions and subscriptions of the manuscripts and to their complete unanimity in their attribution of authorship. As a rule in antiquity the name of the book's author would come first (in the genitive) and be followed by a title indicating content. But in the gospels the title is simply Εὐαγγέλιον κατὰ followed by the author's name. In some manuscripts, such as Sinaiticus and Vaticanus, the title appears without εὐαγγέλιον, and it has been commonly supposed that the titles were originally in this shorter form. Indeed, this is the form given in the 26th edition of the Nestle text. But at an earlier date, in the three papyri in which titles have been preserved all have the longer form, as does the Old Latin, the Coptic, Irenaeus of Lyons, Clement of Alexandria, Tertullian of Carthage and the Muratorian Canon of Rome. 'What is striking here is the complete unanimity over the four titles of the Gospels in a distribution extending throughout the whole of the Roman Empire towards the end of the second century' (66).

This, Hengel maintains, argues against the predominant theory which holds that the gospels were originally anonymous[31] or without titles and that the consistency of their form is explained as being due to the adoption of these names after the fourfold canon had been generally recognised. He argues that canonisation was comparatively late. It can only be clearly seen for the first time in Tatian's Diatessaron of *c.* 170. But even if it was much earlier than that (he rightly maintains), the circulation of individual gospels without titles for even a few years would have resulted in the invention of a diversity of titles. As soon as more than one gospel was in use in a church some method of distinguishing them would have had to be devised. The unanimity that in fact exists cannot have been imposed by authority, for no authority existed capable of effecting such imposition throughout the worldwide church. How then did it come about?

Hengel argues that the attribution of authorship to Mark and Matthew is presupposed in Papias' work (which he thinks was written about 120 or 130), and that this goes back to 'the mysterious presbyter John[32] . . . which brings us to a time between 90 and 100' (69). That is to say, it brings us into the period when the gospels were being composed, which he puts at

69–100. He then boldly argues that the terminology is rooted in Mark 1:1, where εὐαγγέλιον stands in the title. Christian communities, as soon as they had broken away from the synagogue, would set up a book-chest containing Old Testament scriptures and Christian documents suitable for reading during worship. There was, Hengel maintains, a strict scribal discipline and it was the scribes who circulated the Christian books who first invented the title εὐαγγέλιον κατὰ Μάρκον and then gave corresponding titles to Matthew, Luke and John.

Hengel does not explain how this 'discipline' originated and how its rules were so punctiliously observed. The theory, good as far as it goes, clearly has a vital element missing – it demonstrates the early recognition of the traditional authors, but it does not explain how the uniformity of titles arose. Light is thrown on this if our view of the synoptic problem is correct in maintaining that the later evangelists knew, and recognised the authority of, their predecessors. This would mean that from the day of publication of a second gospel (whichever one that was) they would have been known as 'The Gospel according to Matthew' and 'The Gospel according to Mark', and the practice would have been extended on the publication of Luke and John. In other words, the tradition of authorship which was followed with such unanimity could well have been transmitted without a break from the time of publication of the second gospel.

There is one scrap of external evidence to put in the scales against Matthean priority. The fact that Eusebius (who may well be following Papias) mentions the circumstances of Mark's publication before that of Matthew might suggest that Mark is prior. This cannot be held to be a weighty consideration, seeing we have only short extracts from Papias' writings, but in view of the tradition of Matthean priority, it is a consideration to be born in mind (see further p. 269 n1).

All in all the external evidence, which makes the apostle Matthew the author of the first gospel (written apparently in Hebrew) agrees well with our estimate of the internal evidence.

6

ANCIENT TESTIMONY TO MARK'S GOSPEL

Chapter summary

Eusebius quotes Papias, who in turn quotes John the Presbyter (= John the Apostle?), who says that Mark became Peter's interpreter and wrote accurately all that he remembered of the things said or done by the Lord. 'Interpreter' probably means, not that Mark translated Peter's Aramaic words into Greek, but that as a catechist he expounded Peter's teaching. Eusebius contrasts the orderly arrangement of Matthew with the less structured oral teaching of Peter.

Irenaeus tells how Mark the disciple of Peter handed on Peter's teaching after the latter's 'exodus' – probably his death. The Anti-Marcionite Prologue says that Mark *wrote* the gospel in Italy after the 'exodus'. Clement of Alexandria says that Mark wrote at the request of leading Christians in Rome and that Peter later gave his approval. Origen says that Mark wrote on the instruction of Peter. There is thus a solid core of tradition associating Mark with Peter's teaching in Rome.

The eighteenth-century letter of Clement of Alexandria discovered in the Mar Saba monastery telling of a secret version of the gospel of Mark for initiates is of quite doubtful authenticity.

Traditions concerning the second gospel bristle with difficulties. In addition to the well-known quotations in the early fathers which contain knotty problems of interpretation, there are a number of other questions bearing on the subject which are even more debatable. These will be considered in the next three chapters.

136

Papias

As in the case of Matthew, Eusebius has preserved a quotation from Papias in which that father quotes from John the Presbyter. It stands immediately before the reference to Matthew and runs as follows:

> We are now obliged to append to the words already quoted from him [Papias] a tradition about the Mark who wrote the Gospel, which he expounds as follows. 'And the Presbyter used to say this, "Mark became [γενόμενος][1] Peter's interpreter and wrote accurately all that he remembered, not, indeed, in order, of the things said or done by the Lord. For he had not heard the Lord, nor had he followed him, but later on, as I said followed Peter, who used to give teaching as necessity demanded [πρὸς τὰς χρείας ἐποιεῖτο] but not making, as it were, an arrangement [σύνταξιν] of the Lord's oracles [variant readings λογίων or λόγων], so that Mark did nothing wrong in thus writing down single points [ἔνια – certain matters] as he remembered them. For to one thing he gave attention, to leave out nothing of what he had heard and to make no false statements in them."' This is related by Papias about Mark, and about Matthew this was said . . . (*HE* 3.39.14ff)

It is not possible in this quotation-within-a-quotation to be certain where the words of John the Presbyter[2] end. They may not go as far as the above translation by Kirsopp Lake takes them. The 'as I said' sounds more like Papias than the presbyter, so it is probably best to attribute only the first sentence to John, though the comment which follows is of course written on the basis of what Papias had learnt from him. The main thrust of the whole statement appears to be a contrasting of the recollections of Mark derived from the preaching and teaching of Peter with the more orderly arrangement of the gospel of Matthew. Wherever the quotation of the Presbyter ends, the essence of what he has to say is found in that first sentence, which makes four points:

1.) Mark became Peter's ἑρμηνευτής. ἑρμηνεύς and ἑρμηνευτής are not used exclusively of the translator of foreign languages. They are used more generally of one who interprets, expounds or explains.[3] So it is not necessary to take the term 'interpreter' in the sense of 'translator', for Peter was regularly in situations, for example in Antioch (Gal. 2:12) and Caesarea (Acts 10:34), which show that he must have spoken Greek. Greek was the *lingua franca* of the Roman world, and judging by Peter's role as leading apostle in the church he was almost certainly bilingual, and Aramaic and Greek would have served him in all normal circumstances. His preaching would, however, have required careful following up, and Mark as a close and experienced colleague would have been continually engaged in interpreting Peter's message to those who had heard it.

2.) He wrote 'accurately'. He kept a single aim in view: 'to make no false statements'.

3.) He wrote fully. He set down 'all that he remembered', aiming 'to leave out nothing' and including works as well as words: 'the things said or done by the Lord'.

4.) He wrote 'not in order'. The gospel of Matthew with its great sections of discourse is pre-eminently an orderly arrangement (σύνταξις) of the Lord's sayings, which Mark, with its greater emphasis on the Lord's actions, is not. Papias is particularly concerned to bring out Mark's derivation from Peter's relatively unstructured oral teaching, which Peter used to adapt to the needs of his hearers as necessity demanded.[4] It is the stories which formed the staple diet of Peter's teaching that Mark put together in his gospel. It is possible that 'not in order' may have a secondary, apologetic motive. The order of Matthew's pericopes of course differs considerably from that of Mark, and Papias may be attempting to justify the differences. But it has to be said that there is nothing directly to suggest this; even less is there any suggestion that Matthew's order is chronologically more accurate than that of Mark.[5]

Irenaeus

What Irenaeus has to say about Matthew when he recounts the writing of the four gospels, we shall consider on pp. 239–42. Of Mark he says: 'After the death of these [μετὰ δὲ τὴν τούτων ἔξοδον], Mark, the disciple and interpreter of Peter, also has himself handed on to us in writing the things proclaimed by Peter' (*Adv. Haer.* 3.1.2). ἔξοδος is an unusual word for death,

138

and it could mean 'departure' (which is its natural sense) and refer to some unspecified departure of Peter and Paul, say from Rome.[6] But it is used of the forthcoming death of Jesus in Luke's account of the transfiguration (9:31) and of Peter's impending death in 2 Peter 1:15, and 'death' makes admirable sense in the context. The point is the continuity of the apostles' witness before and after their deaths: Mark has handed on in writing the things proclaimed orally by Peter. There is no suggestion that after the apostles had died there had been an interval before Mark's gospel was written. The passage contrasts the traditions of the heretics with the public declarations of the apostles, first preached, then committed to writing and now preserved in the church. Irenaeus does *not* say that after the death of Peter and Paul, Mark *wrote* his gospel, but that he has *handed on* the preaching of Peter to us in writing. Any suggestion of discontinuity between the time of preaching and the time of writing would weaken his argument, and no such notion should be read into it. Of course it does not preclude the possibility that the gospel was written after the death of Peter, but the important point is that the passage does not say so.

The 'Anti-Marcionite' Prologue

In about forty manuscripts of the Vulgate are to be found short introductions to the gospels of Mark, Luke and John (that of Matthew is presumed to have been lost) which are usually referred to by the above title. They were apparently originally written in Greek, but (except in two manuscripts of Luke) they have survived only in Latin. D. de Bruyne[7] (supported by A. Harnack) called attention to them in 1928 and argued that they should be dated 160–80, thus making them a few years earlier than Irenaeus' *Against Heresies*. This view gained wide acceptance,[8] but more recently, especially as a result of an article by R. G. Heard in 1955 and a major treatment by J. Regul in 1969, the tendency has been to date them considerably later.[9]

Since the Markan prologue has similarities to the statement of Irenaeus, it is convenient to consider it at this point:

139

'. . . Mark declared, who is called "stump-fingered", because he had rather small fingers in comparison with the stature of the rest of his body. He was the interpreter of Peter. *post excessionem ipsius Petri descripsit idem hoc in partibus Italiae evangelium*' (text from Aland, *Synopsis* 532). We have here some quite independent matter in the curious reference to Mark's fingers, and we find different terms to express the common tradition concerning Mark's whereabouts: Irenaeus speaks of Peter and Paul preaching 'in Rome', whereas this prologue says 'in the regions of Italy'. On the other hand, Irenaeus and the prologue are at one in making Mark the interpreter of Peter, and the expression *post excessionem* is an exact equivalent of μετὰ τὴν ἔξοδον, meaning 'after the departure', used presumably in the sense of 'after the death' of Peter. *descripsit* suggests what is absent from, or at best ambiguous in, Irenaeus – that Mark wrote down his gospel after Peter's death.

The fact that the prologues are probably translations and of uncertain date should caution us against giving them undue weight. It is generally agreed that de Bruyne was wrong in seeing these prologues as a literary unit, and except in the case of John evidence of an anti-Marcionite tendency is questionable (but see Bruce, p. 275 n9 below). Each prologue must therefore be judged on its own merits. They may contain early traditions, but they should not be regarded as of the same authority as early dateable authors like Irenaeus. In the case of Mark it is quite possible that the author of the prologue or one of his sources simply read into the statement of Irenaeus the idea that the gospel was written after Peter's death, as so many have done since. So the prologue's *descripsit* does not carry great authority.

Clement of Alexandria

Eusebius gives us two quotations from Clement of Alexandria, who was writing at the very end of the second century. Eusebius speaks of his erudition and of his claim to have come near to the successors of the apostles, and to have committed to writing traditions that he had heard from the elders of olden time. (He mentions also that he knew the work of Irenaeus.) He then says:

In the same books [the *Hypotyposeis*] Clement has inserted a tradition of the primitive elders . . . that the Gospel according to Mark came into being in this manner: When Peter had publicly preached the word at Rome, and by the Spirit had proclaimed the Gospel, those present, who were many, exhorted Mark, as one who had followed him for a long time and remembered what had been spoken, to make a record of what was said; and that he did this, and distributed the Gospel among those that asked him. And that when the matter came to Peter's knowledge he neither strongly forbade it nor urged it forward. (*HE* 6.14.6f)

Earlier Eusebius had said with reference to the evil work done by Simon Magus in Rome:

But a great light of religion shone on the minds of the hearers of Peter, so that they were not satisfied with a single hearing or with the unwritten teaching of the divine proclamation, but with every kind of exhortation besought Mark, whose Gospel is extant, seeing that he was Peter's follower, to leave them a written statement of the teaching given them verbally, nor did they cease until they had persuaded him, and so became the cause of the Scripture called the Gospel according to Mark. And they say that the Apostle, knowing by the revelation of the spirit to him what had been done, was pleased at their zeal, and ratified the scripture for study in the churches. Clement quotes the story in the sixth book of the *Hypotyposeis*, and the bishop of Hierapolis, named Papias, confirms him. He also says that Peter mentions Mark in his first Epistle, and that he composed this in Rome itself. (*HE* 2.15.1f)

These two accounts from Eusebius come from the same work of Clement and are evidently his own digests of what he found there. It would suggest that Peter was at first somewhat cool towards the idea of a record of his teaching, but that later, as a result of a revelation by the Spirit, he warmed to the idea and actually ratified Mark's gospel for study in the churches.

Another quotation from Clement is preserved in Latin in which he comments on 1 Peter 5:13. It follows the same general tradition with regard to Mark's association with Peter, but contains extra detail concerning Peter's hearers:

Mark, the follower of Peter, while Peter was preaching the gospel publicly at Rome in the presence of certain of Caesar's knights and was putting forward many testimonies concerning Christ, being requested by them that they might be able to commit to memory the things which were being spoken, wrote from the things which were spoken by Peter the Gospel which is called According to Mark. (*Adumbrationes ad 1 Peter 5:13* – for Latin text see K. Aland, *Synopsis* 539.)

Origen

Eusebius quotes a passage from the immensely erudite Origen's *Commentaries on the Gospel according to Matthew*, in which he says that he has learnt by tradition that there are four gospels, 'which alone are unquestionable in the Church of God', and then refers briefly to Matthew, Mark, Luke and John in turn. Of Mark he says: 'And second, that according to Mark, who did as Peter instructed him, whom also he acknowledged as a son in the catholic epistle' (*HE* 6.25.5). Origen takes us into the earlier part of the third century, and this is about as far as we can usefully go in seeking ancient testimony to Mark.[10]

All these testimonies point to a solid core of tradition, which makes Mark the author of the gospel, which makes him a fellow-worker with Peter, and which makes his book a faithful record of what that apostle taught in Rome. The tradition is not entirely clear as to whether he wrote before or after the apostle's death. Clement specifically states the former. Irenaeus, though frequently cited on the other side, is in fact entirely neutral. Only the Latin translation of the Anti-Marcionite Prologue appears to favour the latter (if *post excessionem* refers to death), and there is doubt about the antiquity of its testimony.

So much for the relatively straightforward quotations from early authors. But there is a crop of more difficult questions to be dealt with below and in the next two chapters.

The Mar Saba fragment

In 1958 Morton Smith announced the discovery of part of a letter of Clement of Alexandria in the library of the monastery of Mar Saba in southern Judea. In 1973 he published facsimiles

142

of the document with translation and commentary.[11] It consists of seventy-two lines which are said to have been written in an eighteenth-century script on the endpapers of a seventeenth-century book. Since the publication of the facsimiles no other Western scholar has had the opportunity of studying the original. (It is not even clear where the book is at the present time.) In it Clement replies to one Theodore who has been troubled by the false teaching of the gnostic Carpocratians, whose licentious ethic claimed to be based on a superior version of Mark's gospel. Theodore has asked Clement to verify certain of their supposed quotations. Clement proceeds to give an account of the writing of the gospel, which, he says, was indeed written in two versions, one for ordinary readers and one 'for the use of those who were being perfected':

> As for Mark, then, during Peter's stay in Rome he wrote an account of the Lord's doings, not, however, declaring all of them, nor yet hinting at the secret ones, but selecting what he thought most useful for increasing the faith of those who were being instructed. But when Peter died a martyr, Mark came over to Alexandria, bringing both his own notes and those of Peter, from which he transferred to his former book the things suitable to whatever makes for progress toward knowledge. Thus he composed a more spiritual Gospel for the use of those who were being perfected. Nevertheless, he yet did not divulge the things not to be uttered, nor did he write down the hierophantic teaching of the Lord, but to the stories already written he added yet others and, moreover, brought in certain sayings of which he knew the interpretation would, as a mystagogue, lead the hearers into the innermost sanctuary of that truth hidden by seven veils. Thus, in sum, he prepared matters, neither grudgingly nor incautiously, in my opinion, and, dying, he left his composition to the church in Alexandria, where it even yet is most carefully guarded, being read only to those who are being initiated into the great mysteries.

Then he tells how Carpocrates with demonic art procured a copy of the secret gospel from a presbyter and mixed 'with the spotless and holy words utterly shameless lies'.

He then proceeds to refute the falsifications by giving the very words of the gospel, quoting two insertions in chapter 10, which are not found in the canonical gospels. After verse 34 there follows:

> And they come into Bethany. And a certain women whose brother had died was there. And, coming, she prostrated herself before Jesus and says to him, 'Son of David, have mercy on me.' But the disciples rebuked her. And Jesus, being angered, went off with her into the garden where the tomb was, and straightway a great cry was heard from the tomb. And going near Jesus rolled away the stone from the door of the tomb. And straightway, going in where the youth was, he stretched forth his hand and raised him, seizing his hand. But the youth, looking upon him, loved him and began to beseech him that he might be with him. And going out of the tomb they came into the house of the youth, for he was rich. And after six days Jesus told him what to do and in the evening the youth comes to him, wearing a linen cloth over his naked body. And he remained with him that night, for Jesus taught him the mystery of the kingdom of God. And thence, arising, he returned to the other side of the Jordan.

On this he comments: 'After these words follows the text, "And James and John come to him," and all that section. But "naked man with naked man," and the other things about which you wrote, are not found.' Finally, he mentions the insertion at Mark 10:46 of:

> And after the words, 'And he comes into Jericho,' the secret Gospel adds only, 'And the sister of the youth whom Jesus loved and his mother and Salome were there, and Jesus did not receive them.' But the many other things about which you wrote both seem to be and are falsifications.
>
> Now the true explanation and that which accords with the true philosophy

At this point, two-thirds of the way down the page, the scribe breaks off.

What are we to make of this? Is there any truth in the notion that there were two versions of Mark's gospel, both approved by the church authorities in Alexandria and one reserved 'only to those who are being initiated into the great mysteries'? Can we believe that Mark wrote the ill-fitting insertions attributed to him, which suggest that Jesus initiated nocturnal 'mysteries' in

144

the nude? That Clement probably did write the letter has been widely accepted, but this must remain very doubtful, both because of the improbability of its contents and also because no other writer alludes to the Alexandrian version of Mark, nor does Clement himself in any of his acknowledged writings. Eusebius tells us that Clement in his *Hypotyposeis* 'has given concise explanations of all the canonical scriptures without omitting the disputed books' (6.14.1), and he gives no hint that there were two versions of Mark, let alone that there was a version containing advanced material for the initiated, which would of course have provided grist to his expository mill.

Of those who accept the genuineness of the letter (and hence the existence of an expanded version of Mark known to Clement) few follow Morton Smith in believing the additions to be the work of Mark himself. Some explain the fragments as belonging to an apocryphal gospel of the common second-century type, some regard them as a pastiche derived from the canonical gospels, some suggest that earlier material has been incorporated into Mark by someone imitating Markan style.[12] If this fragment were authentic, it would confirm the tradition that Mark wrote our canonical gospel in Rome while Peter was still alive, and the tradition of the Alexandrian church that Mark was one of its early teachers. But we would be wise to set no store by its testimony until such time as the original has been scientifically studied by other experts.

$$7$$

THE DATE OF PETER'S
GOING TO ROME

Chapter summary

For many centuries the church of Rome held that Peter arrived
there after his escape from prison in 42. A great weight of
modern authority has been against this, yet there have been
voices on the other side, pre-eminent among them Edmundson,
whose Bampton Lectures of 1913 (*The Church in Rome in the
First Century*) went almost unnoticed. There is a fourfold argument: 1.) There was a world-famous church in Rome in 57 with
which Paul had had contact for some years. 2.) A well-grounded
tradition says that its foundation was laid by Peter in the second
year of Claudius. This agrees with the tradition that the apostles
were dispersed from Jerusalem twelve years after the ascension.
It also explains the remarkable interest in Simon the magician in
Acts. Justin Martyr tells how Simon also went to Rome in the
reign of Claudius and there had a great conflict with Peter. 3.)
This tradition fits without difficulty into the account of Peter in
Acts. 4.) Rome's claim to Petrine foundation was unchallenged
throughout the church.

It is commonly held that Peter only ministered in Rome for a
comparatively short time immediately prior to his martyrdom
in about 67, and that Mark's association with him there must be
placed during that period. But for many centuries the church of
Rome held that Peter in fact arrived there after his escape from
prison in 42 (when it is said that he 'went to *another place*', Acts
12:17)[1] and that he was in some sense the overseer of that
church for twenty-five years. If by any chance the old tradition

146

were correct, it would throw an entirely different light on the dating of Mark's gospel. The substantial truth of the patristic tradition about Mark could be maintained without necessitating a date somewhere after the mid-60s, and a date as early as the mid-40s becomes possible.

Admittedly there is a great weight of modern authority to discourage the taking of the old belief seriously. Here are typical statements by fairly conservative scholars: C. S. C. Williams: 'the Roman Catholic Church claims that Peter went at an early date to Rome and spent twenty-five years there, but there is no evidence for this . . . The tradition . . . is abandoned by the best Roman Catholic scholars.' E. G. Selwyn: 'The tradition . . . is on many grounds improbable.' F. F. Bruce: 'The tradition . . . is contradicted by the evidence of the N.T.' Most important is the verdict of J. B. Lightfoot, whose truly magisterial handling of the material has greatly influenced all subsequent writers: 'It is wholly unhistorical'; 'quite inconsistent with known facts . . . If silence can ever be regarded as decisive its verdict must be accepted in this case.'[2]

Yet there have been voices on the other side. While not going back to 42, T. W. Manson was prepared to argue for a visit *c.* 55.[3] Similarly H. Lietzmann, author of a special study, *Petrus und Paulus in Rom*, also thought that Peter had visited Corinth and had 'quite probably' gone thence to Rome.[4] Of the nine major works on Peter in English this century, seven have been quite disinclined to dismiss the old view. Edmundson in his Bampton Lectures of 1913, *The Church in Rome in the First Century*, offers a sustained defence of the 42 tradition. Foakes Jackson (1927) says: 'That Peter visited Rome after he had escaped from Herod Agrippa's prison is perfectly possible.' Marucchi (1929) argues that Peter arrived in Rome between 41 and 44 and left after the edict of Claudius which expelled the Jews in 49. Underhill (1937) says: 'It seems likely . . . that St. Peter . . . (in 42) made his way to the Eternal City.' Barnes (1938) argues the 42 date in detail. Lowe (1956) says: Peter 'might well have been there earlier' than the date of the epistle to the Romans. Balleine (1958) again argues the case in detail. We have to wait till 1953 (Cullmann) and 1969 (O'Connor) before we find a specialist work on Peter which dismisses the earlier date. O'Connor writes dogmatically:

> It is certain that the proposal concerning the supposed twenty-five year episcopate of Peter was born in the imagination or developed out of genuine confusion . . . It is not known when he came to Rome, how long he stayed, nor what function of leadership he exercised in the Roman Church.

Thiede, on the other hand, writing in 1986, is entirely persuaded that the 'other place' of Acts 12:17 was Rome.[5] Of works not in English, R. Pesch (also in 1986) came out in favour of Peter's arrival in Rome in the second year of Claudius.[6]

It is true that the works which allude to Peter, but do not deal in detail with his movements, frequently set aside the 42 tradition in a peremptory manner, but it is interesting to find that J. A. T. Robinson in 1976 in a general work on the dating of the New Testament had become a convert to Edmundson's view. He concludes:

> One must therefore, I believe, be prepared to take seriously the tradition that Mark . . . accompanied Peter to Rome in 42 as his interpreter and catechist, and that after Peter's departure from the capital he acceded to the reiterated request for a record of the apostle's teaching, perhaps about 45.[7]

There is thus a *prima facie* case for looking at the evidence afresh. Unfortunately it is not possible in the space available to treat it with the fullness that it deserves. To those long accustomed to dismiss the idea as fanciful, it requires a far-reaching reorientation, which is not likely to be achieved on a single reading. One can only make the plea that no one should continue to dismiss the case until they have read with care Edmundson's classic treatment in *The Church in Rome in the First Century*. J. A. T. Robinson in his *Redating the New Testament* constantly refers to Edmundson's erudition and powers of persuasion and to the serious losses incurred by the scholarly world through its almost total ignoring of his work. He speaks of the book as 'scrupulously documented', 'judicious', having 'many merits', exposing error 'in careful argument'.[8]

The argument may be put like this:

1.) There was a large and world-famous church in Rome in 57 with which Paul had had contact for some years.

2.) A well-grounded tradition says that its foundation was laid by Peter in the second year of Claudius.

3.) This fits without difficulty into the account of Peter in Acts.

4.) Rome's claim to Petrine foundation was unchallenged throughout the church.

There was a large and world-famous church in Rome in 57 with which Paul had been in contact for some years

The first point to make clear concerns Acts. Acts is *not* telling the story of how the gospel reached Rome.[9] When Paul arrived in Italy in 60 he found brethren at the great port of Puteoli with whom he stayed for seven days. News of his arrival reached Rome and two deputations came to meet him: 'the brethren there, when they heard of us, came as far as the Forum of Appius and Three Taverns to meet us. On seeing them Paul thanked God and took courage' (Acts 28:13–15). The principal source of our information about the church of Rome in the middle of the century is the epistle to the Romans sent to them three years earlier from Corinth in 57. Judged by this Pauline *Hauptbrief*, as C. H. Dodd says, 'The Church which Paul addressed must have been a large and important one.'[10] There is also information from Acts and from Suetonius. Concerning the account of Suetonius, Edmundson writes:

> disorders seem to have arisen in the Jewish quarter of the city in 50 A.D. of such a threatening character as to force the Government, in spite of its favourable inclination to the Jews, to take strong action. This appears to me to be nothing more than a fair interpretation of Suetonius' words – 'the Jews who were continually rioting at the instigation of Chrestus he (Claudius) expelled from Rome'.[11] To write *Chrestus* for *Christus* was quite natural to a Latin historian, for Chrestus was a name in use at Rome as extant inscriptions show,[12] and both Tertullian and Lactantius[13] tell us that in their time the common pronunciation was 'Chrestus' and 'Chrestianos' . . . Dio

Cassius[14] informs us that the edict of expulsion, owing to the disturbance that it caused, was only partially carried out . . . Among the Jews that were expelled were no doubt the chief leaders of the contending factions. (9f)

Acts 18:1–3 tells us how at Corinth Paul meets Aquila, a fellow-Jew and fellow-native of Asia Minor, who along with his wife Priscilla had 'lately come from Italy . . . because Claudius had commanded all the Jews to leave Rome . . . and because he was of the same trade he stayed with them'. They were evidently Christians before they met Paul and were presumably leaders of the church in Rome prior to their expulsion. Paul's bond with them seems to have been very close, for not only did he live with them in Corinth for eighteen months (18:11), but they came with him to Ephesus (18:18). Their home there soon became a centre of Christian activity (Apollos was instructed by them, 18:26) and Paul probably continued to live with them during his two and a quarter years in Ephesus (19:8, 10), since he sends the fervent greetings of the church in their house to the church in Corinth (1 Cor. 16:19).

Three years later (the edict of Claudius having been allowed to lapse on the emperor's death) we find them back in Rome, presiding again over the church in their home. Paul, now in Corinth, puts them at the top of his long list of greetings in Romans 16, speaking of them in glowing terms – 'my fellow workers in Christ Jesus, who risked their necks for my life [presumably at the time of the Ephesian uproar in Acts 19:23–20:1], to whom not only I but also all the churches of the Gentiles give thanks; greet also the church in their house' (Rom. 16:3–5). 2 Corinthians 1:8–10 gives a vivid idea of the period of 'deadly peril' during which his friends took such risks on his behalf. It seems likely that the friendly Asiarchs (Acts 19:31), who had warned Paul not to venture into the theatre, would have felt it their duty for the sake of the peace of the city to insist that both Paul and his protectors Aquila and Priscilla should leave Ephesus.

It seems probable that a church had met in their home before their expulsion from Rome, and that their property was not confiscated – Dio Cassius (as we have seen) says that the banishment was most leniently carried out. The church (probably consisting of both Gentiles and less conspicuous Jews) would therefore have continued to meet at their house. They, for their part, would have continued to propagate the faith and prosecute their business interests in Corinth and Ephesus, two of the great cities on the main routes of the empire's commerce. (As Dodd says: 'We may put them down as people in a large way of business – just the sort of people who travelled widely in this period.'[15]) Inevitably Christians travelling from Rome would have made a bee-line for their home, with the result that over a period of five or six years Paul would have been in constant personal touch with a stream of Roman Christians. His next step is described by Edmundson:

> St. Paul at the close of his two years' ministry at Ephesus began to look ahead and to plan fresh schemes of missionary activity. His first task was to journey through Macedonia to Corinth, where his presence was called for and needed; his next to pay another visit after a long absence to Jerusalem, but 'after I have been there,' he said, 'I must see Rome' (Acts 19:21) . . . The project of a visit to Rome so long cherished, so often hindered, now began to assume a concrete shape in his mind, and the result was the writing, almost certainly in the early spring of the year 57 A.D., of the Epistle to the Romans. Now this great epistle stands in the forefront of the Pauline writings chiefly as a theological treatise, but apart from its theology it has other claims, as an historical document of the highest evidential value. (13, 14)

Romans tells of the fame of the church. 'I thank my God . . . because your faith is proclaimed in all the world' (1:8). To this Paul adds his own judgement (which would have been an empty compliment if it was not based on personal knowledge of a number of them): 'I myself am satisfied about you, my brethren, that you yourselves are full of goodness, filled with all knowledge, and able to instruct one another' (15:14). His knowledge of the church is not something recently acquired: 'I have longed for many years to come to you' (15:23). 'Many years' probably implies the existence of the church for a decade or more, and the worldwide proclamation of its faith suggests strong growth in spite of the exodus under Claudius.

151

Romans, especially in its greetings, tells of the composition of the church. The right of 16:1–23 to be regarded as an authentic part of the epistle has of course been questioned. But critics are virtually unanimous that it was written by Paul, though some, thinking it improbable that Paul would have been able to greet so many members of a church which he had never visited, have opted for Ephesus (where Aquila and Priscilla are known to have lived, and probably Epaenetus of Asia, Rom. 16:5) as its destination.[16] As we have seen, this is a quite needless speculation.

Note, first, the size of the church implied by Romans 16. Paul greets twenty-five individuals and four groups of Christians. In spite of the comparative ease of travel, the proportion of church members who happened to meet Paul in distant cities must have been a tiny fraction of the total membership. This agrees with the impression given by Suetonius that they were sufficiently numerous to provoke the other Jews of Rome to serious rioting. There is nothing improbable in this. In the ghetto in the Jewish quarter of Rome, Transtiberim, Jewish customs were of course observed. Peter, a devout Jew from the mother-country, would probably have been invited (as Stephen and Paul were) to speak in the synagogues, but when '[God] worked through Peter for the mission to the circumcised' (Gal. 2:8), there would have been sharp tensions and the formation of Christian synagogues. It only required some zealot, like Paul during his former life as a Pharisee in Jerusalem, to be roused in an attempt to suppress the heretics. Nazarene meetings would be broken up, homes wrecked and stones thrown in the streets. With the Christians standing firm and growing in numbers, it is easy to see the riots evoking intervention by the police.[17]

Note, secondly, how far back some of the conversions can be traced. Andronicus and Junia(s) were 'in Christ' before Paul (Rom. 16:7), that is to say, before we know of any evangelisation outside Palestine. This reminds us at once of the existence of the 'visitors from Rome, both Jews and proselytes' to whom Luke calls our attention on the day of Pentecost (Acts 2:10). These 'persons of note' were converted at least as far back as the days of Stephen's activity, and quite possibly in Jerusalem.

Rufus, 'eminent in the Lord' (Rom. 16:13), is probably the Rufus, son of Simon of Cyrene, mentioned by Mark (15:21), which again takes us back to the early Jerusalem church. Simon presumably attended the synagogue of the Cyrenians (Acts 6:9). The family may have found its way to Rome via Antioch, where Paul was at one time a leading member (13:1). We know that the followers of Stephen were scattered as a result of Saul's persecution (8:1) and we know also that Cyrenians were among the first to preach Jesus to the Gentiles of Antioch (11:20). It is not unlikely therefore that Paul's colleague Symeon Niger (13:1) was this same Simon, a dark-skinned man from North Africa.[18] Maybe Rufus' mother, whom Paul greets and describes as 'his mother and mine', was a mother to Paul in that city. The presence of Rufus in Rome as an eminent Christian could well be the fruit of the missionary zeal of the Antioch church.

Concerning the salutations to the households Edmundson says:

> Interesting are the salutations to the households of Aristobulus and Narcissus. These would all be freedmen or slaves. Aristobulus may well have been that grandson of Herod the Great who is described by Josephus as making his permanent home at Rome. This is borne out by the salutation to 'Herodion my kinsman' intervening between those of the two households. The name suggests a member of the family to which Aristobulus belonged. Narcissus can scarcely be any other than the freedman and favourite of Claudius. He had been put to death some three years before this epistle was written, but his slaves and dependents, though they would after his execution be incorporated in the Imperial household, might still retain the distinctive name of *Narcissiani*. It is possible that Aristobulus may have been dead in 57 A.D., and have bequeathed his slaves to the emperor. If so, both these groups would form part of that vast body of freedmen and slaves known as Caesar's Household, to which St. Paul refers writing from Rome to the Philippians: 'all the Saints salute you, specially they of Caesar's Household.'

The two groups of names in verses 14–15 seem to indicate that they were members of two smaller households belonging to private persons. The expression 'all the Churches of Christ salute you' (v.

16) is unique in the New Testament, and when taken in connexion with the language of this epistle elsewhere upon the high repute of the Roman Church may be held (to quote the words of Dr. Hort) to signify that that Church was already 'an object of love and respect to Jewish and Gentile Churches alike.' (26, 27)[19]

Dodd makes the pertinent comment:

When the Neronian persecution broke out, the Christians of Rome were 'a large body' (I Clem. vi.I), 'an immense multitude' (Tacitus, *Annals*, xv.44). Before the end of the first century the evidence of Christian burials is available in the earliest parts of the 'catacombs.' Under Domitian there were Christians among the aristocracy, and even in the imperial family. Perhaps the faith had penetrated upwards from the slaves and freedmen of 'Caesar's household' who were Christians when Paul wrote to Philippi (Phil. iv.22). At any rate, we may infer that the church which in A.D. 64 could be represented as a public danger, and in spite of the persecution made such remarkable progress in the following decades, was already numerous and perhaps influential when Paul addressed the letter to it. (xxviii)

Even taking into account the travellers and refugees from Rome whom Paul must have met in the home of Aquila and Priscilla, it would be surprising if Paul had come to know even one per cent of the church's membership without ever visiting the city. That he knew twenty-nine of them suggests therefore a membership of thousands, rather than scores.[20] (It would have been too artificial to suppose that he sent personal greetings to those he had never met.) It is quite likely that Paul recognised that Jerusalem was doomed and he saw Rome as the future centre of the church.[21] The Jerusalem church was numbered in thousands (Acts 2:41, 47; 4:4; 6:7); Paul knows that the same Spirit of God has been experienced in Rome in great power (Rom. 5:5; 8:2–27; 14:17; 15:13).

According to a well-grounded tradition the foundation of the church in Rome was laid by Peter in the second year of Claudius

A Pauline hint?

In spite of his longing of many years to come to them, Paul was intending only to pay a passing visit to Rome en route for new church-planting in Spain; it was his policy not to preach the gospel where Christ had already been named, lest he 'build on *another man's* foundation' (Rom. 15:20–24). Edmundson thinks that we have here a reference to Peter as the foundation-layer of the Roman church. Indeed he states the matter strongly:

> The meaning of this statement, though the language and sequence of thought are somewhat involved, is . . . as plain and direct as it is possible to be . . . there had . . . been a founder of this great Church of world-wide fame with whom Paul was well acquainted and into whose special sphere of successful preaching he did not think it right to intrude. (28)

But to speak so confidently seems to be reading into the text more than is plainly and directly there. It is not certain that it was anybody or anything in Rome which had hindered Paul from visiting, maybe it was simply the incessant claims of the unevangelised regions and of the churches which he himself had founded. His form of words, however, does *seem* to suggest that Rome had a founder, even though it does not directly say so. ἀλλότριον need not imply foundation by one particular man, as the word is fairly general and could be translated negatively 'not my own'. But it gains force if (as missionary experience in general confirms) the church of Rome did not arise merely through the chance movements of Christian converts, but was in large measure the result of one man's vision and work.[22] Even more so if he was the very man who was to be acknowledged as the leader in the establishment of (predominantly) Jewish churches, while Paul himself was to be acknowledged as the leader in the establishment of (predominantly) Gentile churches (Gal. 2:7–9). In the case of his own churches Paul certainly identifies himself specifically as 'the master-builder' who laid a foundation (1 Cor. 3:10). It makes excellent sense to see here a desire not to trespass in a field for which another man was responsible. Is there a good alternative?

Supposing Paul had nothing of the sort in mind, knowing of no one who was regarded as founder – would he have used the language of inhibition? He would not have been intruding into someone else's province. His sole reason for making only a short visit would presumably have been conscientious scruples about giving time to a church whose foundations he had not laid, while Spain still had no church. Seeing he found time to send them a weighty epistle and time to visit Jerusalem, and he looked forward to bringing them blessing when he came in person, it scarcely seems probable that he would have felt so inhibited. 'Lest I build on another man's foundation' makes good sense and is probably the best translation.

Edmundson 83 and Robinson 113 believe that Paul's inhibitions derived not merely from Peter's ministry in Rome in the early days of Claudius, but from his actual presence there during a further spell of work in the city in 55–56.[23] Be that as it may, Paul had a longing to see his many friends there, and as a 'minister to the Gentiles' he longed to impart some spiritual gift for their blessing, but (it seems) he could not in conscience do so for more than a short visit if he was intruding into another man's sphere of authority.

The tradition

There have been those, moved either by Protestant prejudice or extreme scepticism, who have denied that Peter ever set foot in Rome.[24] But virtually all scholars now agree that he met his end in or near the capital city. When it comes to the question of how long he spent there opinions are divided. Some hold that he spent one short spell in Rome which ended in his death around the year 67. Others hold that he paid more than one visit and that a period of twenty-five years spanned the time from his first arrival to his death.

The twenty-five-year tradition was the standard teaching of the church of Rome probably from the mid-second century till quite modern times,[25] and it is this tradition which Edmundson believes to be sound. One of the most thorough expositions of the contrary point of view is that of D. W. O'Connor, *Peter in Rome: The Literary, Liturgical and Archeological Evidence*, written in 1969, which comes to the conclusion that Peter 'did visit Rome . . . But it is not known when he came to Rome, how long he stayed, nor what function of leadership he exercised in the Roman Church.'[26] It may be well to compare the arguments of these two writers.

O'Connor stresses the divergences in the tradition. Peter's founding and twenty-five-year 'episcopate'[27] of the church in Rome is to be found in the 'extremely influential' *Liber Pontificalis*,[28] which according to O'Connor 32f, was compiled between 514 and 530 and was based on the *Liberian Catalogue* of the Roman Bishops, 'a composite document utilizing material from various traditions'. Concerning this he says,

> By his uncritical appropriation of the *Liberian Catalogue*, the author of the *Liber Pontificalis* reveals that he either did not bother to consult other lists or did not know of their existence. Much of the author's material concerning the life of Peter is derived from Jerome's *De Viris Illustribus* 1.

There are indeed serious inconsistencies in the sources: the *Liber Pontificalis* follows the *Liberian Catalogue* only in parts, and with regard to the dates of the Petrine 'episcopate' follows Jerome, who dates it from the second year of Claudius to the last year of Nero (i.e. 42–67) whereas the *Liberian Catalogue* dates it from the Lord's ascension (i.e. 30) to 55. Consequently L. M. O. Duchesne said that the coming of Peter to Rome under Claudius 'lacks sufficient foundation to win the assent of history'.[29]

Edmundson, on the other hand, points to the convergences (68–72). He notes, first, that Jerome deliberately follows the *Chronicon* of Eusebius, whose episcopal lists are based on those of Hegesippus and Irenaeus, which came from 'documents belonging to the second half of the second century', whereas the *Liberian Catalogue* is based 'on a chronicler, most probably Hippolytus, about fifty years later. Now both the Eusebian Chronicle and the Liberian Catalogue give twenty-five years as the term of St. Peter's "episcopacy", but they differ as to the dates at its beginning and its end.'[30] Secondly, Jerome was secretary to Pope Damasus at the time of the latter's death in 384. Damasus has justly been termed the first Christian archaeologist and he was especially interested in the early history of the church in Rome. Jerome must have had access to the papal archives and he tells us that as a young man he himself visited the sepulchres of the apostles and martyrs. Thirdly, Jerome between 382 and 384 must have met Filocalus, who was the illuminator and probably the editor of the *Liberian Catalogue*. Fourthly, his divergences from the *Liberian Catalogue*, which is 'full of blunders', must be deliberate. Duchesne, who had expressed confidence in the figures given in the *Liber Pontificalis* for the duration of the episcopates only after the time of Xystus (117–26), says nonetheless: 'as regards St. Peter and the figure of his twenty-five years [this] is as well attested as the figures of the years of his successors after Xystus I'.[31]

Tradition claiming the authority of Jerome of the fourth century and apparently of Hegesippus, Irenaeus and Hippolytus of the second century, all of whom had first-hand knowledge of Rome, carries weight. The weightiest objection is the silence of the earliest sources. We shall consider the silence of the New Testament in due course, but what of the absence of other records of the first century and the first half of the second? Humanly speaking it is of course purely a matter of chance whether a writer happens to mention some well-known fact. Clement of Rome, writing to the Corinthians on the evil consequences of jealousy, speaks in chapter 5 of 'those who contended for the faith in our own time'. The names that immediately spring to his mind are 'the greatest and most righteous pillars' Peter and Paul, whom he mentions in that order. He is concerned about their sufferings and death and has no occasion to refer to the time of their arrival in Rome. It should be noted that, although Paul-in-Rome has the immense advantage of clear documentation in Acts and Peter-in-Rome has no explicit scriptural attestation, Peter is always mentioned first in the earliest sources. To quote Edmundson:

Ignatius in his Epistle to the Romans written about 109 A.D. says: 'I do not command you like Peter and Paul; they were Apostles; I am a condemned criminal.'[32] Dionysius of Corinth 171 A.D. writing to Soter bishop of Rome[33] speaks 'of the plantation by Peter and Paul that took place among the Romans and the Corinthians.' Irenaeus a few years later is filled with respect for the 'most great and ancient and universally known Church established at Rome by the two most glorious Apostles Peter and Paul, and also the faith declared to men, which comes down to our own time through the succession of her bishops. For unto this Church, on account of its more powerful lead, every Church, meaning the faithful who are from everywhere, must needs resort; since in it that tradition which is from the Apostles has been preserved by those who are from everywhere. The Blessed Apostles, having founded and established the Church, entrusted the office of the episcopate to Linus. Paul speaks of this Linus in his epistles to Timothy, Anencletus succeeded him, and after Anencletus, in the third place from the Apostles, Clement received the episcopate.' Now Irenaeus, who was a disciple of Polycarp, and acquainted with others who had known St. John, and who in 177 A.D. became bishop of Lyons, had spent some years in Rome. This passage was written, as he tells us,[34] in the time of Eleutherus, probably about 180 A.D. (48f)

This precedence of Peter seems unlikely if his brief residence in Rome was some years after Paul's two years of fruitful work in the city, but quite natural if his overseership lasted twenty-five years.[35] To speak of Peter and Paul as founding the church also seems unlikely if neither apostle appeared on the scene until several years after the faith of the church had become world-famous. It would, however, have been easy to couple the illustrious name of Paul to that of Peter, when in retrospect it was seen how the hand of God had brought both of them to the capital of the empire, not only to establish and build up the church but also to earn a martyr's crown.

A conscientious historian may say that second-century traditions are not good enough and adopt the sceptical attitude of O'Connor and so many others. But if we do so it is possible that we are doing grave injustice to Eusebius, Jerome and other great scholars of the early church. Edmundson stresses the literacy of the age and the wholesale and repeated destruction of Christian documents during the early centuries, especially under Diocletian (45–51).[36] 'But though the documents themselves disappeared, the memory of their contents would remain to be worked up afresh into new narratives tinged with opinions, beliefs and modes of thought of the time at which they were written' (46). It is the task of the historian to eliminate the fancies and to hold fast the memory of the community. Edmundson offers four criteria which should be satisfied before accepting such a tradition as embodying history: 1.) there must have been a great number of witnesses; 2.) the beginning of the tradition must not be too remote from the events; 3.) not long after the first record of the tradition there should appear in the community a general persuasion of its truth; 4.) the facts should be accepted everywhere, even by those who might have desired to reject them. All these criteria are fulfilled by the Petrine tradition. The evidence may be variously assessed, but the tradition should not be lightly dismissed.

Further elements of the tradition pointing to 42

Other elements of the tradition which should be mentioned concern a) the belief that the apostles had instructions to remain in Jerusalem as their centre of operations for twelve years after the ascension of Jesus, and b) the belief that Simon Magus went to Rome in the reign of Claudius and that Peter confronted him there.

A twelve-year stay in Jerusalem

Harnack perhaps exaggerated slightly in declaring the twelve-year residence in Jerusalem to be 'a very old and well-attested tradition'.[37] Our direct early evidence consists of three statements. 1.) Eusebius refers to a book against the Montanists (written about 200?) by Apollonius: 'He says, as though from tradition, that the Saviour ordered His apostles not to leave Jerusalem for twelve years.'[38] 2.) *Acts of Peter*, also to be dated perhaps 180–90, tells of a vision given to Peter in Jerusalem in which he is told to set sail for Rome in pursuit of Simon the sorcerer 'now that the twelve years in Jerusalem which the Lord Christ had enjoined on him were completed'.[39] 3.) Clement of Alexandria in his *Stromateis* of about the same date quotes the lost *Preaching of Peter*: 'Peter records that the Lord had said to the disciples: If now anyone of Israel wishes to repent and through my name to believe in God, his sins will be forgiven him. And after twelve years go ye out into the world that no one may say: "We have not heard [it]." '[40] There are thus three statements from about 200 or earlier, one of them explicitly based on an even earlier document.

This tradition tallies with certain indications in Acts. At the time of Stephen's death the persecution was apparently directed against the Hellenistic Jewish Christian leaders and not against the apostles, whose orthopraxy was evidently not questioned, for we are told 'they were all scattered throughout the region of Judea and Samaria, *except the apostles*' (Acts 8:1). But when Herod Agrippa I came to power in 41 things had changed considerably. According to Josephus,[41] Agrippa had been richly rewarded by Claudius for the important part which he played in securing the emperor's peaceful accession, and:

> He was especially desirous of impressing [his new subjects] with his careful observance of the Mosaic law and his zeal for the national religion, being to some extent suspect through his long residence in Rome and alien descent.[42] Accordingly having gone to Jerusalem to keep the first Passover after his accession, he resolved to give a signal mark of his fervour as a defender of the faith, by the summary execution of James the son of Zebedee. Possibly he was the only one of the Christian leaders on whom for the moment he could lay hands. But finding his action had pleased the Jews, he proceeded to arrest Peter also . . . There is no hint that the Twelve were at Jerusalem at this critical time. St. Peter himself does not seem to have been there when St. James was beheaded. His parting words (Acts 12:17) point to the two conclusions: (1) that the other James, the Lord's brother, was already the recognised head of the Jerusalem community; and (2) that the speaker had no expectation of being able to tell his tale to 'James and the brethren' in person. The explanation however lies to our hand, if we accept the ancient and well-attested tradition of which I have already spoken, that the Lord Jesus had bidden his Apostles to make Jerusalem the centre of their missionary activity for twelve years, after which they were to disperse and go forth to preach to the nations. Already before Herod Agrippa struck his blow the Twelve had begun to set out each one to his allotted sphere of evangelisation. (Edmundson 42, 43)

Even if the supposed instruction by Jesus to stay for twelve years is apocryphal, the tradition may well be a witness to what in fact happened: that there was a general dispersal of the apostles at about this time.[43]

Simon Magus in the reign of Claudius

In Acts 8:4–25 comes the founding of the church in Samaria, in Luke's mind clearly a strategic development (Acts 1:8). Strangely, eleven verses (more than half the narrative) are given to the doings of one Simon, who practised magic arts in the city. Why such interest in this man?

> Eusebius[44] tells us, on the authority of Justin Martyr (a passage of whose 'Apology'[45] he quotes at length), that a certain Simon of the village of Gitton in Samaria, whom nearly all the Samaritans worshipped, confessing him to be the Supreme God, came to Rome in the reign of Claudius Caesar and having there performed many magic rites was regarded as a god. After further describing, this time on the authority of Irenaeus, the character of this man's teaching, as being the fountain-head of all heresy, Eusebius proceeds to say that when in Judaea Simon was convicted of his wickedness by the Apostle Peter, and later journeying from the east to the west arrived at Rome and was there successful in bringing many to believe in his pretensions. 'Not for long, however,' adds the historian, 'did his success continue; for on his steps in this same reign of Claudius, . . . God conducts . . . Peter . . . to Rome.'
>
> With regard to this second century evidence, how is it possible to set aside the statements of Justin Martyr and Irenaeus? The evidence of Justin is of great weight. He was himself born at Flavia Neapolis in Samaria in 103 A.D., a place only a few miles distant from the native place of Simon Magus. His account of Simon's earlier activity and great success in the neighbourhood of his own home must be regarded as first-hand evidence, and it is in exact agreement with the other account of that earlier activity which we have in the eighth chapter of the Acts, an account which it is more than probable that St. Luke derived directly from that best of all witnesses, Philip the Evangelist. I have already pointed out that the emphasis with which St. Luke dwells upon this episode of the encounter between Peter and Simon at Samaria suggests that he had in his mind that later encounter at Rome, which would be fresh in the memories of the first readers of the Acts. Be this as it may, Justin was himself at Rome for some years between 150 and 160

A.D., and wrote his 'Apology' to the Emperor Antoninus Pius in that city. In writing a defence intended for the Imperial eyes it may surely be taken for granted that Justin would not twice over have ventured (for in a slightly different form in ch. 56 he repeats the statement from ch. 26 already quoted) to declare that the magician Simon of Samaria visited Rome in the reign of Claudius and that a statue was erected in his honour and that he was worshipped as a god, unless it were well known that such had been the case.

The evidence of Irenaeus, who was in Rome some ten or fifteen years after Justin, is equally striking. Irenaeus writes at some length about Simon . . . Hippolytus, who is described as a disciple of Irenaeus, spent at least twenty years of his life at or near Rome and also travelled widely. He devotes a long section of his sixth book, which was probably written about 225 A.D., to an account of the heresy of which Simon was the author. Of the man himself he writes: 'This Simon deceiving many by his sorceries in Samaria was reproved by the Apostles and was laid under a curse, as it has been written in the Acts. But he afterwards abjured the faith and attempted [these practices]. And journeying as far as Rome he fell in with the Apostle[s], and to him, deceiving many by his sorceries, Peter offered repeated opposition.'[46] Here then is another absolutely clear statement that Simon went to Rome and there encountered St. Peter. (Edmundson 60–64)

The element of this tradition which is of particular significance to us is its reference to the reign of Claudius. The confrontation with Simon is not connected with the Neronian persecution but with the founding of the church in the days of Claudius.

Edmundson in his account of the earliest days of the Roman church compares them with those in Antioch:

> Events at Rome probably followed on precisely the same lines. Just as the men of Cyprus and Cyrene in the face of persecution made their way back to their own homes carrying with them the message of the Gospel, so would it be with some of 'the sojourners of Rome' belonging to the Synagogue of the Libertines. They would return to the capital inspired by the spirit and example of St. Stephen to form there the first nucleus of a Christian community. As I have already suggested, St. Paul's salutation to Andronicus and Junias seems to point to these two men as the leaders of this first missionary band. Among those converted would be, as at Antioch, both Jews and Gentiles.

163

Some time may well have elapsed before any news of these first small beginnings of Christianity in Rome reached Jerusalem. Possibly St. Peter's intercourse with Cornelius the centurion and his relatives and friends at Caesarea first made him acquainted with the fact that the Gospel had obtained a foothold in the capital, for the body of troops to which Cornelius belonged – the *Cohors Italica* – consisted of volunteers from Italy. From this source too he may in due course have learnt that Simon Magus was in Rome, and that there as in Samaria previously he was proclaiming himself 'to be the Great Power of God' and was leading many astray by his magical arts.

This information in any case, whether derived from Cornelius or from Roman Christians, who came up for the feasts, would reach the Apostles about the time when their twelve years' residence in Jerusalem was drawing to a close, and when, according to tradition, they divided among themselves separate spheres of missionary work abroad. To St. Peter, as the recognised leader, it may well have been that the charge of the Christian Church in the Imperial capital should have been assigned as the post of honour. If so, it will be seen that the persecution of Herod Agrippa only hastened on a journey already planned. After his imprisonment and escape St. Peter's first object would be to place himself out of the reach of the persecutor and to set about his voyage as quickly as possible. If so, his arrival at Rome would be in the early summer of 42 A.D., the date given by St. Jerome. (57, 58)

Archaeology confirms the tradition?

The findings of archaeology consist of a myriad of details insignificant on their own and impossible to present concisely. They have different effects on different people. They are easily dismissed by those who have rejected the Petrine tradition on other grounds, yet to some of those who have given a lifetime to the study of early Christianity in Rome they seem to add weight to the tradition. One of the latter is Orazio Marucchi, who is described by O'Connor as 'the eminent Roman Catholic archaeologist, author of over fifty-five books and articles related to the subject of Peter and Paul in Rome'.[47] His researches and those of G. B. De Rossi and R. Lanciani have obviously deeply impressed Edmundson and Barnes, who consider that they

164

confirm a number of the early traditions. The very frequency of references to Peter in the earliest inscriptions, while not of themselves necessitating an early date for his arrival, suggest 'a considerable residence' in Rome. Of particular interest is an example given by Edmundson:

> On a large number of early Christian *sarcophagi* now in the Lateran Museum the imprisonment of Peter by Herod Agrippa and his release by the angel is represented. The French historian of the 'Persecutions of the first two Centuries,' Paul Allard, was the first to point out that the frequency with which this subject was chosen might be accounted for by the existence of a traditional belief in a close connection between this event and the first visit of St. Peter to Rome. (53)

This tradition fits without difficulty into the account of Peter in Acts

Direct evidence for Peter's movements after the death of Stephen is scanty: we find him at Samaria (Acts 8:14), and moving about among all the growing churches of Judea, Galilee and Samaria (9:31ff); we find him initiating the first Gentile mission at Caesarea (10:1–11:18). During Agrippa's reign (41–44) he escaped from Jerusalem and fled Agrippa's territory (12:1–17). He was in Jerusalem again for the visit of Paul and Barnabas in 46 (Gal. 2:1–10)[48] and for the Apostolic Council of 49 (Acts 15:1–21). He visited Antioch (Gal. 2:11)[49] and had associations with the churches in Asia Minor (1 Pet. 1:1). In 54 Paul can speak of Peter 'leading around a wife', presumably moving from place to place in missionary work (1 Cor. 9:5).

This shows that Peter was not a resident ἐπίσκοπος in Rome for twenty-five years. But before its appropriation by the developing Christian church ἐπίσκοπος was not a technical ecclesiastical term and it would have been a suitable description, for instance, of Paul as non-residential overseer of the churches which he had founded. In Acts 15:36 Paul went with Barnabas on a pastoral visitation (ἐπισκεψώμεθα) of all the cities where he had founded churches. If Peter twenty-five years before his death worked for a time in Rome, evangelising and organising a church with which he kept in touch thereafter, he could rightly have been regarded as its overseer. There is plenty of room consistent with his movements recorded above for residence in Rome in any part of 42–45 or 50–67 (except presumably in 57 when he is sent no greetings in Romans), and we might *possibly* infer his absence from the silence of Paul's prison epistles, *if* any of them were written in Rome. Chronologically the twenty-five year 'episcopate' spans the period from Agrippa to Nero neatly. Agrippa's reign was 41–44 and Nero died in 68, which tallies well with Eusebius who dates the episcopate from 42 to 67. That Peter could have escaped to Rome is clear enough: 'There was no small stir . . . over what had become of Peter. And when Herod had sought for him and could not find him, he examined the sentries and ordered that they should be put to death' (Acts 12:18f). Agrippa was in deadly earnest and Peter in deadly peril. To escape to a neighbouring province would have been to invite extradition, but the ports (where Peter had friends) were full of ships waiting to take the Passover pilgrims home. Peter could have escaped to Egypt, Ephesus, Carthage, Spain, but none of these places claims him. The most likely place in the world to harbour an escaped prisoner was also the home of a vast Jewish population; Rome presented to the one who was later to be described as 'the apostle to the circumcision' an open invitation to an inexhaustible field of work.[50]

We must not attach great importance to the silence of Acts concerning Peter in Rome.[51] It cannot be sufficiently stressed that 'The Acts of the Apostles' is a misnomer. It is a highly selective account of *some* apostles.[52] Although it gives considerable detail about the doings of Paul, it is very selective even about him. His doings between his conversion and his call to Antioch are largely passed over. But that his life at that time was busy and eventful is revealed by chance allusions in his letters. Writing to the Galatians (1:17–2:1) he recalls:

> I went away into Arabia . . . I returned to Damascus . . . after three years I went up to Jerusalem to visit Cephas, and remained with him fifteen days . . . Then I went into the regions of Syria and Cilicia . . . Then after fourteen years I went up again to Jeru-

salem . . . when Cephas came to Antioch I opposed him to his face . . .

Writing to the Corinthians about 56, he can already say

> far greater labours, far more imprisonments, with countless beat-
> ings, and often near death. Five times I have received at the hands
> of the Jews the forty lashes less one. Three times I have been beaten
> with rods; once I was stoned. Three times I have been shipwrecked;
> a night and a day I have been adrift at sea . . . At Damascus . . . I
> was let down in a basket through a window in the wall, and escaped.
> (2 Cor. 11:23–33)

Although there are occasional points of contact between these autobiographical references and Luke's narration in Acts, we are aware of our almost complete ignorance concerning the dozen years of intense toil which followed Paul's return to his native Tarsus and which were concluded by his summons to Antioch to join in the Gentile mission. What Acts gives us in fact is a very incomplete account of the progress of the gospel northwards from Jerusalem to Samaria and thence into Asia Minor; then of Paul's mission westwards to Greece and Italy.

But of the progress of the gospel eastwards and southwards there are only the barest hints. Even of the mission northwards and westwards the account is selective. Galilee, home of most of the apostles and sphere of much of Jesus' work, must have been a Christian stronghold, but its history is passed over. We know that the church of Rome was world-famous by 57, but the story of its founding is left untold. We know that Paul had his sights on Spain, but we are not given the story of its evangelisation. When it comes to Peter, Acts tells us a good deal about him up to chapter 12, but apart from a brief mention in chapter 15, it tells us nothing about where he went or what he did for the rest of his doubtless active life. Of the doings of the other apostles, we are told almost nothing. They are named individually in chapter 1 as witnesses commissioned to go 'to the end of the earth', but where they went Luke does not tell us. Yet surely they and the hundreds of others who were commissioned by Jesus,[53] and many of their converts, were busy telling the good news wherever they went.

167

The ground had been prepared throughout Jewry for the reception of the gospel, as is evidenced by Apollos, who had imbibed the teaching of John the Baptist and knew much of the teaching of Jesus. It seems likely that Luke intends us to understand that many of the visitors to Jerusalem on the day of Pentecost not only listened, but believed – though some mocked, others listened with wondering amazement. Included among them were Jews from the East: Parthia, Media, Elam, Mesopotamia and Arabia. There were probably stories to tell about all these places, but it is not Luke's purpose to relate them. Furthermore, it should not be forgotten that Eusebius at the end of Book 1 and the beginning of Book 2 of his *Historia Ecclesiastica* devotes a great deal of space to the evangelisation of Edessa and the kingdom of the Osrhoenes by Thaddaeus,[54] which he seems to place very shortly after Christ's resurrection. His narrative is taken from the archives of Edessa which he read in the original Syriac. Problematic though it is, there may well be some historical basis for this narrative, but Acts says nothing about it. The same applies to the ancient church of South India, which firmly holds that it was planted by Thomas.[55]

At Pentecost there were Jews also from the South, from 'Egypt and the parts of Libya belonging to Cyrene' (Acts 2:10). Luke tells us that Apollos the Alexandrian later became a fully instructed Christian (18:24–28), and he tells us about a distinguished convert from the court of Candace in Ethiopia (= Sudan) (8:27), who came to Jerusalem an earnest student of scripture and returned home a joyful believer long before Paul had been launched on the imperial highways of Asia and Europe. He tells us also of Stephen's impact on the Cyrenians and Alexandrians in their synagogue in Jerusalem (6:9), men who would inevitably have been in frequent touch with their fellow-countrymen at the great festivals. The letter of Claudius to the Alexandrines dated 41 refers to 'Jews who sail down to Alexandria from Syria' being introduced into the city.[56] As Syria included Antioch and Jerusalem, this is direct evidence of continuous contact between Alexandria and the cradle of Christianity. It is difficult to believe that there were not many Jews in the synagogues of Egypt with some degree of belief in

Jesus within a few years of Pentecost, all ready after proper instruction to be organised into a Christian ecclesia. The fact that Luke does not mention it is neither here nor there. The latter part of Acts is concerned with Paul; Luke sticks to his last and does not stray into the later history of Peter.[57]

Mark in fact fits readily into the pattern of events required by the old tradition. If Peter did go to Rome as suggested, we may believe that he proceeded to evangelise its teeming Jewish population with energy and determination. It is unlikely that he was content to work single-handed. There were many Christian workers who had become mature and experienced in the twelve years since the end of Christ's ministry, of whom Mark was doubtless one. Peter would have left for the 'other place' from Mark's home, and Mark may have gone with him on his journey. If not, he was presumably summoned to join him soon after. This ties in with the witness of Papias, Irenaeus, the Anti-Marcionite Prologue, Clement of Alexandria and Origen, which points to an association of Peter and Mark in proclaiming the gospel in Italy. Others like Rufus and Alexander, sons of Simon of Cyrene (Mark 15:21; Rom. 16:13), seem to have come over to Rome too, since they were known to Mark's readers.

Now while Peter was in Rome, a highly successful work among Gentiles was developing in Antioch, which had begun with the witness of some 'men of Cyprus and Cyrene', and had resulted in 'a great number' believing. Barnabas, himself a Cypriot, was sent down from Jerusalem, and he in turn sought the help of Saul, then at Tarsus (Acts 11:19–30). The development of Gentile work created enormous tensions between Jerusalem and Antioch, and these may well have been the cause of Peter's leaving Rome. Agrippa was dead, and with the church involved in the greatest crisis of its history, the chief of the apostles may have seen it as his duty to leave his own important work in order to tackle the situation. In any case we find Peter in Jerusalem in 46, when Saul and Barnabas brought the famine relief.[58] He took counsel with James and John, and the three of them received Paul and Barnabas and it was then that they came to an understanding about their respective spheres of work.

169

Peter's departure from Rome seems to provide the ideal *Sitz im Leben* for the writing of Mark's gospel. His converts' desire for a permanent record of his teaching, and the uncertainties concerning the future of the Jewish population which culminated in the order for their expulsion from the city in 49, would both have made its writing desirable. It is reasonable to suppose that Peter left Mark behind and that he then wrote his gospel.[59]

It is interesting to speculate whether there might be a particular, deliberate reason for omitting all reference to Peter-in-Rome. A. S. Barnes conjectured that Acts was published in Rome during the Neronian persecution. If this is so (he thinks),

> we can at once see a reason for the complete silence of the writer as to any connection of St. Peter with Rome, and for the absence of any hint that St. Paul had returned to the city. For they, as well-known leaders of the persecuted sect, were both in all probability at that moment fugitives in hiding, liable in case of capture to instant execution.[60]

But it is difficult to see how in these circumstances some accurate knowledge of their former doings (including presumably a successful appeal by Paul to Caesar) could have increased their danger.

A more probable reason is this. If, as we shall argue, Acts was published in Rome while Paul was awaiting trial, it may have been intended not only for the edification of the church, but also for the instruction of those of its members who were in touch with people of influence in the city. We have no means of telling whether the κράτιστος Theophilus was resident in Rome at the time. If he was, he could have been one such. He had been instructed in the faith (Luke 1:4) and, being Luke's literary patron, he was a person of some social standing and was possibly an official.[61] Clement of Alexandria when referring to those in Rome who requested from Mark a written record of Peter's teaching specifically calls them *equites*.[62] More than this, there seem to have been Christian connections with the Imperial house. To quote Edmundson:

> It has generally been assumed that the mass of the early Christians belonged to the lowest classes and that many of them were slaves.

170

This is no doubt to a certain extent true, but not by any means altogether so. Aquila and Prisca may have belonged to the 'freedman' class, but they were well-to-do people, and it is probable that Prisca was Roman by birth and a person of some position. Again, after dismissing all that is worthless and utterly fictitious in the account given of Clement's family and their adventures in the so-called Clementine literature, that literature bears evidence that long after his death Clement was given a place apart among the men of the sub-apostolic age not merely because he was a disciple of St. Peter or the author of a well-known epistle, but because he was connected by ties of relationship with the Imperial house. It seems unlikely that Ebionite writers in Eastern lands should have gone out of their way to lay stress on this relationship, unless it had some foundation in fact. (85)[63]

Rome's claim to Petrine foundation was unchallenged throughout the church

To quote Edmundson once again:

Probably never was any tradition accepted so universally, and without a single dissentient voice, as that which associates the foundation and organisation of the Church of Rome with the name of St. Peter and which speaks of his active connexion with that church as extending over a period of some twenty-five years.

It is needless to multiply references. In Egypt and in Africa, in the East and in the West, no other place ever disputed with Rome the honour of being the see of St. Peter; no other place ever claimed that he died there or that it possessed his tomb. Most significant of all is the *consensus* of the Oriental, non-Greek-speaking, Churches. A close examination of Armenian and Syrian MSS, and in the case of the latter both of Nestorian and Jacobite authorities, through several centuries, has failed to discover a single writer who did not accept the Roman Petrine tradition. (51)

The argument is cumulative. Paul seems to have regarded this large and world-famous church as having a founder. An immensely strong tradition, accepted by the most learned men in the early church, says that its foundation was laid by Peter in the second year of the reign of Claudius. This is indirectly and independently confirmed by the traditions concerning the apostles' twelve-year stay in Jerusalem and concerning Peter's confrontation with Simon Magus in Rome. The movements of Peter and Mark as seen in the rest of the New Testament readily fit in. The tradition was unchallenged throughout the church.

The only objection is the silence of Acts and other very early sources. The argument from silence is worth little, and in this instance it can in any case be satisfactorily explained. J. B. Lightfoot's statement (p. 147 above) that 'If silence can ever be regarded as decisive its verdict must be accepted in this case,' seems to be a powerful illustration of the frailty of such argument. Similarly O'Connor's statement that 'There is not a single clue which points' to Peter as the 'other man' who laid the foundation of the church in Rome (8), seems to betray a historical blind-spot. If this ancient tradition can be re-established as one of the probabilities of history (as I believe it should be), it will revolutionise our understanding of the history of the apostolic church, and will encourage a reconsideration of the dating of the gospels.

8

MARK'S GOSPEL: FURTHER CONSIDERATIONS

Chapter summary

Further external considerations. Coptic tradition makes the undistinguished Mark founder of the church of Alexandria. This is clearly stated by Eusebius, who gives the names of the bishops who succeeded him; also by *The Apostolic Constitutions* and by Epiphanius. P52 gives direct evidence of a church in Egypt early in the second century. There is a whole decade in the 50s when Mark could have been evangelising Egypt and Cyrenaica.

The fragment 7Q5 recovered from Cave 7 at Qumran which was sealed in the year 68 is confidently claimed by O'Callaghan as from Mark 6:52f. He answers two objections: 1.) a *tau* is read at one point where the ordinary text reads *delta*. But this is a common trait in Egyptian biblical papyri. 2.) επι την γην is missing. But this phrase is also missing in some Coptic MSS of Mark. This identification is a possibility which should be taken seriously.

A further internal consideration is the argument of H. D. A. Major which sees in Mark *Reminiscences of Jesus by an Eye-Witness*. This provides an easier explanation of Mark's characteristics than the postulation of literary genius.

Further external considerations

Mark and Alexandria

Another possible source of information about the writing of Mark's gospel is the tradition of the Alexandrian church. We have seen that the dismissal of the age-long tradition of the Roman church by nineteenth-century scholars may have been ill judged. Perhaps the same applies to Alexandria.

There is indeed an interesting tradition, which (if true) would add much to our knowledge of the New Testament church and would underline the selectiveness of Acts, but since it does not greatly affect the dating of the gospel we must deal with it only briefly. Eusebius declares:

> They say[1] that this Mark was the first to be sent to preach in Egypt the gospel which he had also put into writing, and was the first to establish churches in Alexandria itself. (*HE* 2.16)

> [The churches] that are in Egypt and in Alexandria itself, did he [Simon] again, not by his own means, but by those of Mark his disciple, erect, he made his disciple Mark the teacher and fisherman of those in Egypt. (*Theophania* 4.7)[2]

> In the eighth year of the reign of Nero, Annianus was the first after Mark the Evangelist to receive charge of the diocese of Alexandria. (*HE* 2.24)

In addition Eusebius (with his great concern for chronology) is not content with generalisations, he gives the names of the successive bishops of Alexandria at the appropriate places in his narrative, as he does for Rome, Antioch and Jerusalem: Annianus, Abilius, Cerdo, Primus, Justus, Eumenes (*HE* 3.21; 4.1; 4.4; 4.5.5). It is unsafe to infer from the brevity of his references to them that they never in fact existed.

Jerome writes:

> Mark . . . wrote a short gospel at the request of the brethren at Rome . . . taking the gospel which he himself had composed, he went to Egypt and first preaching Christ at Alexandria he formed a church . . . He died in the eighth year of Nero and was buried at Alexandria, Annianus succeeding him. (*De Vir. Ill.8*)

The Apostolic Constitutions (7.46) from fourth-century Syria similarly recall that Annianus was the first of the church of the Alexandrians to be consecrated by Mark the Evangelist. Epiphanius (*Adv. Haer.* 51.6) from fourth-century Cyprus

174

says: 'Mark, having written the gospel, is sent by the holy Peter to the region of Egypt.' The Roman Martyrology for 25 April gives St Anianus (*sic*) as a disciple of Mark and as his successor in the episcopate at Alexandria.[3]

Thus in the fourth century, not only does Alexandria claim Mark as its founder, but this claim is acknowledged in East and West, and it has remained the steadfast tradition of the Coptic church to the present day.[4] When it is remembered that Mark (though connected with Peter and Paul) was not an apostle, that his career as recorded in the New Testament was (to put it mildly) undistinguished, and that his gospel was relatively unesteemed in the early church, this claim, coming from the second city of the Roman Empire, cannot be lightly dismissed.[5] It has become customary not only to dismiss the notion of Mark establishing the church in Alexandria, but to date the establishment of an organised church there much later.[6] But the later the founding of the church is put, the more extraordinary becomes the choice of Mark as its founding father. The church's tradition has a presumption in its favour, unless the counter-arguments prove to be very strong. As with Peter's early visit to Rome, the main counter-arguments are all arguments from silence and are not weighty.[7] It is a case of putting Eusebius' encyclopedic knowledge of the Eastern church together with the solid tradition of the Copts against conclusions based on what Roberts calls 'the jejune and scrappy references'[8] available to present-day scholars in our extant literary sources.

We have, as it happens, one noteworthy piece of direct evidence of a church in Egypt before 150. The oldest generally recognised manuscript fragment of the New Testament comes precisely from Egypt, well up the Nile. The John Rylands Library fragment of John 18:31–33 (P52) is early second century. We do not of course know (as G. D. Kilpatrick points out)[9] that it was actually written in Egypt, but the presumption that it was a product of this (very literary) part of the world, and not an import, must be great. The chance of such a fragment being preserved would be far greater if an organised church had existed for half a century, continually producing scriptures for its members' use, than if it had been the possession of some isolated believer who worshipped in the synagogue or of some visiting Christian from outside Egypt.

Furthermore, the mere fact of the dynamism of the early church at a time when there was busy traffic by land and sea between Egypt and the province of Syria,[10] makes it improbable in the extreme that Egypt did not have its churches at an early stage. That Paul, about to set out for Jerusalem, should say that he no longer had any room for work in these regions and hoped to go to Spain (Rom. 15:23f), seems to confirm this, suggesting, as it does, that at least the eastern section of the African shore of the Mediterranean had been catered for.

Apollos (Acts 18:24f) is a direct witness that some sort of Jesus community existed there – the Bezan text may well be right in saying that Apollos had gained his instruction 'in his own country'. It is of course right and proper that a historian should carefully distinguish between what is directly demonstrated by contemporary evidence and what is derived from less immediate authorities, but it is wrong to suppose that contemporary evidence alone will give a balanced view of the probable course of history. To ignore the testimony of Eusebius and the tradition of the Alexandrian church and to underrate the dynamism of the primitive Christians is to invite a desiccated and distorted account of Christian origins, the blame for which cannot be laid at Luke's door. Acts is as selective in its information about Mark as it is about Peter. There is plenty of room within the known outline of the movements of Mark to fit in the traditions of both Rome and Alexandria. If we assume that all mentions of Mark in the New Testament refer to the same person,[11] we get this sequence: Mark's home in Jerusalem was at the centre of the Christian movement (Acts 12:12) and he must have drunk in Peter's teaching in those early days. He gained some reputation as a useful worker (both in the Jerusalem church and with Peter in Rome?), for after his cousin Barnabas (who was a leader of the work in Antioch) had visited Jerusalem with Paul with famine relief in *c*. 46, Mark went back with him (12:25). He started out on the first missionary journey in *c*. 47, but at Pamphylia he withdrew and returned to Jerusalem, much to Paul's disgust (13:5, 13). (Had his training under Peter made him uneasy at Paul's radicalism?) On the eve of the second missionary journey in *c.* 49 he seems to have been with them again in Antioch, but this time Paul and Barnabas parted, and Mark went with his cousin to Cyprus (15:37–39). This expedition lasted perhaps a year. He appears again at the writing of Colossians (4:10), Philemon (24) and 1 Peter (5:13), usually placed in Rome[12] and not usually dated before the 60s. We get a last glimpse of him in 2 Timothy 4:11.

This gives 42–46 as the limits of Mark's (first) time in Rome and allows somewhere between 44 and 46 for the writing of his gospel there. There is a whole decade in the 50s when he could have been evangelising in Egypt and Cyrenaica, a work to which he could have returned in the later 60s. He might even have left Rome in 44 or 45 and worked in Egypt for a year or two around 44–46.[13]

7Q5

There is one further intriguing possible piece of external evidence which must not be overlooked. It is not often that a small fragment of biblical manuscript hits the headlines of the world's press, but on 16 March 1972, *The Times* of London on its front page carried a headline across five columns: 'Scroll fragments put accepted date of the gospels in doubt.' It referred to the article in *Biblica* 53 (1972) 91–109 by the eminent Jesuit papyrologist, J. O'Callaghan, which reported the identifying of what the author believed to be a fragment of Mark 6:52f, which had come from Cave 7 at Qumran, which had been sealed in the year 68.

There had been a long and unavailing attempt to find an Old Testament passage from which this fragment (known as 7Q5) might have come. The most conspicuous combination of letters in the manuscript was ννησ and it was supposed that it represented some such word as ἐγεννησεν,[14] but no passage in the Greek Old Testament would fit. Then O'Callaghan recollected the passage in Mark 6:52f concerning Gennesaret, and to his astonishment he found that, apart from two queries, it seemed to him to fit. Not only did the fifteen decipherable or partly

177

decipherable letters seem to fit, but there was also a highly significant space (equivalent to nearly three letters) separating verses 52 and 53. In such manuscripts there are normally no spaces between words, but verse 53 starts a new paragraph, and this is indicated in the fragment by this unusual gap. Armed with this totally unexpected clue (for who would have dreamt of finding New Testament fragments as early as 68?), he soon found it easy tentatively to identify several other possible New Testament fragments from the same cave.

Not surprisingly O'Callaghan's announcement was met with no little scepticism by the scholarly world, and it all looked like a flash in the pan. Interest soon subsided and it was even believed that O'Callaghan himself had withdrawn his identifications. But this is in fact quite untrue; O'Callaghan himself has written at least seventeen articles, mostly in Spanish, defending his position. The first of the two queries comes in line 3 where a *tau* is read in place of the usual *delta* in the supposed διαπερασαντες. O'Callaghan shows that this substitution is not infrequent in ancient Greek literature and he gives twenty examples from four biblical papyri of this very change. As these come from Egypt, it would not be surprising to find the same phenomenon in the gospel, if Mark's main centre of operations during the 50s had been Alexandria.

The second query, which at first sight is more serious, is the omission of επι την γην between lines 3 and 4. But early New Testament papyri, often produced quickly and cheaply for private rather than for official use, are full of mistakes, and a scribal error of this order does not invalidate the rest of the identification.[15] In addition, though this omission is not found in any Greek manuscript and is not mentioned in the 25th or 26th editions of Nestle or in Greeven's *Synopsis*, it is to be found in some Coptic manuscripts, which gives independent evidence of the existence of this reading in Egypt.[16] The significant thing about 7Q5 is that there continues to be no satisfactory alternative to Mark 6:52f on offer by way of identification, which means that it must be taken seriously.[17]

If 7Q5 is tentatively identified with Mark 6:52f, some of O'Callaghan's other identifications at once become plausible.

7Q4 fits 1 Timothy 3:16–4:3 (O'Callaghan thinks this certain) and 7Q8 fits James 1:23f. That epistles like 1 Timothy and James, commonly dated round about the end of the century, should have been in the possession of a Christian community in Palestine in 68 is a conclusion almost too shocking to be contemplated! But if the traditional dating of these New Testament documents is in general sounder than the modern dating (as the present book maintains),[18] there is nothing impossible about it. We ought therefore, in spite of the fragmentary nature of the evidence, to keep the possibility in mind.

Further internal considerations

As far as content is concerned, almost the whole gospel deals with events at which Peter was actually present and the remainder with events (such as the crucifixion and the visit to the tomb) at which close associates were present. As far as the book's manner of presentation is concerned, much of it reads either like the oral reminiscences of an eyewitness or as the narrative of an excellent story-teller. J. B. Orchard has argued that Mark's gospel was a record of discourses delivered by Peter in Rome, taken down in shorthand at the time.[19] This, however, is too simplistic a description of the gospel. Though it often seems to recall the spoken word, it does not actually read like a series of discourses. If in fact Peter spoke just as Mark writes, he would have completed his oration in less than two hours – a single session for an eager audience. The matter as it stands is too dense for a sermon or a lecture (see for example, 3:7–19, 23–30; 4:21–34; 8:34–9:1; 9:38–50; 10:1–12; 12:28–40; 13:5–37), but much of it could have been used within a popular discourse which contained fuller explanatory matter. It reads like a book, a book which draws upon oral material.

This point was made forcefully in a work written by H. D. A. Major, entitled *Reminiscences of Jesus by an Eye-Witness* (London: Murray, 1925). Major is probably best known for *The Mission and Message of Jesus* which he wrote in collaboration with T. W. Manson and C. T. Wright, but he was also editor of

179

The Modern Churchman
and had no reputation for conservative views. He writes:

> The experience of reading St. Mark's Gospel many times in the Greek in parallel columns with the corresponding sections of the other Gospels, has not only impressed upon me a number of important points in which St. Mark's Gospel differs from the other Gospels, but has also convinced me of the very primitive and archaic character of this Gospel, and that the primitive and uncontradicted Church tradition which ascribed this Gospel to St. Mark and declared it to contain the actual memoirs of St. Peter is based on fact, and so is worthy of acceptance by modern man . . . [It] enshrines the reminiscences of St. Peter, delivered orally in Aramaic but translated into Greek by St. Mark and transcribed by him. (vif)
>
> Bishop Westcott, in his *Introduction to the Study of the Gospels*, observes that 'there is perhaps not one narrative which he [St. Mark] gives in common with St. Matthew and St. Luke to which he does not contribute some special feature' (chap. 7). An examination of these 'special features' leaves the impression that they are not the skilful invention of the literary artist, but the reminiscences of an eye-witness. They have been called 'Petrine touches'; they might be more accurately named 'Petrine recollections'.
>
> The special features are so numerous that to deal with them fully would require a running commentary on the greater part of the text. (75)

He then proceeds in the next twenty-five pages to give a few examples 'from a vast mass'.

In 1:16–20 the use of the ἀμφίβληστρον, the circular fishing-net which is used from the beach; Jesus speaking to those on the beach and calling to those in the boat; the presence of the hired servants. In 1:41 Jesus emotionally moved, in 1:45 his sternness, in 3:5 his anger. In 2:2, 'There was no longer room for them, not even about the door'; in 3:34, 'looking round on those seated in a circle round him'. In 4:2 there are vivid details (this time also noted by Matthew): 'he got into a boat and sat in it on the sea; and the whole crowd was beside the sea on the land'; in 4:36, 38 Mark mentions the presence of other boats, and how Jesus was in the stern, sleeping on the cushion; in 5:35f Jesus 'overhears' (or perhaps 'ignores') the 'Why bother the Teacher?' – the whole narrative leading up to the Aramaic command *Talitha cumi* is marvellously vivid. So with the feeding of the five thousand in 6:30–44 with all its detail and the narrator's impressionistic συμπόσια συμπόσια and πρασιαὶ πρασιαί. In 6:48 Jesus 'would have passed them by' seems like the recollection of an eyewitness. The healing of the deaf man who had an impediment in his speech in 7:31–37, with the touching, the anointing with saliva, the groaning, the Aramaic *Ephphatha*, the charge to tell no one and the subsequent disobedience, has the same characteristics. And so we could go on traversing well-known ground to the end of the book.

All this may seem to have an old-fashioned ring to it, for it is commonly held that the early Christians were not much concerned about factual accuracy, but with presenting a divine, saving, Messianic figure, and that picturesque detail is in fact characteristic of apocryphal writing.[20] D. E. Nineham, for instance, in a series of influential articles in 1958 and 1960, 'Eye-Witness Testimony and the Gospel Tradition',[21] argued that eyewitnesses 'played little direct part in the development of the Gospel tradition' (13). 'Unless the whole form-critical approach is radically unsound, this tradition can hardly be accepted as it stands, for no plausible reason can be given why recollections derived directly from the living voice of St. Peter should have been cast in the stereotyped, impersonal form of community tradition' (243). He stressed that Markan pericopes are *community* anecdotes (16).

There may well be something in the idea that stories gain a certain smoothness, conciseness and impact through frequent repetition. But this is at least as true of the stories of a single eyewitness in the course of a lifetime of itinerant preaching as it is of a succession of preachers borrowing material from their predecessors. The supposed conclusions of form criticism (which builds on the two-document hypothesis) in fact beg the very questions we are investigating.

The evidence is not compelling to those who are happy with the idea that the gospel of Mark was written by a man of outstanding talents with a flair for developing more or less legendary stories of Jesus current in his Christian community. But to those who believe that a Jesus very like the Jesus of the gospels is necessary to account for the rise of the Christian church and for the emergence of writers who could produce such gospels, it is a different matter. It seems easier to us to believe that the qualities of this gospel spring not from the author's genius, but from his fidelity to the reminiscences of an outstanding eyewitness.

To summarise: the ancient testimony indicates that Mark's gospel is substantially the teaching of Peter, and was the means by which that teaching was handed down to the church after his decease. It also seems to indicate that it was probably written before the apostle's death, quite possibly shortly after a stay in Rome by Peter from 42 to 44 and before Mark started on his missions with Paul and Barnabas. This agrees with the tentative conclusions reached in our study of the relation between Matthew and Mark in Chapter 4, and is confirmed by internal characteristics.

9

ANCIENT TESTIMONY TO LUKE'S GOSPEL

Chapter summary

Testimony is virtually universal that the author of the third gospel was Luke, the beloved physician and companion of Paul. The Anti-Marcionite Prologue says he was a Syrian of Antioch, a disciple of the apostles, unmarried, who died at the age of eighty-four, having written his gospel in Achaia. Theophilus must have known the author's name and it is unlikely to have been forgotten. Hobart's *The Medical Language of St. Luke* (1882) does not in fact prove the author a physician. There is slender, but not negligible, evidence for the late traditions that Luke was one of the seventy, that he was the unnamed disciple of the Emmaus road, that he was Lucius of Cyrene, a kinsman of Paul.

Clement of Alexandria says that 'those gospels were first written which include the genealogies'. This would seem to mean that Luke (and Matthew) were written before Mark (and John). This is the strongest argument in the Griesbach case, for Clement is early (*c*. 150–215) and well informed. Peabody's belief that this view was held by Augustine in later life seems ill-founded. Gamba finds traces of the view in the Monarchian Prologue to Mark and in the writing of Sedulius Scottus of the ninth century. This tradition is not so strong as the Matthew–Mark–Luke–John tradition. If it has to be explained away, it is perhaps easiest to assume that Clement meant that Matthew was composed before Mark and Luke before John.

The main points in the Griesbach and the two-document debate are then summarised.

In our attempts to unravel the synoptic problem there are two matters concerning the gospel of Luke about which we would be glad of light from the church fathers: Who was its author? and, Where does it come in the gospel sequence? The ancient testimony to the authorship of the third gospel may be divided into three very unequal sections. Firstly, there are the testimonies which are universal (viz. that the author was Luke) or nearly universal (viz. that he was a companion of Paul and the beloved physician). Secondly, there is a strongly supported tradition that he was 'the brother whose praise is in the gospel'. Thirdly, there are those which are supported less widely: that he was a) one of the seventy; b) the unnamed disciple of Emmaus; c) Lucius of Cyrene.

Luke: Companion of Paul and beloved physician

The unanimous testimony of the early Christian writers attributes the gospel to Luke. This is found in Irenaeus,[1] the Muratorian fragment, Tertullian,[2] Clement of Alexandria[3] and in those who came after,[4] and is never disputed. They usually make clear that he was the companion of Paul.

The so-called Anti-Marcionite Prologue to Luke spells out a much fuller story and equates the companion of Paul with the beloved physician. Its date (as we saw on pp. 139–40) is disputed, but it has a better claim to be placed early than the other prologues identified by de Bruyne. It alone is in the original Greek and it has interesting features, some of which could not have been derived from the New Testament and which may depend on independent information. It reads as follows:

> Luke is a Syrian of Antioch, a physician by profession. He became a disciple of the apostles and later he accompanied [παρακολουθήσας] Paul until his martyrdom. He served the Lord without distraction, having neither wife nor children, and at the age of eighty-four he fell asleep in Boeotia, full of the Holy Spirit.
>
> Although there were already gospels previously in existence – one according to Matthew written in Judea and one according to Mark written in Italy – [Luke] moved by the Holy Spirit composed

184

the whole gospel in the districts around Achaia. In his prologue he makes this very point clear, that other [gospels] were written before his and that it was necessary that an accurate account of the [divine] plan be set forth for the Gentile believers . . .

Afterwards the same Luke also wrote the Acts of the Apostles. [5]

This prologue identifies Luke with the beloved physician who is said to have been with Paul when he wrote the epistles to the Colossians (4:14) and to Philemon (24), and this identification is found in many other writers. A Luke is also with Paul according to 2 Timothy 4:11. It is natural to assume that these notices of an otherwise undistinguished companion of Paul all refer to the same man. There is, however, nothing in the passages themselves to suggest that he was a chronicler of Paul's doings. Of the very large number of companions of Paul known to us from his epistles and from Acts, there seems no reason why Luke should be picked on as an author who refers to himself in the 'we' passages of Acts.

H. J. Cadbury's argument[6] that some acute second-century critic might have deduced the name of Luke from a study of Acts and the epistles by a process of elimination, is tenuous and is dismissed by Streeter,[7] who points out that Luke's preface would have been meaningless to the original readers unless its author's name had been known. Furthermore, as we have already seen, when a church which already possessed a gospel acquired a second one, the necessity of distinguishing the two would from the very first have prevented the name of either being forgotten.

It is probable that Theophilus' own copy would have been tagged with the author's name. Private libraries were common among the rich, and before placing a book-roll in the library, it was customary to tag it. Unlike oriental practice, Greco-Roman libraries were indexed by the author's name.[8] Thus the authorship of a catalogued book which had no author's name in the text would nonetheless be known beyond doubt to its readers, and this was presumably true of Luke.[9]

There is some slight internal evidence in support of the tradition that the author was a physician. W. K. Hobart in *The Medical Language of St. Luke* argued that both gospel and Acts

185

are permeated by first-century medical terminology. A. Harnack, W. M. Ramsay and several other scholars declared the argument basically sound,[10] but H. J. Cadbury showed that the so-called medical words are also to be found in non-medical authors, like Lucian and Josephus.[11] A. T. Robertson, the grammarian, considered that Cadbury had by no means demolished Hobart's case and that Luke's interests and choice of words did in some measure corroborate the tradition that he was a physician.[12] J. M. Creed also thought that the case retained some weight.[13] L. C. A. Alexander in her thorough investigation of the prologue's genre concludes that the author could well be a physician, but equally well he could be an engineer.[14]

Our discussion of 'the brother whose praise is in the gospel' of 2 Corinthians 8:18 will be deferred till pp. 230–7, where his identity is discussed in connection with the dating of Luke's gospel. Suffice it to say that the belief that he was Luke is found in the great scholars of the early church: Origen, Eusebius, Ephraem, Chrysostom and Jerome; it is found in the subscriptions added to the epistle in the Byzantine-text tradition, and it has been retained in certain liturgies to this day.

The three other traditions of Luke's identity to which we referred are of little value as historical evidence. They do, however, call attention to interesting questions of internal evidence, which suggest that there may be more to these late ideas than at first seems probable. Their full discussion will be found in Wenham *Luke*. At this point we must confine ourselves to summaries.

a) There is a tradition, widely held but not traceable earlier than the late third century, that Luke was *one of the seventy*. If this was so it would explain why Luke dismisses the mission of the twelve in seven verses, but devotes twenty-four verses to the mission of the seventy. This would require that Luke should have been a Jew and not a Gentile as is generally supposed on the basis of Colossians 4:11. Luke's gospel has a strong Hebraic tinge and it is far from certain that Colossians 4:11 requires the usual interpretation. Furthermore, there is a strong case for interpreting the παρηκολουθηκότι ἄνωθεν of the prologue as a claim by Luke to have actually followed the events of the gospel

186

as they took place from a long time back. In the latter part of the gospel and throughout Acts it has been 'notoriously difficult'[15] to identify sources used by Luke. A simple explanation of this would be that Luke did not need sources. He was there.

b) If Luke was one of the seventy, credence is given to a tradition of the Greek church that he was the *unnamed disciple of the Emmaus road*. Though not directly traceable earlier than the tenth century, there are indications in the text of Luke which seem to confirm it. The second-century Muratorian Canon on the other hand says that Luke 'had not seen the Lord in the flesh'.

c) A good case can be made for identifying the Antioch church leader *Lucius of Cyrene* and *Paul's kinsman Lucius* (of Rom. 16:21) with Luke. If this is so, Luke was presumably one of the Cyrenians who fled Jerusalem at the time of Saul's persecution and began to evangelise Gentiles in Antioch.

These identifications play no essential part in our attempted solution of the synoptic problem, but they open up a great range of possibilities as to when Luke began to be an observer of the things he records. He might have joined Paul at the point in the story where the first 'we-passage' begins (Acts 16:10), he might have been an early convert in the Jerusalem church who evangelised the Gentiles of Antioch (11:19, 20), or he might have been (as a literal understanding of παρηκολουθηκότι ἄνωθεν would suggest) an active disciple of Jesus from the time of the Galilean ministry till he saw him risen in Jerusalem. Which it was has no direct bearing on the date of the gospel, though the earlier we envisage Luke participating in the Christian mission the stronger will be the case for taking his narrative as a sound historical source.

Was Luke written before Mark?

The other matter of external evidence which has to be considered concerns the place of the book in the gospel sequence. This is a point of sharp contention in the modern debate. The traditional view (which is of course supported by the modern two-documemt theory) puts Mark first, whereas the Griesbach (or two-gospel) view puts Luke first. Supporters of the latter lay great stress on the evidence of Clement of Alexandria, preserved for us by Eusebius: 'In the same books Clement has inserted a tradition of the primitive elders with regard to the order of the Gospels, as follows. He said that those Gospels were first written which include the genealogies' (*HE* 6.14.5). This is claimed as the earliest reliable testimony to the order of the gospels and (to me at least) it seems to be the strongest plank of the Griesbach platform. Earlier in his book Eusebius stresses the catholicity and apostolicity of the sources claimed by Clement. He quotes Clement as saying:

> This work is not a writing composed for show, but notes stored up for my old age, a remedy against forgetfulness, an image without art, and a sketch of those clear and vital words which I was privileged to hear, and of blessed and truly notable men. One of these, the Ionian, was in Greece, another in South Italy, a third in Coele-Syria [Lebanon], another from Egypt, and there were others in the East, one of them an Assyrian, another in Palestine of Hebrew origin . . . these men preserved the true tradition of the blessed teaching directly from Peter and James and John and Paul, the holy apostles. (*HE* 5.11.3, 4)

The case was stated concisely in 'A Position Paper for the Two Gospel Hypothesis' written in preparation for the 1984 Gospels Conference in Jerusalem and circulated privately:

> The earliest and most reliable testimony bearing on the question of the sequence in which the Gospels were written is from Clement of Alexandria who reports that he has received from the elders the tradition that the Gospels with genealogies, i.e., the *two Gospels*, Matthew and Luke, were written before the others, i.e., Mark and John. The Two Gospel Hypothesis, then, rests upon the secure foundation of the testimony of Clement of Alexandria who witnesses to an unquestioned second-century tradition that the earliest Gospels were Matthew and Luke. Until clearly stated reasons are brought forward which serve to call into question the reliability of this statement attributed to Clement, it is only right to begin with the critical basis laid down in this early witness and then to proceed to test this evidence by other evidence . . . It is of the greatest importance to recognize the peril and ultimate futility of discussing

the relationships of the Gospels in an historical vacuum where only the internal evidence from literary criticism is weighed in the balance of historical judgment. It is, of course, equally dangerous to focus on Patristic tradition to the neglect of internal considerations.

Critical confidence in the essential correctness of the Two Gospel Hypothesis has been strengthened recently by two developments in Patristic studies: *First*, by the discovery that the testimony of Clement was still being recognised and taken seriously in the Church as late as the ninth century (Gamba), and *second*, by the discovery that the 'so-called' Augustinian Hypothesis is a late medieval and modern construction (Peabody).

The contrary view, maintaining that Matthew–Mark–Luke was the true order, was expressed with great force at an earlier date by Zahn, who himself espoused this Augustinian view:

Clement's isolated statement, which seems to say that Luke was written before Mark, must give way before the tradition which represents the two Gospels as having been written in the order Mark–Luke, not only because the witness for the latter view is incomparably stronger, but also because Clement's view might have been the result of critical reflection, which is inconceivable in the case of the opposing tradition. (2.396)

He argued his case like this: Origen in his commentary on Matthew claims to have learnt by tradition the order of writing Matthew–Mark–Luke:

. . . as having learnt by tradition concerning the four Gospels, which alone are unquestionable in the Church of God under heaven, that first was written that according to Matthew, who was once a tax-collector but afterwards an apostle of Jesus Christ, who published it for those who from Judaism came to believe, composed as it was in the Hebrew language. Secondly, that according to Mark, who wrote it in accordance with Peter's instructions, whom also Peter acknowledged as his son in the catholic epistle, speaking in these terms: 'She that is in Babylon, elect together with you, saluteth you; and so doth Mark my son.' And thirdly, that according to Luke, who wrote, for those who from the Gentiles [came to believe], the Gospel that was praised by Paul.[16] After them all, that according to John. (*HE* 6.25.3–6)

189

We should note particularly how he says: 'first was written . . . secondly . . . thirdly'. Origen says this in spite of the fact that the order of the gospels in the codices which seems to have prevailed in Egypt for a long time was John–Matthew–Mark–Luke.[17] Zahn proceeds:

> What Origen gives as a tradition, without any thought of a divergent view, is expressed also by Irenaeus and the author of the Muratorian fragment without the least indication of uncertainty. It continued to be the prevalent view of antiquity, and it was this more than anything else which brought it about, that the arrangement of the Gospels familiar to us displaced more and more the other arrangements in the East from the beginning of the fourth century on, and after Jerome also in the West . . . It is to be noticed, further, that Irenaeus had read Papias' work (Adv. Haer. 5.33.4) . . . [and] was aware that his view regarding the time of the composition of Mark's Gospel was in agreement not only with that of Papias, but also with that of his teacher John the presbyter, who, according to Irenaeus, was the apostle John. (2.393f)

Zahn then looks for ways of explaining Clement away.

The divergence between the two views could hardly be greater and it appears to be a case of both sides pushing the evidence too hard. Two things seem to be clear: 1.) Origen did spell out the tradition as he knew it, which states that the gospels were written in the order Matthew–Mark–Luke. 2.) Clement, Origen's teacher, gives on the most natural reading a view inconsistent with this.

What justification has Zahn for thinking that Origen's tradition is that of the whole church and Clement's tradition is an isolated anomaly? For the period before Origen he quotes the passage from Irenaeus which we have already discussed in detail (pp. 239–42), with its clear sequence: 'Matthew published . . . after the exodus [of Peter and Paul] Mark also . . . and Luke . . . then John' (*HE* 5.8.2f; cf. *Adv. Haer.* 3.1.1). This certainly looks as though it is meant to be a chronological order (H. von Campenhausen in fact says 'it is obviously intended as a chronological order'[18]), but Irenaeus is not as explicit as Origen: 'Mark . . . and Luke' *need* not mean 'Mark . . . and then Luke.' Irenaeus' usual order (in contexts where chronology is not being

discussed) is Matthew–Luke–Mark–John,[19] though when dealing with the symbols of the evangelists he adopts the order
John–Luke–Matthew–Mark.[20] This increases the probability
that on this one occasion Irenaeus is deliberately changing his
usual order into a chronological one. Farmer, on the other
hand, considers that 'there is no reason at all to think that
Irenaeus intended his readers to conclude that Mark was
written before Luke'. He suggests that his reason for mentioning Mark and Luke in that order may have arisen simply
because he has just mentioned Peter and Paul and his desire is
'to establish that these two apostles are also to be credited with
written gospels through their close associates'.[21] This shows
that, if Irenaeus has to be explained away, his statement is not
impregnable.

Zahn, as we have seen, carried back the tradition further,
stressing the importance of Papias:

> Irenaeus had read Papias' work (*Adv. H.* 5.33.4), which contained
> notices regarding the origin of Matthew and Mark . . . With
> reference to Mark, Papias preserved a statement of his teacher,
> John, whom Irenaeus held to be the apostle . . . Since Irenaeus uses
> . . . the same peculiar phrase which [Papias] employed to express
> the relation in which Mark stood to Peter (ἑρμηνευτὴς Πέτρου), it
> is perfectly clear that Irenaeus was aware that his view regarding the
> time of the composition of Mark's Gospel was in agreement not
> only with that of Papias, but also with that of . . . the apostle John.
> (2.394)

Zahn is somewhat inclined to overstatement (e.g. 'perfectly
clear'), but he is right to remind us of the links in the chain
of tradition to which Irenaeus laid claim. The order which
Irenaeus seems to espouse could have come from the aged
apostle.

Zahn also cited the Muratorian fragment, another early
witness (probably from the second half of the second century)
which refers specifically to Luke as the third gospel. The
sections on Matthew and Mark are missing, so that we cannot
know whether their time and mode of composition was stated,
though in the case of John these are narrated in detail. In any
case it adds some weight to the view that Luke is later than

Mark. A counter-suggestion is that towards the end of the second century a canonical order may have been established which was different from the chronological order and was mistaken for it. This, however, could hardly have been the case with Origen since (as we have seen), Matthew–Mark–Luke–John was not the usual order in the early Egyptian codices. So Muratori must be held to favour the main tradition.

For the period after Origen the tradition seems fairly solid in spite of the claims of G. G. Gamba and D. B. Peabody. Eusebius himself, though he does not attempt any reconciliation between Clement and Origen, appears to concur with the latter. He says: '[Matthew] transmitted in writing in his native language the Gospel according to himself . . . and Mark and Luke having already published the Gospels according to them, John . . . at last took to writing' (*HE* 3.24.6, 7). He then (sections 9–11) discusses the content of the gospels in the order Matthew–Mark–Luke–John. Orchard's judgement is: 'He himself did not make a strict synthesis of it [the information about the gospels], though he held all the elements of the synthesis in his own mind, as is clear from the cross references he makes from time to time.' With regard to the fourth-century fathers after Eusebius, Orchard says: 'they all seem quite content with the Gospel order Matthew–Mark–Luke–John, and none of them sought to contrast or to oppose this order with Clement of Alexandria's statement'.[22] This must suggest a strong possibility that Eusebius himself did not regard the sources he quotes as contradictory.

The most celebrated of the later statements was that of Augustine: 'these four Evangelists . . . are said to have written in this order: first Matthew, then Mark, thirdly Luke, lastly John. Thus they have one order as regards knowing and preaching, and another order as regards actual composition (*Concerning the Harmony of the Evangelists* 1.3 – Orchard's translation 212). This is as clear as could be, but it is claimed that Augustine subsequently adopted a different line. Peabody has argued this at length in a rather unlucid article,[23] maintaining that Augustine at the beginning of his book on gospel-harmony bases his conclusions only on a study of the Eusebian canons (hence his view that Mark was the abbreviator of Matthew: 1.4); but by the time he gets to Book 4 Augustine has carried out a careful comparison of the text of the greater part of the gospels and gained a new view. At 4.11 he looks back on the work done and discusses Mark's relation to Matthew and Luke:

> Mark . . . appears to be preferentially the companion of Matthew, as he narrates a larger number of matters in unison with him . . . or else, in accordance with the more probable account of the matter, he holds a course in conjunction with both. For although he is at one with Matthew in the larger number of passages, he is nevertheless at one with Luke in some others. (Peabody's translation; for a more straightforward translation see Orchard 213f)

From this Peabody concludes that 'Augustine's new, more probable view of Mark is that Mark is literarily dependent upon both Matthew and Luke', and that 'Augustine had not *one* but *two* views of the relationships among the gospels.'[24] This last statement is true enough if one is a view of order of composition and the other a view of theological relationship (which is what the passage is all about). Augustine is arguing that Mark has affinities with Matthew in his emphasis on Christ's kingly office and with Luke in his emphasis on his sacerdotal office, and with both in their emphasis (in contrast to John) on his manhood. It requires abstruse (if not perverse) reasoning to see reference to a literary relationship, and Peabody's theory must be judged quite unconvincing.

Gamba, on the other hand, has discovered some small items supporting Clement's witness. He finds a reference to Mark's knowledge of Matthew's and Luke's gospels in the Monarchian Prologue to Mark, which is to be dated at the end of the fourth century. Of Mark it says, *non laboravit nativitatem carnis, quam in prioribus viderat, dicere* (freely translated by Orchard, 'he did not bother with the nativity story which he had seen related in the former [Gospels]'),[25] which would seem to imply that Mark had seen in earlier gospels accounts of Jesus' birth and that therefore he wrote after the other two. Further, Gamba points out:

> the Irish monk Sedulius Scottus in the ninth century A.D., commenting in an *Explanatiuncula*, the not-easy Latin text of the

'Monarchian' Prologue to Mark's Gospel, . . . writes '[Mark] did not find in the two Evangelists that are in agreement between themselves, vid. Matthew and Luke, who, according to some, as the *Ecclesiastical History* relates, wrote their Gospels before Mark.'[26]

This is a clear reference to Eusebius' account of Clement's view. A little further on Sedulius again refers to things which Mark 'knew had already been fully recorded in the earlier Evangelists, namely in Matthew and Luke'.[27] In the Monarchian Prologue to Luke, however, Mark is explicitly given priority: 'after the Gospels of Matthew in Judea and of Mark in Italy had been written down, [Luke] under the impulse of the Holy Spirit wrote this Gospel in Achaia'. Sedulius just accepts this and leaves the two traditions unreconciled.[28] Gamba makes the further point:

Clement is a member of the church of Alexandria, where Mark the Evangelist was acclaimed as founder and first bishop: cf. Eusebius *HE* 2.16.1. He therefore would have no reason at all to place Mark's Gospel after the other two that contain a genealogy of Jesus, unless it was for a definite and grounded persuasion of historical nature.[29]

There are, then, two rival traditions, that of Origen apparently somewhat the stronger, but Clement's by no means negligible. For either to be wholly convincing it would be necessary to explain the other's contrary evidence. Zahn offered two possible explanations of Clement's anomaly. Possibly, he suggests, it was based on the beliefs a) that Peter was only in Rome for a short time before his martyrdom (in perhaps 67) and b) that Mark wrote under his supervision at that time, combined with a deduction about the date of Luke and Acts – namely, that Clement may have reasoned like many other scholars that Acts was written at the point in time where its story ends (about 62) and his 'former treatise' probably earlier. This would have compelled him to believe that Luke was written before Mark. Alternatively, he suggests:

If, in consideration of the general currency of the tradition that the order was Matthew, Mark, Luke, John, one may assume that it was

known to Clement's teachers and to himself, it is noteworthy that
their divergent statement is given without any hint of its opposition
to the common view. It is not impossible, then, that the presbyters
simply meant that Matthew was written before Mark and Luke
before John.[30]

Another attempt to nullify Eusebius' report of Clement
argues that *HE* 6.14.5–7 may have consisted of a tradition
preserved by Clement concerning the relation of Matthew and
Luke to John into which a selection on Mark (from Papias?) has
been inserted.[31] Once one indulges in speculation a number of
conceivable influences come to mind as possible causes of Luke
coming to be put before Mark, e.g. the greater esteem and
wider use of Luke, or possibly a feeling that birth narratives
should come first. Zahn's second possibility (that Clement was
thinking of the gospels in pairs, and meant Matthew was
written before Mark, and Luke before John) has the merit of
simplicity and is perhaps the best option, but there is no
denying that the natural reading of Eusebius at this point puts
Luke first.

If, on the other hand, the Clement tradition is correct, it
seems necessary to suppose that a canonical order had become
established by the time of Origen and that this was mistaken for
an order of composition. Once this had been adopted by
Augustine his influence would have played a big part (at least in
the Western church) in the general acceptance of the erroneous
idea. This is possible, but it seems rather unlikely that a
mistaken view should have established itself so quickly and
universally, when it is remembered that the firmness of the
tradition that Matthew was written first and John last shows
that there was interest in the order of composition in the
church. The Griesbach view of the external evidence still looks
less plausible than the traditional view.

It may be convenient at this point to collect together the main
points in the Griesbach debate. The main arguments in favour
of the Griesbach hypothesis are: 1.) The argument from order,
which (as we saw on pp. 17f) appears to have no validity. 2.)
The testimony of Clement of Alexandria cited above, which has
force but is not decisive. The main arguments against are: 1.)

195

The great improbability of a narrative with the freshness and vigour of Mark being produced in the way suggested (see pp. 12–16). 2.) The small quantity of ready-to-use coincidence in Matthew and Luke adopted by Mark. All the Q-material is omitted by him (p. 17). 3.) The fact that no one seems to have shown that it actually works out in practice. See especially Farmer *SP* 217–19, where a positive correlation between agreement in order and closeness of text between Mark and Luke is argued. Farmer is forced to add: 'It is very important not to think that this correlation can be easily verified. There are places where no correlation seems apparent' (219 n9). Farmer and Orchard felt that they were going forward from the work of Jameson, Chapman and Butler when they discarded the Augustinian view in favour of Griesbach. They would surely have been better advised to have modified the Augustinian view in the direction of the oral theory and not pinned all their hopes on literary relationships.[32]

Let us also attempt to summarise the modern debate concerning the two-document hypothesis.[33] As regards the supposed priority of Mark, the five points in the classical statement of Streeter have continued to form the basis of the case for Markan priority. We saw in Chapter 4 (p. 90f) that Streeter's five heads reduce in fact to two: 1.) Mark is intermediate between Matthew and Luke. 2.) Mark has a more primitive character, which includes matter likely to cause offence. But that Mark is intermediate between Matthew and Luke fits equally the two-document hypothesis, the Griesbach view and the Augustinian view. Also, Mark's supposedly more primitive character is just as well explained by the patristic view which makes Mark a record of Peter's vivid oral instruction in which the apostle does not attempt to hide the disciples' faults. Added to this there are some positive arguments for Matthean priority: e.g. it provides a good rationale for the differences in order between Matthew and Mark (pp. 101–8) and there is evidence of conscious omissions in Mark (pp. 97–100). In the search for literary relationships the most decisive question in this debate is likely to be the weight to be attached to patristic tradition. If it is considered worthless, the purely literary debate is likely to remain indecisive, insufficient to create a new consensus. If it is thought to be of weight, it is likely to tip the scale in favour of Matthean priority.

But the more fundamental question remains, Are we right to look primarily for literary relationships? As we shall see in the next chapter, it is improbable on purely physical grounds that the later evangelists produced their works by redacting one or more scrolls as is generally supposed.

10

HOW WERE THE GOSPELS WRITTEN?

Chapter summary

The early church was eager to pass on the words and deeds of Jesus to both Aramaic-speaking and Greek-speaking hearers. Learning was mostly by rote, but a rigid form of catechising was not adopted. Written records were probably required quite early for a scattered church. The apostle Matthew, as the first author, presumably put in writing what he and his colleagues were accustomed to teach to the stream of visitors who came to Jerusalem. His order was not entirely chronological, as he wished to put the Sermon on the Mount and the mission charge in the forefront of his book. Peter knew Matthew's gospel (either in a Semitic or Greek form) and it is Peter's teaching that Mark records. The physical difficulties of writing, and even more of adapting, a scroll are stressed. It is unlikely that one evangelist worked directly on the scroll of another. Ancient historians relied on their memories and the briefest of notes. Only very rarely did they attempt conflation, and that of the simplest kind. Mark probably wrote in the way that he and Peter were accustomed to teach, basing his order on Matthew and possibly using Matthew in checking his final revision.

Luke probably wrote with a knowledge of the work of Matthew (a from-the-beginning-eyewitness) and of Mark (a minister of the Word) and as a result of long following the words and deeds of Jesus. He followed the order of Mark, making some omissions and a great number of additions, but keeping to his own normal form of words. He also makes small additions from Matthew. His gentle harmonising tendency leaves the Jericho discrepancy untouched, possibly because he was aware of two Jericho settlements. His geography (e.g. re Samaria and

198

Galilee) seems to be sound. Other questions of harmony (e.g. re the genealogies) are considered.

We saw in Chapters 1–4 that it seems necessary to give a place both to the factor of mutual dependence and to a large measure of independence if we are to solve the synoptic problem. In Chapters 5–9 we have seen that the external evidence fits well with the internal evidence and provides some further indications (of varying degrees of probability) which bear on the problem. Is it possible to be more precise as to the part played by dependence and independence in the creation of the pattern of likenesses and differences which we find in the three gospels? The honest answer must be that we are in the realm of speculation, with small means of checking our guesses. The most we can do is to set out the probable situation with its many variables and not attempt the impossible by offering detailed proposals as to the history of the traditions, since the bulk of any such proposals would almost certainly be wrong.[1]

The oral background

We know that Jesus was a preacher and teacher who made a great impact during his short career. His first language was Aramaic, but he was almost certainly capable of using the Greek *lingua franca*, even possibly of using Hebrew.[2] He spoke in a manner intended to be remembered, and we must suppose that those whom he sent on mission were carefully instructed in what to say. In their heralding of the kingdom they would have had particularly in mind the words and deeds of Jesus recently witnessed by the Galilean crowds, and there could already have come into being the beginnings of a standard order and form of words. There is no reason (as we saw on pp. 113f) why notes of Jesus' teaching should not have been made during the time of his ministry.

If Acts is to be believed, there came after Pentecost a great new era of proclamation in which it is virtually certain that there would have been teaching in both Aramaic and Greek, given under the authority of the twelve. In Jewish and in Greco-

199

Roman culture learning by rote provided the backbone of education,[3] and one would expect that ἡ διδαχὴ τῶν ἀποστόλων would have assumed a more or less stereotyped form, both in Aramaic among the Palestinians and in Greek among those who streamed into Jerusalem from the Diaspora. If we had no reason to believe that one evangelist knew the other's work, we could opt for this stereotyping as the sole explanation of the likenesses, as Gieseler, Westcott, Rist, Reicke, Scott and others have done – it is *possible* that such passages as the γεννήματα ἐχιδνῶν utterance might have been transmitted thus accurately down two different lines or been remembered by two different people – but if we have reason to believe that a written source was available, a documentary source is more probable.

It is clear, however, that the early church did not adopt a rigid system of catechising, since this is denied by the huge number of differences in the parallel passages. It is better to imagine careful instruction (with particular attention paid to Jesus' words), given in an atmosphere of spontaneity – the freedom of the Spirit accompanying fidelity of witness. All the preachers would have developed within this constraint elements which reflected their own individuality. Good reasons for making a written record are likely to have arisen quite soon. For instance, a reliable source of instruction would be needed when no qualified teacher was available; it would be felt necessary to secure accuracy in the substance of what was being taught in the scattered Christian communities; probably a need would be felt for a form of witness to those outside the church. Torrey gives a sense of the urgency that characterised the early church:

> The truth *must* be made known to all the Jews, everywhere, and as soon as possible . . . As soon as the adherents of the new faith became a veritable sect, their need of a 'gospel' was imperative. It was a literary age and a literary people, but this was not all. The Israelites were 'a people of the book' (to use Mohammed's term); meaning, that their faith was based on a divine revelation which was written down. Here was a new and most important chapter, to be added to the record. No other means of presenting the new truth with authority and in consistent form could compare, in its appeal to the Jews at home and abroad, with the written announce-

ment . . . In due time . . . the Nazarenes found themselves in possession of formal documents of their faith, 'their "gospel," for which they evidently claimed the character of sacred scripture; . . . inspiration was no longer a thing of the past, and inspired books were again possible.' (Moore, *Judaism* I 244).[4]

Writing Matthew's gospel

According to tradition it was Matthew who wrote the first authoritative gospel. Because of his facility with the pen he was the obvious member of the apostolic company to put in writing the message which they were proclaiming. He would have had his own recollections (and possibly his own first-hand notes) to draw upon, as well as the memories of his colleagues. He may have built up his store of material over a period of years, till the time came when a full statement was called for. It could have been published in Aramaic (as Torrey thought) or in Hebrew (the most suitable language in which to record the fulfilling of the Old Testament scriptures – as Carmignac thought) or in Greek (as the majority of scholars still hold, though in defiance of the patristic tradition). It is probably best to assume that all three synoptic gospels were carefully and unhurriedly composed, for (although literary critics can find fault with the greatest of writers – even Shakespeare) the gospels are clearly fine compositions which have stood the test of time. There is no need to suppose (as Chapman did),[5] that 'Luke hurriedly makes his extracts from Matthew', 'slashing his own manuscript'.

Matthew would perhaps have committed to writing first of all the great discourses. He would not have heard the lengthy instruction given to the four apostles on the Mount of Olives but its contents ('when will the destruction of Jerusalem take place and what will be the sign of your parousia?') would have been of the intensest interest to all the apostles and indeed to the whole church, and we might expect a demand for an accurate record at a very early date.[6] When the idea of producing a comprehensive account of Jesus the Messiah was entertained, Matthew would presumably have given high priority to an account of the passion and resurrection appearances, and would have added other stories of the works of the Messiah which he and his colleagues used regularly in their work. It was probably a common occurrence for Peter and the other apostles to devote two or three hours to the narration of the gospel story to those who visited Jerusalem, and a basic content and outline and even order may have developed. Having this material on papyrus sheets, it would be the task of Matthew to decide finally in what order to arrange it. As he was reporting on a historical person, he would naturally lay out the matter in a broadly chronological order from the conception of Jesus to the final commissioning on the Galilean mountain. But, as we have noticed (p. 107), he (or his fellow-apostles before him) seem to have brought forward the Sermon on the Mount and mission of the twelve somewhat, in order to emphasise the abiding importance of these great statements. His work when completed provided a magnificent handbook for those engaged in Christian work in the Jewish homeland. If the Semitic Matthew was translated into Greek before the writing of Mark, its form of words would probably have been much influenced by the Greek form of the early oral tradition.

Writing Mark's gospel

When we come to the composition of the second gospel, the uncertain variables increase. We argued in Chapter 4 that Mark probably modelled his gospel form on Matthew, and we know that tradition regards its content as substantially the teaching of Peter. But we do not know whether Peter (or Mark) had the use only of a Semitic Matthew or whether they had it in Greek. We do not know whether Mark's record is based upon a particular series of Petrine discourses or whether it is an account of Peter's usual teaching. We do not know how much of the gospel comes direct from the apostle and how much is Mark's own.

To suppose that Peter had only the Semitic Matthew, which he translated (to use the term of Papias) 'as he was able', is one way of accounting for some of the many differences between Matthew and Mark, but it seems most improbable that Peter would have been dependent on Matthew. Carmignac, in *The*

Birth of the Synoptic Gospels, offers another way: he holds that Mark was also originally in Hebrew and that the Hebrew Matthew was based upon it and that a good many of the differences in the Greek versions are the result of varying translations of the same Hebrew. If stress is laid on literary dependence this type of factor may be important. If, however, stress is laid upon the freedom of the individual teachers, their independence will account for an unlimited number of differences. For those who believe in a Semitic Matthew the question of the likenesses between the Greek gospels poses a greater problem than the differences. Zahn's view was that Mark was the first Greek gospel and that Matthew was translated by someone who knew its language well and consciously or unconsciously often adopted its wording.[7] This view was pressed by J.-M. Vosté[8] and is favoured by J. E. Steinmueller, who says:

> [That] the Greek translator of St. Matthew's Semitic original depended upon St. Mark's Gospel for his language and style is shown by the fact that about one fifteenth of the Second Gospel agrees verbally with St. Matthew, and twenty-three rare words are used only by these two Evangelists in parallel passages: then too the citations from the Old Testament which these two Evangelists have in common, agreed in their divergences from the Hebrew text or the Septuagint.[9]

Butler[10] repudiates Vosté and opts for the simpler hypothesis of Mark's direct dependence on an already translated Matthew. The influence of a fairly well-established oral tradition in Greek would seem a feasible alternative adequate to account for Matthew's translator using the same words and phrases as Mark. The adoption by the apostolic church of a somewhat rare Greek word (such as ἐπιούσιος in the Lord's Prayer) as the best solution of a problem of translation could quickly establish itself as the standard rendering.

The question of Old Testament quotations in the two books presents no real problem. Hawkins[11] argued that the form of the Old Testament quotations in Matthew suggested at least two sources. For, where Matthew and Mark are parallel, the quotations approximate rather closely to the Septuagint; but, where Matthew has no parallel, less so. But this does not prove different sources. On the theory of the priority of a Semitic Matthew one would *expect* the translator to use the Septuagint form, so well known to him and his readers, in the passages where it served its purpose adequately, as it did in the Markan parallels and (be it noted) in some of the passages peculiar to Matthew (e.g. 1:23). Where the text demanded a more literal translation he was free to make one. If Mark was following the text of Matthew, his use of the Septuagint form would be quite natural, whether he was copying the Greek or translating a Semitic original.

One idea (espoused by both Chapman and Butler[12]) can be safely discarded. It is hardly likely that Peter made use of Matthew as an *aide-mémoire* in his preaching. The apostle had been incessantly telling the story of Jesus for years and would have felt no need for such help. Nor is the idea that Mark is a transcript of a series of lectures taken down in shorthand (as Orchard supposed[13]) likely. As we have seen (p. 179), the gospel is too short and concise to be a full record of the preached word, even though Mark's account continually seems to recall the preacher's language.

How are we to suppose that Mark went to work? It is anachronistic to think of him working like a modern author with well-referenced sources, convenient writing materials and plenty of space. A quotation from A. Dain, the eminent French authority on manuscripts, will illustrate the point:

> With very rare exceptions, one always sees the copyist in a quite characteristic attitude: he does not execute his copy on a desk or reading-stand – nor à fortiori on a table – but he writes on his knees, usually but not always, with a board serving as a writing-surface for him . . . It is astonishing that the professional copyists should not have used a table for their work. The truth is that Antiquity did not know what we call a writing-table. The table virtually serves only for eating, and it is always very low. It is only in the second part of the Middle Ages that one finds representations showing copyists writing on a desk, or even on a table . . . There is then a classical copyist position: κάλαμος μ' ἔγραψε, δεξιὰ χεὶρ καὶ γόνυ, one reads on a papyrus of the first century . . . The person is seated, his left leg bent; his right leg is vertical and his knee supports the little

writing board on which [he] writes. With the right hand he traces the written marks, while with the left he holds the sheet of parchment.[14]

This is borne out by B. M. Metzger's subsequent study 'When did Scribes Begin to Use Writing Desks?' in which he shows that desks, tables and stands are traceable only to the ninth century.[15] He adds useful information about note-taking:

> . . . when a scribe was making relatively brief notes on a wax tablet or on a sheet of papyrus or parchment, he would usually stand and write while holding the material in his left hand. When a scribe had a more extensive task, such as the copying of a rather lengthy manuscript, he would sit, occasionally on the ground but more often on a stool or bench, supporting the scroll or codex on his knees. (123)

He discounts the idea that the 'table' in the scriptorium at Qumran, which was solid and only seventeen and a half inches high, could have served as a writing-desk (136). Nothing could give a more vivid idea of the awkwardness of redactional work than a study of Plates III–XIX in Metzger's book, which show how cramped scribes were even when they began to have desks to work at. In the first century tables and chairs such as we know them did not exist. Diners reclined, propped up on an elbow, at the low tables. To consult more than one scroll[16] an author would presumably have had to spread them out on such a table or on the floor and either crawl around on hands and knees or else repeatedly crouch down and stand up again, looking at first one and then another. He could either make notes or commit what he read to memory before writing the matter up on a sheet of papyrus or vellum, or, possibly, sitting down and transferring it direct to his new scroll. Finding the place, unless he was prepared seriously to deface his scrolls, would be difficult. Handling a reed pen dipped in ink (or moistened to get ink from a dry ink-cake) to write on a surface made of strips of papyrus pith was a skilled operation – which Paul seems usually to have left to an amanuensis. In a community where most had small, dark, crowded homes, finding a room suitable for the task, and reasonably free from distractions, would not be easy.

In ideal conditions it was not particularly difficult for a
trained scribe simply to copy a scroll, though (as Dain points
out) it required great concentration. Copying with some adaptation was also common in the ancient world, but it was the work
of highly educated scholars. For one who was not a professional
to take a lengthy manuscript with no chapter, verse or even
word divisions and select, rearrange and revise it was a formidable task. It is highly unlikely that one gospel was produced as
the result of an author working directly on the scroll of another;
even less that he worked on two or three at once.[17]

F. G. Downing, in a most valuable article 'Compositional
Conventions and the Synoptic Problem',[18] has uttered a strong
protest, on the basis of contemporary educational methods and
of known compositional procedures, against complex compositional hypotheses. He quotes recent research into the methods
adopted by Livy, Plutarch, Hieronymus of Cardia, Lucian and
Josephus. He says:

> We are in a position to tell with a considerable degree of certainty
> what compositional procedures for making use of existing writings
> would have been readily available in the first century. We can tell
> on the basis of many examples of practice and some indications of
> theory: even the most highly literate and sophisticated writers
> employ relatively simple approaches to their 'sources.' . . . Con-
> flation was itself only rarely attempted, and then very simply
> effected . . . the long debate on the sources of the Synoptic Gospels
> seems to have been conducted without paying much or any atten-
> tion to this issue of whether any indications of 'sensible' compo-
> sitional procedures in the first century C.E. are available. (70)

He quotes Pelling: 'Livy read widely, but nevertheless followed
a single source for a single section; within these sections he
would occasionally add supplementary items from other
sources, but he would not use a number of sources to weave
together a coherent and independent account of his own.'[19] He
refers to J. Hornblower, who concludes that in classical studies
in the field of composition 'hypotheses involving complex
composition have been largely abandoned as unfruitful'.
He again quotes Pelling, who gives a sketch of an author at
work:

A writer would not normally refer back to [earlier] reading to verify individual references, and would instead rely on his memory, or on the briefest of notes . . . Stray facts and additions would be recalled from the preliminary available reading, but it would be a very different matter to recall the detail of an episode's presentation . . . Such a procedure seems less perverse in view of the physical difficulties of working with papyrus rolls . . . [with] non-existent or rudimentary . . . indexing, chapter-headings, line- and column-numbering . . . Even if, for example, a slave held a second roll for an author to compare accounts, or the author himself used a book-rest, combining versions would still be awkward. (92f)

Downing then comments:

If this general picture be accepted for a fairly sophisticated and wealthy writer's preparations for writing, then the implications for the study of the Synoptic Gospels is clear. Even had one of our evangelists wanted to emulate the well-staffed and well-equipped compositional procedures of a sophisticated literary figure, nothing would have suggested that he should begin by analysing his source material, nor on that or any other basis that he should plan some complex conflation of his sources. (73)

Downing thinks that the two-document hypothesis 'fits snugly' (85) into the contemporary background, but his evidence in fact argues for even less literary dependence than he admits. He favours Streeter's model, but Streeter gives considerable space to the overlapping of Q and Mark, which he believes to have been conflated, particularly by Matthew (Streeter 186–91).

So it is unlikely that a gospel-writer worked directly on the scroll or scrolls of his predecessors. It is more likely that he started by writing down the words and deeds of Jesus after the manner of his normal oral instruction and that he then used the written word of the earlier evangelist to check and improve what he had written. Possibly Mark worked something like this:

1.) He thought out the broad outline of how he wanted to present the good news of Jesus, Christ and Son of God. (This is where Mark's fine and original mind laid its stamp upon the book that was to be.) His intention was to write another account of Jesus on the lines pioneered by Matthew, but reflecting the manner and substance of Peter's missionary instruction in Rome. (This was not to replace Matthew, but to provide the church with a second apostolic portrait of Jesus.)[20] He wished to take the main topics of Peter's preaching and weld them into a coherent story, emphasising the cross and the cost of discipleship and looking forward from the resurrection to the parousia.

2.) He wrote in vellum notebooks or on separate sheets of papyrus or parchment his various recollections of Peter's teaching.

3.) He read through Matthew, making a table of its contents.

4.) In this table he bracketed the items which were not part of Peter's regular teaching and which he did not intend to use (see p. 105 above). This list provided him a guide to the Matthew scroll, and a preliminary guide to the contents of his new book.

5.) He drew up a table of contents for the new book based on Matthew, but incorporating the three changes of order (see pp. 101–8 above) and the extra little items which he wished to include.

6.) He arranged his sheets in this order.

7.) He proceeded to read through Matthew again, with a view to improving what he had written. He would not have worked in the spirit of one forestalling twentieth-century biblical critics, but he would have been concerned with accurate and united apostolic testimony. Probably a large majority of his sheets were entirely satisfactory and were left untouched, but Matthew would occasionally suggest omissions to be remedied, possible misunderstandings to be corrected or harmonisations to be effected. Hence there would be a gentle harmonising influence operating which may partially account for the closeness of sense of the two gospels.

8.) Finally, he edited his revised drafts ready for professional copying.

Writing Luke's gospel

When we come to the composition of the third gospel, we have Luke's prologue to help us. Luke tells us that many had already attempted to write an account of the events fulfilled in their midst. All had attempted to write in accordance with the tradition which the from-the-beginning-eyewitnesses and ministers-of-the-word had delivered to the church (καθὼς παρέδοσαν ἡμῖν οἱ ἀπ᾽ ἀρχῆς αὐτόπται καὶ ὑπηρέται γενόμενοι τοῦ λόγου). This form of words (which is discussed in greater detail in Wenham *Luke*) may well betray a knowledge of the first two gospels. These bearers of a common tradition appear to be one group having two sections: apostles and their assistants. Matthew's gospel would represent the first section, though it was probably not merely the witness of one man, it was the witness of one man working in close association with eleven others, acting as their penman and with their approval. Mark's gospel represents the second section, for although it was the witness of Peter we owe its writing to his ὑπηρέτης (cf. Acts 13:5). Luke (it would seem) knows and acknowledges the authority of these two works, but he has much additional information in which he has entire confidence, which it seems good to him to write up for the benefit of Theophilus. We must leave it an open question (see Wenham *Luke*) whether Luke was claiming by his παρηκολουθηκότι to have been present during the ministry of Jesus or simply to have been the recipient of much incontrovertible information. Whichever it was, he is evidently a Christian teacher of long standing, who has confidence in what he is accustomed to teach.

So Luke has Matthew, Mark and his own material. How are we to suppose he set to work? He evidently wished to write a fully rounded gospel which included most of the material common to Matthew and Mark, and which covered the great events from the promise of the forerunner to the ascension. He had big stores of information and he knew that to keep his material within the limits of one scroll[21] would require much self-denial. So he decides to leave out most of the peculiarly Matthean material and concentrate on his new matter, only using Matthew to fill out an occasional thin spot. He then presumably did with Mark much as we suppose Mark to have done with Matthew. He listed the contents of Mark and then decided how to fit together blocks of Mark with his great new blocks of L. He then wrote up his sheets and revised them in the light of his readings of Mark and Matthew. It was probably when he came to the final editing that he discovered that he had considerably exceeded the length of a scroll and decided that something must be dropped. It was natural to hold on to all the new material and drop something from the Galilean ministry, hence the Great Omission of Mark 6:45–8:26, which apart from the healing of a blind man at the end is fully covered by both Matthew and Mark.[22]

In Luke's revised sheets there would again have been the same gentle harmonistic tendency. But he would not have been scrutinising every parallel passage with such care that there would never be any possibility of misunderstanding. When he came to Mark's Jericho story he may not even have noticed that Mark had referred to it as taking place ἐκπορευομένου αὐτοῦ ἀπὸ Ἰεριχώ (10:46), while he had said that it was ἐν τῷ ἐγγίζειν αὐτὸν εἰς Ἰεριχώ (18:35).

This trivial discrepancy calls for explanation whatever synoptic theory is proposed. Ellis thinks that Luke changes the locale of Mark's story of the healing of the blind man so that he may link it with his Jericho story about Zacchaeus. He is prepared to do this because he is more concerned with thematic arrangement than with locale and chronology.[23] There is, however, no obvious reason why he should not have put Zacchaeus before Bartimaeus and left Mark's note of time and place untouched. It is more likely that having written his own version he saw no need to change it when he read Mark's – and this for a surprising reason.

At the time of Jesus there were two inhabited Jericho settlements in addition to the deserted Tell-es-Sultan, which hid the ancient Jericho excavated by Kathleen Kenyon and others.[24] From Elisha's Fountain, which issues from the ground at this point, there flows a watercourse eastward to the Dead Sea, providing irrigation for a considerable area in the hot and barren rift valley. It was along this watercourse that the houses lay which made up the later Old Testament Jericho, the city of palm trees (2 Chron. 28:15). In the time of Herod the Great a new group of buildings was established centred on his winter

210

palace in the valley of the Wadi Qilt a mile or so to the south of the ancient city. This place got its water by aqueduct from a different source. It is here that the well-to-do like Zacchaeus would have lived. At pre-Herodian Jericho roads from the north meet the road from across the ford of Jordan. Travellers to Jerusalem would proceed about a mile from this road junction, before crossing the Wadi Qilt and beginning the long climb up to the capital. Not enough is known of the precise limits of the two settlements to say dogmatically that there was a point where the road to Jerusalem could be said to be going out of the older Jericho and to be drawing near to Herod's Jericho. Josephus does not speak of two separate Jerichos, he describes the Jericho area simply in terms of the fertility deriving from Elisha's spring. But it seems likely enough that there was a section of the road where the older houses came to an end and the new buildings began, and that Luke knew the place himself.

Luke's supposed ignorance of Palestinian geography has been gratuitously deduced from his earlier remark that as Jesus 'was going to Jerusalem διήρχετο διὰ μέσον (or μέσου) Samaria and Galilee' (17:11). H. Conzelmann regarded this as impossible geography, taking it to mean 'that Luke imagines that Judaea and Galilee are immediately adjacent, and that Samaria lies alongside them, apparently bordering on both the regions'.[25] *BAG* likewise says that διὰ μέσον 'probably can only mean through Samaria and Galilee'.[26] But nearly all the atlases[27] show a roughly triangular section of the Decapolis in the Valley of Jezreel to the west of the Jordan which thrusts its apex between the two territories. Along this valley runs a road down which would proceed Galilean pilgrims who wished to avoid travelling through the main Samaritan centres. They would pass through Scythopolis (described by Josephus as the greatest city of the Decapolis),[28] turn south and follow the course of the Jordan, probably crossing to its eastern bank[29] and going on until they reached the ford which brought them to Jericho. The RSV translation 'passing along between Galilee and Samaria' precisely fits this location.[30] At no place would it be more likely that Jesus would meet a mixed group of lepers, which included a Samaritan.

The crasser cases of supposed disharmony between Luke and Matthew were evidently not regarded as such by Luke himself. The infancy narratives of Matthew and Luke, in spite of their few points of contact, are not difficult to harmonise when they are seen as accounts from two quite different angles, one from Joseph's and the other from Mary's.[31] A good case can still be made for the genealogies being one of Jesus' legal descent from his adoptive father Joseph and the other of his physical descent through Mary. J. S. Wright said concerning this famous discrepancy:

> The simplest explanation is that the genealogy in Luke 3 is that of Mary, since the early chapters of Luke's Gospel are clearly written from Mary's point of view. In Luke, Joseph is the son of Heli [some prefer the spelling Eli], whereas in Matthew's Gospel he is described as the son of Jacob.
>
> Let us suppose, then, that Mary's father was Heli. Mary had a sister; we are told that 'standing by the cross of Jesus were his mother, and his mother's sister' (John 19:25). We are nowhere told of a brother. If, therefore, Heli had two daughters only, the line, which was always traced through the male line, would have died out. The regulations quoted in Numbers 27:1–11 and 36:1–9, were that, when daughters only survived, their possessions and their family name required a male relative, or at least someone of the same tribe, to carry them on. Even if Joseph was not a (near) relative of Mary, he was one of the line of David, and, in marrying her, he carried on the line of Heli, thus becoming the son of Heli.[32]

In other words the opening sentence of Luke's genealogy is to be interpreted: 'Jesus . . . being as it was supposed son of Joseph, who was the son of Heli *by virtue of his marriage to Mary.*' Luke has made it abundantly clear that Jesus had no physical derivation from Joseph, but (to maintain the conventional male sequence) he inserts the name of Joseph, who was at once Heli's heir and Jesus' father (both legally and practically). Even if no levirate factor was involved and Mary had brothers, Joseph would still have become a son of Heli by virtue of his marriage to her. Geldenhuys points out how beautifully it all fits once a rigid literalism concerning Joseph is dropped.[33] On this

212

view we see Luke once again adding valuable new information about Jesus.[34] I have written at length elsewhere about the disharmonies of the resurrection narratives, which appear to me to be reconcilable without any forcing.[35]

The whole edifice of modern gospel criticism is based on the belief that the true Jesus is to be found by a critical elimination of those elements of the gospels which are not true and by trying to make a careful distinction between historical event and theological interpretation. Great efforts are made to analyse the documents and to bring to light their inconsistencies.[36] Harmonisation is somehow regarded as the enemy of exegesis. Yet harmonisation is a perfectly proper procedure for a historian who believes that he has reliable witnesses, and if our view of the method of the composition of the gospels is right, harmonistic exegesis may in fact be quite in tune with the evangelists' own approach to one another.

It will be noticed that in this treatment of the synoptic problem I have refrained almost entirely from attempting to identify the particular influences which have moulded the authors' forms of words. This is a necessity of truth, because we cannot pretend to know how much comes from literary dependence, how much from oral tradition, how much from assimilation of phraseology in well-known accounts of similar events, how much from an individual author. The strongest position is to go no further than the evidence and to be content with what we have. In our last two chapters I think it will be found that we have a great deal.

Additional Note on the genealogies of Jesus

In the so-called pre-critical era a vast literature was devoted to the problem of the two genealogies, but nowadays many scholars have no interest in looking for a reconciliation between them, not regarding them as sources of historical information. M. D. Johnson, the author of *The Purpose of the Biblical Genealogies* (Cambridge UP, 1969), is a noteworthy example. He has summarised his views in his *ISBE* article 'Genealogy of Jesus':

213

the genealogies probably arose in Jewish-Christian circles from a need to historicize this item of belief. On this view both lists fall into the category of midrash . . . both are apologetic attempts to express more fully the Christian conviction that Jesus is the fulfillment of the hope of Israel.

There have, however, been numerous scholars in modern times, who, like F. F. Bruce, would say: 'It is most improbable that the names in either list which have no OT attestation were simply invented by the Evangelists or their sources' ('Genealogy of Jesus Christ' *IDB*). In addition to that given in the text two other theories have been adopted. The most venerable is the one relayed to us by Julius Africanus (*c.* 160–240) and quoted by Eusebius (*HE* 1.7.2–16), which, Julius says, is supposed to have come from members of the Saviour's family:

> Whether this be so or not no one could give a clearer account, in my opinion and in that of all well-disposed persons, and it may suffice us even though it is not corroborated [εἰ καὶ ἀμάρτυρός ἐστιν] since we have nothing better or truer to say: in any case the gospel speaks the truth . . . Matthan of the line of Solomon begat Jacob. On the death of Matthan, Melchi of the line of Nathan begat Eli from the same woman. Thus Eli and Jacob were step-brothers with the same mother. When Eli died without children, Jacob raised up seed for him, begetting Joseph as his own natural son but the legal son of Eli. Thus Joseph was son of both. (Kirsopp Lake's text and translation)

Some (e.g. B. W. Bacon, 'Genealogy of Jesus' *HDB* II 138 col 2) have taken this to mean that the theory is 'unsupported by [any] testimony' and that therefore it did not come from Jesus' family. But Julius says, 'This is neither devoid of proof, nor is it conjecture, for the human relatives of the Saviour have handed on this tradition' (para 11). He does not make it clear whether he got it direct from them, but he evidently believes that they were the source of the explanation, which satisfies him and 'all well-disposed persons'. He appears to be drawing a contrast between the gospel which certainly speaks the truth and the tradition which has only uncertain human testimony. Since Julius was not only a man of wide learning, but he had 'good critical powers' ('Julius Africanus' *ODCC*), his explanation has considerable authority, and it satisfied the church for many centuries. Though complex, it is possible.

Even so, there are difficulties. If one of the evangelists wrote with knowledge of the different list in an earlier gospel, it is hard to see what he intended to achieve by appearing thus to contradict it without giving any explanation.[37] If, on the other hand, they wrote without knowledge of each other and were not inventing, it is surprising that members of Joseph's family should have given different lists to the two evangelists. Furthermore, it needs to be remembered that the interval of perhaps eight generations between the birth of Jesus and the writing of Julius allows plenty of time for the true story to have got lost. Origen, writing against Celsus (2.32) says that the incompatibility of the genealogies had been an occasion of derision to many an earlier opponent of Christianity. This suggests a strong motive for thinking up possible explanations for the discrepancy and for attributing the tradition to Jesus' family. (What started as speculations could easily have become traditions without any conscious falsification.) Julius himself is obviously passing on the best information at his disposal, which could perfectly well have been passed on by James the Lord's brother or other members of the family who occupied positions of influence in the Jerusalem church, but his sources may not have been as good as he thought. The first gospel harmony, Tatian's Diatessaron (*c.* 150 or a little later), appears to have solved the problem by omitting both genealogies, but whether this was because Tatian knew no solution or because it would have gone against his principles to insert an explanation in the text we do not know. (See J. H. Hill, *The Earliest Life of Christ*, Edinburgh: T. & T. Clark, 1910, for an English translation of the (Arabic) text.) What may have been well known to Luke's first readers could have given way before the pressure of a literal interpretation of Luke's text in the second century, as it has done in the twentieth; Lagrange (*Évangile selon St Luc* 116) complains of non-literal interpretations: 'il faut changer le text'. (So also R. E. Brown, *The Birth of the Messiah*, London: Chapman, 1977, 89.) It is possible that the levirate factor which appears in the complex scheme of Julius is a relic of genuine history which originally took the form of the simpler scheme of J. S. Wright.

The second view, favoured by F. F. Bruce, J. G. Machen, *The Virgin Birth of Christ* (London: Marshall, 1930) and many moderns, holds that Matthew gives the line of royal descent (where a sovereign's successor is not always his son) from David to Joseph, and Luke gives the natural succession back from Joseph to David (and Adam). On this view one would expect frequent coincidences between the two genealogies, but these are in fact notoriously few. In any case the Jewish monarchy does not seem to have been regulated by a strict theory of primogeniture like the royal houses of Europe. A boy's concern would simply have been whether or not he was a descendant of David and therefore a possible heir to the Messianic promises.

The view given in the text that Luke's list is Mary's was held by Luther, Bengel, J. Lightfoot, Wieseler, Godet, B. Weiss, A. T. Robertson, N. Geldenhuys and many others. It is sometimes said (e.g. Marshall *Luke* 158) to be the theory of Annius Viterbo (*c*. 1490), but Lagrange 119 claims to trace it back to the fifth century. Luke's taking the genealogy back to Adam fits well with the 'last Adam' theology of his travelling companion Paul (1 Cor. 15:45). This information about Mary's descent provides a valuable complement, theologically as well as historically, to what Matthew has told us.

11

JESUS-TRADITION ORAL AND WRITTEN

Chapter summary

If the gospels were written very early, why are they not referred to in the rest of the New Testament? This is a problem for all who maintain the substantial reliability of the Jesus-tradition in the synoptic gospels. M. B. Thompson thinks that Paul could assume some knowledge of it on the part of ordinary church members. Bultmann thought such knowledge minimal. Resch saw over a thousand gospel allusions in the Pauline letters. Yet implicit appeals to dominical sayings are rare. This thinness of appeal to the gospels persists into the sub-apostolic age, when the existence of the gospels is no longer debatable. Luke in Acts, having at least twenty-four chapters of Jesus-tradition in his mind, does not refer to it. Hebrews, James, 1 and 2 Peter, 1 John and the Apocalypse all presuppose knowledge of the tradition. 1 Timothy 5:18 appears to be an actual quotation from Luke 10:7.

Factors militating against the establishment of written norms include: 1.) As long as apostles could be *heard* there would be little incentive to refer to their writings. 2.) The Christians had no synagogue schools in which to teach their scriptures. 3.) Verifying of quotations by either writer or reader would be difficult. 4.) It was some time before the regular reading of 'epistle' and 'gospel' took root, and with it the idea of New Testament scripture. 5.) There was no central authority to define canonicity, a concept which developed gradually. From *c.* 40 to *c.* 160 written and oral tradition circulated side by side. The special authority of the former, being less subject to change, was recognised as the apostolic era passed away.

217

The argument of this book has been pointing towards the possibility of an extremely early date for Matthew and very early dates for Mark and Luke. But this raises the question, Why is there no direct reference to them in the rest of the New Testament? In particular, if Matthew was written first, by the apostle, with the approval of the rest of the from-the-beginning-eyewitnesses, should we not expect it to have achieved something like canonical status almost at once? Yet neither the later gospels, nor Acts, nor the epistles, nor the Apocalypse, make any appeal to it. This is an objection from silence, which needs for that reason to be treated with caution; but at first sight it seems a formidable hurdle for the theory to surmount.

It is a problem which to some extent faces all who maintain the substantial reliability of the Jesus-tradition in the synoptic gospels. It has been explored in depth by M. B. Thompson in a 1988 Cambridge PhD thesis on *The Example and Teaching of Jesus in Romans 12:1–15:13*. He maintains in the case of Paul that he himself knew a great deal of Jesus-tradition and could assume at least some knowledge of it on the part of ordinary church members – careful instruction in the life, teaching, death and resurrection of Jesus was probably the normal foundation of Christian faith.[1] Since Paul's apostleship did not derive from a call of the earthly Jesus, one might have expected concern with this tradition to have been relatively slight in his churches. But this is not so. Though there have been minimalists like R. Bultmann, who have held that 'the teaching of the historical Jesus plays no role, or practically none, in Paul and John,'[2] and there have been maximalists like A. Resch, who thought he could recognise 1,158 gospel allusions in the Pauline letters,[3] there seems little doubt that both Paul and his converts knew a good deal of this tradition. W. D. Davies, an eminently moderate scholar, having discussed Resch in *Paul and Rabbinic Judaism* (London: SPCK, 1948, 137) was prepared to say in 1966: 'a careful reading of the Pauline Epistles reveals again and again that there are echoes of the Sayings of Jesus constantly creeping into the apostle's words. For example it has been estimated that at over a thousand points the words of Paul recall those of Jesus.'[4] If Resch was over-zealous in his quest for allusions,[5] Bultmann was unreasonable to be dismissive of so much material. Yet Paul makes explicit and unquestionable appeal to dominical sayings only three times, on marriage and divorce (1 Cor. 7:10f), on the right of gospel preachers to material support (1 Cor. 9:14)[6] and on the Lord's Supper (1 Cor. 11:24ff), and then not in the precise form found in the gospels. He never refers to a written record, except possibly in his reference to 'The labourer deserves his wages' in 1 Timothy 5:18 (which he describes as 'scripture' and which is identical with Luke 10:7), and seemingly he refers in an incidental way to a gospel in 2 Corinthians 8:18.[7]

How are we to account for the richness of the knowledge of Jesus-tradition and the paucity of explicit appeals to it in the early literature? The first point to notice is that the thinness of appeal to the Jesus-tradition is not confined to the literature written at a time when the existence of the gospels is debatable, but it continues into the period of the apostolic fathers,[8] when their existence is virtually undeniable, showing that silence does not necessarily mean non-existence. The fallacy of the argument from silence is seen most clearly in the case of Luke. He knew all the Jesus-material of his gospel, yet when he came to write Acts he did not repeat it there, though he could have done so frequently when describing the work of the apostles and their helpers. Further, if our understanding of τὰ λόγια in Polycarp and Papias is correct (see pp. 128–30) the use of this expression bears direct witness to the existence of Christian scriptures even when they are not quoted. In the case of Papias this witness should apparently be dated before the end of Trajan's reign in 110.[9]

Thompson, having argued the presupposition of earlier instruction, offers five main suggestions to account for this state of affairs (48ff). 1.) Language which echoes the gospels is commonest in paraenesis. But in paraenesis, where argument ceases and exhortation begins, Paul has no need to cite sources. 2.) The occasional nature of the epistles means that their purpose is not to present the ABCs of Christian tradition for neophytes, but to give particular answers to particular problems. 3.) Paul's own chief experience of Christ was on the

Damascus road, and his supreme concern continues to be with Christ as he is, rather than as he was. 4.) The cross outshone all other examples of love and humility, and the resurrection outshone all other examples of power. The whole Jesus-tradition was necessary to make the gospel claim intelligible, but in paraenesis all was secondary to its great climax. 5.) Christianity was built on Judaism and this remained a source for much of what Paul taught. So it is that he had no occasion to tell his readers that Jesus habitually spoke in parables, that he healed the sick and ministered in Galilee, that he was baptised, tempted and transfigured.[10]

What is true of Paul's letters is also broadly true of Hebrews, James, 1 and 2 Peter, 1 John and the Apocalypse[11] – all presuppose a knowledge of Jesus-tradition. Much of this tradition approximates to what is written in the canonical gospels, but how much of it derives from written gospels and how much from oral tradition is the subject of endless and fruitless debate, since verbal identity could be preserved in oral transmission and major differences of form could occur as a result of inexact quotation from or deliberate adaptation of the written word. Only explicit reference to a written source can be decisive, though generally speaking the closer it is to the canonical form the more likely it is to be using a written gospel. This favours the view that the 'scripture' in 1 Timothy 5:18 is an actual quotation from Luke 10:7.

A number of more general factors militated against the establishment of specifically Christian written norms in the church:

1.) In the first two generations of the church, those who had *heard* the living voice of Spirit-filled apostles were unlikely to appeal to their written words. It would be unnatural to regard living traditional material as something written, simply because written versions had come into being.

2.) The church was a mixed Jewish-Gentile body, with the proportion of Gentiles steadily increasing. The Jewish system of education had been based on a verbatim knowledge of the scriptures, the community's most treasured possessions. Copies were kept in every synagogue and Jewish boys were thoroughly drilled in their contents. In the increasingly Gentile church there was nothing that quite corresponded to the synagogue-school. It would have been a long time before gospels became common in Christian homes.

3.) In the earliest stages of the church's life it was far easier to instruct orally than to bother with lengthy scrolls which were difficult to find one's way around. Also, may there not have been a reluctance to give specific attribution to a passage, which though well known was not known verbatim, and which could only be verified with considerable trouble?[12] It was probably not till the codex came into common use in the second century that works of gospel-length became relatively easy to handle.

4.) Though most of the New Testament books were intended for reading in the assembly (1 Thess. 5:27; Col. 4:16; Rev. 1:3) and were doubtless repeatedly read in the churches to which they were first sent, it was some time before the practice established itself throughout the churches of the regular reading of 'gospel'[13] and 'epistle', which caused the idea of New Testament scriptures to take deep root in the minds of church people.

5.) The development of the concept of apostolic authority into that of canonicity could only have progressed slowly since there was no central authority directing the churches as to whether an edifying writing should be regarded as γραφὴ θεόπνευστος.[14] The larger churches no doubt wished to acquire the texts known to be in use in other churches and were able gradually to build up their collections. But the precise authority of the various books only became clear by slow degrees.

I shall argue in the next chapter (pp. 230–7) that there is some direct evidence that Luke's gospel was highly valued throughout the Pauline churches in the mid-50s, and I am inclined to believe that Matthew and Mark are referred to in Luke's preface,[15] but this does not mean that they were functioning in the church in the way that the Old Testament books functioned in contemporary Judaism. 2 Peter 3:16 (which I believe we should date before 70)[16] indicates that Paul's letters were widely known in the church and could be categorised as γραφαί. This was a big step towards the canonisation of the Pauline epistles, but it was still a long way from the notion of a New Testament canon.[17] These indications of the existence of New Testament books and of their regard in the church are occasional in their nature and serve only to give chance glimpses of their value and function. Matthew's gospel must in fact have been more influential than Luke in the early days, to explain the preponderance of echoes of his Sermon on the Mount in the apostolic fathers and the gospel's predominance in the second-century church.[18] Textual criticism also bears out the gradualness of growth of the idea of canonicity, since the great majority of significant textual variants date back to the first two centuries, which suggests that much of the copying in the early days was done without a belief in the sanctity of the very wording of the books as the oracles of God.[19]

These factors account for the paucity of references to the gospels as manuals of instruction and show that in practice reliance was placed for a long time on oral instruction rather than on written texts. Only gradually did confidence in the process of oral transmission wane and the superiority of written apostolic traditions establish itself. This is common ground for all who uphold the substantial historicity of the synoptic gospels, whether they favour very early dates or not. D. A. Hagner in his 'The Sayings of Jesus in the Apostolic Fathers and Justin Martyr' adopts the conclusion of R. C. P. Hanson, 'the situation of the Church in the years *circa* 60 to *circa* 160 A.D. is precisely this one, when written and oral tradition are circulating in the Church side by side'.[20] Our dating of the gospels simply means emending the span of years to read '*circa* 40 to *circa* 160' and saying: 'The situation of the Church in the years *circa* 40 to *circa* 160 was one where written and oral tradition were circulating in the Church side by side.' For a balanced understanding of the way in which Jesus-tradition was transmitted we need to grasp the importance, both of the careful training in an oral tradition coming from the authorised leadership, which was the normal mode of instruction; and, the written accounts of which there were 'many', pre-eminent among which were 'the dominical oracles', the gospel-scriptures. The latter were far the less accessible, but as they were also far less subject to change they carried a special authority, which came to be recognised more and more clearly as the apostolic era passed away.[21]

12

WHEN WERE THE GOSPELS WRITTEN?

Chapter summary

On the face of it the synoptic apocalypse makes a date before 70 probable for all three gospels – there is no suggestion of Jesus' momentous prophecy having been fulfilled. Dodd argues that Luke's version of the apocalypse reflects Old Testament prophecies rather than recent history. Hemer's *The Book of Acts in the Setting of Hellenistic History* makes a reconsideration of the 62 date of Acts necessary. Harnack moved from a post-70 date to 62; Bruce has moved in the opposite direction for insufficient reasons. One reason for discrediting Acts as history has been the supposed inconsistency of its portrait of Paul when compared with that derived from his epistles, and some have seen this as a reason for dating the book late. Much more decisive has been the supposed necessity of dating Luke's gospel (and Mark before it) well after 62. Luke and Acts are separate works. The former could have been written during Paul's imprisonment in Caesarea, but 2 Corinthians 8:18 suggests an even earlier date. The 'brother whose fame in the gospel is throughout the churches' is evidently Luke, and his fame derives from his gospel-book. (This usage of εὐαγγέλιον was to be expected any time after Mark 1:1 had been written.) It makes 55 the latest possible date for Luke.

Mark is to be dated *c.* 45, after Peter's first visit to Rome in 42–44.

Matthew is to be dated before the dispersal of the apostles in 42. Irenaeus is often misinterpreted in favour of a date after Paul had reached Rome.

223

Finally, a summary of conclusions to be drawn from the book
as a whole brings the volume to an end.

It is impossible without unduly lengthening the book to attempt
an exhaustive discussion of the many theories concerning the
dates of the gospels. I shall not attempt to refute the scholars
who adopt extremely late dates since the ground has been
adequately covered by scholars of a more moderate persuasion.[1]
I shall confine the discussion to the debate with the centre party.

Before or after AD 70?

There are two considerations which bear on the question of
whether the synoptics should be dated before or after 70. First
is the dating of Jesus' eschatological discourse. Most scholars
adopt a date after 70 for at least Matthew and Luke. But it needs
to be said with great emphasis (as Robinson has shown in
chapter 4 of his *Redating the New Testament*) that on the face of it
none of the synoptists suggest this. The eschatological discourse foretells the shocking disaster which forty years later was
to engulf the Jewish people, yet not one of them tells us that
Jesus' prophecy was fulfilled. Luke tells us of the fulfilment of
Agabus' prophecy of worldwide famine (Acts 11:28), but of the
fulfilment of this disaster, which to the Jews was incomparably
greater, he says not a word. It is true that many believe Luke to
betray a knowledge of the sack of Jerusalem, even though he
does not explicitly mention it. But this is based on flimsy
evidence, as C. H. Dodd showed when he affirmed of Luke
19:42–44 and 21:20–24:

> Not only are the two Lucan oracles composed *entirely* from the
> language of the Old Testament, but the conception of the coming
> disaster . . . is a generalized picture of the Fall of Jerusalem as
> imaginatively presented by the prophets. So far as any historical
> event has coloured the picture, it is not Titus's capture of Jerusalem
> in A.D. 70, but Nebuchadnezzar's capture in 586 B.C.[2]

D. Wenham has argued that a pre-synoptic tradition lies behind
the three synoptists, and that Luke probably did not change
'abomination of desolation' into 'armies', but that he used an

224

earlier tradition which contained reference both to armies surrounding the city and to sacrilege in the holy place of the temple.[3] It is worth noting, further, how in Paul's last visit to Jerusalem in 57, accompanied as he was by Luke (Acts 21:17), everything is going on as usual and Luke somehow refrains once again from any reference to the catastrophe which (were he writing after 70) he must have known was so soon to strike the city.

The date of Acts

The second consideration bearing on the question of whether the synoptics should be dated before or after 70 is the dating of Acts. The starting-point of serious study of Acts must now be C. J. Hemer's magnificent work *The Book of Acts in the Setting of Hellenistic History*, published posthumously in 1989. Hemer shows how the debates concerning historicity initiated by W. M. Ramsay, who 'in his own field . . . represents the beginning of modern knowledge' (4), 'were truncated unresolved' (9) by the First World War. The interests of the post-war generation of critics (particularly in Germany) were quite different, with the result that the discussion based on the detailed findings of epigraphy was by-passed in favour of form criticism and style criticism (8, 311). Hemer shows that there has been a vast accumulation of knowledge in the last hundred years concerning the historical background of the first century AD, which in good conscience must be taken seriously before writing off the historicity of Acts. He shows in chapter 3 that 'our patronizing stance of cultural superiority is not warranted' (85), since among ancient historians there was a 'consciousness of the distinctive rigour which their best practitioners required of history' (93).[4] Chapters 4 and 5 show the detailed links between Acts and its historical background. Chapter 6 deals with the theoretical notion that because the Pauline epistles are primary sources and Acts is secondary, therefore the latter is of little value as history (even if the author is participating?) and then proceeds to show that in fact they throw much light upon one another and even make possible a credible chronology. This involves for Galatians 1.) a South Galatian destination; 2.) a date before the apostolic council of Acts 15; 3.) an identification of the Jerusalem visit of Galatians 1 with that of Acts 9. Chapter 7 discusses the uses of 'Galatia' and 'Galatians' fully. Hemer inclines (346) ever so slightly towards Ramsay's view that Luke may have been the 'man of Macedonia' of Acts 16:9 and in chapter 8 shows how such a person might have gathered reliable information about the matters recorded in Acts.

In chapter 9 reasons are given for dating Acts before 70. This is based on general indications (376), on the ending of the book (383) and on the 'immediacy' of the later chapters (388). Hemer adduces fifteen general indications, of varied weight but cumulative in their effect. Thirteen, I think, should be noted: 1.) There is no mention of the fall of Jerusalem; 2.) no hint of the outbreak of the Jewish War in 66; 3.) no hint of the deterioration of Christian relations with Rome involved in the Neronian persecution. 4.) Acts has an optimistic tone. 5.) The author betrays no knowledge of Paul's letters. The very disjunction between Acts and the epistles is best explained by an early date. 6.) There is no hint of the death of James at the hands of the Sanhedrin in 62, which would have suited Luke's apologetic to a Roman audience. 7.) Gallio's tolerant attitude to Paul in Acts 18:14–17 does not seem to be obsolete. 8.) The prominence of the Sadducees belongs to the pre-70 situation; 9.) as does the relatively sympathetic attitude to the Pharisees; 10.) as does the prominence of 'God-fearers' in the synagogues; 11.) as do details (he mentions nine) pointing to an early milieu. 12.) The controversies over the temple have greater relevance pre-70. 13.) The use of 'Jesus' and 'Christ' seems primitive. Hemer lays considerable emphasis on the 'immediacy' of the later chapters of Acts, claiming: 'It is our contention that these inconsequential details are hard to explain except as vivid experiences recalled at no great distance in time' (388f).[5]

When he looks for greater precision he comes down firmly on the date 'about 62' (390). This date in an earlier generation was particularly associated with Harnack, who had an immense reputation as a scholar and who changed his mind in the course of thirty years' study of the question. In his *Chronologie* of 1896

226

(the fruit of fifteen years' study) he dated Acts with some confidence between 78 and 93. By 1911 he had come to the painful conclusion that it was 'in the highest degree probable' that it should be dated in 62. His whole treatment in *The Date of Acts and the Synoptic Gospels* merits careful attention, but a single quotation must suffice:

> Throughout eight whole chapters St Luke keeps his readers intensely interested in the progress of the trial of St Paul, simply that he may in the end completely disappoint them – they learn nothing of the final result of the trial! Such a procedure is scarcely less indefensible than that of one who might relate the history of our Lord and close the narrative with his delivery to Pilate, because Jesus had now been brought to Jerusalem and had made his appearance before the chief magistrate in the capital city![6]

This conclusion has commended itself to many readers,[7] but few have felt able to accept it, simply because this date for Acts requires an even earlier (and seemingly impossible) date for Mark.

F. F. Bruce has changed his views about the date of Acts in the reverse direction to that of Harnack. He says:

> a sufficient time has elapsed for the author to look back in tranquillity over the course of events and present them in a more balanced perspective than would have been possible for one writing *in mediis rebus*. The outstanding personages of the narrative – Peter, Paul and James of Jerusalem – had all died (I think) by the time of writing, and the author was able to stress their respective contributions to the rise and progress of Christianity rather than the temporary controversies in which they had been involved one with another . . . the author wrote a decade or two later than the last events he records.[8]

I cannot see that composition thirty years after the council of Jerusalem of 49 is in any way preferable to composition thirteen years after. That council ended with warm and brotherly accord which was felt to have been the work of the Holy Spirit (15:25–28). There is no reason to think that deep-seated animosities clung to the church leaders in the ensuing period. Bruce sees Acts as 'an intelligible history of the rise and progress of

Christianity . . . sure of reception among the intelligent reading public – or rather listening public – of or in Rome'.[9] Yet, as we have seen (p. 149), this is precisely what it does not do. *It gives no hint as to the founding and vicissitudes of the world-renowned church in Rome.* Bruce admits that his is a subjective judgement,[10] but by adopting this later date for Acts he throws away the obvious explanation of its ending.

Of the alternative ways of explaining the end of Acts, probably the favourite is to claim that the arrival of Paul in Rome to spend two full years proclaiming the kingdom of God to all without hindrance is a fitting climax to the book; the story has been told of the spread of the gospel from Jerusalem, through Judea and Samaria, and now it has reached the capital of the empire. As a matter of history this is quite erroneous, since (we must reiterate) we know from Romans 1:8 that the faith of the church in Rome was world-famous long before this. And even if Acts is discarded as a source of history, the idea that it is telling the story of how the gospel got to Rome breaks down on the grounds of internal inconsistency. When Paul arrived at Puteoli the news soon reached Rome and brethren from there came the forty miles to the Forum of Appius to meet him (28:14). The author of Acts makes it as clear as can be that there was a lively church in Rome before Paul arrived. He is not telling the story of how the *gospel* got to Rome, but of how *Paul* got there.[11] Yet the myth of the late date of Mark has driven Lukan studies into this absurdity. In the circumstances of 62 Acts has a thoroughly fitting end, it brings the story of Paul up to date and tells how the apostle to the Gentiles preached in the capital, without hindrance, to both Jew and Gentile. But in circumstances later than the trial, the Neronian persecution or Paul's martyrdom it is hard to credit an author ending this way.[12] P. W. Walasky has made the further point: it is difficult to imagine the author of Acts giving so favourable a view of the Roman authorities after the horrors of Nero's persecution in 64. He argues that 'Luke has carefully consistently and consciously presented an *apologia pro imperio.*'[13]

Among the various secondary reasons given for dating Acts late in the century the following may be mentioned. Acts is said

228

to present a picture of Paul so different from that in his epistles that it must be unhistorical. This applies to matters factual; some scholars, for instance, say that at almost every point Acts and Paul disagree; this is illustrated particularly in the difficulties in harmonising Paul's visits to Jerusalem as given in Acts and Galatians. It applies also to matters theological – differences are seen between the approach of Paul and Luke to natural theology, the law, Christology and eschatology;[14] and the Lukan writings are said to reflect an early catholic rather than a primitive stage in the church's development.

As to matters factual, the researches of W. M. Ramsay (and now of Hemer) need to be borne in mind. They have shown conclusively how accurate Luke's record is in many particulars.[15] The harmonisation of Acts and Galatians is not very difficult, as Bruce and Hemer have shown.[16] The supposed theological irreconcilability between Paul and Luke seems to stem from two errors: one is the underrating of the versatility and adaptability of Paul, who knew how to be all things to all men when he was trying to convince them of his point of view. The other is the failure to distinguish between the theological emphases of Luke and of Paul. There is no reason to think that one was a carbon-copy of the other. The author of Luke–Acts, whose writing occupies more space in the New Testament than all the Pauline epistles put together, was (in spite of his self-effacingness) a great man, and his individuality must be recognised. As to the supposed early catholicism of Luke, C. K. Barrett sees little trace of it.[17] These objections do not in fact stand up to close examination and they lead to a new set of difficulties, for one would expect any late admirer of Paul to base his story on the epistles, which quite evidently the author of Acts did not do.

The decisive reason for rejecting 62 for the dating of Acts has been the dating of Luke (and lying behind that the dating of Mark).

The date of Luke

It has become almost a datum in modern Lukan scholarship to hold that Luke's gospel and Acts are two volumes of one book.[18] This seems to be a baseless assumption. τὸν πρῶτον λόγον more naturally refers to an earlier work than to part of the present work now appearing for the first time. The two books are of course the product of one mind and they show a unity of outlook and a common theology, but Luke 24 and Acts 1 do not read like successive parts of one book. The gospel says nothing of resurrection appearances over forty days and can be read simply as an account of a single day. Although Acts does not detail the πολλὰ τεκμήρια of the forty days, it makes it clear that the gospel account is not of just one day. It hardly seems likely that this explanation of what happened between the resurrection and the ascension, which looks clumsy in a continuous narrative, was written as part of a single book, but it is very natural as the introduction to a new work, written for a church which knew from other sources of many resurrection appearances. Furthermore, there is absolutely no evidence of the two books being put together in the manuscript tradition. Luke always belongs with the other three gospels, not with Acts.

An attractive way of dating Luke, if it must be dated no later than 62, is to place it during the time of Paul's imprisonment in Caesarea: 57–59. This is related in a we-passage which records the arrival of Paul and Luke in Jerusalem: 'When we had come to Jerusalem' (21:17), and their departure from Caesarea: 'we put to sea' (27:2). During this long stay in Palestine, Luke would have had ample opportunity for interviewing scores of witnesses and building up an accurate body of information to put in his gospel. It is perfectly possible that Luke did this, but there is evidence to suggest that we should look for an even earlier date.

'The brother whose praise is in the gospel'

A tradition, far from universal yet strongly supported in the early church, identifies Luke with 'the brother whose praise is in the gospel' of 2 Corinthians 8:18, who carried Paul's letter from Macedonia to Corinth. According to Acts Luke was present during the second missionary journey in about 49 (according to Hemer 269), when, in response to Paul's vision of the man of Macedonia calling for help, Luke tells us, 'immediately we sought to go' (16:10). He accompanies Paul to Philippi, where Lydia is baptised and the slave girl is exorcised. Paul and Silas are briefly imprisoned and the story continues in the third person as these two travel to Thessalonika, apparently leaving Luke behind in 49 or 50. Paul goes to Athens and to Corinth in Achaia, staying in the latter 'many days', before paying a hasty visit to Palestine. His third journey involves a long stay at Ephesus, whence he writes his first epistle to the Corinthians, and makes a further visit to Macedonia and Corinth, before retracing his steps to Philippi. On his return journey in 57 (Hemer 255) he is joined by Luke, who accompanies him to Jerusalem (20:3–21:17), evidently bearing the collection for the poor. There is thus a period of some seven or eight years, beginning and ending in Macedonia, where Luke drops out of the Acts story. But tradition has something to say about his movements at this time.

The second epistle to the Corinthians was written from Macedonia in about 56, a couple of years after the first. It was taken to Corinth by three messengers: Titus; συνεπέμψαμεν δὲ μετ' αὐτοῦ τὸν ἀδελφὸν οὗ ὁ ἔπαινος ἐν τῷ εὐαγγελίῳ διὰ πασῶν τῶν ἐκκλησιῶν; and another well-tested brother (8:16–22). There are noteworthy references in the great early fathers, Origen, Eusebius,[19] Ephraem,[20] Chrysostom,[21] Jerome,[22] identifying the brother 'whose praise in the gospel had spread through all the churches' with Luke. The subscription 'The second epistle to the Corinthians was written from Philippi διά Titus and Luke' is found in most Byzantine-type manuscripts at the end of the letter.[23] It was incorporated in many editions of the Authorised Version and the tradition continues right up to modern times[24] – it still has a place in the collect of St Luke's day in the English Book of Common Prayer. At least one scholar of the last two centuries has mildly opposed the identification,[25] some have been content to leave the matter entirely undecided,[26] a good many have been prepared to say that Luke has a somewhat better claim than others,[27] while a few have been unashamedly convinced that the old tradition is right.[28]

At first sight the task of identifying the brother seems

231

hopeless, for Paul had so many fellow-workers besides Luke, and commentators have suggested a bewildering number of possibilities. Luther and Calvin, following Chrysostom, Theodoret and Theophylact, suggested *Barnabas*, who is associated with Titus and Luke in the subscriptions to a few cursives. But there is no evidence that Barnabas was with Paul at this time, nor is it likely that he would have been left unnamed (cf. 1 Cor. 9:6). There is no evidence that *Mark* was there at the time. *Silas* is unlikely, because he was well known to the Corinthians and had been already named in the letter (1:19; Acts 18:5) and would hardly have been referred to thus cryptically; similarly *Timothy*. In addition, though Timothy is called ὁ ἀδελφός in the salutation, the fact that he was co-author of the letter means that he would not have delivered it himself.

Furthermore, writers who have suggested these names seem to have over-looked the context in which the brother is introduced. The passage is all about the collection for the relief of the poor saints in Jerusalem, and it goes on to say that the brother

> has been appointed by the churches to travel with us in this gracious work which we are carrying on, for the glory of the Lord and to show our good will. We intend that no one should blame us about this liberal gift which we are administering, for we aim at what is honourable not only in the Lord's sight but also in the sight of men.

This surely means that we must look for the brother among those who were taking the offerings to Jerusalem with Paul. Acts is silent about the collection, apart from Paul's statement to Felix that he had come to Jerusalem 'to bring to my nation alms and offerings' (24:17), but the matter for two or three years had been greatly occupying Paul's mind,[29] and presumably the men entrusted with the task of taking their churches' contributions to Jerusalem are to be found in Acts 20:4f: 'Sopater of Beroea . . . the Thessalonians, Aristarchus and Secundus; and Gaius of Derbe, and Timothy; and the Asians, Tychicus and Trophimus. These went on and were waiting for us[30] at Troas.'

Of these, *Sopater, Aristarchus, Secundus* and *Gaius* were Macedonians who seem[31] to be ruled out by 2 Corinthians 9:4: 'lest if some Macedonians come with me and find that you are not ready, we be humiliated – to say nothing of you – for being so confident'. Hughes comments:

> Paul envisages the possibility that some Macedonians (those, no doubt, designated to travel with the money collected by the Macedonian churches) may accompany him to Corinth. Tasker may well be right in declaring that Paul's language here, although it appears hypothetical to us, is in fact under the influence of Semitic idiom, and actually means that a number of Macedonians will quite definitely come with him. (As parallel instances of such usage he cites Jn. 12:32 and 1 Jn. 2:28.) If that is so, then we may suppose that the Apostle was waiting in Macedonia, not merely to give the Corinthians an opportunity for completing their charitable undertaking, but at the same time to enable the Macedonians to make the final arrangements concerning their own collection, now completed (perhaps the selection by the congregations of suitable men to travel with Paul to Jerusalem), before he came on with the latter to Corinth. It would be most unfortunate and a source of embarrassment both to himself and (he delicately suggests) to the Corinthians, if these Macedonians whose zeal had been fired by the earlier enthusiasm of the Corinthians should arrive in Achaia to find the collection there in a state of disorganization.
>
> It was this situation which, as he points out in the next verse, convinced Paul of the necessity of sending Titus and the other two brethren on ahead so that this business might be efficiently supervised. We may deduce from what Paul says here that neither of the brethren who accompanied Titus was a Macedonian, for otherwise there would have been little point in the admonition concerning the regrettable effect that a discovery of Corinthian unreadiness would have on any Macedonians who came with him. (325f)

The Asians, Tychicus and Trophimus are not disqualified, but *Trophimus* is perhaps an unlikely candidate as being rather insignificant. (He is just mentioned as being with Paul in Jerusalem in Acts 21:29, and as being sick at Miletus in 2 Timothy 4:20.) *Tychicus*, however, is quite a strong candidate. Hughes says:

> Paul's bond of friendship and confidence with Tychicus is clearly displayed elsewhere in his letters. Thus he is commended to the Ephesians as 'the beloved brother and faithful minister in the Lord' (Eph. 6:21) and to the Colossians as 'the beloved brother and

faithful minister and fellow-servant in the Lord' (Col. 4:7), and it is apparent that Paul placed such trust in him that he was in the habit of sending him as his emissary and the bearer of his epistles to different churches or persons (cf. Eph. 6:21f.; 2 Tim. 4:12; Col. 4:7f.; Tit. 3:12). In view of all this, Tychicus is as likely as any to have been one of those chosen by Paul to travel with Titus on this mission to Corinth. (315)

So it seems to be a case of two main contenders: Luke with a strong backing of tradition behind him versus Tychicus with none. Is not the ideal solution, then, to accept as well grounded the tradition that 'the brother whose praise in the gospel has spread through all the churches' is Luke; and to adopt as a plausible conjecture the hypothesis that the third messenger, the 'often tested' and 'earnest' brother, is Tychicus?

So far so good. But what does it mean to say of Luke οὗ ὁ ἔπαινος ἐν τῷ εὐαγγελίῳ? The great distinction between the views of the early writers and of the writers of more recent times is that the former said (as far as I know, to a man) that Luke was famous for his gospel-book, while the latter say (*almost* to a man[32]) that εὐαγγελίῳ does not refer to a book. This denial is based on one or other or both of two affirmations: 1.) εὐαγγέλιον was not used in the sense of gospel-book at the time Paul wrote; 2.) Luke's gospel was not in existence at that time.

As to the former, it is generally conceded that there are no indisputable examples of this use before Justin Martyr in about 155,[33] but there are a good many examples where the sense of gospel-book is entirely compatible with what is said. In 2 Clement, the oldest surviving Christian sermon outside the New Testament, probably of the early second century, we have:

> For the Lord says in the gospel, 'If you fail to guard what is small, who will give you what is great? For I say to you, He who is faithful in a very little is faithful also in much.' (8:5)

Ignatius writing to the church in Smyrna about 107 says:

> They were not persuaded by the prophecies or the law of Moses or, thus far, by the gospel. (5:1)

> Pay attention to the prophets and specially to the gospel, in which the passion has been explained to us. (7:2)

The Didache, the date of which has been placed as late as the fourth century or, in J.-P. Audet's learned commentary,[34] as early as 50–70, says:

> As the Lord commanded in his gospel, pray thus: Our Father . . . (8:2)
>
> Concerning the apostles and prophets, act in accordance with the precept of the gospel. Let every apostle who comes to you be received as the Lord. (11:3)
>
> Reprove one another, not in anger but in peace, as you find it in the gospel. (15:3)
>
> Perform your prayers and your acts of charity and all your actions as you find it in the gospel. (15:4)

This shows that the transition from the meaning 'good news' or 'gospel message' to that of a book dealing with the life and teaching of Jesus was natural and almost imperceptible.

It is probable that the greatest influence in effecting this transition was Mark 1:1. The exegesis of this verse is difficult, and when Mark headed his book Ἀρχὴ τοῦ εὐαγγελίου Ἰησοῦ Χριστοῦ he probably had no intention of coining a new usage for the word; for him εὐαγγέλιον meant the message of the entire work. But once written it stood there (as we have already noted) for ever after looking for all the world like the title of a book. Indeed J. A. T. Robinson calls 'the Gospel of Jesus Christ the Son of God' Mark's 'own title'.[35] M. Hengel similarly writes of 'Mark, who composes his work as the *evangelium Jesu Christi* . . . his history is . . . a *evangelion*.'[36] He quotes with approval W. Marxsen: 'εὐαγγέλιον is set over the entire work as a kind of "title".'[37] M. D. Goulder says: 'Mark calls his book "the Gospel".'[38] It was inevitable that this usage, together with the early description of these books as 'The Gospel according to . . .', should give to the new genre of writing the name 'gospel'. There is therefore no reason to doubt the possibility that εὐαγγέλιον might have been used to describe a written gospel at any date subsequent to the publication of Mark.[39]

As to the confidently made assertion that Luke's gospel could not have been written at this date, we have a millennium and a half of Christian belief contradicting it, which belief we have tried to show well grounded. It can, I think, be shown that the traditional exegesis of ἐν τῷ εὐαγγελίῳ is more satisfactory than its rivals. Two questions need to be asked: How is it that the brother has earned praise in all the churches? And: Why is he introduced anonymously?

'In the gospel' has been taken by many (e.g. RSV) to mean 'for his preaching of the gospel' and by others (e.g. NEB; cf. NIV) to mean 'for his services to the gospel'. But it is curious to introduce this unnamed brother as the one famous among all the churches for his preaching. It seems almost to suggest an invidious comparison between Titus, who formerly did a spell of preaching among the Corinthians, and this other man who could *really* preach. Furthermore, how was it possible to gain fame as a preacher in *all* the churches? Even allowing for a measure of hyperbole, such fame could only be gained before the days of mass media by going in person to a large number of them. As we know from Paul's experience this was a long and arduous business and there must have been few who earned such a reputation. The incongruity of thus seeming to compare the preaching abilities of Titus and his colleague presumably the lies behind the alternative translation 'for his services to gospel', for this might suggest the gifts of an administrator or organiser or personal worker. But is it likely that one particular man in Macedonia had gained such a reputation that he would be recognised in Achaia as *the* brother famed for his services to the gospel? Neither suggestion has plausibility. If, on the other hand, Luke's gospel had been circulating in the churches of Greece for a year or two, he would indeed have been famous for one very special service to the gospel. Here was the author of 'the most beautiful book in the world'[40] coming to Corinth in person. If Luke's gospel existed, the Gospel according to Mark had almost certainly existed even longer and was probably known by that title. Even if Paul was not consciously using εὐαγγέλιον in the sense of gospel-book (which he may not have been), the existence of such a book would give a convincing reason for the universal fame of its author in the cause of the gospel.

As to why he is introduced in this indirect way, one can at this distance do no more than guess at what factors influenced Paul. Possibly Titus is named because he has already served the church at Corinth and is well known to its members, whereas Luke may not have visited them before. More probably it was little more than a whim of the moment which caused Paul to commend him by reminding them of his fame rather than simply using his name.

So then, this piece of external evidence, if we have assessed it correctly, would give us our first firm gospel date: the gospel of Luke was written before 56, the approximate date of 2 Corinthians. It is difficult to say how long it would take for the fame of the book to spread through 'all the churches'. The expression suggests more than just the churches of Macedonia and Achaia, so we should probably allow at least a year, and say therefore that its writing had taken place by 55 at the latest.

We should note also the possible quotation of Luke's gospel in 1 Timothy 5:18, which cites verbatim the dominical saying 'The labourer deserves his wages' after the quotation from Deuteronomy 25:4 'You shall not muzzle an ox when it is treading out the grain', introducing both by the quotation-formula 'the scripture says'. The saying could of course have been known by oral tradition, but its wording is exactly that of Luke 10:7. Such exactitude of quotation is striking, since (as we saw in the last chapter) apparent allusions to the words of Jesus in the gospels are seldom verbatim even in the apostolic fathers. Such precision of wording with reference to a saying from 'scripture' certainly suggests quotation of a writing. On almost any date suggested for the Pastoral Epistles it could have been a quotation of Luke's written word. Even its citation as 'scripture' would be perfectly possible after a few years of use in the Christian assemblies and of known apostolic approval.[41]

As far as Acts is concerned we know nothing about Luke's movements between his time with Paul at Philippi in Acts 16 in about 50 and his arrival in Corinth in about 56. During this period Paul was engaged in much journeying, which took him to Thessalonika, Beroea, Athens, Corinth, Ephesus, Caesarea, Antioch and eventually back to Macedonia. There is no positive indication to show that Luke accompanied him (though it needs to be stressed that the absence of 'we' is no proof of the absence of Luke). There could well have been both the opportunity and the incentive during the years 50–55 to compose his gospel for the use of the growing and multiplying churches, as our interpretation of 'the brother whose praise is in the gospel' presupposes.

It could not (on my view) have been earlier than the publication of Mark (which could hardly have been earlier than 44 – see next section). If, as I have tentatively argued,[42] Luke was one of the seventy and in personal touch with the events he describes right up to the time of his joining Paul, there is no decisive reason why he should not have published his gospel any time after 44. But since Luke appears to have been in Macedonia and Achaia between 50 and 56 (not travelling with Paul, as far as we know), and since the 'Anti-Marcionite' Prologue and other early writers[43] make Achaia the place of writing, the likeliest date for its composition would seem to be somewhere in the early 50s.

The date of Mark

Our main discussion bearing on the date of Mark has already been given in Chapters 6 and 7 above. There we saw the strength of the tradition which makes Mark the recorder of the teaching which Peter used to give in Rome, and we gave reason to believe that Peter and Mark were in Rome together from 42 to 44. We suggested (p. 169f) that Peter's return to the East after Herod's death in 44 might well have been the occasion that called forth this record of his teaching, probably while Mark himself was still in Rome in (say) 45. Any date between 44 and the writing of Luke in the early 50s is, however, possible. The tradition that he had already composed it before his Alexandrian mission (in the 50s? see p. 177) seems likely enough.

The date of Matthew

Dates assigned to Matthew vary between the 30s of the first century and the middle of the second century. Cosmas of

Alexandria (died *c*. 550) put it during the persecution which followed the death of Stephen, which might be as early as 33.[44] Eusebius (writing probably at the very end of the third century) is of greater importance. He says of Matthew: 'when he was on the point of going to others he transmitted in writing in his native language the Gospel according to himself, and thus supplied by writing the lack of his own presence to those from whom he was sent' (*HE* 3.24.6). There is a suggestion here that the writing of the gospel preceded the departure of Matthew from Palestine. As we have seen (pp. 160–62) there was a widespread belief that the apostles were dispersed from Jerusalem twelve years after the crucifixion. Acts may perhaps hint that this had taken place by the time Peter was released from prison in 42, James the apostle having been killed and James the brother of the Lord having become head of the church there (Acts 12:2, 17). In his *Chronicon* Eusebius places the writing of the gospel in the third year of the reign of Caligula, that is, in 41.

Dates like these in the 30s and 40s (which we might describe as 'Eusebian') were favoured by many orthodox scholars right down into the nineteenth century.[45] Others, following the common (but apparently erroneous) interpretation of Irenaeus, favoured the 60s.[46] We need therefore to look at Irenaeus' witness.

The witness of Irenaeus

The tradition of the fathers concerning the authorship, priority and language of Matthew is solid and weighty, but when it comes to the question of date there is no firm tradition. Papias says nothing. Irenaeus, however, is commonly thought to have pronounced upon the dates of the gospel. In the passage already quoted, and which we study below, he is understood to say that Matthew wrote at the time when Peter and Paul were preaching at Rome and that Mark wrote after the death of these apostles. It is unlikely, however, as Chapman has shown,[47] that he intended to supply his readers with either of these pieces of information. It can be dangerously misleading to read only the extract preserved by Eusebius without paying attention to the

239

context in which it stands in *Adversus omnes Haereses*. Irenaeus' statement appears in fact to be very general. He is contrasting the unwritten, private traditions of the heretics with the public declarations of the apostles, first preached and then committed to writing and preserved in the church.

His words merit quotation at length:

Ὁ μὲν δὴ Ματθαῖος ἐν τοῖς Ἑβραίοις τῇ ἰδίᾳ διαλέκτῳ αὐτῶν καὶ γραφὴν ἐξήνεγκεν εὐαγγελίου, τοῦ Πέτρου καὶ τοῦ Παύλου ἐν Ῥώμῃ εὐαγγελιζομένων καὶ θεμελιούντων τὴν ἐκκλησίαν. Μετὰ δὲ τὴν τούτων ἔξοδον, Μάρκος ὁ μαθητὴς καὶ ἑρμηνευτὴς Πέτρου, καὶ αὐτὸς τὰ ὑπὸ Πέτρου κηρυσσόμενα ἐγγράφως ἡμῖν παραδέδωκε. Καὶ Λουκᾶς δέ, ὁ ἀκόλουθος Παύλου, τὸ ὑπ' ἐκείνου κηπυσσόμενον εὐαγγέλιον ἐν βιβλίῳ κατέθετο. Ἔπειτα Ἰωάννης ὁ μαθητὴς τοῦ κυρίου, ὁ καὶ ἐπὶ τὸ στῆθος αὐτοῦ ἀναπεσών, καὶ αὐτὸς ἐξέδωκε τὸ εὐαγγέλιον, ἐν Ἐφέσῳ τῆς Ἀσίας διατρίβων. (*Adv. Haer.* 3.1.1, as quoted in *HE* 5.8.2–4)

As Chapman showed, any precise dating is quite foreign to Irenaeus' intentions: 'he is simply explaining that *the teaching of the four principal apostles has not been lost, but has been handed down to us in writing*'. (Note the emphasis) καὶ γραφήν, ἐγγράψως, ἐν βιβλίῳ, ἐξέδωκεν.)

He is not in the least concerned to defend the authenticity of the Gospels, still less to give their dates. The Valentinians accepted them all, and St. Irenaeus is merely urging upon them the fact that each Gospel is the written record of the matter preached by an apostle.

Irenaeus is answering the question: 'How has this preaching come down to us in writing?' The reply is: 'Two of the apostles wrote down their own teaching, while two others were reported by a follower.' Chapman translates the passage literally (adding explanatory comments):

Matthew among the Hebrews in their own language published a writing also of the Gospel [besides preaching it], Peter and Paul preaching the Gospel [not to Jews but] at Rome [without writing it down], and founding the church there [whose testimony I shall give presently – 3.3]. But [although they died without having written a Gospel] after their death [their preaching has not been lost to us,

240

for] Mark, the disciple and interpreter of Peter, has handed down (perfect tense) to us, he also in writing [like Matthew] the things which were preached by Peter.

And Luke besides, the companion of [the other,] Paul, set down in a book the Gospel preached by that apostle.

Finally, John, the disciple of the Lord, he also published a Gospel, while he was living in Ephesus of Asia.

In other words, 'we know what they preached for we have written records of what they preached in Palestine, Rome and Asia'. Dating is foreign to the argument; there would be no motive for pointing out a synchronism between the writing of Matthew and the preaching of Peter and Paul. εὐαγγελιξομένων cannot be pressed to mean that in a given year Matthew wrote and Peter and Paul preached. The most that can be inferred is that both events occurred in the same period – when the apostles had gone forth on their worldwide preaching. There is indeed no evidence that Irenaeus intended to add to the information which he had read in Papias.

Chapman's article has not received the attention it deserves, in spite of the fact that Harnack wrote:

> To Chapman belongs the credit of having first correctly interpreted this passage, which hitherto had been a veritable *crux*, because it did not seem to fit in with the other chronological traditions . . . He [Irenaeus] had no further information . . . than what could be read in Papias. All that is additional is only in seeming, but Irenaeus did not even intend to give an appearance of more detailed knowledge.[48]

It should be noted that no later fathers interpret Irenaeus as meaning that Matthew was written after Paul's arrival in Rome or that Mark was written after the deaths of Peter and Paul. Eusebius' *Chronicon* is the most precise, putting the publication of Matthew's gospel in 41. This is immediately accounted for by the fact that those of them who had read Irenaeus would have had his complete text in front of them. They would have had the good sense not to read out of Irenaeus matters with which he was not concerned and which contradicted current traditions. In any case they knew that Irenaeus does not say that after the deaths of Peter and Paul Mark *wrote* his gospel, but that he *handed down* in writing the things preached by Peter. The only clear item of chronology in the passage concerning the dates of writing comes from ἔπειτα, which shows that John wrote last. Incidentally, it is ironical that so much weight should have been given to supposed chronological references of Irenaeus, when it is well known that chronology was not Irenaeus' strong point. He believed that Jesus lived to be nearly fifty years old and that his public ministry lasted at least ten years![49]

Dates in the region suggested by the apparently erroneous interpretation of Irenaeus were adopted by many, including (as we have seen) by Zahn.[50] A recent exponent of Matthean authorship and a pre-70 date is R. H. Gundry.[51] I shall not occupy space by repeating arguments for the 'Irenaean' position, which Gundry has so ably stated (and which usually presuppose the priority of Mark), but will just mention one objection that is raised to the very early date demanded by the 'Eusebian' position. Matthew twice uses the expression 'to this day', referring to the name attached to the so-called Field of Blood and to the currency of the report that the disciples stole Jesus' body (27:8; 28:15). Does not this suggest a date of writing long after the event? It is true that in the Old Testament there are many instances of such a use, but always in a context which shows clearly that the time of writing was long after the event or that the speaker was referring to a process begun long ago. But the phrase could be used of any period, whether it be two years or two thousand years.[52] As T. Townson said,

> *Palpable lies*, and *new names* of places, which have had others from ancient usage . . . are beings of such a perishable nature . . . that a single year was sufficient to give propriety to the observation that they then continued, it was more memorable that the *name* had fastened on the field, and strange that the *lie* had lasted so long.[53]

That the story of the stealing of the body was current 'to this day' seems in fact indicative of an early date, for Matthew gives it as part of his apologetic. He adds to the evidence of the appearances reported by Christians the further evidence of the guards as to the disappearance of the body and the counter-evidence concocted by the chief priests. As serious apologetic this extra evidence would have had limited value outside Jerusalem, but in Jerusalem itself in the early days the story would have been known to almost everyone, and the true version of the story would carry weight. As Birks says,

> The fact that this gospel alone records the watch, and the report spread among the Jews, implies naturally that it was written earlier than the others, when the fact of the watch being set was most likely to confirm the evidence of the resurrection, from being familiarly known; and when the counter-explanation, being also well known, would stand most in need of refutation by a simple, unadorned statement of the events themselves.[54]

Conclusions

The argument of *Redating Matthew, Mark and Luke*, which has eight major stages, has been cumulative:
1.) Verbal synoptic likenesses and differences are best explained by independent use of the primitive form of oral instruction.
2.) Genre and order are best explained by a literary relationship.
3.) In particular, Luke knew Mark's gospel.
4.) Dates should be reckoned by working back from Acts, the natural date of which is 62.
5.) Luke's gospel was apparently well known in the mid-50s.
6.) According to tradition Mark's gospel gives Peter's teaching in Rome.
7.) Peter's first visit to Rome was probably 42–44 and Mark's gospel was probably written about 45.
8.) The universal tradition of the early church puts Matthew first, which means a date around 40.

As was made clear in the previous chapter, we have not attempted to work out the detailed tradition-history of more than a handful of gospel parallels, believing it to be an impossible task, a game of sophisticated guesswork which is more likely to be wrong than right. This may be unsatisfying to those who would like greater precision, but the best scholarship

243

knows that our nearest approach to truth comes when we try to go as far as the evidence leads, but no further. Our 'solution' to the synoptic problem does not give the sort of answers that some are looking for, but it gives us much for which to be thankful. It confirms the general soundness of early tradition, showing the external evidence and the internal evidence to be in remarkably close agreement. It gives us two gospels containing the teaching of apostles and a third by one who had followed everything closely for a long time. These were written at dates when many were alive who could confirm or contradict what was written.[55] This means that the Christian is fully justified in accepting anything that is written in these books until it is proved beyond reasonable doubt to be in error.[56] It confirms the right of the Christian church to maintain its traditional stance with regard to the foundation documents of the faith without impairing its integrity – and for that we should be thankful indeed.

NOTES

Introduction

1. Chapman. (Where bibliographical references to modern authors are incomplete, see pp. vii–xv for full particulars and abbreviations.)

2. Zahn 1909; Jameson 1922; Butler 1951; P. Parker, *The Gospel Before Mark* (University of Chicago Press, 1953); L. Vaganay, *Le problème synoptique* (Tournai: Desclée, 1954); A. M. Farrer, 'On Dispensing with Q' in D. E. Nineham (ed.) *Studies in the Gospels* (Oxford UP, 1955); N. Turner, 'The Minor Verbal Agreements of Matthew and Luke Against Mark' in *Studia Evangelica* I, TU 73 (Berlin, 1959); A. W. Argyle, 'The Agreements Between Matthew and Luke' *ExpT* 73 (1961/2) 19; 'Evidence for the View that St. Luke used St. Matthew's Gospel' *JBL* 83 (1964) 390; R. T. Simpson, 'The Major Agreements of Matthew and Luke against Mark' *NTS* 12 (1965/6) 273; Farmer *SP* 1964; Sanders 1969; Lindsey 1971; P. Benoit and M.-É. Boismard, *Synopse des quatre évangiles en français* II (Paris, 1972); Rist 1978. The most persistent ground for dissent is the seemingly undue number of agreements of Matthew and Luke against Mark, which these writers deal with in different ways. (On the theory of a common oral tradition partially espoused by Rist the problem does not of course arise, we should expect any two gospels often to agree against the third.)

3. Cf. the quotation on p. 189:

> It is of the greatest importance to recognize the peril and ultimate futility of discussing the relationships of the Gospels in an historical vacuum where only the internal evidence from literary criticism is weighed in the balance of historical judgment. It is, of course, equally dangerous to focus on Patristic tradition to the neglect of internal considerations.

4. e.g. Manson 38ff suggested the possibility of dating Mark before 60. Reicke 180 dates all the synoptics *c*. 60. Gundry 608 dates Luke 63, Matthew before Luke and Mark before Matthew. Hemer 358 n85 says of Mark, 'I should not exclude a date earlier than 60, nor advocate it.' Torrey 39f dated Mark 40. Carmignac 71 thought our Greek gospels to be: Luke *c*. 50, Matthew *c*. 60, Mark before 64, but all based on earlier written Hebrew.

5. W. G. Kümmel, for instance, dates Mark around 70, Matthew 80–100, Luke 70–90. (Kümmel 98, 120, 151.)

6. It is of course commonly held that Luke and Acts were two volumes of one work. Reasons for rejecting this are given on pp. 229f.

7. See W. W. Gasque, *A History of the Criticism of the Acts of the Apostles* (Tübingen: Mohr, 1975) for the views of scholars up to 1974. This book has been republished with an updating supplement under the title *A History of the Interpretation of the Acts of the Apostles* (Peabody, MA: Hendrikson, 1989). On the place of presuppositions in the forming of historical judgements, see the additional 'Note on Presuppositions' on pp. 247–50.

8. The Alands like to speak of the new Standard Text. (K. and B. Aland, *The Text of New Testament*, Grand Rapids: Eerdmans; Leiden: Brill, 1987, 30.) In the great debate between Westcott and Hort on the one side and Burgon and Scrivener on the other, which resulted in texts heavily weighted in favour of B and the Alexandrian text-type and almost totally rejecting the Syrian/Byzantine text-type, it is by no means clear that the Alexandrians deserved so sweeping a victory. This was demonstrated by G. Salmon, *Some Thoughts on the Textual Criticism of the New Testament* (London: Murray, 1897). G. D. Kilpatrick, 'The Greek New Testament Text of Today' in the G. H. C. Macgregor *Festschrift*, H. Anderson and W. Barclay (edd.), *The New Testament in Historical and Contemporary Perspective* (Oxford: Blackwell, 1965) 205 came to the 'principal conclusion . . . that the Syrian text is frequently right'. H. A. Sturz, *The Byzantine Text-type and New Testament Textual Criticism* (Nashville: Nelson, 1984) 23, through a study of the papyri, 'seeks to show that the Byzantine text should be recognized as having an important and useful place in textual criticism because it is an independent witness to an early form of the New Testament text'. Sturz is favourably discussed in J. K. Elliott, 'The Text of Acts in the Light of Two Recent Studies' *NTS* 34 (1988) 250–58. W. N. Pickering, *The Identity of the New Testament Text* (Nashville: Nelson, rev. ed. 1980) and J. van Bruggen, *The Ancient Text of the New Testament* (Winnipeg: Premier, 1976) argue that the Byzantine is the best text-type. Z. C. Hodges and A. L. Farstad (edd.), *The Greek NT According to the Majority Text* (Nashville: Nelson, 1982) is based in part on a stemmatic use of Byzantine MSS. H. Greeven (1981) and J. B. Orchard (1983) in their gospel synopses do not adopt the Nestle-Aland text. I have given reasons for questioning the modern critical texts at two major points, and one minor one: 'Why do you ask me about the Good? A

Study of the Relation between Text and Source Criticism' *NTS* 28 (1982) 116–25; on the ending of Mark: *Easter Enigma* 45f, 147f; 'How Many Cock-Crowings? The Problem of Harmonistic Text-Variants' *NTS* 25 (1979) 523–25.

9. See also Bruce *Chronology* 273–95.

10. See p. 275 n1, below. There are tables setting out the Pauline chronology as seen by fifteen scholars from Petavius to Tenney in Williams 33f.

11. See Bruggen p. viii.

12. Hemer 251–70. Bruce and Hemer base their chronology on a belief that Acts is good history, and they carefully correlate the Pauline epistles, Acts and the chronology of secular history. The views of those like J. Knox (*Chapters in a Life of Paul*, New York, 1950; London: SCM, 1987) and G. Lüdemann (*Paul, Apostle to the Gentiles: Studies in Chronology*, ET, London: SCM, 1984), who see little value in Acts for chronology, necessarily lead into paths of great uncertainty. Lüdemann is criticised in Hemer 167 n18.

A Note on Presuppositions

This is not the place for detailed discussion, but some general remarks are called for. The first thing to stress is that much of the argument of the book is not greatly affected by the author's standpoint, so it is to be hoped that those with different presuppositions will not be deterred from reading it. It is in fact very tempting to write such a book without openly confessing one's biases, so making a pretence of neutrality. But important parts of the argument are affected by differences of standpoint.

For instance, to many scholars trained in a modern secular university much in the gospels is self-evidently legendary. An honest historian, it is said, must write off most of the recorded miracles as unhistorical, and therefore it is nonsense to argue that the stories may have been accurately transmitted from the start. At some points the pious must have been inventive. R. Morgan and J. Barton, for example, cite D. F. Strauss (an early and influential critic) who 'argued that the Gospels must be judged unhistorical . . . because heirs to a modern scientific (mechanistic) view of the world do not believe in angels, demons, voices from heaven, walking on water and other interferences with the laws of nature' (Morgan 47).

Similarly Bultmann wrote:

The historical method includes the presupposition that history is a unity in the sense of a closed continuum of effects in which individual events are connected by the succession of cause and effect . . . This closedness means that the continuum of historical happenings cannot be rent by the interference of supernatural transcendent powers and that therefore there is no 'miracle' in this sense of the word. Such a miracle would be an event whose cause did not lie within history . . . [Historical science] cannot perceive such an act and reckon on the basis of it; it can only leave every man free to determine whether he wants to see an act of God in a historical event that it itself understands in terms of that event's immanent historical causes. It is in accordance with such a method as this that the science of history goes to work on all historical documents. And there cannot be any exceptions in the case of biblical texts . . . (R. Bultmann, 'Is Exegesis Without Presuppositions Possible?' *Existence and Faith*, New York, 1960, 291f)

To others, however, secular presuppositions seem quite false. The Christ of the gospels has captured our minds and imaginations so completely that we worship him. We do not find the miracles incredible or believe that they were invented. They seem to be the outworking of the greater miracle of the incarnation. In the New Testament we see God visiting his people. Consequently we have a bias in favour of believing that the God who took the trouble to become incarnate also took the trouble, for the sake of those who came after, to leave a dependable account of the amazing happenings.

Thus what to one person looks self-evident looks to another quite perverse. This does not mean that we should not listen to one another's historical arguments (we should be foolish not to), but we must not expect to arrive at the same conclusions. We will naturally hope that those who share our presuppositions will find the case satisfying, but we must be content if others say: 'I cannot at present accept your conclusions, but on your presuppositions the case is cogently argued.' Those who are committed to neither presupposition can weigh up the arguments and let them play their part in guiding them towards a decision as to who or what Jesus was.

Put another way, the question may be asked whether this book is a work of apologetics; that is to say, is it the defence of a preconceived position or is it an attempt to solve a problem? In all honesty, it is the latter – during the course of the study my views have changed considerably. But everyone works in the light of his own presuppositions and (he hopes) with the help of those presuppositions – for if they are true they will provide a framework into which the data will fit in an unforced and coherent way. The presupposition that the New

Testament gives us dependable accounts has long been out of fashion, but I believe it to be a helpful safeguard against ill-considered criticism. This is not a licence for facile harmonisation (which is thoroughly objectionable), but it accepts sober harmonisation as a useful historical tool. Where good witnesses seem to disagree the historian should first try to harmonise their witness before resorting to rejection. As Hemer 86 says, 'The best course is to strike a balance in which historians are honest about their presuppositions and allow them to be present, even influential, in their thought, yet recognize the primacy of the documents, allowing the evidence to call those presuppositions into question.'

Hemer further rightly declares the impact of presuppositions to be 'subtle and complex' (16). It is difficult to exaggerate the influence of the Enlightenment on contemporary thought. Descartes' principle of systematic doubt has penetrated deeply, not only into non-Christian thought, but also into the thought of Christians engaged in critical biblical studies. It has produced a sceptical climate quite different from that of historic Christianity, a climate which first questions and then often rejects many of its traditions. Hence the widespread rejection of the traditional authorship of the gospels and many of the epistles, the low esteem of Acts as history and the slight value accorded to patristic tradition. In the process such long-established beliefs as the early dates of the gospels, the going of Peter to Rome in 42 and Mark's evangelisation of Alexandria have gone by the board. On Christian presuppositions all these matters deserve reconsideration, comprehensively and in detail.

Five examples of the way Christian presuppositions will affect historical judgements may be mentioned. 1.) The traditional Christian will not countenance in either the gospels or Acts arguments based solely on the improbability of miracle. 2.) He will not date documents on the assumption that Jesus could not foresee future events. 3.) To him it will probably seem more plausible to attribute the vividness of Mark to the dynamism of Peter than to a story-teller's art (pp. 179–82). 4.) He will have a bias in favour of harmonistic exegesis – letting the gospels throw light on one another's meanings and letting Acts illuminate the epistles. 5.) He will respect arguments which show how hypotheses fit into a postulated historical situation, as for instance in Mark's postulated rearrangement of Matthew 3:1–4:22 (pp. 101ff) – appeal is made to what actually appears to have happened. Hemer in this connection speaks of 'the simple interlocking of ostensible evidence' (409), and of the importance of

249

'considering whether the different strands together contribute to the enlargement of a broadly consistent picture' (48).

If this confession deters readers, I would reiterate that *much of the argument is not greatly affected by differences of standpoint*, and I would solicit an open-minded hearing.

1 The Intractable Problem

1. Even his complex colour code does not show all the significant relationships. (See Neirynck 41 n135.)

2. In Britain Streeter's four-document hypothesis, which is a modification of the two-document scheme (see p. xxvii fig. 2 and 3), has been popular.

3. See especially H. Palmer, *The Logic of Gospel Criticism* (London: Macmillan, 1968), who has looked at the synoptic question strictly from a logician's point of view.

4. The focus of dissatisfaction in the vast majority of cases has been the agreements of Matthew and Luke against Mark, which seem to be too many in two books which are supposed to have used Mark independently. Many nineteenth-century critics met this difficulty by following an idea of Lessing, who postulated an apostolic Ur-gospel (or Ur-Marcus) from which all three canonical gospels differed in varying degrees. Streeter thought that he could eliminate Ur-Marcus and devoted a chapter of *The Four Gospels* (293–331) to explaining the Matthew and Luke agreements. Farmer devotes much of chapters 2–4 of *The Synoptic Problem* (esp. 118–52) to the subject. In his exhaustive treatment Neirynck 40 rightly regards Farmer's criticism of Streeter as 'the focal point' of his book. Neirynck's 330 pages illustrate the depth of concern which these agreements have caused a host of scholars. Fitzmyer 73 considers this concern exaggerated.

5. Bellinzoni 438.

6. M. D. Goulder, 'Some observations on Professor Farmer's "Certain Results . . ."' Tuckett *SS* 99.

7. For this see Palmer, *Logic*. That most directional evidence can be made to cut both ways is borne out by the endless discussions of the various protagonists as they try to justify their positions.

8. Alford 1.6. T. H. Horne, *An Introduction to the Critical Study and Knowledge of the Holy Scriptures* (London, 4th ed. 1823), IV 285, was representative of an earlier generation that argued for entire independence without stressing a common form of oral instruction.

9. B. F. Westcott, *An Introduction to the Study of the Gospels* (London: Macmillan, 7th ed. 1887).

10. We shall consider a modern form of the oral theory in Chapter 10.

11. Stoldt gives a careful account of the work of Wilke, Weisse, Holtzmann, Wernle and Bernhard Weiss, who established the two-document theory in Germany. See also W. Sanday (ed.), *Studies in the Synoptic Problem* (Oxford: Clarendon, 1911), which gives the fruits of the Oxford seminars which began work in 1894.

12. The massive work of B. de Solages, *A Greek Synopsis of the Gospels*, ET (Leyden: Brill, 1959) is a noteworthy example.

13. It is true of all the scholars mentioned on p. xxi, except for Rist. Fee 24–28 is one of the many who give an important place to oral tradition *alongside* written sources: 'Biblical scholarship, by and large, has for nearly two hundred years had a "documentary mentality." Every verbal correspondence was turned into documentary borrowing . . . one must not assume Luke . . . to have been laboring slavishly with documents.'

14. Farmer *SP* 49 n1 (latter half). See further, n29 of this chapter.

15. For their treatment of the synoptic problem, see Sanders and Davies 51–119. For diagram of Boismard's view see figure 7 on p. xxviii above.

16. See further p. 77. Sometimes the common use of parentheses in parallel passages is taken as evidence of a literary relationship, e.g. Stein 37ff, who cites Mark 5:8, 28; 14:2, 10, 43; 15:10. All these are explicable just as easily by oral tradition. 13:14 suggests written material, which is probable on other grounds (see p. 27).

17. Before Rist's book was announced I had come to the conclusion that in many of the pericopes Matthew was not based on Mark nor Mark on Matthew. I wrote 'Independent' against the pericopes in Huck's *Synopse* which begin in the case of Mark with the following verses: Mark 3:23; 4:10; 4:13; 4:30; 4:35; 5:1; 5:21; 6:6; 7:1; 7:24; 8:1; 8:11; 9:14; 9:30; 9:33; 9:42; 10:1; 10:13; 10:17; 10:46; 11:1; 11:20; 12:1; 12:13; 12:28; 12:35; 12:38; 13:1; 13:9; 14:1; 14:10; 14:12; 14:53; 15:6; 15:16; 15:21; 15:42; 16:1.

I was more inclined to believe that Luke was often actually using Mark. Yet sometimes his treatment seems very free and quite often he has echoes of Matthew (the agreements against Mark). This struck me with particular force in the Feeding of the 5,000 in 9:12–17. Luke's freedom can be seen in the fact that (according to Farmer's *Synopticon*) of the 145 words of Mark 6:35–44 he has only fifty in the same form.

In the introduction to the story where Matthew and Mark speak of withdrawal 'to a desert place', Luke says 'to a city called Bethsaida' (v. 10). Where Mark says he taught them 'many things' Luke says 'he was speaking to them about the kingdom of God' (v. 11). Only Luke records that 'the twelve' tell Jesus to send the crowd away so that καταλύσωσιν καὶ εὕρωσιν ἐπισιτισμόν (v. 12). Verses 12, 13, 14 have major differences. Non-Markan echoes of Matthew are οἱ ὄχλοι ἠκολούθησαν αὐτῷ (v. 11), οἱ δὲ . . . βρώματα (v. 13), ὡσεί (v. 14), in two other references to ὄχλος or ὄχλοι (vv. 12, 16), τὸ περισσεῦ (σαν) (v. 17). In verse 13b the disciples (as in Matthew) reply with a statement, not a question (as in Mark). Markan phrases are missing in both gospels: 'many . . . ran . . . and got there ahead of them' (Mark 6:33), 'because they were like sheep without a shepherd; and he began to teach them many things' (v. 34), συμπόσια συμπόσια, χλωρῷ (v. 39), ἀνέπεσαν πρασιαὶ πρασιαὶ κατὰ ἑκατόν (v. 40), καὶ ἰχθύας ἐμέρισεν πᾶσιν (v. 41). This hardly looks like Luke adapting Mark and incorporating bits of Matthew or Q. Has not Luke told this story countless times at the Breaking of Bread?

18. M. D. Goulder, *JTS* 30 (1979) 266f.

19. J. B. Orchard, *Heythrop Journal* 20 (1979) 191f; T. R. W. Longstaff, *JBL* 100 (1981) 130; W. R. Farmer, *Perkins Journal* (Spring 1979).

20. This figure is based on the Unit-Sequence Comparison chart at the back of J. B. Orchard's *Matthew, Luke and Mark* (Manchester: Koinonia, 1976).

21. I regard this thesis of 509 pages very highly. Indeed I have been challenged by it more than by any other work on the synoptic problem, but it is not easy of access for purposes of study. Its arguments should be made available in some published form.

22. My tutor, Edwyn Hoskyns, once spoke of the tantalising nature of Luke's preface – how it just fails to answer the questions we so urgently want to put to it.

23. A new recruit to the oral theory is B. Chilton. In an original book, *Profiles of a Rabbi: Synoptic Opportunities in Reading About Jesus* (Atlanta: Scholars Press, 1989), he utters a strong protest against 'the failure of Sanday and his colleagues to engage Westcott's work directly and seriously' (43). He castigates the theses of both Streeter and Farmer: 'Both those theses, the first accepted by a (sometimes unreflective) majority of scholars, the latter by a vociferous and growing minority, represent elegant applications . . . of the axiom of the generation of documents from documents' (4). It is refreshing to

meet this independence of mind and his shrewd criticisms, but whether his rabbinic parallels will be considered sufficiently close to carry conviction is more doubtful.

24. Romans 16 and see p. 152 below.

25. Note Mark's and Luke's contacts with one another: Col. 4:10, 14; Phm. 24; 2 Tim. 4:11. The evangelists could conceivably have known each other's gospels, yet decided to make no use of them, but this gratuitously throws away an easy explanation of their order. Reicke seems to attribute the concord in pericope-sequence in Mark and Luke to their personal contacts (165, 170).

26. Scott in a private communication said, 'I date Luke in the (probably early) 50s, Matthew in the 50s or early 60s and Mark in the (probably mid) 60s.' With composition spread over a decade, is it not almost certain that an evangelist working on his book would have known about, and, in view of the seriousness of his task, would in all probability have procured a copy of his predecessor's work?

27. Augustine *Harmony* 1.4 writes, 'each of them is found not to have desired to write in ignorance of his predecessor'. (See Orchard 220, 212 for text and translation.)

28. This confidence in literary solutions was illustrated also by a remark made in the SNTS Synoptic Problem Seminar by a leading authority, who said that in a court of law the kind of evidence provided by the synoptists would be clear proof of plagiarism. I am sorry that on that occasion I was not aware of the case of Florence Deeks. It is so relevant that it deserves to be recounted at length. 'Plagiarism' of course to the modern ear has a pejorative sound, but in the ancient world unacknowledged use of someone else's material (which is what we are concerned about) would not be regarded as reprehensible. The account of Miss Deeks below is taken from an article by H. E. Irwin, K.C., 'Testing the Higher Criticism in the Law Courts', *Bible League Quarterly*, 1933, reprinted in S. M. Houghton (ed.), *Truth Unchanged, Unchanging* (The Bible League, 1984; Larkhill House, 4 Godwyn Close, Abingdon, OX14 1BU) 422ff. W. A. Irwin, the biblical critic in the case, was sufficiently distinguished for four of his books (and a *Festschrift* in his honour) to gain a place in the Bodleian Library, Oxford.

The Strange Case of Miss Florence Deeks

Shortly before the First World War, a Canadian woman of literary ability wrote the story of woman's part in world history. She took the voluminous manuscript, which she entitled *The Web*, to the Macmillan Company of Canada, in whose hands it lay for some eight months.

At about the end of this period the Anglo-Saxon world was flooded with H. G. Wells' loudly heralded *Outline of History* from Macmillan of England, which he had written for publication in instalments at terrific speed during the period when Miss Deeks' work was in Macmillan's possession. When she read *The Outline*, the author of *The Web* was convinced that she recognised so many of her own original ideas, and such frequent repetitions of her own sequence of events in narration, that she felt assured that the author of *The Outline* had appropriated many parts of it and incorporated them in his book. She consulted eminent counsel, and brought an action for 500,000 dollars (*sic*) damages against H. G. Wells, and against the Macmillan Company. On behalf of the defendants (Mr. Wells and his publishers) it was stated that the manuscript of *The Web* had never been in the hands of the author of *The Outline*, that no copy of it or any portion of it had ever, by any other means, been made available to him. They affirmed that it had never been out of the custody of the Toronto house and that the author of *The Outline*, which was written in England, had not been in Canada during the period when the manuscript of *The Web* was in the hands of Macmillans.

The plaintiff had no evidence wherewith to offset this denial. How then, was she to prove to the satisfaction of a Court of Justice that her unpublished book had been plagiarised? That was a question to stagger the most optimistic of advocates. Someone suggested that she seek the aid of a biblical critic, skilled in the identification of literary sources and in the study of their interrelation. She took her case to Professor W. A. Irwin, an Old Testament scholar of some distinction in Toronto and later in Chicago. He said in a signed statement filed in court:

> Miss Deeks called upon me, told me the story of her manuscript and her belief that Mr H. G. Wells had used it in writing his *Outline of History*, and asked me to undertake a study of the two works for evidence bearing upon this contention. I consented, in considerable measure because this is the sort of task with which my study of ancient literature repeatedly confronts me, and I was interested to test out in modern works the methods commonly applied to those of the ancient world.

He said on oath that:

> by his analysis and comparisons, and by the application of the rules of Biblical Criticism, it is established beyond a doubt that:
> 1 . . . the author of *The Outline* had access to the manuscript of *The Web*.
> 2 . . . the manuscript was at hand as he wrote.

254

3 . . . the manuscript was constantly available, lying close at hand on his work table, and referred to repeatedly if not steadily throughout the course of his writing.

4 . . . Sometimes it lay open before him and his writing was palpably a disguised copying of a passage from *The Web*.

In addition to giving his evidence by way of oral answers to questions of counsel, he was permitted to file with the court a sixty-page statement of his findings, with the reasons therefor.

The verdict was given by the judge in these words:

> If I were to accept Professor Irwin's evidence and argument, there would only remain for my consideration the legal questions involved in the piracy of a non-copyright manuscript. But the extracts I have quoted, and the other scores of pages of Professor Irwin's memorandum, are just solemn nonsense. His comparisons are without significance, and his argument and conclusions are alike puerile. Like Gratiano, Professor Irwin spoke 'an infinite deal of nothing.' His reasons are not even 'two grains of wheat hidden in two bushels of chaff.' They are not reasons at all.

The court dismissed the action and gave the defendants their large costs.

But this is not the end of the story. So convinced was Miss Deeks of the rightness of her cause that she took the case to appeal and finally to the Privy Council. The result: All the learned judges were agreed on 'the utter worthlessness of this kind of evidence'. For a condensed account of the proceedings see *Dominion Law Reports*, 1930, vol. 4, pp. 513–24; 1931, vol. 4, pp. 533–48).

This seems a very impolite way of dealing with the methods which biblical critics had developed with such immense toil, but it is salutary to see what happens when our procedures are taken out of the abstract world of academia and tested in the world where money and reputations are at stake. It is a matter of judgement to decide how close is the analogy between the case of the two world histories and the case of two synoptic evangelists. In both instances we have two writers attempting to describe the same facts and ideas from their own individual points of view and in both instances we have the same literary critical methods applied with painstaking thoroughness. Maybe Irwin was over-confident and not the most judicious of critics, but at least he had the courage of his convictions, and his effort provides a cautionary tale for all of us who attempt this sort of critical work.

A closer analogy to the situation envisaged by the oral theory would be provided if two pupils were independently to write accounts of a beloved teacher. That they included some of the same anecdotes and that they gave accounts of his teaching with many examples of verbal identity would in fact be evidence of careful listening or recording, not of plagiarism. An additional factor of course in the earliest days of the church would have been the continuing programme of repetitive instruction in Jerusalem given by the apostles to visitors from the diaspora.

2 Building a Synoptic Theory: (1) The Relation of Luke to Mark

1. Lindsey (Introduction, esp. 27–38) also maintained this, and his views have influenced M. Lowe and D. Flusser, who adopt a modified Griesbach position in which a Hebrew Proto-Matthew (which, incidentally, they date not much later than 36) is said to have been interwoven with Luke to form Mark. See their 'Evidence corroborating a modified Proto-Matthean Synoptic Theory' *NTS* 29 (1983) 25.

2. See, for example, H. D. A. Major, pp. 179–81 below.

3. D. L. Dungan, 'The Purpose and Provenance of the Gospel of Mark according to the Two-Gospel (Owen-Griesbach) Hypothesis' in Farmer *NSS* 414.

4. J. B. Orchard, 'Why THREE Synoptic Gospels?' *Irish Theological Quarterly* 46 (1979) 241ff. See also Orchard 266–72.

5. R. Morgenthaler, *Statistik des neutestamentlichen Wortschatzes* (Zürich: Gotthelf-Verlag, 1958) 164.

6. W. R. Farmer, 'Modern Developments of Griesbach's Hypothesis' *NTS* 23 (1977) 280, 293.

7. D. L. Dungan, 'Mark – the Abridgement of Matthew and Luke' in Buttrick 63 n5.

8. Tuckett, 'Arguments from Order' in Tuckett *SS* 204. The appropriate formulae by which his figures are arrived at give $4 \times \frac{6}{80} \times \frac{74}{79} \times \frac{73}{78} \times \frac{72}{77}$ (= 0.246) and $\frac{74}{80} \times \frac{73}{78} \times \frac{72}{78} \times \frac{71}{77}$ (= in fact 0.7275) respectively. In layman's terms this means that the odds are roughly 3 to 1 (0.25) against the first happening and 3 to 1 (0.75) in favour of the second, whereas it would need to be something like 19 to 1 (0.05) against to be significant. The whole article represents a characteristically thorough and careful investigation of the arguments from order. Tuckett is criticised by A. J. McNicol, 'The Two Gospel Hypothesis Under Scrutiny: A Response to C. M. Tuckett's Analysis

of Recent Neo-Griesbachian Gospel Criticism' *Perkins Journal* 40 (1987) 5–13.

9. For further discussion of the Griesbach hypothesis, see below p. 195.

10. For the assumption that scrolls, not codices, were used, see Chapter 10 n16 below.

11. This is based on sample counts of passages in Category 1. Every word added or omitted or changed is regarded as a difference, and a transposition is regarded as a single difference however many words are involved. Tyson and Longstaff 169–71 as quoted by Stein 115 give this statistic: Luke omits three-fourths of the Markan vocabulary, substituting 6,244 of his own words for the 8,038 words of Mark that he omits. But this includes both Category 1 and Category 2.

12. J. M. Creed says, 'The words of Jesus are generally reproduced without material change' (Creed lxiii). Goulder 76 calls Luke 'a cautious editor' in these passages.

13. See Luke 9:3 discussed on p. 27. There is also a small change of sense, according to most modern editors, at Luke 9:50, where ὑμῶν ('he who is not against *you*') is substituted for ἡμῶν, but, since both texts are uncertain and the interchange of ἡμεῖς and ὑμεῖς is one of the commonest of textual corruptions, it is precarious to regard this as a Lukan change. There is also in the narrative passage concerning the blind man at Jericho Luke's ἐν τῷ ἐγγίζειν (18:35) for Mark's ἐκπορευομένου, which is discussed on p. 210f.

14. For a convenient look at the Chronicler's work, see R. Somervell, *The Parallel History of the Jewish Monarchy* (Cambridge, 2nd ed. 1901). Notice how he can introduce only a handful of tiny changes in a passage of twenty-seven verses (see 2 Chron. 18:4–30 and 1 Kings 22:5–31).

15. θέλω, καθαρίσθητι (5:13); ἀκολούθει μοι (5:27); σὺ λέγεις (23:3).

16. 18:16f.

17. σου (6:10); τοίνυν (20:25); καί (18:16f – this is a saying of thirty-six identical words apart from the καί).

18. δέ (21:23).

19. ὄχλοι (9:18) for ἄνθρωποι; εἰσπορεύονται (18:24) for εἰσελεύσονται; ἀνάβλεψον (18:42) for ὕπαγε – this is really a subtraction and addition.

20. e.g. 5:14; 6:8; 8:30; 9:23, 24 – the addition of καθ' ἡμέραν interprets the sense of ἀράτω; 9:41; 18:22, 25, 27; 20:3, 4, 46; 21:27, 29–33; 22:10–12, 52, 53a.

21. 5:22, 23; 8:48; 20:3, 4.

22. This is not meant to suggest that the finer points of detail are all easily harmonised, but taking the sequence as a whole it is obvious how the various sections fit together and there are no striking contradictions. For a thorough discussion of the discourse which argues the coherence of the whole, see D. Wenham. His suggested reconstruction of the discourse is on 360–64.

23. The Lukan version seems to have been understood and acted on before the siege, since the flight of the Jerusalem Christians to Pella (as recorded in *HE* 3.5.3) suggests that they took warning from the approach of the armies and did not wait for the desecration of the temple.

24. The Byzantine text (and A) favour the plural ῥάβδους in Luke, which would seem to harmonise the three accounts: Matthew says, 'Procure no [spare] sandals or staff'; Mark, 'Take nothing [extra], only a staff and sandals'; Luke, 'Do not take more than one staff.'

25. In the charge to the Seventy (10:4) they are told not to carry (βαστάζω) sandals.

26. See further n29 below.

27. This still applies if the shorter reading is followed at Luke 22:19f.

28. The charge of circular reasoning is made with some justice by Goulder with regard to Vincent Taylor's handling of his sources in the passion narrative. His own methods show extraordinary flights of imagination. He takes as his 'model' (123) of Luke's compositional powers his 'working up a masterpiece of his own out of half a dozen words in Matthew's Two Sons' (76). That is to say, he gets the twenty-two verses about the two υἱοί of the prodigal son parable (Luke 15:11–32) out of the two τέκνα of Matthew 21:28. He does not consider that 'a high incidence of words in common with Mark' (76) is a safe criterion for assessing the literary relationship. In the end he concludes that virtually none of the non-Markan material in Matthew and Luke comes from Jesus-tradition (77). Seemingly he substitutes for the greatness of Jesus the genius of two gospel-writers.

29. There are two cases which, although they have some words and actions in common, belong to neither Category 1 or 2, since they do not appear to be referring to the same event:

7:36–50 – The sinner anoints Jesus

There are here some similarities to the anointing story of Mark 14:3–9

258

– they are at a table, a Simon is mentioned, a woman appears with ἀλάβαστρον μύρου and complaints are made about her. But Luke (if he knew Mark's gospel) is clearly distinguishing two incidents. In the events leading up to the passion Luke follows the Markan sequence from 18:15 till he reaches the plot to kill Jesus. At this point Mark tells the story of the anointing in Bethany, but Luke leaves it out. The time and location of Mark's story (in Judea at the end of Jesus' ministry) is clear; the time and location of Luke's story (in Galilee at an earlier date) is also clear and quite different; in form and content the two stories differ throughout. Luke is placing his account in a manner which forbids their identification. We are not to suppose that Luke has here rolled his Mark scroll forward seven chapters in order to take out a pericope, only to alter it wholesale. They are not, therefore, in the category of pericopes which cover more or less the same ground. They do, however, provide a useful reminder that the coincidence of a few words and some similarities of action are not enough to prove a common origin. I have discussed the relation between these two incidents in my *Easter Enigma* ch. 2.

22:24–30 – Who is the greatest?

There are strong echoes here of the earlier incident recorded in Matthew 20 and Mark 10, but omitted by Luke, in which places of honour are sought for James and John in the kingdom. In response to the resentment of the ten, Jesus spoke in words similar to those recorded here by Luke which were addressed to the twelve at the last supper:

Mark 10:41–45

41 Καὶ ἀκούσαντες οἱ δέκα ἤρξαντο ἀγανακτεῖν περὶ
42 Ἰακώβου καὶ Ἰωάννου. καὶ προσκαλεσάμενος αὐτοὺς ὁ Ἰησοῦς λέγει <u>αὐτοῖς</u>· οἴδατε ὅτι <u>οἱ δοκοῦντες ἄρχειν τῶν ἐθνῶν</u> κατακυριεύουσιν <u>αὐτῶν</u> καὶ οἱ μεγάλοι αὐτῶν κατεξουσιάζουσιν
43 <u>αὐτῶν. οὐχ οὕτως δέ</u> ἐστιν ἐν <u>ὑμῖν· ἀλλ'</u> ὃς ἂν θέλῃ μέγας γενέσθαι <u>ἐν ὑμῖν</u>, ἔσται ὑμῶν

Luke 22:24–27

24 Ἐγένετο δὲ καὶ φιλονεικία ἐν αὐτοῖς, τὸ τίς αὐτῶν δοκεῖ εἶναι μείζων.
25 ὁ δὲ εἶπεν <u>αὐτοῖς</u>· οἱ βασιλεῖς <u>τῶν ἐθνῶν</u> κυριεύουσιν <u>αὐτῶν</u>, καὶ οἱ ἐξουσιάζοντες <u>αὐτῶν</u>
26 εὐεργέται καλοῦνται. ὑμεῖς δὲ <u>οὐχ οὕτως, ἀλλ</u>· ὁ μείζων ἐν <u>ὑμῖν</u> γινέσθω ὡς ὁ νεώτερος, <u>καὶ</u> ὁ ἡγούμενος ὡς ὁ

44 διάκονος, καὶ ὃς ἂν θέλῃ ἐν
   ὑμῖν εἶναι πρῶτος, ἔσται
   πάντων δοῦλος·

27 διακονῶν. τίς γὰρ μειζων, ὁ
   ἀνακείμενος ἢ ὁ διακονῶν; οὐχὶ
   ὁ ἀνακείμενος; ἐγὼ δὲ ἐν μέσῳ
   ὑμῶν εἰμι

45 καὶ γὰρ ὁ υἱὸς τοῦ ἀνθρώπου
   οὐκ ἦλθεν διακονηθῆναι ἀλλὰ
   διακονῆσαι καὶ δοῦναι τὴν
   ψυχὴν αὐτοῦ λύτρον ἀντὶ
   πολλῶν.

ὡς ὁ διακονῶν.

Luke continues (vv. 28–30) with a passage not found in Mark concerning their judging of the tribes of Israel which has echoes in Matthew 19:28. In spite of the occasional (underlined) verbal coincidences with the other gospels, Luke appears to be quite independent of them. He seems deliberately to have omitted one incident and included a later one which had some similar features – so this passage does not belong to Category 2.

3 Building a Synoptic Theory: (2) The Relation of Luke to Matthew

1. The exegesis of the preface is discussed in Wenham *Luke*.
2. Orchard ('The Solution of the Synoptic Problem' *Scripture Bulletin* 18.1 (1987) 14 n23) adds a further point:

> Apart from the fact that no two scholars agree on its content, 'Q' stretches credulity to the limit – to imagine that in the first Christian century a document, so highly treasured and copied so carefully and lovingly by both Matthew and Luke quite independently, should have disappeared without leaving a single trace or any real objective clue to its existence and nature.

3. See the articles 'The Order of Q' and 'The Original Order of Q' reprinted in V. Taylor, *New Testament Essays* (London, 1970) 90–118. Tyson, attempting an evaluation of the best arguments in the synoptic debate, says that Taylor's efforts show 'the remarkable ingenuity of a modern scholar', but he considers that 'observations on order lack probative value' (Bellinzoni 443f).
4. Bellinzoni 406f, in which is reprinted W. R. Farmer, 'A Fresh Approach to Q' from J. Neusner (ed.), *Christianity, Judaism and Other Greco-Roman Cults*, Part 1 (Leiden: Brill, 1975) 39–50.
5. Tuckett *SS* 204.

6. Taylor *Mark* 236; C. E. B. Cranfield, *Gospel according to Saint Mark* (Cambridge UP, 1959) 133.

7. It will be remembered that Tuckett *SS* 26 allows four changes of pericope order, but the other two are even less plausible than the two just cited. The Nazara pericope of 271 words (Luke 4:16–30) has precisely fourteen words in common with Mark 6:1–6, and the catch of fish pericope of 207 words (Luke 5:1–11) has eighteen words in common with Mark 1:16–20 according to Farmer's *Synopticon* – scarcely the foundation for a theory of literary dependence.

8. R. Morgenthaler, *Statistische Synopse* (Zurich: Gotthelf-Verlag 1971) 83.

9. Tuckett *SS* 111–30.

10. Streeter 183.

11. Goulder sets out these correspondences in a table (Tuckett *SS* 129f):

13.34f.	Jerusalem, Jerusalem	Matt. 23.37–39
14.1–14	Pharisaic legalism, best seats, humility	Matt. 23.6–12
14.15–24	The Great Dinner, based on	Matt. 22.1–14
14.25–35	The Tower-Builder and Embassy, based on	Matt. 21.33f.
15.1–31	Pharisees and Sinners: The Two Sons, based on	Matt. 21.28–32
16.1–13	The Steward who remitted debts, based on	Matt. 18.23–35
16.14–31	Harder for the rich to enter heaven . . .	Matt. 19.9, 16–26
17.1–10	Offences, Forgiveness, Faith	Matt. 18.6–21; 17.20
*17.11–19	Ten lepers, based on	Matt. 17.14–23
*17.20–18.8	The Coming of the Son of Man, based on	Matt. 16 with 24

(*signifies: not found in Aland's 'Conspectus Locorum Parallelorum' *Synopsis* 564–65. Also, of the eighteen verses of 16:14–31, only the one verse Matt. 19:9 is cited as parallel.)

Goulder has elaborated his ideas in his *magnum opus*, *Luke: A New Paradigm*. This, as the title suggests, is a radical attempt to overthrow the whole two-source paradigm. With its emphasis on midrashing, it is as far removed as possible from any scissors-and-paste idea of literary relationship. The need for a new paradigm has been shown by both Farmer and Goulder, but neither of them has found a satisfactory one. For all the implausibility of his conclusions, (which stem from his failure to distinguish between the Category 1 and Category 2 passages, as expounded on pp. 18–39 above), Goulder's critique of the Q-hypothesis in his second chapter is immensely valuable. He argues 'that Q is indistinguishable from Matthew not only in language, but in date, presupposition, attitude and theology' and calls the Q-hypothesis 'The grandfather of all synoptic errors' (27). For his treatment of the argument from order, see 48–51. The agreements of Matthew and Luke against Mark always provided a weak point in Streeter's exposition of the two (four)-document hypothesis. These are so numerous and often so weighty that it was necessary to postulate an overlap of Mark and Q in passages where Mark is supposedly being followed. This would be all right if Q could be firmly delineated. But in fact it cannot be. As long as Q fails to emerge clearly as a document, the agreement of Matthew and Luke against Mark constitute an argument against Matthew's and Luke's independence of one another.

12. E. P. Sanders, 'Argument from Order and the Relationship between Matthew and Luke' *NTS* 15 (1969) 249–61, studying the order of the smaller items common to Matthew and Luke, argued that they were not to be explained by a Q-document, but rather by the likelihood that one (probably Luke) knew the other. I would argue that the small likenesses and differences are rather evidence of independence.

13. See S. Neill and T. Wright, *The Interpretation of the New Testament 1861–1986* (Oxford UP, 2nd ed., 1988), ch. 1 'Challenge to Orthodoxy', esp. 4–10.

14. A. C. Headlam, *The Life and Teaching of Jesus the Christ* (London: Murray, 3rd ed., 1936) 8f.

15. Streeter xx.

16. W. Wrede, *The Messianic Secret*, ET (Cambridge and London: James Clarke, 1971).

17. Morgan 334 calls these 'gems'.

18. N. Perrin, *What is Redaction Criticism?* (London: SPCK, 1970) 14.

19. Bultmann 1926 340f.

20. Ellis *GC* 52ff.

21. Comparable to the Apocalypse; cf. Rev. 1:1–3; 3:22f. See also Ellis on the Christian prophet (Ellis *Luke* 170ff).

22. 1 Corinthians 7:25; 11:23; 15:3.

23. In addition to the close correspondences in the passages discussed on pp. 55–66 which on my reckoning contain some eighty-seven such verses or part verses, there are other parallels at 12:10–12; 13:28a; 14:27; 17:27.

24. In the discussion that follows reference will be made to Fitzmyer and Marshall *Luke*.

25. In the Byzantine text as printed in Hodges and Farstad, there are only 25 differences as compared with the 35 of the Aland text. This could be a case of assimilation after the writing of the gospels, though it is possible that the Byzantine form may itself be a good text.

26. See my 'Synoptic Independence and the Origin of Luke's Travel Narrative' *NTS* 27 (1981) 512f, from which this section is taken by permission of the Cambridge University Press.

27. The topographical and chronological notices of Luke's Central Section are too slight to allow a confident reconstruction of the history. I (in common with H. W. Hoehner, *Chronological Aspects of the Life of Christ*, Grand Rapids: Zondervan, 1977, ch. 3) incline towards the view expounded (according to Hoehner) by K. Wieseler, *Chronologische Synopse der vier Evangelien* (Hamburg, 1843) 316–32, adopted by A. T. Robertson, *A Harmony of the Gospels* (London: Hodder, 1922) 276–79, and worked out by A. Edersheim, *The Life and Times of Jesus the Messiah* (London and New York: Longmans, 1883), vol. 2, bk 4, chs 4–23, which correlates Luke's Central Section with the fourth gospel. If, as advocated by J. A. T. Robinson, *The Priority of John* (London: SCM, 1985), the fourth gospel is adopted as the framework into which the synoptists are to be fitted (if possible), we should not understand Jesus' setting his face to go to Jerusalem as signifying one simple journey, but as the decisive turning of his back on his home and his home-country of Galilee. Jesus undertook an extended campaign which included Samaria (Luke 9:52) and Perea (cf. Matt. 19:1), and which ended seven months later with his final entry into Jerusalem. Luke's three notices of movement towards Jerusalem (9:51; 13:22; 17:11) are correlated with three journeys mentioned by John (7:1–11; 11:7–20; 11:55–21:1). Reicke 116–27 gives considerable importance to a ministry in Transjordan.

28. Kümmel seeing doublets as 'decisive evidence' for Q (66) is thus wholly fallacious.

29. He does not eliminate all repetitions – see the ten small Lukan doublets discussed in Hawkins 81–86. The case for Luke himself having been one of the seventy is argued in Wenham *Luke*.

30. I do not rule out the possibility that Matthew's great discourses were composed from smaller units brought together as a literary device by the evangelist, but it is more straightforward to take the settings in their natural sense unless there is strong evidence to the contrary. D. Guthrie regards it as 'certainly not improbable' that Jesus 'spoke all this teaching on one occasion' (*New Testament Introduction: Gospels and Acts*, London: Tyndale, 1965, 28).

31. Birks 97–101 argued that these were two different sermons, Matthew's being the earlier.

32. Augustine regarded the order of the temptations as of no real consequence, provided it be clear that all these incidents did take place (Augustine *Harmony* 2.16.33, p. 238). The probability is that all three temptations were harassing Jesus throughout the forty days and that they reached a climax towards the end, and that then he clearly formulated his final answer to them.

33. If the Byzantine text is followed an extra sixteen verbal identities would be added to Farmer's total of 163.

34. For a discussion of παρηκολουθηκότι ἄνωθεν in Luke 1:3, see Wenham *Luke*.

35. This category overlaps with 1.) and 4.) since some of them are embedded in passages otherwise dissimilar, suggesting that they were uttered on more than one occasion.

36. This estimate is again based on a sample count – of 135 verses. Tyson and Longstaff 169–71 (as quoted by Stein 115) reckon that Matthew substitutes 6,469 of his own words for the 6,593 words of Mark that he omits. These figures take no account of transpositions of order, and sometimes it would be incorrect to regard a Matthean addition as a substitute for a Markan omission, hence the true total of changes is higher than the number of Markan words omitted.

37. I do not include the many passages in which new matter is introduced which does not conflict with the sense of the original (e.g. Matt. 16:17–19).

38. See my article 'Why do you ask me about the Good? A Study of the Relation between Text and Source Criticism' *NTS* 28 (1982) 116–25.

39. On the question of text here, see my 'How Many Cock-Crowings? The Problem of Harmonistic Text-Variants' *NTS* 25 (1979) 523–25.

40. There is no reason, however, to think that Luke organised his special material into a proto-gospel which he conflated with Mark, as Streeter thought.

4 Building a Synoptic Theory: (3) The Relation of Matthew to Mark

1. W. F. Albright, coming to the subject from the background of a different discipline, reached the same conclusion, suggesting that 'Mark and Matthew may represent two quite separate collections of tradition.' See W. F. Albright and C. S. Mann, *Matthew*, Anchor Bible (New York: Doubleday, 1971) xlviii.

2. Lachmann himself, believing in an Ur-gospel behind all the synoptists, was not in fact guilty of this fallacy. See Farmer *SP* 66. According to Dungan, Neirynck explicitly rejects the Lachmann fallacy, but adopts the 'Lachmann Gambit' instead! (Farmer *NSS* 416 n15).

3. Butler ch. 5 referring to Streeter ch. 7, quotation from Streeter 157. His main exposition of the fallacy (62–67) concerns Streeter's 'heads of evidence' 1–3; he dismisses head 5 on pp. 67f.

4. E. A. Abbott, *The Fourfold Gospel: Section 1 – Introduction* (Cambridge UP, 1913) 11f.

5. C. F. D. Moule, *The Birth of the New Testament* (London: Black, 3rd ed., 1981). Strangely an earlier version (1962) of Styler's essay has been reprinted in Bellinzoni, along with other defences of Markan priority by Streeter, Kümmel, Wood, Neirynck and Fitzmyer. Fitzmyer's article was a paper given at the Pittsburgh Festival of the Gospels and published as 'The Priority of Mark and the "Q" Source in Luke' in Buttrick 131–70. Fitzmyer's nine objections to the Griesbach hypothesis are answered by Farmer in 'Modern Developments of Griesbach's Hypothesis' *NTS* 23 (1977) 283–293, with a fair measure of success. Fitzmyer's objections have even less validity on an Augustinian view. See also Farmer's 'A Response to Joseph Fitzmyer's Defense of the Two Document Hypothesis' in Farmer *NSS* 501–523. Sanders' comment on Styler is interesting: 'The basis for deciding on a solution to the Synoptic problem is somewhat elusive. Thus Styler, in referring to an article by Farmer, grants that the arguments for Mark's priority which were used in the past are "insecure". He nevertheless remains convinced of Mark's priority' (Sanders 277). This illustrates Tyson's conclusion: 'The two-source hypothesis has been damaged, but its adherents have not surrendered' (Bellinzoni 438).

6. Sanders 274. Though Sanders refers primarily to fictitious details, the addition of eyewitness details from an apostle would be relished by a Christian audience.

7. H. G. Jameson wrote his impressive book arguing Matthean

priority, *The Origin of the Synoptic Gospels*, published by Blackwell of Oxford in 1922, and apparently unknown to Chapman. This book is not to be found in the Bodleian library in Oxford and is not mentioned by name by Streeter in his book of 1924. Farmer says of this:

> Jameson . . . had already been made aware of Streeter's views on the Synoptic Problem through Streeter's article in Peake's *Commentary on the Bible* published in 1920, and had taken Streeter's arguments into account in his book in 1922. In this book Jameson refuted most of the essential arguments which Streeter incorporated into his 'Fundamental Solution' in 1924. Streeter's refusal to acknowledge the serious and responsible work of Jameson, in which the logical fallacy of Streeter's arguments had been exposed, constitutes in the history of the Synoptic Problem the single most unparalleled act of academic bravado on record. Jameson refuted the argument from order and showed that it could be used quite as well to argue for the Augustinian hypothesis. (Farmer *SP* 152f; cf. 287–93)

8. Butler 105, 83, 91. For its esteem in the early church, see the 877 pages of Massaux. The popularity of Matthew is seen again in the frequency of its use in the Nag Hammadi literature, see C. M. Tuckett, *Nag Hammadi and the Gospel Tradition* (Edinburgh: T. & T. Clark, 1986).

9. e.g. W. D. Davies, *The Setting of the Sermon on the Mount* (Cambridge UP, 1964) ch. 4 'The Setting in the Contemporary Judaism' dates Matthew between 70 and 100 (191) and cautiously suggests that it is 'the Christian answer to Jamnia', 'a formulation of the way of the New Israel at a time when the rabbis were engaged in a parallel task for the Old Israel' (315).

10. John 12:42 says explicitly that 'many ἐκ τῶν ἀρχόντων believed in him,' but then goes on to say, 'but because of the Pharisees they did not confess it, lest they should be put out of the synagogue.' While making it clear that the chief opposition came from the Pharisees, it does not necessarily imply that none of these timid leaders came from that group.

11. Stoldt 187f. For the relation between Peter and Mark, see also Hengel *Mark* 50–53 and the excursus in the same book by R. Feldmeier, 'The Portrayal of Peter in the Synoptic Gospels' 59–63.

12. Chapman 16f; cf. France 88f:

> The inclusion of the story about the temple tax . . . implicitly approves the payment . . . Before AD 70 this would have been a meaningful gesture of solidarity with Israel, but after AD 70 it would carry a quite different connotation, for the tax was not abolished when the temple was destroyed,

but rather diverted to the temple of Jupiter in Rome . . . it was now resented as a contribution to idolatry.

In 'St Paul and the Revelation to St Peter, Matt. 16:17' *Revue Benedictine* 29 (1912) 133–47 Chapman also argues the primitive character of the famous Petrine passage, as do Butler 131–32; G. Maier, 'The Church in the Gospel of Matthew' in D. A. Carson (ed.), *Biblical Interpretation and the Church* (Exeter: Paternoster, 1984) 45–63; B. F. Meyer, *The Aims of Jesus* (London: SCM, 1979) 185–97 and D. Wenham, 'Paul's Use of the Jesus Tradition: Three Samples' in D. Wenham (ed.), *The Jesus Tradition Outside the Gospels*, Gospel Perspectives vol. 5 (Sheffield: JSOT, 1984) 24–27. The last named, referring to J. Dupont, 'La Révélation du Fils de Dieu en faveur de Pierre (Mt 16, 17) et de Paul (Ga 1, 16)' *Recherches de science religieuse* 52 (1964) 411–20, says that Dupont 'adduces weighty arguments to support Chapman's case'. These writers have an impressive variety of different approaches.

13. Walker 393f.

14. Matthew on reaching 2:1 moves forward to 4:35, then back to 2:1 to take three of Mark's controversy stories, forward again to 6:6b (passing over the Nazareth visit of 6:1–6a), then adding his own section on sheep without a shepherd, forward to 6:7 for the commission of the twelve, then adding his own form of the names of the twelve, forward to 6:8 for the missionary discourse which he intended to adapt and expand, then adding his chapter 11, before going back to 2:23 to take up the other two controversy stories. Then he adds the sections about the gathering of the crowds at 3:7–12, passes over 3:13–21 and substitutes the healing of the man blind and dumb, then takes the Beelzebul section at 3:22, adds in three sections on the tree and its fruits, Jonah, and the return of the unclean spirit, before taking the passage about Jesus' mother and brothers at 3:31 and then writing an enlarged version of the parables section of 4:1–34. Finally he goes forward to pick up the Nazareth passage, 6:1–6a, which he had passed over.

15. Walker 394.

16. οὐϱανός: LSJ.

17. οὐϱανός: Kittel-Friedrich, v. 510.

18. Butler 149. Luke's Hebraisms are well known. ἰδού is one of them, used eighty times in Luke-Acts.

19. Chapman 193.

20. J. Carmignac, *La naissance des Évangiles Synoptiques* (Paris:

O.E.I.L. 1984) gives a preliminary account. This is now in English as *The Birth of the Synoptic Gospels* (Chicago: Franciscan Herald Press, 1986).

21. E. J. Goodspeed, *Matthew, Apostle and Evangelist* (Philadelphia: Winston, 1959).

22. W. M. Ramsay, *Expositor* (1907) 424; G. Salmon, *The Human Element in the Gospels* (London: Murray, 1907) 275.

23. R. H. Gundry, *The Use of the Old Testament in St. Matthew's Gospel* (Leiden: Brill, 1967) xii.

24. M. Lowe and D. Flusser, 'A Modified Proto-Matthean Synoptic Theory,' *NTS* 29 (1983) 47 n88.

25. Alexander 146. This point is relevant if (as I have tentatively argued: Wenham *Luke*) Luke was present during the ministry of Jesus. F. F. Bruce in a private communication writes: 'In my Greek *Acts* (p. 377) I say that Luke almost certainly heard Paul's farewell speech at Miletus, "and may even have taken shorthand notes." The only thing Haenchen could do with such an extraordinary suggestion was to quote it *verbatim* and follow it with "(!)".'

26. D. A. Carson, *Scripture and Truth* (Leicester: IVP; Grand Rapids: Zondervan, 1983) 124, 378; cf. R. Riesner, *Jesus als Lehrer* (Tübingen: Mohr, 3rd ed., 1988). H. Schürmann's article 'Die vorösterlichen Anfange der Logientradition' in H. Ristow and K. Matthiae (edd.), *Der historische Jesus und der kerugmatische Christus* (Berlin: Evangelische Verlagsanstalt, 1960) is discussed by Stein, 203–5. After noting the mnemonic forms in the traditions and showing it 'probable that memorization played a considerable part in Jesus' instruction', Stein concludes 'there is furthermore no need to think that this material was simply memorized by the disciples. Some of Jesus' teaching could well have been written down in brief note-book-like memoranda for use during their mission'; cf. Walker 394, who speaks of 'Matthew's diary in Aramaic'.

27. E. E. Ellis, 'Historical-Literary Criticism – After Two Hundred Years' *Proceedings of the Conference on Biblical Inerrancy 1987* (Nashville: Broadman) 417; 'Reading the Gospels as History,' *Criswell Theo. Rev.* 3 (Fall 1988) 7.

28. 'The Gospels and Jewish Tradition' in R. T. France and D. Wenham (edd.), *Studies of History and Tradition in the Four Gospels*, GP I (Sheffield: JSOT, 1980) 87, 98.

5 Ancient Testimony to Matthew's Gospel

1. In this and subsequent quotations of Eusebius the Loeb library translations of Kirsopp Lake and J. E. L. Oulton are used unless otherwise stated. The dates of the fathers quoted are taken from *ODCC*. For the date of Papias' *Expositions* see n11 below. The fact that Eusebius records Papias' words about Mark before those about Matthew has been taken as possible evidence that this was Papias' belief about the order of composition (see C. M. Tuckett, *The Revival of the Griesbach Hypothesis*, Cambridge UP, 1983, 57; Gundry 613f; France 57). But conjectures which run counter to the views which Eusebius directly cites (e.g. Origen's) are of little value.

2. This passage is discussed in detail below on pp. 239–42 in connection with Matthew's date.

3. So says Alford 1.27, though without giving references. Mention should also be made of the Anti-Marcionite Prologue to John's gospel (see Aland 533) which describes Papias as a beloved disciple of John and as the amanuensis to whom John dictated his gospel. See France 55f for the significance of this.

4. For a brief discussion see G. Howard, 'A Primitive Hebrew Gospel of Matthew and the Tol'doth Yeshu' *NTS* 34 (1988) 60–70. For the critical edition of the complete text: G. Howard, *The Gospel of Matthew According to a Primitive Hebrew Text* (Macon: Mercer UP, 1987). The Talmud itself seems to bear witness to a time when gospels (the word used, *gilyon*, is an abbreviation of εὐαγγέλιον) were being read with approval in the synagogues in either Hebrew or Aramaic. *Tosephta Yadaim* II 13, attributed by G. F. Moore and C. C. Torrey to Johanan ben Zakkai, who flourished mid-century and was head of the College at Jamnia (Jabneh) 70–80, says: 'The Gilyonim and the writings of the Minim [sectaries] do not defile the hands. The writings of Ben Sira, and whatever books have been written since his time, do not defile the hands.' Torrey then quotes Moore: 'This ruling implies . . . that by many Jews of good standing the Gospels had been thus ranked [as holy scripture] and that the fact was well known', C. C. Torrey, *Documents of the Primitive Church* (New York: Harper, 1941) 94. (L. Ginsberg *JBL* 41 (1922) 115 took a contrary view, maintaining that the problem arose from the Old Testament quotations in the gospels. Did *they* constitute a defiling property? He thinks there was never any question of the gospels having had such a status.) Furthermore, Torrey speaks of 'numerous allusions to the Gospels' in the Talmud (93). If Moore and Torrey are right, it would seem that

such a use of the gospels must have substantially antedated the full rupture between church and synagogue, otherwise the matter would not have attained sufficient importance to become a subject of debate in the Talmud. That Matthew (as we know it) in Hebrew should have disappeared is not surprising. The works of the Jew Josephus were preserved in Greek by Christians and his Aramaic version disappeared.

5. Gundry *Matthew* 610. This strength of tradition reinforces the wise words of E. E. Ellis: 'one must resist the modern tendency to assume that in early Christianity only unknowns knew how to write' (*GC* 47 n114).

6. For a good discussion see Hennecke 1.117ff, from which the quotations that follow are taken and whose guidance I largely take.

7. Jerome's other quotations are collected in Hennecke 146–50, 163–65.

8. Carmignac 65 describes the story as 'trop invraisemblable pour n'être pas vérédique!' To Eusebius Pantaenus is no shadowy figure. He devotes a lengthy passage to his zeal, learning and fame and to his influence on Clement (*HE* 5.10f).

9. *Adv. Haer.* 3.3.4, cf. Eusebius, *HE* 5.20.6.

10. M.-J. Lagrange, *Évangile selon Saint Matthieu* (Paris: Gabalda, 1923) xvf. Streeter believed that the whole tradition of a Hebrew Matthew derived from Papias. This is conceivable, rather than probable – certainly not to be claimed as a fact. Zahn 2.517f repudiates the notion. A. C. Perumalil, 'Are not Papias and Irenaeus competent to report on the Gospels?' *ExpT* 91 (1980) 332–37 shows how Irenaeus had associations with many leading Christians of apostolic and sub-apostolic days in Asia Minor and Rome, and concludes: 'It becomes clear that Irenaeus was in a position to report things independently of Papias. Both Papias and Irenaeus, therefore, are competent to give us reliable and independent information about the gospel origins.' The same view is trenchantly expressed by Petrie, see n13 below.

11. Gundry *Matthew* 610f. R. W. Yarbrough, in a clear and concise article: 'The Date of Papias: A Reassessment' *Journ. Evan. Theo. Soc.* 26 (1983) 181–91 also opts for a date *c.* 95–110 for his five treatises.

12. F. F. Bruce writes in a personal communication: 'J. Rendel Harris (*Testimonies* I [Cambridge, 1916] 119f) has an interesting argument pointing to the possibility that the description σφόδρα . . . σμικρὸς ὢν τὸν νοῦν may be Papias's own self-depreciatory comment. The phrase seems to have become a cliché, going back to Plato's *Gorgias* 500c, σμικρὸν νοῦν ἔχων ἄνθρωπος.' Harris 119 says, 'this

description of Papias as a person of quite inferior intelligence was contradicted (apparently) by another passage in which he is described by Eusebius as ἀνὴρ λογιώτατος'. Unfortunately he does not say in which passage this description of 'a very learned man' is to be found.

13. This seems to be the main source of the current undervaluing of external evidence. Kümmel (*Introduction to NT*, 1966) 44, for instance, regarded the priority of the Greek Mark as a 'fact'. Hence his conclusion that it is 'advisable to leave Papias' notices, in spite of their great age, out of consideration', because they do 'not correspond to the literary facts of the case'. But with the reopening of the synoptic problem such 'facts' must be looked at again and the fathers must be given a better hearing. C. S. Petrie, in an article which seems to have been unjustly overlooked, 'The Authorship of "The Gospel according to Matthew": A Reconsideration of the External Evidence' *NTS* 14 (1967) 32, comes to precisely the opposite conclusion with regard to the value of Papias' testimony, which he declares 'is on much firmer ground than the best speculative guesses of the twentieth century . . . it is not to be dismissed because of its inconvenience for current hypotheses. If it does not accord with these hypotheses, it is the hypotheses that must be considered anew.' Sanders and Davies 8–12 gives their treatment of Papias.

14. V. Taylor, *The Gospels* (London: Epworth, 4th ed., 1938) 92.

15. The full paper has been printed in Tuckett *SS* 187–96.

16. See, for instance, 'Eusebius' *ODCC* 473:

> his *Ecclesiastical History* . . . contains an immense range of materials on the E. Church . . . largely in the form of long extracts taken over bodily from earlier writers. If Eusebius's interpretation of these documents was sometimes in error, this is to be explained by his want of critical judgement and not by conscious perversion of the facts.

Even more authoritative is J. B. Lightfoot's pronouncement, which he italicises: 'In no instance which we can test does Eusebius give a doubtful testimony', *Essays on the Work Entitled 'Supernatural Religion'* (London and New York: Macmillan, 1889) 49. See also P. W. L. Walker, 'Gospel Sites and "Holy Places": The Contrasting Attitudes of Eusebius and Cyril' *Tyn B* 41.1 (1990) 89–108, and his *Holy City, Holy Places? Christian Attitudes to Jerusalem and the Holy Land in the Fourth Century* (Oxford UP, 1990).

17. He devotes an extraordinary amount of space to the arguments of Dionysius, who regards John of the apocalypse as being different from the apostle John of the gospels and epistles (*HE* 7.25). It will be

271

remembered that Eusebius does not put the Apocalypse among the disputed books, but among both the recognised and the rejected books, which seems to suggest that the Apocalypse of John was very generally recognised, although he himself wished to reject it (*HE* 3.25). *HE* 6.25.10 asserts that the same John is author of both books.

18. The story of the 'two tombs at Ephesus both called John's', which Eusebius quotes in support of his theory, is flimsy evidence on which to postulate a second John, otherwise unknown. It is not something of which Eusebius has first-hand knowledge or reliable testimony (his information evidently came from Dionysius, bishop of Alexandria (died *c*. 264), who had it on hearsay: *HE* 7.25.16); in a later work, written after the final edition of *HE*, he in fact refers to '*the* sepulchre . . . which is in Ephesus' (*Theophania* 4.7: ET by S. Lee 1843, p. 221); and it is not even certain that μνήματα means 'tombs', it could refer to memorials of other kinds. Even if the story was true, the fact that two memorials (or even tombs) of the great man should be shown to visitors to Ephesus two hundred years after his death would be of no proof that in fact there were two Johns. F. F. Bruce believes that there probably were two tombs at Ephesus associated with the same John – a temporary one and a permanent one, the latter on the site still marked by the Justinian's basilica. See his *Men and Movements in the Primitive Church* (Exeter: Paternoster, 1979) 139–41. Irenaeus, who had read Papias, seems not to believe that there were two Johns, since he calls Papias 'the hearer of John' (*HE* 3.39.1–4), suggesting by his unqualified reference that he had actually heard the great and only apostle John. If this is so, Eusebius is overstating the case when he says that Papias 'makes plain that he had in no way been a hearer and eyewitness of the sacred Apostles'. The elderly John may have been an exception. Indeed when Eusebius says that Papias 'had actually heard [Aristion and] the presbyter John' and that 'he often quotes them by name', he may be bearing witness to statements of Papias now lost to us, but available to him and Irenaeus. In that case, if John was both presbyter and apostle (as seems likely) Papias received some of his apostolic information without any intermediary, he was literally a 'hearer of John'. Irenaeus is often held responsible for confusing the two Johns, see Hengel *Johannine Q* 2–4.

19. Stoldt 48. Stoldt traces Schleiermacher's influence on K. Lachmann and C. H. Weisse and on the whole development of the two-document hypothesis.

20. Published first in *Presbyterian and Reformed Review* XI (1900) 217–60, it was reprinted in *Revelation and Inspiration* (New York:

Oxford UP, 1927) 335–91. In a personal note Bruce writes: 'if the word were diminutive it would probably be accented λογίον'. This interpretation does not seem to have occurred to scribes and editors. In general agreement with Warfield against Schleiermacher are Zahn 2.509ff, Chapman 3, Petrie 31f (see n13 above; he cites also Jülicher, Bacon, Kittel, Kilpatrick, Lightfoot and Stonehouse), Kümmel 44, J. C. O'Neill *NTS* 21 (1975) 283 n1, Orchard 191 n12, Reicke 8, 157f, and Goulder 33, who speaks of 'a virtual consensus . . . Papias meant Matthew's Gospel'. F. F. Bruce, *The Books and the Parchments* (Basingstoke: Pickering and Inglis, 1984) 259 and Robinson 97 seem still to favour reference to a Q.

21. R. Gryson, 'À propos du témoignage de Papias sur Matthieu: le sens du mot *logion* chez les Pères du second siècle' *Ephemerides Theologicae Lovaniensis* 41 (1965) 530–47.

22. This point is made by A. F. Walls, 'Papias and Oral Tradition' *Vigiliae Christianae* 21 (1967) 137–40. The concern of Papias is with apostolicity. He is suspicious of works of whose apostolic origin there is no proof, preferring the living voice of those who had been verifiably in touch with the Lord or with any of the twelve.

23. G. D. Kilpatrick, *The Origins of the Gospel according to St Matthew* (Oxford: 1946) 138f.

24. K. Stendahl, *The School of St Matthew and Its Use of the Old Testament* (Philadelphia: Fortress, 2nd ed. 1968).

25. This does not mean that Matthew composed his gospel without reference to others. There is every likelihood that he wrote in consultation with his fellow apostles and other ministers of the word and published with their endorsement.

26. It has been suggested that Ματθαῖος μὲν οὖν may imply that it is only an inference, see Birks 334.

27. J. Kürzinger, 'Das Papiaszeugnis und die Erstgestalt des Matthäusevangeliums' *Biblische Zeitschrift*, Neue Folge 4 (1960) 19 –38 and 'Irenäus und sein Zeugnis zur Sprache des Matthäusevange-liums' *NTS* 10 (1963) 108–15.

28. Gundry *Matthew* 619f.

29. R. T. France, *Themelios* 8.3 (April 1983) 31. Kümmel 55 n30 says that the proposal of Kürzinger is 'scarcely tenable'.

30. Hengel *Mark* ch. 3. Titles are discussed in Reicke 150ff.

31. Anonymity is stressed in Sanders and Davies 21–24.

32. Hengel, persuaded of two Johns, weaves an elaborate story around the presbyter in *The Johannine Question*. Reicke 161f declares decisively against a second John. Petrie (see n13 above) says:

Here we have the genesis of 'John the Elder', that elusive mythical figure that for so long has bedevilled students of the Fourth Gospel. We must see just how Eusebius brings him into the picture and why; and then, after wondering at the fuss he has been allowed to cause, consign him to oblivion. (20)

6 Ancient Testimony to Mark's Gospel

1. γενόμενος. J. A. T. Robinson 95 n42 rightly questions the translation of Lawlor and Oulton: 'having *been*', which implies 'that he was the "late" interpreter of Peter, who was by then dead. But it is best not to prejudge this.'

2. The Presbyter (as we saw on p. 123) is identified as John in *HE* 3.39.4.

3. LSJ gives ἑρμηνεύω: *interpret* foreign tongues, *translate, explain, expound, put into words, express, describe.* (cf. BAG: *explain, interpret,* also means simply *proclaim, discourse on.*) ἑρμηνευτής = εύς: *interpreter* especially of foreign tongues, *dragoman, matrimonial agent, go-between, broker . . . expounder.* Zahn 2.442f forthrightly repudiates the notion that Mark was Peter's translator. Kümmel 54: 'It is unlikely that Peter used an interpreter in his preaching.' For the view recently upheld by Hengel that Mark was literally Peter's translator, see Thiede 156, 247 n256. Having a Jewish name John and a Roman name Marcus suggests that he was at home in both cultures.

4. R. O. P. Taylor 29f, 75–90, suggested that πρὸς τὰς χρείας should be translated 'for the Chreiai', a chreia being a short maxim suitable for memorising. This suggestion is ingenious. Robinson 95 n43 finds it attractive, but does not adopt it, whereas it has been adopted by Farmer *SP* 266–70, Orchard 190 and others. Bruce *Date* 75 n22 inclines to this view. J. R. Butts 'The Chreia in the Synoptic Gospels' (*Biblical Theology Bulletin* 16, 1986, 132–38) thinks that it should no longer be doubted that the synoptic evangelists were familiar with the chreia-form and the compositional techniques taught by the rhetoricians. While it is quite possible that the evangelists knew something of elementary rhetoric, it is doubtful whether it makes sense to say that 'Peter used to give teaching for the Chreiai.' Is there evidence that Christians ever had collections of sayings known as Chreiai? Would the hearers of the Presbyter or Papias have naturally inferred this meaning? Sanders and Davies 146–62 devote a chapter to Chreiai. It still strikes me as more likely that for a time Matthew was only in a language not widely used and that the early preachers had

this as their text, which made it necessary for them when addressing Greek-speaking audiences to translate as best they could.

5. Alternatively Papias might be thinking of the far greater differences between the chronology of Mark and the fourth gospel; cf. Bruce *Date* 76.

6. Manson 40 argues this.

7. D. de Bruyne, 'Les plus anciens prologues latins des Évangiles' *Revue Bénédictine* 40 (1928) 193–214.

8. e.g. it was accepted by Taylor *Mark* 3.

9. R. G. Heard, 'The Old Gospel Prologues' *JTS* n.s. 6 (1955) 1–16. J. Regul, *Die antimarcionitischen Evangelienprologe* (Freiburg: Verlag Herder, 1969). H. Greeven, *Synopsis of the First Three Gospels* (Tübingen: Mohr, ET 1981) ix considers Regul's case 'proved'. See also E. Haenchen, *The Acts of the Apostles*, ET (Oxford: Blackwell, 1971) 10 n1. Orchard 155f is more reserved in his judgements. In a personal communication F. F. Bruce writes:

> When all due attention is paid to Regul's arguments (to which I attach sufficient importance to have bought his book a few years ago), the individual prologues are all worthy of careful study. I believe the *Lukan prologue is anti-Marcionite as well as the Johannine one*: the emphasis on the relevance of the initial sections dealing with John the Baptist to the message of Luke as a whole reflects the fact, I believe, that Marcion omitted all reference to the Baptist as irrelevant to the true gospel of Christ.

10. The mutilated fragment from the Muratorian canon (dated perhaps 170–90) is too incomplete to be of value, except as evidence that Mark was regarded as the second gospel in Rome at that time.

11. Morton Smith, *Clement of Alexandria and the Secret Gospel of Mark* (Cambridge, Mass.: Harvard, 1973).

12. For Morton Smith's own comments on these explanations, see his article 'Clement of Alexandria and Secret Mark: The Score at the End of the First Decade' *HTR* 75.4 (1982) 449–61. For a critical survey see E. Osborn 'Clement of Alexandria: A Review of Research, 1958–82' *The Second Century* 3 (1983) 223–25.

7 The Date of Peter's Going to Rome

1. In Eusebius' *Chronicle* 153 the date is the second year of Claudius, i.e. 42. (References are to the end section of *Eusebii Chronicorum Liber Prior*, edited by A. Schoene, Berlin, 1875. This section is entitled 'Eusebii Chronicorum Canonum Liber' and its

pages separately numbered. This section is also published separately as: J. K. Fotheringham (ed.), *Eusebii Pamphili Chronici Canones* (London, for Oxford UP, 1923) 261.) Jerome's Latin text reads: 'Petrus apostolus cum primum Antiochenam ecclesiam fundasset Romam mittitur. Ubi evangelium praedicans XXV annis eiusdem urbis episcopus perseverat.' Peter's escape is sometimes dated 44 (e.g. apparently by F. F. Bruce, *Acts*, Greek Text, London: Tyndale, 1951, 55, who puts the death of James, escape of Peter and death of Herod under 'Spring 44') on the ground that his departure in Acts 12:17 is closely linked with Herod's death in 12:23 which occurred in that year. διέτριβεν of verse 19, however, seems to hint at an interval between the two events. Bruce probably only intended 44 to apply to the death of Herod. In Bruce *Chronology* 276 he thinks 42 or 43 most probable, 44 possible (n16).

2. Williams 149f; E. G. Selwyn, *The First Epistle of Peter* (London: Macmillan, 1947) 61; Bruce, *Acts* Greek (1951) 248 – in his 1990 revision he says: 'Lactantius is probably right in saying that Nero was already emperor when Peter came to Rome (*De mort. persec.* 2.5). A date early in Nero's principate is probable' (287). J. B. Lightfoot, *Apostolic Fathers*, Pt. I. *S. Clement of Rome* I (London: Macmillan, 1890) 340; II, 490f. Cullmann says concerning Peter's episcopal status: 'All these statements [about Peter receiving the episcopal office] stand in such flagrant contradiction to The Acts and the letters of Paul that it is unnecessary even to discuss them' (113 n72). But on the question of a visit to Rome in 42, he seems to leave open the barest possibility: 'The wording does not permit the identification of the "other place" with Rome . . . [It] can be identified with any city of the Roman Empire' (39). The latest conservative writer to voice the negative view is J. R. W. Stott: 'This was definitely not Rome' (*The Message of Acts*, Leicester: IVP, 1990, 211).

3. T. W. Manson, *BJRL* 28 (1944) 130f. F. F. Bruce also inclines to this view, *The Pauline Circle* (Exeter: Paternoster, 1985) 78; Bruce *Date* 77.

4. H. Lietzmann, *Beginnings of the Christian Church*, ET (London: Lutterworth, 1949) 111.

5. For particulars of publication of Edmundson, Marucchi, Barnes, Balleine, Cullmann, O'Connor, Thiede, see pp. xi–xviii. Other references: F. J. Foakes Jackson, *Peter: Prince of the Apostles* (London: Hodder, 1927) 195; Marucchi, ch. 5; F. Underhill, *Saint Peter* (London: Centenary, 1937) 207; J. Lowe, *Saint Peter* (Oxford UP, 1956) 28; O'Connor 5.50; Thiede 153–8. P. Boylan, *St. Paul's*

Epistle to the Romans (Dublin, 1934) xvi, accepts Peter's oversight of the church in Rome from 42–67.

6. R. Pesch, *Die Apostelgeschichte* (Apg 1–12) (Zürich/Neukirchen, 1986) 368f. I am indebted to I. H. Marshall for this note concerning Pesch and other recent writers:

> He accepts the dating of the episode in AD 41: 'In favour of this date we also have the early church tradition of the 12-year apostolate of Peter in Jerusalem, his 25-year episcopate in Rome, and his first arrival there in the second year of Claudius (before 25 Jan., AD 43). Luke is silent – possibly deliberately, since he preserves the wider spread of the gospel for Paul – that Peter, who went to "another place" according to 12:17, reached Rome by way of Antioch at an early date before he temporarily returned to Jerusalem after the death of Agrippa I, where he was present at the apostolic council (see on Acts 15).' Pesch refers for this to S. Dockx, whose essay on 'Chronologie de la vie de saint Pierre' appeared in his book *Chronologies néotestamentaires et vie de l'Église primitive* (Louvain, 1984) and was then published in German translation in C. P. Thiede, *Das Petrusbild in der neueren Forschung* (Wuppertal, 1987) 85–108. But other recent German commentators (A. Weiser, J. Roloff and H. W. Neudorper) all say that we cannot draw conclusions. Equally sceptical is R. E. Brown and J. P. Meier, *Antioch and Rome* (New York, 1983) 97f., which follows O'Connor.

The Dominican scholar, S. Dockx, referred to above, fully accepts Peter's ministry in Rome in the reign of Claudius.

7. Robinson 114.

8. Robinson refers to Edmundson at least thirty-eight times. The above quotations will be found on pp. 112–14, 145, 329. There is a fascinating account of this versatile and brilliant man on p. 349 n4.

9. Marshall says 'Luke's purpose was to show how the gospel reached Rome' (*Acts* 47, cf. 27).

10. Dodd xxviii.

11. Suetonius, *Claudius* 25. The text of this and the four following quotations are given by Edmundson in the original Latin and Greek on pp. 9, 10.

12. e.g. *Corpus Inscriptionum Latinarum* 6, 10233.

13. Tertullian, *Apology* 3: 'Even when it is wrongly pronounced by you "Chrestianus".' Lactantius, *Inst. Divin.* 4.7: 'the error of the ignorant, who by a change of a letter are accustomed to call him Chrestus'. This mode of spelling still survives in the French 'Chrétien'.

14. Dio Cassius, *Roman History* 60.6.6 He says of the Jews: 'by reason of their multitude it would have been hard without raising a

tumult to bar them from the city, [so] he did not drive them out, but ordered them . . . not to hold meetings'. Bruce *Chronology* 281, following E. M. Smallwood, *The Jews Under Roman Rule* (Leiden: Brill, 1976) 210–16, believes that the accounts of Suetonius and Dio refer to two separate actions: 'At the beginning of his principate Claudius tried to curb Jewish rioters in the capital by imposing limited restrictions on them; when, some years later, those limited restrictions proved to be insufficient, he took the more drastic step of banishing the Jewish community from the capital.'

15. Dodd xxi.

16. Textual evidence for the omission of chapter 16 or of 15 and 16 is slender. Marcion was possibly responsible for such omission. For careful discussions see C. E. B. Cranfield, *Romans*, ICC (Edinburgh: T. & T. Clark, 1975) 5–11; L. Morris, *Romans* (Grand Rapids: Eerdmans; Leicester: IVP, 1988) 21–31; H. Gamble, *Textual History of the Letter to the Romans* (Grand Rapids: Eerdmans, 1977) in Studies and Documents 42.

17. This point is made by Balleine 155.

18. If Luke can call Peter both Simon and Symeon (Acts 11:13; 15:14), he could call the Cyrenian both Simon (Luke 23:26) and Symeon (Acts 13:1).

19. The greeting from all the churches of Christ was particularly apt when representatives of so many churches were joining Paul in preparation for their journey to Jerusalem (Acts 20:4).

20. E. E. Ellis writes in a personal communication: 'A better argument can be built on the size of church a house meeting could accommodate. I argue 100 or 150 or even 200. Thus a church up to 1,000 – and there may have been house churches unknown to Paul.' See his *Pauline Theology* (Grand Rapids: Eerdmans/Exeter: Paternoster, 1989) 142–4. This seems to me likely to be an underestimate, if Paul is only greeting those with whom he has had personal contact.

21. On this see H. Chadwick, *The Circle and the Ellipse* (inaugural lecture, Oxford 1959).

22. It is altogether likely that there was a group of Christians in Rome before 42 – Jews like Andronicus and Junia(s) who had come to believe in Jesus as Messiah perhaps as a result of a visit to Jerusalem. Peter would probably have known about them and gone straight to their house-church. But it is unlikely that these untrained Christians would have established the world-famous church of which Paul speaks. It was for just such a task that the chief of the apostles had been trained. The specific mention of a twenty-five-year episcopate is

first found in the Latin of Eusebius' *Chronicle*, which was based on various second-century sources no longer extant. For an account of the papal lists of Hegesippus, Epiphanius, Irenaeus, Julius Africanus, Hippolytus, Eusebius, see O'Connor 27–35. He quotes J. B. Lightfoot as believing that the second-century list of Hegesippus 'did contain the length of office' (28). After Eusebius the twenty-five-year period is the standard and uncontradicted tradition (Jerome, *Liberian Catalogue, Liber Pontificalis*, etc.). The *Chronicle* of Eusebius may be consulted in Migne *PG* vol. 19 *Eusebii Caesariensis Opera* 539f or in A. Schoene (ed.), *Eusebii Chronicorum libri duo* (Berlin, 1875). The Latin version may have been by Jerome and altered by him (R. M. Grant, *Eusebius as Church Historian*, Oxford: Clarendon, 1980, 2).

23. Barnes 27 inclined, on the other hand, to the view that Peter perhaps went to Corinth from Rome with Aquila and Priscilla at the time of the expulsion. The presence of a Cephas party in Corinth, however, does not require the presence of Peter on Pauline territory, only the presence of his converts. A number of those expelled from Rome may have been such. See my article 'Did Peter go to Rome in AD 42?' *Tyn B* (1972) 100f.

24. e.g. P. W. Schmiedel in 1909 and K. Heussi in 1936. See Cullmann 71–77 for references and the modern debate.

25. O'Connor 6 says: 'By the middle of the second century the Roman Church, rightly or wrongly, certainly affirmed that Peter had come to Rome and that he was the founder and first bishop of the Church.' A church so flourishing in 57 (when Romans was written) *must* have been founded several years earlier.

26. O'Connor 50b.

27. Though writers of the second century and later probably thought of a continuous, resident episcopate it would be anachronistic to think in those terms during Peter's lifetime. See further p. 165.

28. 'Liber Pontificalis' *New Catholic Encyclopedia VIII* (New York, 1967) 695a.

29. O'Connor 4 n14, quoting L. M. O. Duchesne, *Histoire ancienne de l'Église* (Paris, 1906–10) 55, cf. ET, *The Early History of the Christian Church* (London: Murray, 1909) I 41: 'too insecure to be sanctioned by history'.

30. Edmundson 72.

31. *La Liber Pontificalis* I (Paris, 1886) ccxlvi col 2 n1 as translated by Edmundson 71.

32. Ignatius, *Romans* 100.4.

33. Eusebius, *HE* 2.25.

34. Irenaeus, *Adv. Haer.* 3:3; *HE* 5:6.

35. This would also apply, though not so strongly, if Peter's first visit was *c.* 55 as T. W. Manson thought.

36. Edmundson points out that Jerome must have had access to the *Chronography* of Julius Africanus, the *Chronicle* of Hippolytus, the *Memorials* of Hegesippus and other lost works (50 n2); cf. n25 above.

37. A. Harnack, *Constitution and Law of the Church* (London: Williams & Norgate, 1910) 31. J. B. Lightfoot also took the tradition seriously (*Galatians*, London: Macmillan, 10th ed., 1896, 127 n1).

38. Eusebius, *HE* 5.18.14.

39. *Acts of Peter* 2.5, as given in Hennecke II 282.

40. Clement, *Stromateis* 6.5.43 as translated in Hennecke II 101.

41. Josephus, *Ant.* 19.4ff; *War* 2:2–6.

42. Josephus, *Ant.* 19.6.

43. The legend which won almost universal acceptance in the middle ages of how the twelve, equipped with different languages at Pentecost, composed the Apostles' Creed and then set forth to proclaim God's word to the nations, is vividly described by J. N. D. Kelly, *Early Christian Creeds* (London: Longmans, 1950) 1–6. Nothing so neat is in the least probable. That any general dispersal was not complete and final is suggested some seven years later by Acts 15, with its repeated references to 'the apostles'. Peter is back in Jerusalem; he alone of the twelve is mentioned by name, but he is not the only 'apostle' present. The other Jerusalem leaders mentioned by name are James (the Lord's brother), Judas Barsabbas and Silas. It is possible, however, that Luke is using 'apostle' in a wider sense than 'one of the twelve'. See my discussion of the term 'apostle' in Wenham *CB* 114ff: The word 'apostle' is used in at least two senses in the New Testament. It is used of the delegates sent by the churches to take the collection to Jerusalem (2 Cor. 8:23; Phil. 2:25). It is also used of the twelve, whom Jesus called and upon whom, as foundations, the New Jerusalem was built (Luke 6:13; Rev. 21:14). In the one case the apostle is just a representative of his local church, with a temporary commission. In the other his commission is to the church universal. In between these two uses are others not so easily defined. Pre-eminent is Paul, who regarded himself as an apostle in the fullest sense (prepared publicly to oppose Peter). Once Barnabas is called an apostle (Acts 14:14), probably also James, the Lord's brother (Gal. 1:19; 1 Cor. 15:7), possibly Silvanus and Timothy (1 Thess. 1:1; 2:6; Acts 16:1–4; 17:14). See also Ellis *GC* 47 n108.

44. Eusebius, *HE* 2.13,14.

45. Justin, *Apology* 1.26.
46. Hippolytus, *Refutation of All Heresies* 6.20.2.
47. O'Connor 5. Marucchi is probably best known for his *Éléments d'archeologie chrétienne* of 1899/1900, translated into English as *Manual of Christian Archeology* (4th ed., 1933). I have not seen these.
48. The question arises whether Acts 12:17–25 allows room for Mark to go to Rome in 42, write his gospel and return to Jerusalem by 46. There is in fact no difficulty since the time-references are quite imprecise. The section from 11:19 to 12:25 consists of a main narrative and a parenthesis concerning Herod. It covers a long span from Paul's conversion (*c.* 33) to his second visit to Jerusalem (*c.* 46) – i.e. fourteen years reckoned inclusively (Gal. 2:1). The time-note in the main narrative ('in these days', 11:27), therefore, is not at all a precise date. Luke (in Acts 12:1–22) squeezes his whole account of Herod's reign (41–44) between the mention of Barnabas and Saul going to Jerusalem with famine relief and the mention of their return to Antioch accompanied by Mark (11:30; 12:25). This parenthesis is also introduced by an imprecise phrase, 'About that time' (12:1).
49. It is possible that the occasion of Paul's confrontation with Peter was not a passing visit, but that Peter made Antioch his headquarters when he left Rome. Peter was long recognised in the West as having been bishop of Antioch as well as bishop of Rome. The Roman Calendar, before it was revised in 1970, celebrated the Feast of the Chair of St Peter at Rome on 18 January and the Feast of the Chair of St Peter at Antioch on 22 February. In the East we find Origen calling Ignatius 'the second bishop of Antioch after Peter' (*Homily On Luke* 6.4). Eusebius similarly calls him 'the second after Peter to succeed to the bishopric of Antioch' (*HE* 3.36.2; cf. 3.22). Jerome says, 'after having been bishop of the church of Antioch and having preached to the Dispersion . . . [he] pushed on to Rome in the second year of Claudius to overthrow Simon Magus, and held the sacerdotal chair there for twenty-five years until the last . . . year of Nero' (*De Vir. Ill. 1*). This is a witness to his 'bishopric' in Antioch, but Jerome must surely be wrong as to its timing. There was not time for such extensive activities. Presumably he went first to Rome, then to Antioch, and later returned to Rome. Dockx (*Chronologies* 146, see n6 above) opts for two spells in Antioch, one before going to Rome and one after. He envisages on the first visit in 41/42 one year in Antioch, followed by a few months evangelising Asia Minor (1 Pet. 1:1) and a short visit to Corinth en route for Rome. Not only does there not seem to be time for the evangelisation of such a vast area, but to have

worked openly in Syria would have been to leave himself exposed to Herod's agents who were out to kill him. Dockx sees the second visit as covering the seven years 49–56. The tradition of his Antioch episcopate is jealously guarded by the Melkite Christians to this day.

It is understandable that Peter should choose Antioch as his base. It was the third city of the empire; it was the flash-point of the Jewish–Gentile tension in the church; it was within fairly easy reach of Jerusalem, yet it did not intrude on James' jurisdiction; it was a good base for work among the peoples of Pontus, Galatia, Cappadocia, Asia and Bithynia, whom he addresses in his first letter. For further references, see Thiede 245 n244; S. Dockx, *Chronologies néotestamentaires et vie de l'église primitive*, Louvain, 1984, 135. Dockx postulates a stay in Antioch from March 41 to April 42.

50. With regard to the sentence in Acts 12:17, 'then he departed and went to another place,' Hemer 207 n90 says, 'The story is rounded off with the statement, in effect, that he went into hiding' (cf. 360, 'most likely simply to signify "into hiding"'; Bruce *Acts* NICNT 238, 'went underground'). He says that 'τόπος is not commonly used of a "city" as . . . in English' (208n). See, however, Luke 10:1; Acts 27:8; 1 Cor. 1:2. He cites no other example of εἰς ἕτερον τόπον being used for 'into hiding'. Similarly Marshall *Acts* 211 says, 'As for Peter, the text may imply merely that he went into hiding until it was safe for him to return to Jerusalem (*i.e.* after the death of Herod).' It is hard to imagine that a man like Peter, famed for his boldness and conscious of the Christian's call to suffering (1 Pet. 4:12–19), would have gone into hiding for many months. No, he went to some place out of Herod's reach where he could continue to witness.

51. Thiede 154 argues that the apparent silence of Luke concerning Peter's destination in fact hides a cryptogram which clearly points to Rome. In Ezek 12:3 LXX the prophet is told to go εἰς ἕτερον τόπον, 'the identical expression used by Luke for Peter's destination. "The other place" is Babylon (Ez. 12:13), and Babylon is Rome.' It is difficult to know whether a significant proportion of Luke's readers might be expected to pick up such an allusion. If they knew that the other place was Rome it is possible.

52. In a title the anarthrous Πράξεις Ἀποστόλων could mean *The Acts of the Apostles*, *Acts of the Apostles* or *Acts of Apostles*.

53. See Wenham *EE* 112ff.

54. According to Eusebius (and the Syriac sources, which call him Addai) this Thaddaeus was not the apostle, but was one of the seventy,

sent on this mission by Thomas (*HE* 1.13.4; 2.1.6). It is possible that Thaddai and Addai have been confused.

55. C. B. Firth, *Introduction to Indian Church History* (Madras: Christian Lit. Soc. 1976) ch. 1; S. Neill, *A History of Christianity in India* (Cambridge UP, 1984) ch. 2. This tradition is taken for granted by Gregory of Nazianzus in the fourth century, *Orations* 33 (Migne *PG* 36, Col 228; Greg. Naz. *Discours 32–37*, ed. C. Moreschini, Sources Chrétiennes, vol. 318, Paris 1985, 181; *Nicene and Post-Nicene Fathers*, vol. 7, 332).

56. H. I. Bell, *Jesus and Christians in Egypt* (Oxford, 1924) 25.

57. Incidentally, it ill behoves those who date Acts after the death of Peter and Paul to use the argument from silence. The silence about Peter's going to Rome is less remarkable than the double silence about the martyrdom of the two apostles. In Paul's case his death is ignored in spite of the great attention paid to his arrival.

58. Galatians 2:1–10. This assumes that Galatians was written before the apostolic council in Acts 15. If it was written after, it would involve the improbable conclusion that Paul ignored the findings of the council, in spite of the fact that they lent massive support to his argument against the necessity for Gentile circumcision. In contrast, when Romans came to be written eight years after the council, the question had ceased to be a burning issue. See further, F. F. Bruce, 'Galatian Problems I: Autobiographical Data' *BJRL* 51 (1968/69) 292–309; II: 'North or South Galatians?' 52 (1969/70) 243–56.

In P. T. O'Brien and D. G. Peterson (ed.), *God Who is Rich in Mercy* (Homebush West NSW; Anzea and Grand Rapids: Baker, 1986), the *Festschrift* to D. B. Knox, Bruce writes on 'The Conference in Jerusalem' and concludes:

> Dr. Broughton Knox's earliest published contribution to theological scholarship was an article on 'The Date of Galatians' in *The Evangelical Quarterly* for October 1941. In that article he argued for an early date and defended the identification of the conference visit of Gal. 2:1–10 with the famine-relief visit of Acts 11:30. His arguments commanded my eager assent then; they still do.

So did they mine, and they still do.

59. Objection to a date as early as 45 has been raised by a correspondent on the ground that Simon would have been too young to have had sons old enough to warrant mention in the gospel. The Roman soldiers in 30, it is said, would probably have picked on a muscular young man to carry Jesus' cross. But a) the cross-bar was not

difficult to carry, and anyone up to the age of forty-five could have been chosen; b) marriages were customarily entered upon at an early age, and Simon's sons could have been well into their twenties by 45; c) it is not necessary to demand that Rufus and Alexander should have been distinguished, merely well known to the Christian community; they could have been under twenty. Since Paul had a particular affection for their mother and by 57 Rufus had gained some eminence in the church (Rom. 16:13), the family was probably already well known in 45. So there is at least twenty-five years to spare – Simon could have been anywhere between fifteen and forty-five at the crucifixion, and his sons anywhere between fifteen and forty in the year 45.

60. Barnes 6.

61. See BAG κράτιστος.

62. Clement, *Adumbrationes*. The Latin text is given in Aland 539.

63. Edmundson then relates the case of Julia Pomponia Graecina, the wife of Aulus Plautius, the conqueror of Britain. Tacitus (*Annals* 13.32. 3–5) tells how this distinguished lady was accused of some foreign superstition and lived a life of unbroken melancholy from the time of Claudius. Her melancholy was due to the murder of her friend Julia, daughter of Drusus, at Messalina's instigation in 43; she remained in mourning until her death forty years later. It seems likely that the foreign superstition was Christianity and that she was related to the Claudian family. In his final lecture (222–37) and Note D (250–58) Edmundson discusses the Domitian persecution of a generation later and 'the many high and influential persons (i.e. Christians) whom the tyrant visited with death or banishment' (224). This is also discussed at length by Barnes, who includes a genealogical table of the Flavian family in which he discerns fourteen men and women probably Christian (142). See also Marucchi ch. 6.

8 Mark's Gospel: Further Considerations

1. 'They say' could refer to Clement of Alexandria and Papias, whose witness is discussed in the preceding paragraph; or it could mean 'it is said'/'tradition says'.

2. This quotation is from the translation of S. Lee (Cambridge, 1843).

3. *Martyrologium Romanum ad Novam Kalendarii* (Paris, 1607). In the Coptic calendar Mark is commemorated on 30 April as 'evangelist,

first patriarch of Alexandria', N. Nilles (ed.) *Calendrier d'église copte d'Alexandrie* (Paris, 1898) 16.

4. The *Liber Pontificalis* of the Coptic church is *The History of the Patriarchs of the Coptic Church of Alexandria*, the text of which is to be found in Arabic, with English translation by B. Evetts, in *Patrologia Orientalis*, Tome 1, Fasc. 2 (Paris, 1903–5). Most Western scholars write it off as worthless. It was put together by Bishop Severus in Arabic in the tenth century. He says, however, that it was compiled from Greek and Coptic documents found in the monasteries of his country, which he translated with the help of certain 'clerks'. Its quality is most uneven, often fantastic tales lying side by side with sober narrative. Sound historical method must begin by eliminating the tall stories and then judge the rest on its merits. Since Severus does not identify his different sources, it is impossible to know whether the remaining plausible sections are historically based or not. It is equally wrong to assert either that they are or that they are not. One can only say that they *may* be, and that the possibilities which they present should not be ignored. This is particularly so since Severus' account is very close to the oral traditions which E. L. Butcher found were still being passed on by the village Copts at the end of the last century (*The Story of the Church in Egypt*, London, 1897). For a modern Coptic view which takes *The History* seriously, see A. S. Atiya, *A History of Eastern Christianity* (London: Methuen, 1968).

5. J. J. Gunther, 'The Association of Mark and Barnabas with Egyptian Christianity' *EQ* (54. 1982 and 55. 1983) gives, according to I. H. Marshall, a 'careful presentation and discussion of the evidence'. Gunther believes emphatically that Mark evangelised Egypt. His argument that Barnabas was associated with him in this is flimsy. Barnabas plays a distinguished part in the New Testament and is even called an apostle in Acts 14:14. It is unlikely that the Coptic church would have claimed Mark as their founder if Barnabas was available.

6. An important introduction to early Christianity in Alexandria is C. H. Roberts, *Manuscript Society and Belief in Early Christian Egypt* (Oxford UP, 1979). This is to some extent a reply to the thesis of W. Bauer, *Rechtgläubigkeit und Ketzerei im ältesten Christentum* (Tübingen, 1934); ET, *Orthodoxy and Heresy in Earliest Christianity* (London: SCM, 1972), who thought that the church in Egypt made so small a mark on Christian history because it was thoroughly Gnostic in origin and its early history was hushed up as discreditable. Bauer thought that the Eusebian list of bishops came ultimately from Demetrius, the first noteworthy 'orthodox' bishop in Alexandria. At

that time, he says, 'There was being cultivated in Alexandria that branch of theological endeavour which fought heresy by appeal to episcopal succession' (55) – which is a way of saying that episcopal lists were being invented. It is difficult to think of an endeavour more likely to be counter-productive – Alexandrian Christians would at once have recognised as bogus a list of Christian bishops of whom they had never heard! Roberts considers that Alexandria would have been a primary target for Christian mission (1) and sees early evidence of organised orthodox Christianity there (53). For a critique of Bauer, see also the 1954 Bampton Lectures by H. E. W. Turner, *The Pattern of Christian Truth: A Study in the Relations Between Orthodoxy and Heresy in the Early Church* (London: Mowbray, 1954). The second lecture is devoted expressly to Bauer, and pp. 46–59 to Alexandria. Bauer is also examined by D. A. Carson, 'Unity and Diversity in the NT' in D. A. Carson and J. D. Woodbridge (edd.), *Scripture and Truth* (Leicester: IVP, 1983) 66–72. In a review (*EQ* 62.3, 1990, 282f) D. F. Wright describes T. A. Robinson, *The Bauer Thesis Examined. The Geography of Heresy in the Early Christian Church*, Studies in the Bible and Early Christianity II (Lewiston, NY: Edwin Mellen, 1988) as 'most substantial' and 'very welcome'. See also H. I. Bell, 'Evidences of Christianity in Egypt during the Roman Period' *HTR* 37.2 (July 1944) 199–203; L. W. Barnard, 'St. Mark and Alexandria' *HTR* 57 (1964) 145–50.

7. The silence of Acts, the supposed lack of tangible evidence for an organised church in Alexandria before the middle of the second century and (more seriously) the silence of the voluminous Clement and Origen. As regards the last, it is important to notice that they do not refer to any alternative tradition either – the Mark tradition is entirely uncontradicted. And as Roberts points out: 'Origen set very little store on Mark, shows little familiarity with it, [and] once in *Contra Celsum* appears to have forgotten it' (148). Thus in his biblical studies (which was his all-consuming interest) he had little reason to call attention to Mark's part in the founding of the church.

8. Roberts 1.

9. G. D. Kilpatrick, *ExpT* 87 (1976) 1, in a review of J. Finegan's book, *Encountering New Testament Manuscripts*, says: 'All we know is that the Rylands papyrus was written about A.D. 125 and was found in Upper Egypt in the twentieth century. We do not know where it was written. If it was written outside Egypt we do not know when it came to Egypt.'

10. See p. 168.

11. J. J. Gunther argues this in detail: *EQ* 54 (1982) 223–25. (See n5 above).

12. The oral tradition of the Coptic church takes Peter and Mark to Babylon on the Nile. In spite of the great prestige of the interpretation which identifies the Babylon of 1 Peter 5:13 with Rome (an interpretation natural enough to someone like Eusebius who knew the Apocalypse of John and who believed that Peter was the founder of the church in Rome), it is quite difficult to imagine the author of a non-symbolic book sending his message to his widely dispersed readers in such a cryptic form, when there were two literal Babylons of which they would know. E. F. F. Bishop remarks: 'Why so often does the less likely come to be the predominant theory in Western N.T. scholarship? There is surely as good a case for the "Babylon" of 1 Pet 5:13 being the Egyptian Bablun, close to old Cairo, as the one farther east or as meaning "Rome"!' ('Simon & Lucius: Where did they come from?' *ExpT* 51, Dec. 1939, 149f). G. T. Manley, 'Babylon on the Nile' *EQ* 16 (1944) 138–46 argues that this was both a Jewish and a Christian centre and probably where 1 Peter was written.

13. It has been said that 'the references to Mark in the Pauline and Petrine epistles do not at all sound like references to an evangelist, church-founder and bishop. Isn't it more likely that he went off to Alexandria after Peter's death?' I cannot see that the references tell one way or the other. By 46 Mark had gained a reputation which made him appear a suitable choice as an evangelist on Paul's first missionary journey. Apart from the stay of the apostles in Jerusalem we have no knowledge in New Testament times of a church-founder or church overseer remaining long in one place. There seems no reason why Mark should not have worked among the Jews in Egypt as well as acting as assistant to Peter and Paul in their work among the Gentiles. The initial founding of a church is 'a day of small things' and there would be no reason for referring to it in the casual references to Mark in the epistles. It is difficult to believe that Egypt, next door to Palestine, had to wait more than thirty years before it was evangelised.

14. This suggestion was made by M.-E. Boismard 144, who contributed the section on 7Q5 to the *editio princeps*: M. Baillet, J. T. Milik, R. de Vaux (edd.), *Discoveries in the Judaean Desert* (Oxford, 1962), III, vol. 1; for the facsimile, see vol. 2, planche XXX.

15. See E. C. Colwell, 'Scribal Habits in Early Papyri: A Study in the Corruption of the Text' in J. P. Hyatt (ed.), *The Bible in Modern Scholarship* (New York: Abingdon, 1965) 370–89.

16. Aland's *Synopsis* gives it as the Sahidic and Bohairic reading.

According to *The Coptic Version of the New Testament* (Oxford: Clarendon, 1911) 451 the MSS vary. It relegates the reading corresponding to ἐπὶ τὴν γῆν to the margin, and adopts the shorter reading in the text.

17. Among sharp critics of O'Callaghan are G. D. Fee, 'Some Dissenting Notes on 7Q5 = Mark 6:52, 53' *JBL* 92 (1973) 109–12 and C. J. Hemer, 'A Note on 7Q5' *ZNW* 65 (1974) 155–57. F. F. Bruce writing in 1972 considered O'Callaghan's thesis conclusively refuted, on the basis of a study of the papyrus fragments themselves (as distinct from photographs), by P. Benoit, 'Note sur les fragments grecs de la grotte 7 de Qumran' *RB* 79 (1972) 321–23. See Bruce *Date* 78 n27. However, in a private communication in 1989 he described the matter 'as still *sub judice*'. Apart from O'Callaghan's own articles, defences of his position will be found in Pickering 155–58 and in C. P. Thiede, '7Q – Eine Rückkehr zu den neutestamentlichen Papyrusfragmenten in der siebten Höhle von Qumran' *Biblica* 65 (1984) 538–59 and *idem*, *Die älteste Evangelien Handscrhift?* (Wuppertal: Brockhaus, 1986) which give full references to the earlier debate. The latter has an enlarged photograph of the fragment.

In reply to a personal enquiry Professor O'Callaghan has kindly written in a letter dated 13 November 1989: 'I entirely agree with what you have written. If you want the best up-to-date information about my works, you can read the article by C. P. Thiede, *Schriftfunde vom Toten Meer* published in the III volume of *Das grosse Bibellexicon* (ed. Brockhaus), Wuppertal/Zürich 1989, pp. 1405–1407. In the bibliography the enlarged edition of Thiede, *The oldest manuscript of the Gospels?*, which will appear in 1990, is mentioned.'

18. Able defences of the Pauline authorship include J. N. D. Kelly, *The Pastoral Epistles*, BNTC (London: A. & C. Black, 1963); D. Guthrie, *The Pastoral Epistles and the Mind of Paul* (London: Tyndale, 1956); *The Pastoral Epistles*, TNTC (Leicester: IVP, 1957); and *New Testament Introduction* (Leicester: IVP, 3rd ed., 1970) 584–622, 632–34; C. Spicq, *Les épîtres pastorales* (Paris: Gabalda, 4th ed. 1969) 157–214. A stream of works in English have affirmed that the epistle of James was written by the brother of the Lord at a very early date: A. Plummer (1891), J. B. Mayor (1892), F. J. A. Hort (1909), G. H. Rendall (1927), A. T. Cadoux (1944), A. Ross (1954), R. V. G. Tasker (1956), C. L. Mitton (1966), J. A. Motyer (1970), J. B. Adamson (1976), R. Longenecker (1975), P. H. Davids (1982), D. Moo (1985). O'Callaghan thought that the minute fragment 7Q10 might come from 2 Peter 1:16 – a very long shot! The case for its

apostolic authorship is well argued by E. M. B. Green, *2 Peter and Jude*, TNTC (Grand Rapids: Eerdmans; Leicester: IVP, 2nd ed., 1987).

19. For his later exposition of this theme see Orchard 266ff.

20. Bultmann and Dibelius held that increasing detail was a characteristic of a developing tradition, which suggested that supposed eyewitness touches in a narrative were probably nothing of the sort. Sanders (ch. 3) has challenged this generalisation on the basis of a study of textual transmission and of developments in apocryphal and patristic tradition, which shows that in these fields it is often so, but by no means always. It is in any case doubtful whether conclusions drawn from textual criticism and from New Testament apocrypha are relevant to the question of the eyewitness origin of Mark. If Mark reflects the spoken word of Peter, vividness of detail will be evidence of the fact, regardless of any findings in these other fields.

21. D. E. Nineham, *JTS* n.s.9 (1958) 13–25; 243–52; 11 (1960) 253–64. Nineham's position is criticised in Stein 178, 183, 195f, 212.

9 Ancient Testimony to Luke's Gospel

1. *Adversus Haereses* 3.1.1.

2. *Adversus Marcionem* 4.2.4, 5.

3. *Stromateis* 5.12.

4. Fitzmyer 40 mentions Origen, Eusebius, Jerome, Ephraem Syrus, Adamantius, Monarchian Prologue, Prologue to Vulgate.

5. For text see Aland 533.

6. H. J. Cadbury 'Commentary on the Preface' in F. J. Foakes Jackson and Kirsopp Lake (edd.), *The Beginnings of Christianity* (London: Macmillan, 1922) 2.260f.

7. Streeter 560.

8. F. G. Moore, *The Roman's World* (New York: Columbia UP, 1936) 223; Ellis *Luke* 63.

9. cf. also what was said on pp. 133–35 about the early date of the titles.

10. W. K. Hobart, *The Medical Language of St. Luke* (London: Longmans, 1882; reprinted Grand Rapids, 1954); A. von Harnack, *Luke the Physician* (London: Williams & Norgate, 1907) 175–98; W. M. Ramsay, *Luke the Physician* (London: Hodder, 1908) 16. Fitzmyer 52 adds Albertz, Behm, Geldenhuys, Gut, Knowling, Lagrange, Michaelis, Wikenhauser, Zahn as approving the argument.

11. H. J. Cadbury, *The Style and Literary Method of Luke* (Cambridge, Mass. 1920) 39–72.

12. A. T. Robertson, *Luke the Historian in the Light of Research* (Edinburgh: T. & T. Clark; New York: Scribner, 1920) 11, 12, 90–102.

13. Creed xixff. Hemer 310–12, while acknowledging the failure of Hobart's hypothesis, sees value in his evidence and points out that Cadbury's criticism 'does not amount to disproof of its essential contention'. G. H. R. Horsley, *New Documents Illustrating Early Christianity*, Volume 2: *A Review of the Greek Inscriptions and Papyri published in 1977* (Ancient History Documentary Research Centre, Macquarie University, North Ryde, N.S.W. 2113, Australia, 1982) 24 calls attention to Greek epitaphs for itinerant doctors which are consistent with Luke practising his profession on the move with Paul (see *NovT* 26, 1984, 88).

14. Alexander 156.

15. Hemer 206, 335 referring to J. Dupont, *The Sources of Acts. The Present Position*, ET (London: Darton, Longman & Todd, 1964) 167, from *Les sources du livre des Actes, État de la question* (Bruges: Desclée de Brouwer, 1960).

16. Note Origen's assumption that the brother of 2 Corinthians 8:18 praised for his gospel was Luke, and that εὐαγγέλιον in the context refers to his gospel-book.

17. Zahn 2.393.

18. H. von Campenhausen, *The Formation of the Christian Bible*, ET (London: Black, 1972) 195.

19. ibid. 195 n243. *Adv. Haer.* 3.9.1–3.11.7; 4.6.1.

20. *Adv. Haer.* 3.11.8.

21. Farmer *NSS* 12. Farmer conjectures that between Clement and Origen lies an act of ecclesiastical authority by which 'the four-fold gospel canon was fixed and published in Rome under the influence of Irenaeus's "history of salvation" theme' (14). He and G. G. Gamba set great store on the possibilities that might accrue from a rigorous re-examination of the patristic evidence (*NSS* xxiii, 17). He argues the Clement case skilfully on pp. 6–15. Gamba (26, 33) thinks that the Mark–Luke order is unchronological, deriving possibly from Peter's primacy in the church. Contrast Farmer *NSS* 12.

22. Orchard 194; 214. Zahn 2.399 n8 gives references from Epiphanius, Jerome, Ephraem, Chrysostom.

23. Farmer *NSS* 37–64.

24. Farmer *NSS* 61; 62.

25. Farmer *NSS* 22. Orchard 209.
26. Farmer *NSS* 23, with the translation of *NSS* 24n18.
27. Farmer *NSS* 24 n19.
28. Farmer *NSS* 23 n14.
29. Farmer *NSS* 21n10. 'Ambrosiaster' (probably late fourth century) has also been cited as a witness to Clement's view. However he gives a theological justification for the order Matthew-Luke-Mark, and specifically distinguishes this from the order of composition. For text see *NSS* 25.
30. Zahn 2.395; 400 n9.
31. See H. Merkel, 'Clemens Alexandrinus über die Reihenfolge der Evangelien' *Ephemerides Theologicae Lovaniensis* 60 (1984) 382 –85; see also the discussion of G. Kennedy, 'Classical and Christian Source Criticism' in W. O. Walker (ed.), *The Relationships Among the Gospels. An Interdisciplinary Dialogue* (San Antonio: Trinity UP, 1978) 147–52 by Farmer, *NSS* xxix; 7 n7. C. M. Tuckett, *Revival of Griesbach Hypothesis* (Cambridge UP, 1983) 59 and 199 n33 deals with Clement's view, but Farmer thinks he 'does not discuss even-handedly the evidence' (xxix).
32. A considerable literature both for and against this hypothesis has grown up since Farmer published *SP* in 1964. A useful collection of articles and extracts from seminal books is Bellinzoni.
33. See the summary in Bellinzoni 15.

10 How Were the Gospels Written?

1. See the discussion of tradition-criticism on p. 84.
2. For discussion of Jesus' language, see J. Barr, 'Which Language did Jesus Speak? Some Remarks of a Semitist' *BJRL* 53 (1970) 9–29; J. A. Emerton, 'The Problem of Vernacular Hebrew in the First Century AD and the Language of Jesus' *JTS* ns 24 (1973) 1–23. The Jerusalem school, of whom D. Flusser and R. L. Lindsey are the best-known members, believe that a Hebrew *Life of Jesus* provided the basis of all three synoptic gospels. For a popular account see D. Bivin and R. B. Blizzard, *Understanding the Difficult Words of Jesus* (Makor Foundation, Arcadia, California 91006, 1983). These two date the Hebrew original 'within five years of the death and resurrection of Jesus' (94) and say: 'Like the other rabbis of the first century, he would certainly have communicated his parables in Hebrew' (76). C. F. Burney, *The Poetry of Our Lord* (Oxford UP, 1925), argued that

the poetic traits in Jesus' teaching 'must have been intended by our Lord as an aid to memory' (6).

3. For learning by rote in the Greek world, see R. O. P. Taylor 23ff; among the Jews, see H. Riesenfeld, 'The Gospel Tradition and its Beginnings' in *Studia Evangelica* (1959) 43–65, and B. Gerhardsson, *Memory and Manuscript* (Lund: Gleerup, 1961). R. Riesner, 'Jüdische Elementarbildung und Evangelienüberlieferung' in R. T. France and D. Wenham (edd.), *Gospel Perspectives*, I (Sheffield: JSOT, 1980) 209–23 argues that the mode of oral tradition in Jesus' day is to be compared not with the sophisticated rabbinic schools of later date, but with the widespread ancient style in popular instruction of learning by rote – inculcated through home, synagogue and elementary school. See further Riesner's *Jesus als Lehrer* (Tübingen: Mohr, 1984).

4. Torrey 95f. As to whether the evangelists wrote under a sense of impulsion by the Spirit, as some think, we are in the realm of speculation and I should not wish to base any conclusions on that assumption. But there is little doubt in my own mind that all the evangelists gave themselves to long and earnest prayer during the planning and execution of their books. And I do not doubt that God answered their prayers. They may well have laid down their pens with a realisation that what they had been moved to write were scriptures of the church of the new covenant, but we are nowhere told so and I do not assume it.

5. Chapman 179, 140.

6. D. Wenham argues in detail for a pre-synoptic version.

7. Zahn 2.601ff.

8. J.-M. Vosté, *De Synopticorum mutua relatione et dependentia* (Rome, 1928).

9. J. E. Steinmueller, *A Companion of Scripture Studies*, vol. 3 (New York: Wagner, 1943) 128. Vosté 15 gives as examples of *verba rara*: τὸ πτερύγιον τοῦ ἱεροῦ (Matt. 4:5), λέγει τῷ παραλυτικῷ (9:6), οἱ υἱοὶ τοῦ νυμφῶνος (9:15) ἐπίβλημα (9:16), γεύσωνται θανάτου (16:28), κολοβόω (24:22), and see parallels.

10. Butler 159ff.

11. Hawkins 125.

12. Chapman 91; Butler 168.

13. Orchard 266ff.

14. A. Dain, *Les Manuscrits* (Paris: Société d'édition "Les Belles Lettres", 1964) 24. He evidently means that the left leg is gently flexed, while the right leg below the knee is vertical, so providing a firm base on which to write.

15. This is ch. 12 of *Historical and Literary Studies* (Leiden: Brill, 1968) which is vol. 8 of 'NT Tools and Studies'.

16. I am assuming that the gospels were originally on scrolls. Roberts says 'The use of the codex goes back to the beginning of the Christian book' (10), 'from earliest times' (76). It is not clear, however, that we should take this back earlier than the second century (47). In any case a codex without word divisions would have been almost as difficult to handle.

17. Of course Tatian in the latter half of the second century wove together four gospels with meticulous thoroughness. But his work was in some respects the antithesis of what is attributed to redacting evangelists. He had a simple and clearly defined aim: he tried to ensure that everything in all the accounts was blended into a continuous narrative. Nothing was to be unnecessarily changed. By contrast Luke is supposed to have altered Mark five thousand times and Matthew to have altered it eight thousand times. Tatian's was the unhurried work of a scholar. It is easy to imagine how he operated. He would have decided which pericopes belonged together and copied out the different versions on to manageable sheets. These he would have studied carefully and then, with much trial and error, would have worked out a harmony. Finally he would have put his sheets together in order. It would have been an arduous task which may have taken years to complete. It shows nothing of the inventiveness and spontaneity of the supposed redactors, whose aims seem neither simple nor clearly defined. Though the work has been carefully done, the gospels read more like the lively teachings of gospel preachers than laborious literary adaptations.

18. F. G. Downing, 'Compositional Conventions and the Synoptic Problem' *JBL* 107 (1988) 69–85.

19. C. B. R. Pelling, 'Plutarch's Method of Work in the Roman Lives' *Journal of Hellenic Studies* 99 (1979) 92. That writers made one of their sources primary and the rest very much secondary undermines the thesis of A. M. Honoré, 'A Statistical Study of the Synoptic Problem' *NovT* 10 (1968) 95–147. He argues his probabilities on the assumption that an author would work on his sources randomly without bias, which is almost certainly the precise opposite of the known procedure.

20. Perhaps the commonest objection to the priority of Matthew is what N. B. Stonehouse calls the 'quite baffling' omissions which this requires of Mark (*Origins of the Synoptic Gospels*, London, Tyndale, 1964, 71). But Mark is not a replacement for Matthew, it is a supplement.

21. F. G. Kenyon, 'Writing' *HDB* 4.946 col. 1 says: 'No Greek literary papyrus is known which exceeds thirty feet.'

22. This was a sensible omission since there are obvious similarities between Mark 4:35–6:44 and 6:45–8:10. There are two feedings of a multitude, followed in each case by a voyage, a conflict with Pharisees and an act of power. Many (including so conservative a scholar as A. C. Headlam, *The Life and Teaching of Jesus the Christ*, London: Murray, 3rd ed., 1936, xii) have seen the passages as two versions of a single cycle of events. Not only is there a host of differences in the pairs of events, but it requires the deliberate invention at some stage of the exchange between Jesus and his disciples in 8:19, 20.

23. Ellis *Luke* 220.

24. For the topography of Jericho, see J. L. Kelso, 'Jericho' *IDB*; M. Avi-Yonah, *Encyclopedia of Archeological Excavation in the Holy Land*, vol. 2, 564; Josephus *War* 4.452ff.

25. H. Conzelmann, *The Theology of St. Luke* (London: Faber, 1960) 68ff.

26. *BAG* μέσος 2.

27. e.g., G. E. Wright and F. V. Filson (edd.), *Westminster Historical Atlas to the Bible* (London: SCM, 1945) 82; J. H. Negenman, *New Atlas of the Bible* (London: Collins, 1969) 151; Y. Aharoni and M. Avi-Yonah, *Macmillan Bible Atlas* (New York, rev. ed., 1977) 140, 148; *Reader's Digest Atlas of the Bible* (London, 1981) 177; H. G. May (ed.), *Oxford Bible Atlas* (New York: OUP, 3rd ed., 1984) 86; J. B. Pritchard, *The Times Atlas of the Bible* (London: Times Books, 1987) 163; J. Rhymer, *The New Illustrated Bible Atlas* (Leicester: Magna, 1988) 92; J. C. Laney, *The Concise Bible Atlas* (London: Marshall Pickering; Grand Rapids: Baker, 1988) 201; C. G. Rasmussen, *The NIV Atlas of the Bible* (London: Marshall Pickering; Grand Rapids: Zondervan, 1989) 170; T. Dowley, *The Student Bible Atlas* (Eastbourne: Kingsway, 1990) Map 20.

28. Josephus *War* 3.446.

29. Y. Aharoni and M. Avi-Jonah (edd.), *The Modern Bible Atlas* (London: Allen & Unwin, rev. ed., 1979) 148 (Map 234) illustrating Jesus' visits to Jerusalem, shows a crossing point some fourteen miles south of Scythopolis. Negenman 151 says: 'He preferred instead the more round-about way through Perea, the Jewish country of Antipas on the far side of Jordan.' *Westminster Atlas* 86 calls this 'the usual Galilean custom'.

30. This explanation is favoured by M.-J. Lagrange, *Évangile selon St Luc* (Paris, 5th ed., 1941) 457, Marshall *Luke* 650 and Ellis

Luke 209. M. Hengel, *Between Jesus and Paul* (London: SCM, 1983) ch. 6, 'Luke the Historian and the Geography of Palestine in the Acts of the Apostles', has much of interest on this subject, particularly on the difficulty of geographic accuracy before the development of cartography.

31. Sanders and Davies say 'the moves between Nazareth and Bethlehem cannot be harmonized' (32). The one difficulty of harmonisation derives from Luke's omission of any reference to the flight into Egypt. But since he only intends to relate two incidents (the return to Nazareth and Jesus' visit to Jerusalem at twelve years old) between the rites of purification in the temple and the appearance of John the Baptist some thirty years later (3:23), there is no reason why he should have referred to the short stay in Egypt.

32. J. S. Wright, *Our Mysterious God* (Basingstoke: Marshalls, 1983) 105.

33. N. Geldenhuys, *Commentary on the Gospel of Luke* (London: Marshall; Grand Rapids: Eerdmans, 1950) 152f.

34. For further discussion of the genealogies, see the Additional Note at the end of the chapter.

35. Wenham *EE*; where see p. 127 for a short note on harmonistic exegesis.

36. See, for instance, Morgan, especially ch. 2, 'Criticism and the Death of Scripture.'

37. This is true also, but to a lesser degree, of the view that it is Mary's genealogy. It is easier to make this simple inference than to infer something like the scheme of Julius involving step-brothers in one generation and a levirate marriage in the next.

11 Jesus-Tradition Oral and Written

1. J. A. Baird, in a study of λόγος in the New Testament and early fathers, 'The Holy Word' *NTS* 33 (1987) 585, reinforces this point: 'There is an abundance of evidence to support the thesis that the teachings of Jesus, what the early church called "The Holy Word", functioned as the basis of Christian doctrine and practice from the beginning of the Christian era at least as far as Eusebius.' He shows a progression from the words of Jesus to the word of Jesus to Jesus the Word and the word about Jesus.

2. R. Bultmann, *Theology of the New Testament*, vol. 1, ET (London: SCM, 1952) 35; cf. 188.

3. A. Resch, *Der Paulinismus und die Logia Jesu – Texte und Untersuchungen*, neue Folge 12 (1904).

4. W. D. Davies, *The Sermon on the Mount* (Cambridge UP, 1966) 97.

5. D. L. Dungan, *The Sayings of Jesus in the Churches of Paul* (Philadelphia: Fortress, 1971) speaks of Resch's 'fantasies' (150).

6. Paul's use of these two sayings is discussed at length by Dungan, op. cit.

7. See the discussion on pp. 230–37 above.

8. Thompson (ch. 2) finds two inexact citations of synoptic sayings in 1 Clement (13:2; 46:8), one he thinks probably dependent on oral tradition, the other derived from Matthew or Matthew's special source; Barnabas echoes Jesus once (5:9) and quotes a written source (probably Matthew) once (4:14); the Didache refers to a saying of the Lord (9:5) and quotes the Lord's Prayer as something commanded by the Lord ἐν τῷ εὐαγγελίῳ αὐτοῦ (8:2) – which expression could well refer to Matthew; Ignatius knows many details about Jesus, but he has only one direct citation of a dominical saying (*Smyrn.* 3:2), the source of which (though not specified) is evidently Luke 24:39; Polycarp is full of echoes of the New Testament, but he only quotes Jesus in *Phil.* 2:3 and 7:2, showing knowledge probably of Matthew and Luke, and in 7:1 he warns against perverting τὰ λόγια τοῦ κυρίου; Hermas has echoes of Jesus-tradition (notably *Man.* 4.1.6 on divorce) and knows that Jesus spoke in parables (*Sim.* 5.4.3), but does not quote from the gospels. It is only when 2 Clement is reached that we begin to find numbers of quotations (eleven in all), and even here quotation is quite free. Thompson is scrupulously careful not to overstate his case, and there are many more instances which are not quotations, but which might be considered clear echoes of the gospels: 1 Clem. 24:5; Barn. 12:11; Didache 1:3, 4, 5; 3:7; 7:1; 10:5; 13:2; 16:1; Ignatius, *Eph.* 6; 14; *Phil.* 7; 9; *Smyr.* 1; 6; Hermas, *Sim.* 9:20.

9. See ch. 5 n11.

10. In any case, in view of his firmly declared independence of the twelve, one would perhaps hardly expect Paul to quote them. Indeed, one would seldom expect one apostle to quote a fellow-apostle whose authority was no greater than his own. Peter's reference to Paul in 2 Peter 3:15, 16 is a striking exception.

11. According to Thompson 23 the author of Hebrews clearly knows some details about the 'days of his flesh' (5:7) from the narrative tradition, including Jesus' descent from the tribe of Judah (7:14), the fact that he was tempted (2:18; 4:15), suffered (2:10, 18)

and died outside Jerusalem (13:12). The last supper tradition may be reflected in his comments about the covenant established by Jesus' blood (10:15–19; 12:24), though the source could equally well be the liturgical tradition. The reference to Jesus' prayers with loud cries and tears in 5:7 suggests knowledge of the Gethsemane experience. He mentions Jesus' faithfulness and endurance (3:2–6; 12:2), his learning obedience (5:8–10), and implicitly, his humility (5:5).

For James, cf. 5:12 with Matthew 5:24 and see the fuller discussion in P. H. Davids, *The Epistle of James* (Exeter: Paternoster, 1982) 15f, 47–50. For 1 Peter's knowledge of both synoptic and Johannine Jesus-tradition, see R. H. Gundry, '*Verba Christi* in 1 Peter: Their Implications Concerning the Authorship of 1 Peter and the Authenticity of the Gospel Tradition' *NTS* 13 (1967) 336–50, of which the final paragraph says:

> By way of summary, then, the presence of numerous *verba Christi* in 1 Peter is universally acknowledged. Examination of the gospel-passages where they appear shows that in most instances the Apostle Peter is a specially active participant in the narrative contexts. At other times the motif would have special meaning for the Peter portrayed by the evangelists. Because of mathematical improbability this Petrine pattern cannot be attributed to chance. Because the allusions to *verba Christi* are beneath the surface, the author of the epistle did not cleverly choose and deliberately insert them for the sake of verisimilitude – an explanation which would require far too much ingenuity on the part of the pious forger anyway. Only Petrine authorship of the epistle and authenticity of the gospel-passages adequately account for the Petrine claim of the epistle and in favour of the gospel tradition. This is not reasoning in a circle. It is the self-consistency we expect from historically reliable material.

Gundry's views were challenged by E. Best in '1 Peter and the Gospel Tradition' *NTS* 16 (1969/70) 95–113, and Gundry replied with 'Further Verba on *Verba Christi* in First Peter' *Bib* 55 (1974) 211–32. The subject was further discussed by G. Maier in 'Jesustradition im 1. Petrusbrief?' in D. Wenham (ed.), *Gospel Perspectives* 5 (Sheffield: JSOT, 1985) 85–127. Thompson's comment is, 'If Best is too restrictive in his judgments, Gundry and Maier seem too eager to find parallels (especially with John's Gospel); the truth probably lies somewhere in between' (22 n10).

For 2 Peter's rich collection of references to the life and teaching of Jesus (including of course the transfiguration), see E. M. B. Green, *2 Peter and Jude*, TNTC (Leicester: IVP; Grand Rapids: Eerdmans, rev. ed., 1987) 21ff.

For 1 John, see C. H. Dodd's Moffatt Commentary *Johannine Epistles* (London: Hodder, 1946): 'He often echoes the teaching of the Lord as reported in the Fourth Gospel . . . some striking resemblances . . . strongly suggest that he was acquainted with an oral tradition of the Sayings similar to that which underlies the Synoptic record' (xxxviii). He then gives twelve examples.

For the Apocalypse, cf. 2:7a etc. with Matt. 11:15; 3:3 = Matt. 24:43; 3:5 = Matt. 10:32; 13:10 = Matt. 26:52; 21:6c and 22:17c = John 4:10 and 7:37b. See also R. J. Bauckham, 'Synoptic Parousia Parables and the Apocalypse' *NTS* 23 (1977) 162–76.

12. In addition it should be remembered that the first-hand recollections of the apostles would probably have been to teaching in Aramaic, rather than Greek.

13. The reading of the apostolic memoirs was well established in Justin Martyr's time (*c.* 155), see *Apol.* 1.66, 67.

14. For a discussion of how the New Testament canon 'quietly and unhurriedly established itself in the church's life', see Wenham *CB* 149–63. It is not widely realised that the first council purporting to be ecumenical which specified the canonical books was the Council of Trent in the sixteenth century. The Protestant confessions gave a different list! (161).

15. See Wenham *Luke*.

16. That 2 Peter is by the apostle is well argued by E. M. B. Green, *2 Peter and Jude*, TNTC (Grand Rapids: Eerdmans; Leicester: IVP, 2nd ed., 1987). R. J. Bauckham, *2 Peter and Jude* (Waco, TX: Word, 1983) maintains that the epistle is an example of a testamentary genre which made no pretence of apostolic authorship and which would at once have been recognised as pseudepigraphic by the first readers. But there is no evidence that it was so recognised by them, and it certainly was not by later generations in the early church, which refused to recognise pseudepigraphs as canonical.

17. J. Carmignac's belief that τῆς παλαιᾶς διαθήκης of 2 Corinthians 3:14 properly means the Old Testament and implies already the existence of an embryo New Testament ('2 Corinthiens 3:6, 14 et le Début de la Formation du Nouveau Testament' *NTS* 24, 1978, 384–86) cannot be sustained. Paul is simply referring by metonymy to the scriptures in which the old covenant is found; there need be no implication that the new covenant was to be found in a corresponding body of scriptures. The new covenant was brought to mind pre-eminently at the Lord's Supper.

18. See Massaux.

19. The view of Pickering 106–16 that most significant alterations were made in the interests of heresy is incapable of proof. D. A. Hagner in D. Wenham (ed.) *Gospel Perspectives* 5 speculates: 'it may be that many of the textual variants . . . were originally caused by a copyist's knowledge of the same saying of Jesus through local oral tradition' (256).

20. ibid. 251, quoting R. C. P. Hanson, *Tradition in the Early Church* (London, 1962) 21.

21. It will be noticed that I have paid little attention to the valuable work of B. Gerhardsson (e.g. *Memory and Manuscript*, Lund: Gleerup, 1964) and H. Riesenfeld (e.g. *The Gospel Tradition*, Oxford: Blackwell, 1970) who demonstrate the possibility of accurate oral transmission. This I accept as an important element in the spreading of a knowledge of Jesus, but it is peripheral to the concern of this book, which is the documents. Preaching, catechising and the written gospels all played their part in handing on the Word.

12 When Were the Gospels Written?

1. I have in mind scholars like D. Guthrie, R. P. Martin and J. A. T. Robinson who have written on the New Testament as a whole; F. F. Bruce, E. E. Ellis, W. W. Gasque, C. J. Hemer, I. H. Marshall on Luke/Acts; J. Carmignac, D. A. Carson, D. Flusser, R. H. Gundry, M. Hengel, J. B. Orchard, R. Riesner on the synoptics.

2. C. H. Dodd, *More Synoptic Studies* (Manchester UP, 1968) No. 6 'The Fall of Jerusalem and the "Abomination of Desolation"' 79. See similarly Reicke 175: 'he merely quoted ancient prophecies'. C. C. Torrey, the eminent Semitist of Yale, said in 1941: 'I challenged my NT colleagues [in 1934] to designate even *one* passage from any of the four Gospels giving clear evidence of a date later than 50 A.D. . . . The challenge was not met, nor will it be, for there is no such passage' (91). Typical of the opposite view is Schuyler Brown: 'The references to the destruction of Jerusalem in Matthew and Luke seem clear enough for these works to be dated with confidence after 70. In the case of Mark, however, opinions differ as to whether his gospel was written just before or just after that fateful year' (*The Origins of Christianity*, New York, Oxford UP, 1984, 23).

3. D. Wenham 217, and see whole section 180–218. Cf. pp. 26f above.

4. Thucydides, who is often quoted to contrary effect, was in fact an advocate of such rigour (421).

5. He is on less sure ground in discussing the διετία of Acts 28:30, of which he says: 'The mention of this defined period implies a terminal point, at least impending, but almost certainly past' (383). He seems to base this on the aorist ἐνέμεινεν which he says 'may suffice to connote a completed period' (383 n43). But the completed period could just as well last to the time of writing as to the time of Paul's release. If it refers to the latter (which could have been in the third year of Paul's captivity) one would expect, as we have already argued, that Luke would have mentioned it.

6. Harnack 95f.

7. This view is approximately that of Eusebius, *HE* 2.22.65. Among moderns who have held it are Robinson 87–92 (an excellent brief statement) and Williams 13–48, who quotes D. Plooij: 'The only really easy explanation of the "abrupt" ending is that Acts has been written just on the point of time where it ends' (18). He avoids the difficulty of dating Luke's gospel so early by postulating a proto-Luke before Acts and a completed gospel after.

8. 'Chronological Questions in the Acts of the Apostles' *BJRL* 68:2 (1986) 273. This quotation would suggest that the spirit of F. C. Baur, who greatly exaggerated the tensions among the leaders of the apostolic church, has not yet been fully exorcised.

9. Bruce *Acts* NICNT 12.

10. Bruce is followed by Marshall *Acts* 46–48, who considers a date 'towards AD 70' to be preferred – Luke 'looks back' on Paul's career 'with a certain sense of perspective'.

11. Even the cautious Guthrie says, 'The gospel has reached Rome and this forms a natural climax to the history of the primitive period' (*New Testament Introduction: The Gospels and Acts*, London: Tyndale, 1965, 310). G. N. Stanton, *The Gospels and Jesus* (Oxford UP, 1989) 99 writes, 'Luke ends his story on a triumphant note: the word of God has reached the heart of the Empire.' Cf. p. 277 n9 above.

12. For eight other explanations of the ending see Hemer 383–87. Hemer does not perhaps give full weight to R. P. C. Hanson's argument in *Acts*, New Clarendon Bible (Oxford, 1967) 34f which accounts for the end of Acts by stressing Rome as the place of publication. Hanson suggests that Acts is silent about the outcome of the trial because all his readers in Rome knew what had happened and did not need to be told. This notion, which 'does not quite satisfy' Hanson, has two weaknesses: 1.) as Hemer remarks, if the argument

'is valid at all, it could be saying too much, for an audience which knew the outcome presumably knew much of the situation which produced that outcome' (384). 2.) More important, it is surely virtually certain that Luke, having taken so much trouble in their writing, intended both his books to be read widely, and not only in Rome.

13. P. W. Walasky, *And so we came to Rome* (Cambridge UP, 1983) 64.

14. For the great influence of P. Vielhauer and the large body of opinion in Germany which sees the Paul of the epistles at odds with the Paul of Acts, see Ellis *Luke* 45–52, who gives a concise reply, in which, according to Marshall 42, his case is 'convincingly destroyed'.

15. e.g. W. M. Ramsay, *St. Paul the Traveller and the Roman Citizen* (London: Hodder, 1895); *The Bearing of Recent Discoveries on the Trustworthiness of the New Testament* (London: Hodder, 1914). In the English-speaking world there has been a strong body of opinion upholding the historical value of Acts, of which Hemer is only the latest example. The attitude of Roman historians is illustrated by A. N. Sherwin-White, *Roman Society and Roman Law in the New Testament* (Oxford UP, 1963) 189: 'Any attempt to reject its [Acts'] basic historicity even in matters of detail must now appear absurd. Roman historians have long taken it for granted.'

16. Hemer ch. 6 or, more popularly, 'Acts and Galatians Reconsidered' *Them.* 2 (1976/7) 81–88. For Bruce, see p. 283 n58 above.

17. C. K. Barrett, *Luke the Historian in Recent Study* (London: Epworth, 1961) 70–76.

18. e.g. Kümmel 156 calls Acts 'the second part of a complete historical work'. Bruce, *Acts* NICNT 7: 'the twofold work'. J. Dawsey, 'The Literary Unity of Luke-Acts: Questions of Style – A Task for Literary Critics' *NTS* 35 (1989) 48–66 on the other hand gives weighty reasons for doubting the narrative unity of the two books.

19. Origen, *First Homily on Luke* 6; cf. Eusebius, *HE* 6.25.6.

20. Ephraem, *Commentary on Epistles of Paul* 103.

21. Chrysostom, *Homily 18 on 2 Corinthians*: 'Some indeed say Luke, because of the history which he wrote; but some Barnabas.' Chrysostom prefers the latter.

22. Jerome, *De Vir. Ill.* 7.

23. See Nestle-Aland text.

24. Alford 2.683 refers to Ambrose, Pelagius, Primasius, Anselm, Cajetan, Grotius, Olshausen and Birks as upholders of this tradition.

25. E. Renan, *St Paul* (Paris: Michel Lévy, 1869) 454f writes:

2 Cor. 8:4 empêche de songer aux Macedonien de Ac 20:4. Luc serait le personnage qui conviendrait le mieux; mais alors la brièveté de Ac 20:1–3 comparée à la prolixité qui domine à partir de Ac 20:4 ff, ne s'explique pas. Luc ne rentra dans la compagnie de Paul qu'au dernier passage à Philippes.

26. e.g. Alford 2.683.

27. e.g. A. Plummer, *A Critical and Exegetical Commentary on the Second Epistle of St Paul to the Corinthians*, ICC (Edinburgh: T. & T. Clark, 1915) 248: 'Luke seems to be the best guess.' Hughes 313: 'the balance of opinion is, if anything, in favour'. Zahn 3.56: 'may have a basis in fact'. In this and the two following paragraphs I am much indebted to Hughes.

28. G. H. Rendall, *The Epistles of St. Paul to the Corinthians* (London: Macmillan, 1909) 79: 'hardly short of demonstrable that this was none other than S. Luke'. According to Plummer (lvii, 248), Bachmann in Zahn's *Kommentar* (Leipzig, 1909) strongly supports it.

29. 1 Corinthians 16:1–4; 2 Corinthians 8:1–9:15; Romans 15:25–28.

30. It is interesting that Luke seems to stress his own fulfilment of the task by mentioning his presence at the beginning and at the end of the journey. He was with Paul before the others (apparently starting from Greece (= Corinth?)) and he was with him in Jerusalem when they went in to James and the elders (Acts 20:2–5; 21:18). (Incidentally, the need to look for the brother among the delegates carrying the collection rules out the recent suggestion of R. P. Martin 275 that he might be Apollos – see n39 below.)

31. V. P. Furnish, *2 Corinthians*, Anchor Bible (New York: Doubleday, 1984) 434 says that Paul's wording 'does not preclude identifying this brother as a Macedonian'. It does not preclude it absolutely, but it makes it unlikely.

32. There are some nineteenth-century exceptions, e.g. C. Dunster, *Tracts on St. Luke's Gospel* (London: Rivington, 1812) 106–69; G. Gleig, *Directions for the Study of Theology* (London, 1827) 366–77.

33. Justin Martyr, *Apol.* 1.66.

34. J.-P. Audet, *La Didachè: Instructions des Apôtres* (Paris: Gabalda, Études Bibliques, 1958) 199.

35. Robinson 115. This has been argued at length by Zahn 2. 457.

36. M. Hengel, *Acts and the History of Earliest Christianity* (London: SCM, 1979) 32.

37. W. Marxsen, *Mark the Evangelist* (Nashville: Abingdon, 1969) 131.

38. M. D. Goulder, *The Evangelists' Calendar* (London: SPCK,

302

1978) 2. J. Sergeant, *Lion Let Loose: The Structure and Meaning of St. Mark's Gospel* (Exeter: Paternoster, 1988) 12 says also that Mark 'actually calls his book a "Gospel"'. C. A. Blomberg, in R. Keeley, et al. (edd.), *Jesus 2,000* (Oxford: Lion, 1989) 42: 'Mark introduces his book by actually calling it a Gospel.'

39. For a full statement of the case against εὐαγγέλιον being used of a document before the time of Marcion, see H. Koester 'From the Kerygma-Gospel to Written Gospels' *NTS* 35 (1989) 361–81; cf. R. P. Martin on 2 Corinthians 8:18: 'Is it a reference to a Gospel-writer (e.g., Mark, Luke)? The last-named is ruled out by the fact that there is no clear evidence before AD 150 of τὸ εὐαγγέλιον . . . being used of a written composition; it is ministry by personal deed and word that is in view' (*2 Corinthians*, Word Biblical Commentary vol. 40, Waco: Word Books, 1986, 274). There may be no indisputable evidence for an earlier use, but neither is there indisputable evidence against, so the interpretation is not ruled out. Indeed the case we have stated for its early use seems quite sound.

40. J. E. Renan, *Les Évangiles* (Paris, 1877) 283: 'le plus beau livre qu'il y ait'. If this was the judgement of the sceptical Renan after eighteen centuries, what must its impact have been on its first believing readers!

41. Even Robinson's tentative date of 55 for 1 Timothy (352) would not rule it out. This date is also favoured by Bruggen 31–35.

42. Wenham *Luke*.

43. e.g. Gregory Nazianzen, *Opera Omnia* II (Paris, 1840) 275 xxii line 1; Jerome: in Achaiae Boeotiaeque (v.l. Bithyniaeque) partibus volumen condidit (*Praefatio in comm. in Mattheum* – for text and also for Lukan preface see Aland 546f). The presence there of Luke (and Lucius: Rom. 16:21 – see Wenham *Luke*), together with the patristic tradition, make a good case for Achaia as the place of writing of the gospel, *pace* Marshall's 'Achaia . . . has nothing positive in its favour' (35).

44. E. O. Winstedt (ed.), *The Christian Topography of Cosmas Indicopleustes* (Cambridge UP, 1909) 205. J. Mumitiz, Master of Campion Hall, Oxford has kindly shown me a pre-publication translation of *The Letter of the Three Patriarchs*. This letter was said to have been sent by the Patriarchs of Alexandria, Antioch and Jerusalem (the highest authorities in the church) to the Emperor Theophilus (the highest authority in the state) in the year 836. In it they recall that the Gospel according to Matthew was composed in Jerusalem eight years after the ascension, that according to Mark in Alexandria ten years

after, that according to Luke in Rome fifteen years after. (The Greek text was published by I. Sakkelion in Εὐαγγελικὸς Κῆρυξ (Athens, 1864).) Theophylact of the eleventh century, *Praef. in Matt.*, put it in the eighth year after the ascension, which in our chronology would be 38. The entirely independent tradition of the Copts puts Mark's composition twelve years after the crucifixion (A. S. Atiya, *History of Eastern Christianity*, London: Methuen, 1968, 26). Writers of the sixth, ninth and eleventh centuries have little value for establishing a date, but they remind us that there is no trace of a tradition which dates the gospel in the last decades of the first century.

45. T. H. Horne (*Introduction to the Critical Study and Knowledge of the Holy Scriptures*, London, 1823, IV. 227, 229) opts for 37 or 38 and cites Baronius, Grotius and Wettstein as favouring 41 'after Eusebius', Cave 48, Benson 43, Owen (inventor of the Griesbach theory) and Tomline 38, Townson 37. In more recent times Torrey 92 favoured a date 'hardly later than the year 50, perhaps earlier'. He put Mark *c.* 40. Reicke makes quite a point of the use of the present tense when listing the apostles in Matthew 10:2: 'The names of the twelve apostles *are* these.' He says, 'The readers were in fact treated as contemporaries of that group' (101). Mark and Luke use the aorist. The language of Matthew would be particularly appropriate if he wrote before the death of James, the first apostle martyred, in 42. No great weight can be put on this, especially since the knowledge of the death of Iscariot is implied in all the lists. Nonetheless the choice of tenses is striking.

46. Zahn 2.571 speaks of 'the tradition that it was written between 61 and 66'. This appears to be merely a reference to Irenaeus, for he also says: 'According to Irenaeus' idea of the chronology, the Hebrew Matthew appeared between 61–66, Mark not long after 66 or 67' (2.394). Similarly France *Gospel* 29 says: 'Irenaeus confidently dates it while Peter and Paul were still preaching in Rome.'

47. J. Chapman, 'St. Irenaeus on the Dates of the Gospels' *JTS* 6 (1905) 563–69.

48. Harnack 130f. J. E. Steinmueller, *A Companion to Scripture Studies*, III (New York: Wagner, 1943) 65 n82 adds Cladder, Dausch, Holzmeister and Curran as those who (like himself) endorse Chapman's interpretation. This particular passage does not demand any knowledge other than that derived from Papias, but it does not preclude the possibility that Irenaeus had the same information from more than one source. F. F. Bruce remarked to me that Chapman's article had been unjustly overlooked. Hengel, *Johannine Q* 2–5,

though dealing with Irenaeus and appreciative of Chapman's book *John the Presbyter and the Fourth Gospel*, seems unaware of this article.

49. *Adv. Haer.* 2.22.5, 6.

50. See n46 above. Horne 229 cites Mill, Michaelis, Percy, Moldenhawer as favouring 61 or 62, Hales 63, Lardner and Hewett 64.

51. Gundry 599–609.

52. In Genesis 26:33 the origin of the name Beersheba is put in the days of Abraham in a book which records the death of his great-grandson Joseph (cf. Gen. 32:33; Judg. 1:21). On the other hand, 1 Samuel 29:3 covers a short period when David took refuge among the Philistines; Numbers 22:30 refers to part of the lifetime of a donkey; Joshua 6:25 to the time between the death of Joshua and the writing of the book, when Rahab is said to be still alive.

53. T. Townson, *Works* (London: Rivington, 1810) 117f.

54. Birks 297. The notion that the story of the guard was invented to strengthen the Christian apologia hardly makes sense. As France *Gospel* 71 says in a different connection, 'it would be a strange apologetic which invented "facts" in order to defend them'.

55. In 65 there would have been a fair number of people in their fifties or over who had heard Jesus in their teens or later, and a few of these would have had very retentive memories. By 85 they would have been reduced to a tiny handful of scattered geriatrics. Even so, the Jesus-tradition could have been carefully taught and accurately transmitted, but the onus of proof is somewhat on those who hold dates of this order. Dates in the 40s and early 50s throw the onus of proof the other way (cf. 1 Cor. 15:6).

56. The traditional, 'pre-critical' view of the Bible would go further and maintain that inspiration rules out the *possibility* of anything which can properly be called error. (See N. M. de S. Cameron, *Biblical Higher Criticism and the Defence of Infallibilism in 19th Century Britain*, Lewiston/Queenston: Edwin Mellen, 1987.) But this would not rule out a discussion of the matter, since a) what is meant by error is a subject of debate and b) the logical processes by which a belief in inerrancy is arrived at may themselves contain error. (See my 'Fifty Years of Evangelical Biblical Research' *Churchman* 103.3, 1989, 209–18, for the twentieth-century debate.)

INDEX OF BIBLE REFERENCES

Index of Bible References

INDEX OF ANCIENT AUTHORS

(Italic numbers signify a substantial entry)

312

INDEX OF MODERN AUTHORS

(Italic numbers signify a substantial entry)

313

314

Index of Modern Authors

315

INDEX OF SUBJECTS

317

Index of Subjects